Dante Alighieri

THE DIVINE COMEDY

A NEW PROSE TRANSLATION, WITH

AN INTRODUCTION AND NOTES BY

H. R. HUSE

Holt, Rinehart and Winston, Inc.

NEW YORK • CHICAGO • SAN FRANCISCO • ATLANTA • DALLAS
MONTREAL • TORONTO • LONDON • SYDNEY

Typography by Stefan Salter

Library of Congress Catalog Card Number: 54-7242

SBN: 03-008690-6

Printed in the United States of America
01234   68   29282726252423222120

INTRODUCTION

The three poets who have most deeply stirred men's imaginations —Homer, Dante, and Shakespeare—are, as Grandgent points out, remote and evasive figures. Little is known about the lives of any. In the case of Dante the established facts are few.

Dante Alighieri was born in Florence in 1265 of a family that had a slight claim to nobility. He began to write poetry early, fought in an important military campaign, and, like many poets of that day, took part in the political life of his city. In 1300 he became one of the six priors in charge of the government. But in 1302, while Dante was away from Florence, probably on a diplomatic mission to Rome, an opposing political faction took control of the city. This faction was supported by Pope Boniface VIII, whose secular ambitions Dante bitterly opposed, although he always affirmed the authority of the papacy in spiritual matters. To secure its position the new government brought various charges, including that of taking graft, against Dante and his friends, fined him heavily, and exiled him from the city. A later sentence condemned him to death if he were ever found on Florentine territory.

After a brief effort, together with numerous other exiles, to regain power, an attempt which led only to disappointment, Dante began his life as a wanderer. He never saw his wife or city again. During his exile he secured the patronage of several noble families in north-central Italy, and engaged in various negotiations for his patrons. There is a legend that he visited Paris and even England, but no certain proof of this exists. It is said also that after he had become well known as a poet the Florentines invited him to return, but under conditions which he proudly refused to accept.

He died in 1321 and was buried in Ravenna, where his tomb is one of the principal monuments. The Florentines have tried on many occasions to secure his remains, but he is still, in a sense, an exile from his home and city, from his *bel San Giovanni,* as he refers affectionately to his parish church.

In his youth Dante wrote love poems. Then, under the influence of a cultural movement which tended to fuse the two cur-

rents of courtly, chivalric love with philosophical, spiritual, or
divine love, he began to devote his writings to a certain Beatrice
Portinari, whom he chose as a symbol or representative of Divine
Beauty or of Divine Wisdom.

There has been much dispute as to whether Beatrice was just
a symbol, an allegorical figure, or a real person. Most commenta-
tors now agree that she was both real and ideal. The two aspects
are intimately fused. Thus, when Beatrice smiles or speaks or
wears a crimson dress, she is Beatrice Portinari, but when she
spreads a light that makes even the angels rejoice, she is a symbol
of something absolute and greater. The change in aspect may
come from one line to the next or even in the same line. Without
this understanding the poems on Beatrice would be almost in-
comprehensible or at least very strange.

When the inspiration came to Dante to make Beatrice a symbol
he had already written a number of poems, some to her and some,
obviously, to other ladies. To give an apparent unity to all of this
work, he composed a commentary on it, trying to show the rela-
tionship of all the poems to Beatrice, and tracing, in a curious
and artificial framework, the development of his conception of
her. The poems together with the prose commentary he called the
Vita Nuova (New Life).

Thus the *Vita Nuova* is an account partly fictive, partly real,
of the love of Dante for Beatrice. He tells how he met her at the
age of nine, how she greeted him some nine years later, how on
the occasion of a marriage (which some have suggested might
have been her own) she made fun of his embarrassment. This
tragic moment is a crisis in the work. Dante suffers acutely: it is
then, perhaps, or shortly after that he decides to transmute this
Beatrice Portinari whom he had loved so hopelessly into an ideal
and to write only in praise of her, placing his joy then "in some-
thing that could never fail him." Later he tells of her death, of
his momentary devotion to the *donna pietosa,* who has been taken
as the symbol of Philosophy, and finally of his unreserved and
definitive return to Beatrice, who is now enshrined in eternal
glory.

This is a bare outline of the story of the *Vita Nuova.* It is a
curious work, a composition in which we can trace the poet's
progress in using the Italian language.

In the last paragraph of the *Vita Nuova* Dante mentions a

marvelous vision, perhaps the vague starting point of the *Divine Comedy*. To prepare himself for revealing it, he intends to study, he says, and he hopes, if he lives, to write about Beatrice "what never before has been said [in praise] of mortal woman." The *Divine Comedy* is the magnificent fulfillment of this promise.

After completing the *Vita Nuova* at the age of about 27, Dante studied intensely and became one of the most learned men of the Middle Ages. He threw himself also into political life; he was exiled, he traveled, he saw the infinite disorders caused mainly by greed. A new cause presented itself together with that of praise of Beatrice, namely, to show the men of his day the road to salvation, to salvation on earth as well as in Heaven. This is the double theme of the *Divine Comedy*.

Two of his works, the *Convivio* (Banquet) and *De Vulgari Eloquentia*, both incomplete, are evidence of his dedication. The former is an encyclopedic work presented by Dante as a feast of learning in which all who could read Italian might share. In *De Vulgari Eloquentia* (written in Latin, the medieval language of scholars) Dante argues for the use of the vulgar tongue, Italian, as a literary language and for some unification of the many dialects into which Italian speech was then divided.

But what most fascinated Dante's interest were the political problems of his age, especially the great conflict between the Roman Catholic Church and the Holy Roman Empire—the struggle that rocked all western Europe in the late Middle Ages and that led in part to his exile. Dante's political views are set forth systematically in a treatise which he wrote in Latin and called *De Monarchia* (On Monarchy). This work presents the lesson of Dante's political experience: his conclusion that unless a world state were established to govern in temporal matters as the universal Church of his time ruled in spiritual matters, men would never enjoy peace and happiness in the world, and few men would escape sin and reach heaven. On this subject, however, as on all subjects that interested him, Dante says the final word in the *Divine Comedy*.

In the *Comedy*, the story of the journey through the future world is in the form of an elaborate allegory in which the characters and things have double or triple meanings, just as Beatrice had in the *Vita Nuova*. Thus Dante himself represents Mankind; Virgil, Dante's guide, Reason or Philosophy and sometimes the

Roman Empire; Beatrice is Revelation or Theology or the Church; Cato stands for Free Will; the sun for God or Divine Enlightenment or Righteous Choice, and so on. The punishments likewise are symbolic, as are the physical features, the rivers, rocks, swamps, deserts, fire, and water.

The allegorical element is only one feature of the enormous complexity of the work. It has an architectural structure based on the relationship of three, as in the Trinity (or of nine, the square of three) to One, the Unity (or to the perfect numbers ten and a hundred which are related to this unity).

The total number of cantos is 100, divided into three groups of 34 for the *Inferno,* 33 for the *Purgatory,* and 33 for the *Paradise.* But the first canto is an introduction to the whole work, so that the arrangement is really 1–33, 33, 33. The poem is written in three-line stanzas with triple rime. Each part of the three future worlds has ten divisions. In Hell there are nine circles plus the vestibule; in Purgatory, nine divisions plus the Garden of Eden; in Paradise, nine revolving heavens plus the Empyrean, the final and absolute Heaven. There are three main guides, three groupings of the various sections of Hell, Purgatory, and Paradise. And so on. From this viewpoint the *Divine Comedy* is a vast architectural structure, with all parts fitted symmetrically together.

In his cosmogony Dante followed the Ptolemaic system, but added certain symbolic elements. Around the earth, the center of the universe, the various heavens with their planets revolve, and beyond all, embracing all, is the infinite Empyrean. In the middle of the hemisphere of land is Jerusalem, and directly opposite, on the other side of the earth, is the mountain of Purgatory, crowned with the Garden of Eden. At the center of the earth, the material center of the universe, the point farthest removed from the spiritual good of Heaven, we find Satan, cold, silent, and repulsive, frozen to above his waist in the ice. Only his vast batlike wings move, creating a freezing blast of Ignorance, Hatred, and Impotence. The rivers of Hell, which may symbolize the tears of man's suffering, flow down toward the center to torment those who caused them to be shed. Even Lethe, the river of forgetfulness, flows down to Hell from the Garden of Eden, carrying with it the last trace, the very memory, of sin.

At the beginning of the journey Dante represents himself as lost in a wood of worldliness or sin. He spends a night in this wood in darkness and in the morning tries to climb unaided the Mountain of Righteousness. But he is attacked by various beasts, a leopard which stands (in the interpretation adopted here) for luxury; a lion, pride; and finally a she-wolf, the symbol of avarice or greed, the main factor in most of the individual and collective crimes men commit. Dante, as Mankind, could probably have got by the first two, but at the sight of the wolf he despairs and falls back.

At this critical moment the shade of Virgil (Reason, Philosophy) appears and proposes to act as a guide. Reason can show the way to earthly felicity represented in the Garden of Eden; the guide to heavenly beatitude must be Beatrice, that is, Revelation or Theology or the Church.

The journey through Hell under the guidance of Reason is intended to show the consequences of our sins. To get rid of them we must first see what they look like, how repulsive they are: a new mental vision must be the preliminary to reform.

The punishments that Dante imagines are always related to the evil itself: usually they represent symbolically what happens to us when we indulge in the sin in question. Thus a person who becomes a glutton may live in luxurious surroundings but, in spite of outward semblances, he makes a pig of himself, he lives bestially. That condition is symbolized by the sty-like mire in which gluttons suffer in Dante's Hell.

In the same symbolic manner illicit lovers are blown about by the winds, as they are in our life by their passions. Dante takes them at their word; he requites their wishes; he lets them be together for an eternity, like Paolo and Francesca; but they long for rest, for the peace and security they can never know.

The hypocrites also get what they ask for. They wear gilded gowns, brilliant outwardly, but made of lead, and so heavy that the wearers groan under the weight. So it is with those who assume a pose here in our life. They can never be themselves; they must watch their words, their looks, their gestures. All this can become a heavy burden.

Thus in the *Inferno* Dante portrays certain relationships of cause and effect that are true and significant in all ages and in all societies.

When Dante reaches the bottom of Hell he has seen what sin looks like, how repulsive it really is. This is a first stage in his (and Mankind's) redemption. With a new, less obscured vision he can more easily tear himself away from evil habits and practices, and that effort is symbolized by the long climb from the center of the earth to the foot of Purgatory, which Dante imagines as an island peak in the hemisphere of water, directly opposite Jerusalem.

Dante and Virgil enter Hell on the evening of Good Friday and emerge at the foot of Purgatory just before sunrise on Easter Sunday. The action of the *Inferno* takes place therefore, appropriately, in the time between the Crucifixion and the Resurrection. In this interval Dante has torn himself away from the habits of sin. But he still has within him a tendency or inclination toward the capital vices—pride, envy, anger, sloth, avarice, gluttony, and lust, all capable of producing the sins punished in Hell. Dante's task in Purgatory is to get rid of these inclinations; and the punishments or disciplines there are intended precisely to remove them.

On each ledge of the mountain of Purgatory are seen or heard examples of the vice being removed and of the opposite virtue. The souls must contemplate constantly these visions of ugliness on the one hand and of beauty and goodness on the other. In addition there are various disciplines. The proud get practice in bending their stiff necks; they carry heavy weights, so that the heads they once held high are now low. The envious have their eyelids sewn together, since sight is the sense organ most implicated in envy: they accustom themselves to the use of other faculties. The angry are blinded by the fumes of their wrath. The gluttonous gain practice in abnegation. And so on. As Dante passes from ledge to ledge he removes one of the capital vices. At the top he is free, really free, as no one on earth can be. Not only are the bad habits gone which had conditioned his will, but also the potentiality of ever forming them again.

This undoing of our inheritance is symbolized by the entrance into the Garden of Eden which Dante places on top of the mountain of Purgatory. After being bathed in the waters there, Lethe and Eunoë, Dante returns to the state of mankind before the Fall. He is completely innocent, unweighted even by the memory of sin, and he can mount in the spiritual world of Heaven without effort or turning aside, just as a light body rises in the water.

Virgil leaves Dante before Beatrice (Revelation, Theology)

appears. In Paradise it is she who serves as the guide. The rise through the various heavens to the Empyrean represents a progress in joy and in understanding. The climax comes in the very last lines. Dante, possessed of a new and exalted vision, sees the Trinity as a Unit and in its separate aspects. And in a flash the complicated puzzle of life is resolved. He sees, in his own words, "contained, bound with love in one volume, what is scattered on leaves throughout the world."

Dante is unable to verbalize fully this experience, to compose in our imperfect words a formula which can be the equivalent of such a vast comprehension. But he tells us that he did understand momentarily, and that with the understanding came a smile of pleasure, a joy that is absolute. The happiness of Dante's heaven is primarily intellectual: it consists in immediate contemplation of the magnificence of God and of His creation, and in comprehending both.

The sketch above is a bare outline of the *Divine Comedy*. It is a vast structure, like a modern skyscraper. To reveal all the details it contains, the halls with their decorations and exhibits, the diverse tragedies enacted in the various compartments, as in the rooms of some Grand Hotel, would require much space. An introduction can only summarize a few of the wonders.

First, science. For a long time Dante's work appeared as one of profound learning, almost as a scientific treatise. Whenever the occasion arises the poet expounds philosophical, astronomical, physical, and theological theories. From this viewpoint, the *Divine Comedy* is an encyclopedia of the knowledge of the Middle Ages. This material is not extraneous to the unity of the work, since the allegory involves precisely such a knowledge of both man and the world.

Another subject with which Dante deals extensively is history, especially that of the Roman Empire, of the papacy, of Florence, and of Italy. In this he is not interested merely in the details, but in the significance of the general movement of events. He considered the Roman Empire divinely ordained to prepare the world for Christianity and still necessary as a kind of world government to end the anarchy of little sovereignties and constant wars. There is much material also on medieval customs and institutions.

Dante's political views at times seem prophetic. He diagnosed the disease of the world, the source of most crime and disorder, as greed. He demanded a separation of powers between the ecclesiastical authority, whose business he conceived as spiritual guidance, and the temporal power. He thought that men must and will be guided, and wished that the guidance should be adequately motivated and responsible. Many of his views concerning empire were based, not on idealistic dreaming, as some have supposed, but on a consideration of the Roman peace, the *pax romana*, which had lasted for two hundred years.

In all that depends upon the direct observation of men, Dante's knowledge was great. It is shown in the numerous and varied characters with which he peoples the worlds he describes and who appear with a curious definiteness, like statues. He generally chose for special treatment persons he knew personally or whose memory was recent. From this viewpoint the *Divine Comedy* is a vast gallery of figures, tragic, heroic, comic; and in them we have represented the dominant emotions, love, hatred, patriotism, desire for fame, for justice, for scientific discovery, and so on.

Dante's ability to create characters amounts almost to magic. Just as a cartoonist with a few lines represents persons by choosing one or two dominant traits, so Dante does in his portraits. Through his sense of dramatic situations, his skill in characterization by means of dialogue, Dante belongs with the great dramatic artists of all times. Such a figure as Francesca da Rimini—and she is only one of many—tells her story in thirty-eight lines. In just four lines Dante creates the character of La Pia and tells the drama of her life.

We encounter not only noble types, but also distortions of body and of mind—cripples, epileptics, those with such diseases as dropsy, fever, and paralysis. We see different types of insanity, maniacs, the depressed and melancholy, the demented, the hallucinated, and the suggestible. These are presented in a few lines, sketched briefly as we continue steadily, almost without turning aside, on our long journey.

Just as historical realism is represented by the persons, a material realism is shown in the descriptions of places. There is nothing vague about the Hell and Purgatory Dante creates. Even a mildly attentive reader comes to know well the geography of those regions, the rivers, cliffs, bridges, walls, tombs, swamps, deserts, and the light and the darkness. There are also descriptions of buildings, of works of art, of customs, of industries, and of astronomical and meteorological phenomena.

Descriptions of nature, too, appear occasionally. We see little scenes like that of the peasant on a summer evening looking down at the fireflies in the valley, the scene of the busy shipyards of Venice in winter—all sketched with the economy of means we find sometimes in Japanese drawings.

In addition to all this, in reading the *Divine Comedy* we become acquainted with the poet himself. While maintaining an extraordinary reticence concerning the objective facts of his life, he draws necessarily upon the impressions he has gained; and so we have occasional reflections of the events of his youth, his military experience, his friendships, and his delight in music and in the various arts. The lyric element is not dominant in the *Divine Comedy,* but it appears occasionally.

The first characteristic of Dante's style is perhaps its plainness, its simplicity. In the *Divine Comedy* almost nothing depends upon mere phrasing or upon the sound or prestige of words. Words for Dante are the humble servants of his thought, and the language rises only as the thought pulls it up. Another characteristic of his style is what Italians call *determinatezza* or clearness. He avoids abstractions instinctively: even ideas with him tend to assume a concrete form. And finally, as an artist of the classic spirit, he felt as much as any ever has *lo fren dell'arte,* the sobriety and restraint that classic art demands.

Dante's work was the first important composition in Italian. He was obliged largely to create his own literary tongue on the basis of the popular speech of Florence. There is some French influence, and there are many Latinisms. The work of two other Florentines, Petrarch and Boccaccio, following that of Dante, assured the supremacy of the Tuscan dialect as a literary language for the whole of Italy.

Dante called his great work simply *Commedia* (Italian for "comedy") or *Comedia* (the Latin form of the same word) because it begins in a fearful or unpleasant situation and ends happily, and because the language is popular and the characters are commonplace. The notions of comedy and tragedy as we understand them were unknown to Dante and to his age generally. Boccaccio, some forty years after Dante's death, used the term "divine" to characterize the work, but it was not until the sixteenth century that the full title, now universally applied, appeared on the frontispiece of the poem.

The three parts of the *Divine Comedy* are different in tone and in spirit. The damned in Hell keep the emotions which dominated them in our life. The *Inferno,* therefore, seems to most readers the most intimately human. The *Purgatory* is characterized by a religious feeling, the human aspiring to the divine. The *Paradise* presents a spiritual world which Dante constructs out of such materials as light, sound, color, movement, and with symbols, like that of the cross, the imperial eagle, Jacob's ladder of contemplation, and the mystic rose.

In the *Inferno* the violent passions dominate, and the tone of the poem varies with them. There are noble figures, admiration, reverence, and also satire, irony, invective, and even physical violence on the part of the poet. In the *Purgatory* the gentler emotions prevail, those of friendship, family, art, pity, and pardoning. In the *Paradise* there are a peace and an intellectual enjoyment unperturbed. From an artistic viewpoint the *Purgatory* appears to many as superior to the *Inferno,* and the great passages of the *Paradise* bring to a climax this product of the imagination, this soaring dream.

The popular conception of Dante as cruel and vindictive is curiously wrong. He condemns as his faith and observation direct, but he chooses often the most striking, the most sympathetic examples he can find. There is indignation against the sins, but a dominant sympathy for the victims. His bitterness is reserved mainly for the avaricious and the fraudulent, those whose vices are incompatible with any compensating or generous virtues.

The *Divine Comedy* is difficult, almost impossible, to read without the help of notes or commentaries. It contains countless allusions, some purposely blind, a vast amount of learning, various symbols and levels of meaning. Some of the difficulties are due to remoteness in time: since Dante's day the heavens and earth have changed as well as the conventional knowledge on which all communication must be based. But many problems existed even for Dante's contemporaries, so that the need for interpretation was felt immediately.

Moreover, in contrast to modern journalism, the *Divine Comedy,* like many poetic works, requires active cooperation on the part of the reader. It is intended to evoke thoughts, pictures, and experiences, to suggest as well as to be explicit. It must grow and unfold in the reader's mind. It should be read slowly, a few cantos at a time.

The impression conveyed by the *Divine Comedy* is profound and complex. As Rossi points out, it appeals to both the mind and the heart. It is a synthesis in popular form of the thought and feeling of the most glorious period of the Middle Ages. A deep understanding of man and of civil morality pervades the work, and this makes it profoundly meaningful to men of all countries, of all faiths, and of all times. The greatness and universality of the content are matched by the beauty of the form. For many, a careful reading of the *Divine Comedy* is not just a literary experience, but a life experience. There is hardly a situation in which a knowledge of Dante does not offer some help or guidance.

Chapel Hill, N. C.　　　　　　　　　　　　H. R. HUSE
February, 1954

THE PRESENT TRANSLATION

The present translation, although intended as prose, is printed in the typographical form of the original verse. Besides diffusing and lightening the text, the method followed here keeps the original tercets. These usually have a unity of thought which demands also a certain unity of form.

The loss of rhyme and meter will seem great to some, of less importance to others. Probably for a majority of modern readers of narrative, philosophical, and didactic works, rhyme and the division into a certain number of syllables (the meter) are less vital than the style or rhythm of the phrases.

In many editions of the *Divine Comedy* a brief summary or "argument" appears at the beginning of each canto. Unfortunately these explanations can hardly be kept in mind until they are needed. If the reader omits them or fails to look back, as often happens, the text presents recurring and cumulative frustrations. To obviate this difficulty the explanations here are inserted in the text close to the point where they are needed.

Most readers of a translation want a version as similar to the

original as possible. The present work tries to meet this legitimate
demand. If the aim has been realized to any considerable extent,
it is largely because of the form chosen, which imposes no con-
straint.

ACKNOWLEDGMENTS

The translator gratefully acknowledges his indebtedness to many
commentators, notably Grandgent, Carroll, and Sinclair, to men-
tion only a few names; to Rossi's *Storia della letteratura italiana;*
and to the recent editions of Rivalta and Momigliano. Professors
R. W. Linker and A. G. Engstrom have generously helped with
the proofs. Thanks are due also to Messrs. Henry Paolucci and
John M. Pickering for suggestions pertaining to the Introduction.

A NOTE ON INTERPRETATIONS

The interpretations of allegorical figures and of other matters
vary somewhat with different commentators: those offered in this
work are, for the most part, widely accepted, but at best they can
only be suggestions or opinions, not statements of fact.

BIBLIOGRAPHICAL NOTE

The text followed in this translation is that of the *Società Dan-
tesca Italiana* (The Italian Dante Society).

The bibliography on Dante is probably greater than that on
any other author, ancient or modern. The catalogue of the Fiske
collection at Cornell University alone requires two volumes and
a supplement.

For background information, the standard scholarly work is that
of Karl Vossler, *Die Göttliche Komödie*, which has been trans-
lated into English under the title *Medieval Culture*, Constable,
London, 1929. Of the general introductions to Dante for English
readers, the following are generally available: E. H. Wilkins,

Dante, Poet and Apostle, University of Chicago Press, Chicago, 1921; J. B. Fletcher, *Dante,* Holt, New York, 1916; C. H. Grandgent, *The Power of Dante,* Jones, Boston, 1918, and *Dante,* Duffield, New York, 1916; G. Papini, *Dante Vivo* (English translation), Macmillan, New York, 1915; E. G. Gardner, *Dante* (in Temple Primers), Dent, London, 1900; C. A. Dinsmore, *Aids to the Study of Dante,* Houghton Mifflin, Boston, 1903; Alice Curtayne, *A Recall to Dante,* Macmillan, New York, 1932. An excellent essay is contained in George Santayana, *Three Philosophical Poets,* Harvard University Press, Cambridge, 1910. Especially for Dante scholarship, B. Croce, *The Poetry of Dante,* Holt, New York, 1922, is noteworthy. More detailed studies are contained in W. W. Vernon's *Readings on the Inferno, Purgatorio, and Paradiso,* each part in two volumes, Methuen, London, 1889, 1906, 1909. P. J. Toynbee, among other works, has published *A Concise Dictionary of Proper Names and Notable Matters in the Works of Dante,* Clarendon Press, Oxford, 1914. For Dante's influence in various countries, see W. P. Friederich, *Dante's Fame Abroad,* Edizioni di Storia e letteratura, Roma, 1950. On Dante's political thought, A. Passerin d'Entrèves, *Dante as a Political Thinker,* Clarendon Press, Oxford, 1952.

For an adequate understanding of the *Divine Comedy* the reader is urged particularly to consult the commentary in the three volumes of John D. Sinclair, *The Divine Comedy,* Lane, London, 1939, 1948; and the three volumes of John S. Carroll, *Exiles in Eternity, Prisoners of Hope,* and *In Patria,* Hodder and Stoughton, London, 1903, 1906, 1911.

For Dante's *Vita Nuova,* see *Poems and Translations* by Dante Gabriel Rossetti, in "Everyman's Library," or Mark Musa, *La Vita Nuova,* Rutgers University Press, 1957.

CONTENTS

PARADISE   327

GLOSSARY   483

INFERNO

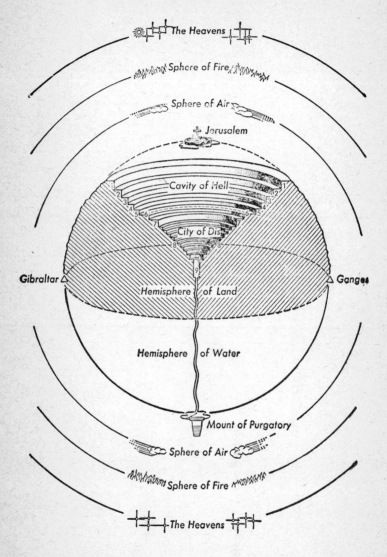

The Heavens

Sphere of Fire

Sphere of Air

Jerusalem

Cavity of Hell

City of Dis

Gibraltar △

△ Ganges

Hemisphere of Land

Hemisphere of Water

Mount of Purgatory

Sphere of Air

Sphere of Fire

The Heavens

A DIAGRAM OF THE EARTH IN THE CENTER OF THE UNIVERSE

OUTLINE OF THE INFERNO

Upper Hell, Incontinence [handwritten: lack of control over the natural appetites;]

Region	Sinners	Punishments
	[handwritten: modify if especially]	
Vestibule	Trimmers, neutrals	Stung by insects, run after banners
Circle I	[Virtuous pagans, unbaptized infants]	Melancholy, desire without hope
Circle II	The lustful	Blown forever by storm winds
Circle III	The gluttons	Discomfort, all senses punished
Circle IV	The avaricious and the prodigal [handwritten: greedy / wasteful]	Pushing rocks, useless labor
Circle V	The angry and the sullen	The angry thrashing about helplessly; the sullen submerged, emitting bubbles

Lower Hell, Malice (Violence and Fraud) [handwritten: or abuses of mental faculties]

Region	Sinners	Punishments
Circle VI	[Heretics] [handwritten: first circle]	In burning tombs
Circle VII	The violent	
Round 1	against neighbors, fellow men	Submerged in hot blood
Round 2	against self (suicides)	Enclosed in new bodies, as trees and bushes

3

OUTLINE OF THE INFERNO (Continued)

Lower Hell, Malice (Violence and Fraud)

Region	Sinners	Punishments
Round 3	against God (blasphemers, sodomites, us-urers)	On burning sand in rain of fire
Circle VIII	Fraud against those who have no special trust raewt	
Bolgia 1	Panders and seducers	Whipped by devils
Bolgia 2	Flatterers	Covered with filth
Bolgia 3	Simonists—days in sell church offices	Upside down in holes, feet on fire
Bolgia 4	Soothsayers	Heads twisted, turned backward
Bolgia 5	Barrators— how church office plate	Covered by boiling pitch
Bolgia 6	Hypocrites	Wearing leaden mantles
Bolgia 7	Thieves— lose identity	In snake pit, transformations
Bolgia 8	Evil counselors	Concealed in flames

4

OUTLINE OF THE INFERNO (Continued)

Lower Hell, Malice (Violence and Fraud)

Region	Sinners	Punishments
Bolgia 9	Sowers of discord	Wounds, mutilations
Bolgia 10	Falsifiers (alchemists, impersonators, counterfeiters, liars)	Diseases (leprosy, madness, dropsy, high fever)
Circle IX	Fraudulent against those who have special trust	
Caïna	Murderers of kindred	In ice to necks, heads bent forward
Antenora	Traitors to party or country	In ice to necks
Tolomea	Murderers of guests	In ice to necks, heads bent backward
Giudecca	Traitors to lords and benefactors	Completely submerged in ice

At the Center of the Earth (Universe)

Lucifer with Judas, Brutus, and Cassius in his three mouths, with three sets of wings sending forth a freezing blast of impotence, ignorance, and hatred.

NOTE: The souls in Circle I and Circle VI are outside of the classifications of Incontinence and Malice. They are guilty only from a Christian viewpoint, and Dante has to fit them as well as he can into the Aristotelian classification.

The opening tercets from Canto I will give readers an idea of the language and form of the original work.

Nel mezzo del cammin di nostra vita
    mi ritrovai per una selva oscura,
    chè la diritta via era smarrita.

Ah quanto a dir qual era è cosa dura
    esta selva selvaggia e aspra e forte
    che nel pensier rinnova la paura!

Tant'è amara che poco è più morte;
    ma per trattar del ben ch'io vi trovai,
    dirò dell'altre cose ch' i' v'ho scorte.

Io non so ben ridir com'io v'entrai,
    tant'era pieno di sonno a quel punto
    che la verace via abbandonai.   12

Ma poi ch'i' fui al piè d'un colle giunto,
    là dove terminava quella valle
    che m'avea di paura il cor compunto,

guardai in alto, e vidi le sue spalle
    vestite già de' raggi del pianeta
    che mena dritto altrui per ogni calle.

Allor fu la paura un poco queta
    che nel lago del cor m'era durata
    la notte chi'i' passai con tanta pièta.

E come quei che con lena affannata
    uscito fuor del pelago alla riva
    si volge all'acqua perigliosa e guata,   24

così l'animo mio, ch'ancor fuggiva,
    si volse a retro a rimirar lo passo
    che non lasciò già mai persona viva.

CANTO I

Virgil

The story begins on Thursday night, April 7, 1300. Dante, at the age of thirty-five, having completed half of man's traditional three-score years and ten, awakens to find himself in the forest of worldli-ness or sin. He cannot recall how he entered it: he had sunk, as men do, gradually and imperceptibly into sinful habits.

The night passes, and the sun (Divine Enlightenment or Righteous Choice) rises behind the Mount of Rectitude.

In the middle of the journey of our life
    I came to my senses in a dark forest,
    for I had lost the straight path.

Oh, how hard it is to tell
    what a dense, wild, and tangled wood this was,
    the thought of which renews my fear!

So terrible it is that death is hardly worse.
    But to reveal the good that I found there,
    I will speak first of other things.

I cannot tell how I entered it,
    so heavy with slumber was I at the moment
    when I abandoned the true way.   12

But when I had reached the foot of a hill,
    there where the valley ended
    which had filled my heart with fear,

I looked up, and saw its shoulders
    clothed already with the rays of the planet
    which leads men straight on every path.

Then the fear was somewhat quieted
    which had lasted in the lake of my heart
    during the night I had passed so piteously.

NOTE: Passages enclosed between [. . .] may be omitted by those concerned with only the main course of the narrative.

And as a seafarer, who has escaped from the storm
    to the shore, turns with wearied breath
    to the turbulent waters and gazes,   **24**

so I, still fleeing in my mind,
    turned back to look at the pass
    which no one before had ever left alive.

*As Dante starts to climb the hill, a leopard, the symbol of luxury or
lust, appears. It offers some opposition, but the early hour and the
buoyant influence of Spring, the season when the universe was sup-
posed to have been created, give him hope. Then a lion (Pride)
assails him, rushing on with such fury that the very air around seems
to tremble. And finally a she-wolf, the symbol of avarice or greed,
the most widespread of vices. Dante (Mankind) feels that he could
overcome the others, but at the sight of the wolf, he despairs.*

After I had rested a little my weary body,
    I took my way over the lonely slope
    [climbing] so that the firm foot always was the lower.

And behold! almost at the beginning of the rise,
    a leopard, light, and very nimble,
    which was covered with a spotted hide!

It did not move from in front of me,
    but instead so blocked my way
    that several times I turned to go back.   **36**

The time was the beginning of the morning,
    and the sun was rising with those stars
    that were with it when Divine Love

first set those beautiful things in motion,
    so that I found cause for good hope
    concerning the beast with the gaily spotted hide

in the hour of the day and in the sweet season;
    but even so I feared again
    at the sight of a lion that confronted me.

It appeared to be coming at me
    with head erect and with ravenous hunger,
    so that the air seemed afraid of it,   **48**

and a she-wolf came also, burdened

in her leanness with all cravings,
and which has indeed made many live in sorrow.

The sight of her brought such fear
and such distress upon me
that I lost hope of the ascent.

And as a gambler who gladly wins,
but when the time comes for him to lose,
weeps and is saddened in all his thoughts,

so I changed as the restless beast advanced
against me, and little by little
drove me down to where the sun is silent. 60

*At this critical moment, Virgil (Reason, Philosophy), whose voice has
long been unheard, appears. Dante forgets for a moment his despair,
and bends reverently before his master. Then he mentions the wolf
which has blocked his (and mankind's) reform. Virgil explains the
nature of the greed for which the wolf stands: it is an element in
nearly all the crimes men commit. But a "hound," a redeemer (vari-
ously identified), possibly from between the towns of Feltro and
Montefeltro, will ultimately come.*

While I was falling back to a lower place
someone appeared before me whose voice
from long silence seemed faint.

When I saw him in that desolation,
"Have pity on me!" I cried to him,
"whoever you are, whether a shade or a real man."

He answered, "Not a man now,
a man once I was, and both my parents
were Lombards, Mantuans by city.

I was born *sub Julio*[1] although late,
and I lived in Rome under the good Augustus
at the time of the false and lying gods. 72

I was a poet and sang of [Aeneas] that just son
of Anchises who came from Troy
after proud Ilion had been burned.

But why do you return to such misery?

---

[1] "At the time of Julius Caesar."

Why not climb the delightful mountain
  which is the beginning and the source of all joy?"

"Now are you that Virgil, that spring
  which pours forth so broad a stream of speech?"
  I answered him with bashful brow,

"Oh, honor and light of other poets,
  may the long study and great love help me
  which made me search through your volume!   84

You are my master and my author;
  you alone are the one from whom I took
  the style which has done me honor.

See the beast because of which I turned;
  save me from her, famous sage,
  for she makes my whole body tremble!"

"You must take another road," he answered
  after he had seen me weep,
  "if you want to escape from this wild place;

for the animal of which you complain
  lets no one pass along her way,
  but so hinders that she kills,   96

and she has a nature so vicious and perverse
  that she never satisfies her greedy desires,
  and after feeding is hungrier than before.

Many are the animals with which she mates,
  and there will be still more until the Hound comes
  that will make her die in pain.

He will not feed on earth or pelf,
  but on wisdom, love and virtue,
  and his nation will be between Feltro and Feltro.

He will be the savior of that humbled Italy
  for whom the virgin Camilla,
  Euryalus, Turnus, and Nisus died of wounds.

He will hunt her through every town
  until he has driven her back to Hell,
  whence Envy [of man's happiness] first released her.

*Now Virgil proposes to lead Dante through Hell and Purgatory, and
outlines the course of the journey. In Heaven, Beatrice (Revelation,
Theology) will be the guide.*

*In his humble submission to the mystery of Divine Justice, Virgil
accuses himself of "rebellion" against God's law. There is a note of
sadness in his words, condemned as he is, for having lived before
Christ, to an eternity of longing. Dante generously suggests his apology
by a reference to the God the ancient poet did not and, of course,
could not know.*

Therefore I think it best for you
 to follow me, and I will be your guide
 to take you through an eternal place [Hell]

where you will hear despairing cries
 and will see the tormented spirits
 each of whom proclaims the second death [damnation],

and you will see [in Purgatory] those who are contented
 in the fire, because they hope to come,
 whenever it may be, among the blessed,   120

to whom, then, if you wish to ascend,
 a guide worthier than I will take you:
 to her I will entrust you when I leave,

for that Emperor who reigns up there,
 because I was rebellious to His law,
 does not want me as a guide to His city.

Everywhere He reigns and there He rules;
 there is His seat and His high throne,
 O happy are those whom He chooses!"

And I to him, "Poet, I beg you
 by that God you did not know, in order
 that I may flee from this evil and worse,   132

take me where you have said,
 so that I may see St. Peter's gate
 and those you proclaim so sad."

Then he moved on, and I followed him.

CANTO II

Beatrice

It is now the evening of Good Friday. The sun which had cheered
Dante is going down, and the animals on earth (all workers in God's
universe) are returning home from their labors of the day. In this
dark moment, Dante's courage fails, and he wonders about the advis-
ability of the journey. It is true, he reflects, that both Aeneas and
St. Paul, the "Chosen Vessel," visited the future world; but Aeneas'
visit led to the founding of the Roman Empire, divinely ordained to
be the seat of the papacy, and St. Paul brought from Heaven a con-
firmation of the true faith. Dante disclaims any such mission.

The day was departing, and the darkening air
    was taking the creatures that are on earth
    from their daily toil, and I alone

was preparing to endure the hardship
    both of the journey and of the pity
    which unerring memory will relate.

O Muses, O lofty genius, aid me now!
    O mind which inscribed what I saw,
    here your worth will be revealed.

I began, "Poet, you who guide me,
    consider my strength, whether it is great enough
    before you commit me to the arduous journey.   12

You say that [Aeneas] the father of Sylvius,
    still subject to corruption,
    went bodily to the eternal world;

but that the Adversary of all Evil [God]
    should be gracious to him, thinking of the result
    and of who and what he was,

does not seem unreasonable to a thoughtful man;
    for he was chosen in the Empyrean heaven
    to be father of glorious Rome

and of her empire, both of which
    were established for the holy place
    where the successors of St. Peter sit.   24

On this journey through which you honor him,
    he heard things which led to his victory
    and to the papal mantle.

Afterward the Chosen Vessel [St. Paul] went there
    to bring comfort to the faith
    which is the beginning of the way of salvation.

But why should I go? Who grants it?
    I am not Aeneas, nor am I Paul;
    for that neither I nor others believe me worthy.

Therefore, if I allow myself to go,
    I fear the journey may be folly: you are wise
    and understand better than I can speak."   36

And, as a person unwills what he wills,
    and with new thoughts changes purpose,
    holding back from what he has started,

so I became on that dark slope,
    for, by thinking, I delayed the undertaking
    -that I had begun so quickly.

*Not deceived by this rationalizing, Virgil reproves Dante for being
afraid. Then, to reassure him, he describes the occasion of his coming,
a scene in the first circle of Hell where the souls of the virtuous pagans
are "in suspense," longing for an understanding of God and of the
mystery of life, with the realization that they can never attain it.*

"If I have understood your words rightly,"
    answered that magnanimous shade,
    "your resolution is dulled by cowardice

which often distracts a man
    and turns him away from honorable deeds;
    as imperfect sight causes an animal to shy.   48

To free you from this fear, I will tell
    why I came and what I heard
    when I first took pity on you.

I was among those who are in suspense.

and a lady [Beatrice] called to me
so blessed and beautiful that I asked her to command.

Her eyes shone more than the stars,
and with an angelic voice,
softly and sweetly she spoke to me,

O courteous Mantuan soul whose fame
still lasts on the earth, and will last
as long as the world,   60

my friend, but not the friend of Fortune,
is so impeded on the deserted slope
that in fear he has turned back,

and, from what I have heard in Heaven,
I am afraid he is already so lost
that I have come too late for his relief.

Now go to him, and with your eloquent speech
and with all else needful for his escape
help him, so that I may be consoled.

I am Beatrice, bidding you to go;
I come from a place to which I would return;
Love moved me and makes me speak.   72

When I am in the presence of my Lord
I will praise you often to Him.'
She was silent then and I began,

O lady of virtue [Revelation] through whom alone
the human race excels all creatures contained
within the heaven of the smallest orbit [all on earth],

your command so pleases me that complying
if already begun would seem slow;
you need only to reveal your desire;

but tell me why you do not shrink
from descending to this depth from the broad expanse
to which you are eager to return.'   84

Beatrice explains how, although pitying Dante, she can feel no distress at the working of Divine Justice.

The formal allegory of the scene in Heaven she then describes is as follows: Mary (Divine Mercy) sends Lucia (Illuminating Grace) to

prepare the way for Beatrice (Revelation) whom Dante (Mankind)
will perceive when Virgil (Reason) makes him ready to behold her.

'Since you wish to know so much
    I will tell you briefly,' she answered,
    'why I do not fear to come here.

We should be afraid only of things
    which can harm, not of others,
    since they are not fearful.

Through God's grace I am formed in such a way
    that your misery does not touch me,
    nor does a flame of this burning hurt me.

There is a gentle lady in Heaven [Mary]
    whose pity is aroused by the distress of him
    to whom I send you, and who tempers harsh judgment.   96

She called upon Lucia and said in her request,
    "Your faithful one now has need of you,
    and I recommend him to you."

Lucia, the enemy of all cruelty,
    arose and came to where I was
    seated by the ancient Rachel.

She said, "Beatrice, true praise of God,
    why do you not help him who loved you so much
    that through you he rose above the common crowd?

Do you not hear the pity of his cries?
    Do you not see Death struggling with him
    on the river [of evil] not less terrible than the sea?"   108

On earth men were never so swift
    to seek gain and flee from harm
    as I was after these words were spoken

to come here from my blessed seat,
    trusting in your noble speech
    which honors you and those who have heard it.'

After she said this to me
    she turned away her shining eyes in tears,
    which made me still readier to go,

and to you I came as she desired.

I freed you from that beast
    which had cut off the short way up the fair mount.   120

So what is it? Why, why do you hold back?
    Why keep such cowardice in your heart?
    Why are you not bold and free,

since three such holy ladies
    care for you in the court of Heaven,
    and my words promise you so much good?"

As little flowers, bent down and closed by the frost of night,
    stand up, all open on their stems,
    when the sun comes back to warm and brighten them,

so I revived my failing strength,
    and so much boldness rushed into my heart
    that I began like one set free,   132

"O compassionate lady who gave aid to me!
    O courteous shade who obeyed so quickly
    the true words she spoke to you!

You have disposed my heart
    with such desire for going by your account
    that I have regained my first intent.

Now go, for one wish is in both of us,
    you my leader [guide], my lord [superior], my master
        [teacher]!"
    Thus I spoke to him, and when he started

I followed on the deep and wild way.

CANTO III

The Entrance

In the faint light of the evening of Good Friday, the anniversary of the Crucifixion when, according to the Creed, Christ "entered into Hell," the two travelers move on to the gate over which appears a fearful inscription pointing out the woe within, the eternal pain, the people lost even to hope. Divine Justice (incomprehensible to reason alone) moved God in his three-fold attributes of Power, Wisdom, and Love to create Hell. It was made when only eternal things (the elements, the heavens, and the angels) existed, and it also will last and function eternally.

On reading these words Dante begins again to doubt, but, ashamed to confess his fear, he seeks delay or assurance by asking about their meaning which, incidentally, is painfully explicit. Virgil, undeceived, reproves Dante for his weakness.

THROUGH ME YOU GO INTO THE CITY OF GRIEF,
    THROUGH ME YOU GO INTO THE PAIN THAT IS ETERNAL,
    THROUGH ME YOU GO AMONG PEOPLE LOST.

JUSTICE MOVED MY EXALTED CREATOR;
    THE DIVINE POWER MADE ME,
    THE SUPREME WISDOM, AND THE PRIMAL LOVE.

BEFORE ME ALL CREATED THINGS WERE ETERNAL,
    AND ETERNAL I WILL LAST.
    ABANDON EVERY HOPE, YOU WHO ENTER HERE.

These words of a dark coloring
    I saw written above a gate; whereupon I said,
    "Master, their meaning is hard for me."   12

Then he spoke like one who understands:
    "Here you must give up all distrust,
    here all cowardice must end.

We have come to the place where I said
    that you would see the woeful people
    who have lost the good of the intellect.

And after he had taken me by the hand,
    with a cheerful look which comforted me,
    he drew me within the secret place [the eternal world].

On entering, Dante sees little because of the darkness, but hears sounds which he distinguishes gradually as cries, languages, words, accents, voices, and finally as the dull noise of blows. Virgil contemptuously refuses to waste words on the souls here. They are the trimmers, the mediocre, the poor in spirit, the neutrals, joined with the angels who refused to take sides in the revolt against God. They

*are in a kind of vestibule, outside of Hell proper. Their punishment
is slight compared to those which come later, yet they are envious of
every other lot.*

There, sighs, lamentations, and deep wailings
    resounded through the starless air,
    so that at first I began to weep.   **24**

Diverse tongues, horrible languages,
    words of pain, accents of rage,
    voices loud and hoarse, and the sounds of blows

made a tumult which moved forever
    in that air unchanged by time,
    as sand eddies in a whirlwind.

And I said, my head girt with horror,
    "Master, what is it that I hear,
    and who are these people so overcome by pain?"

Then he to me, "This miserable fate
    afflicts the wretched souls of those
    who lived without infamy and without praise.   **36**

They are joined with that choir of wicked angels
    who were neither rebellious
    nor faithful to God, but for themselves.

The heavens, to remain beautiful, drove them out,
    nor would deep Hell receive them
    lest the wicked gain pride by comparison."

And I, "Master, what is so burdensome
    that it makes them lament loudly?"
    He answered, "Briefly I will tell you.

They have no hope of death,
    and their blind life is so debased
    that they are envious of every other lot.   **48**

The world does not grant them any fame;
    pity [of Heaven] and justice [of Hell] alike disdain them.
    Let us not speak of them, but look and pass on."

*Some of these souls, neutral and perhaps sedentary in life, are con-
demned now to active partisanship. The poet recognizes one, but will
not distinguish him with a name. Most commentators have identified
him as Celestine V, a pope who, by his refusal to keep his office,*

*allowed Dante's great enemy, Boniface VIII, to rise to power. There
are less scandalous interpretations, however, notably as Pontius Pilate,
who refused justice to Christ and who offers a better motivation for
the extreme contempt shown here.*

And I, looking, saw a banner
    which, circling, moved so fast
    that it seemed to scorn all rest,

and behind it came such a throng of people
    that I never would have believed
    that death could have undone so many.

After I had recognized some of them,
    I saw and knew the shade of him
    who, through cowardice, made the great refusal.   60

At once I understood and was certain
    that this was the sect of the wicked
    displeasing both to God and to His enemies.

These wretches, who had never really lived,
    were naked and stung constantly
    by hornets and wasps that were there.

These made their faces stream with blood
    which, mixed with tears, was consumed
    by loathsome maggots at their feet.

*When Dante asks about a crowd in the distance, Virgil tells him to
wait and see. Taking this as a reproach, our poet remains silent for a
long time.*

*As the travelers move on, Charon appears, the ancient boatman of
the Styx, who prophesies Dante's ultimate salvation and whom Virgil
appeases with a kind of conjuring formula.*

When I began to look farther on
    I saw people on the shore of a great river;
    whereupon I said, "Master, now grant   72

that I should know who they are
    and what makes them so ready to pass over,
    as I discern through the faint light."

And he to me, "These things will be known to you
    when we stay our steps
    on the sad bank of the Acheron."

Then with eyes ashamed and lowered,
    fearing that my words might have offended him,
    I kept from speaking until we reached the stream

And behold! coming toward us in a skiff
    an old man, white with ancient locks,
    shouting, "Woe to you, depraved spirits;   84

hope not ever to see Heaven.
    I come to take you to the other shore
    into eternal darkness, into heat and cold.

And you there, living soul,
    get away from these who are dead."
    But when he saw that I did not leave,

"By another way, at other ports," he said,
    "you will come ashore, not here;
    a lighter boat will carry you."

And my guide, "Charon, do not be disturbed;
    this is wished for where the power is
    to do what is wished; and ask no more."   96

Then were quieted the woolly cheeks
    of the boatman of the livid marsh
    who, around his eyes, had rings of flame.

*The souls are impelled by a kind of instinct to seek their proper place,
since sin leads inevitably to its own results, its own suffering.*

*We are not told how Dante crosses the river. There is a flash, an
earthquake, and he falls unconscious. On awakening he is on the
other bank.*

But those weary and naked souls
    changed color and gnashed their teeth
    as soon as they heard the cruel words.

They cursed God and their parents,
    the human race, and the place, time, and seed
    of their begetting and of their birth.

Then, all together they withdrew,
    weeping loudly, to the accursed shore
    which awaits every man without fear of God.   108

Charon the demon, with eyes like glowing coals,

beckoning to them, gathered them in,
and hit with an oar any who delayed.

As in autumn the leaves fall
one after the other, until the branch
sees all its spoils upon the ground,

so, the evil seed of Adam
fell to that shore, one by one, and at signals,
as the falcon does at its recall.

Thus they go over the dark water,
and before they have landed on the other shore,
again on this side a new crowd assembles.   120

"My son," said the courteous master,
"those who die in the wrath of God
gather here from every country,

and they are ready to pass the river,
for Divine Justice so spurs them
that fear is changed into desire.

Along here no good spirit ever passes;
therefore, if Charon complains of you,
you can understand what his words imply."

When he had ended, the dark country
trembled so that from fright
my memory bathes me still with sweat.   132

The tearful land produced a blast
which flashed a crimson light
conquering all my senses;

and I fell, like one overcome by sleep.

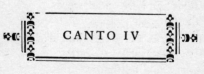

CANTO IV

Limbo

*When Dante awakens from his swoon he is in Limbo, the first circle
of Hell. He interprets Virgil's pallor as due to fear, but learns that it*

*comes from pity for those in the ancient poet's own circle. Although
Dante still refrains from questioning, Virgil is anxious to point out
that the shades here committed no sin, but died unbaptized or lived
before Christ. Their damnation is an article of faith, beyond man's
understanding. Here there is no torment other than a sense of unful-
fillment, a feeling that expresses itself in melancholy, in suspense, in
a vague longing for knowledge of God and for a solution of the mystery
of life without hope of ever having either.*

The deep sleep into which I fell was broken
    by heavy thunder, so that I started,
    like one awakened by force,

and having risen, I glanced around
    and looked intently with rested eyes
    to discover where I was.

In truth, I found myself on the brink
    of the dolorous valley of the abyss
    which resounds with the sound of countless cries.

It was so dark, deep, and cloudy
    that in looking toward the bottom
    I could discern nothing.   12

"Now, let us go into the blind world,"
    the poet began all pale,
    "I will be first and you second."

And I, noticing his color, said,
    "How shall I come if you are afraid,
    you who always comfort me in my doubt?"

And he to me, "The anguish
    of the people down there paints on my face
    the pity which you mistake for fear.

Let us go, for the long way impels us."
    Thus he moved on and made me enter
    the first circle which girds the abyss.   24

Here, so far as one could tell by listening,
    there was no lament, but only sighs
    which made the eternal air tremble.

They came from the sadness without torment

felt by the great crowd
of children and of women and of men.

My good master said to me, "You do not ask
what spirits these are. Now,
I want you to know before you go farther

that they did not sin, but having merit
was not enough, for they lacked baptism,
which is a portal of the faith you hold;

and if they lived before Christianity
they did not worship God rightly;
among such as these am I myself.

For such defects, not for other faults,
are we lost, and afflicted only
in that we live in longing without hope."

Great grief gripped my heart when I heard this,
for I knew that people of much worth
were in that Limbo in suspense.

*Dante now risks a timid question. He wants to know about the
"Harrowing of Hell," when Christ was supposed to have gone to
Limbo to release the ancient Hebrews who had believed in His
coming. After the explanation the poets move on to a special region
reserved for the great men of the past. Virgil (as Reason) approves
the recognition of Dante as the sixth in rank of the world's poets.*

"Tell me, Master, tell me, sir," I began,
wishing to be assured of the faith
that destroys every error,   48

"did any ever through his own merit
or another's leave here to be blessed?"
And he, understanding my veiled speech, answered,

"I was new in this condition
when I saw a Powerful One [Christ]
crowned with the sign of victory [the cross as an aureole].

He took from here our first parent,
Abel his son, and Noah,
obedient Moses, the lawgiver,

the patriarch Abraham, and David, the king,
    Israel [Jacob] with his father and his sons,
    and Rachel for whom he [Jacob] did so much,   60

and many others, and he made them blessed,
    and I wish you to know that before then
    no human souls were ever saved."

We did not stop because of his remarks,
    but kept passing through the forest—
    the forest, I mean, of crowded spirits.

Our way had not yet taken us far
    after my slumber when I saw a light
    which dispelled a hemisphere of darkness.

We were still distant from the glow
    but not too far for me to discern
    that notable people occupied that place.   72

"O you who honor every science and art," I said,
    "who are these whose great merit
    separates them from the others?"

And he answered, "The deserved fame
    which still honors them in your life
    gains favor in Heaven, and thus promotes them."

Meanwhile a voice was heard, saying,
    "Honor the greatest poet;
    his shade which had left is returning."

When this voice was silent
    I saw four great figures come to us,
    their faces neither sad nor gay.   84

My good master began to speak:
    "See that one with sword in hand,
    coming ahead of the others as their lord.

He is Homer, the sovereign poet;
    the other, following, is Horace, the satirist;
    Ovid is the third, and Lucan the last.

Since each shares with me the title 'poet'
    which the single voice pronounced,
    they do me honor, and in doing this do well."

Thus I saw assembled the school
    of that lord of the lofty song who soars
    above the others like an eagle.   96

After they had talked together a little
    they turned to me with signs of greeting,
    and my master smiled at that.

And still more honor they showed me
    by making me one of their group,
    so that I was the sixth among such sages.

*The poets now come to the Castle of Wisdom or Fame, surrounded by
the walls of the cardinal and speculative virtues and defended by a
moat which may represent eloquence or desire for knowledge. They
pass through the gates of the seven liberal arts. On a kind of enameled
meadow within, the great spirits of the past appear: first the Trojans,
Greeks, and legendary figures of early Rome; then philosophers, sci-
entists, mathematicians, and doctors; and finally the Moorish scholar
Averroës.*

Thus we continued toward the light,
    speaking of matters concerning which silence
    is as fitting now as speech was then,

and we arrived at the foot of a noble castle,
    seven times encircled by high walls,
    defended all around by a fair rivulet.   108

This we crossed as if on solid ground.
    Through seven gates I passed with these sages
    and we arrived on a meadow of fresh verdure.

There we saw people dignified and grave,
    of great authority in their semblance;
    they spoke seldom, and with soft voices.

Afterward we withdrew to one side
    to an open place, luminous and high,
    from which all could be seen.

There, standing on the green enamel,
    the great spirits were shown to me,
    to have seen whom I feel exalted.   120

I saw Electra with many companions.

among whom I recognized Hector and Aeneas,
   and Caesar clad in arms, with hawklike eyes.

I saw Camilla and Penthesilea
   on the other side, and I saw the Latian king,
   sitting with Lavinia, his daughter.

I saw that Brutus who expelled the Tarquin,
   Lucretia, Julia, Marcia, and Cornelia;
   and alone, to one side, the Saladin.

When I had raised my eyes a little higher
   I saw the Master of the Knowing [Aristotle]
   sitting with his philosophic family.   132

All looked at him, all did him honor;
   there I saw Socrates and Plato
   who stood ahead of the others closest to him:

Democritus, who thought the world due to chance;
   Diogenes, Anaxagoras, and Thales,
   Empedocles, Heraclitus, and Zeno;

and I saw the good compiler of the qualities [of plants],
   Dioscorides, I mean; and Orpheus,
   Tully [Cicero], Linus, and Seneca, the moralist;

Euclid the geometer, and Ptolemy,
   Hippocrates, Avicenna, and Galen,
   and Averroës who made the great commentary [on
      Aristotle].   144

I cannot enumerate them all fully;
   my long theme so drives me on that many times
   my words fall short of the facts.

The sixfold company diminished to two [Virgil and Dante];
   by another way my wise guide took me,
   out of the quiet into the trembling air,

and I came to a place where no light shines.

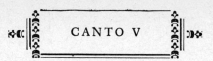

CANTO V

Francesca da Rimini

Since Hell is like an inverted cone, the circumference of each succeeding circle diminishes.

The guardian of the second ring is Minos, the ancient judge of the dead, represented by Dante as having some of the characteristics of a medieval demon. Like Charon, Minos offers a slight opposition which is overcome by the conjuring formula.

Thus I descended from the first circle
    down to the second which encloses less space
    but so much more pain that it moves to tears.

There Minos stands, horrible and snarling,
    examining the offenses, judging,
    and sending down as he girds himself—

I mean that when an ill-born soul
    comes before him, it confesses wholly,
    and that discerner of sin,

seeing what place in Hell belongs to it,
    encircles himself with his tail as many times
    as the degrees he wants it to descend.   12

Always many stand in front of him;
    they come in turns to their judgment,
    confess and hear, and then are hurled below.

"O you who come to the painful refuge,"
    Minos said when he saw me,
    interrupting the work of his great office,

"consider how you entered and in whom you trust;
    do not let the breadth of the entrance deceive you."
    And my guide to him, "Why do you cry out?

Do not impede his fated going.
    It is wished for where the power is
    to do what is wished; so ask no more."   24

The poets hear and see the shades guilty of lust. A landslide caused by an earthquake at the time of the Crucifixion perhaps reminds the restless souls as they pass of the impossibility of their redemption. Dante pities more than blames these victims of the flesh and of the imagination. They pass like birds in autumn flight.

Now I begin to hear the sad notes of pain,
    now I have come to where
    loud cries beat upon my ears.

I have reached a place mute of all light
    which roars like the sea in a tempest
    when beaten by conflicting winds.

The infernal storm which never stops
    drives the spirits in its blast;
    whirling and beating, it torments them.

When they come in front of the landslide,
    they utter laments, moans, and shrieks;
    there they curse the Divine Power.   36

I learned that to such a torment
    carnal sinners are condemned
    who subject their reason to desire.

And, as starlings are borne by their wings
    in the cold season, in a broad and dense flock,
    so that blast carries the evil spirits.

Here, there, up, and down, it blows them;
    no hope ever comforts them
    of rest or even of less pain.

And as cranes go chanting their lays,
    making a long line of themselves in the air,
    so I saw coming, uttering laments,   48

shades borne by that strife of winds.

Dante is eager to know who is punished here. No vulgar examples are cited but only glamorous figures of the ancient and medieval past whom love too completely mastered. Perhaps our poet suspects already that Francesca da Rimini and her lover are here. In any case he asks to speak to two who seem unusually light and is told to address them in the name of love, to which, in a nobler form, all his own life was a dedication. The real appeal, however, is in the sympathy ex-

*pressed by the words, "O wearied souls!" Like doves borne on by desire,
Francesca and Paolo leave their company, so responsive are they still
to the slightest note of affection.*

I asked, "Master, who are these people
    whom the black air so punishes?"

"The first of those about whom
    you want to know," he said to me,
    "was an empress over many peoples,

by the vice of luxury so subdued
    that she made lust lawful in her decrees
    to take away the blame she had incurred.

She is Semiramis who, we read,
    succeeded Ninus, her spouse;
    she held the land that now the Sultan rules.   60

The other is she [Dido] who killed herself
    after breaking faith with the ashes of Sichaeus;
    next comes luxurious Cleopatra.

See Helen [of Troy] for whom
    so many bad years revolved, and the great Achilles
    whose last battle was with love.

See Paris, Tristan,"—and he pointed out and named
    more than a thousand shades
    whom love had taken from our life.

After I had heard my teacher
    name the knights and ladies of olden times,
    pity overcame me, and I felt dismayed.   72

I began, "Poet, willingly would I speak
    with those two who go together
    and seem so light upon the wind."

And he to me, "Wait until they come closer,
    then entreat them by the love
    which impels them and they will come."

As soon as the wind brought them to us,
    I raised my voice, "O wearied souls,
    come speak to us if it is not forbidden."

As doves summoned by their desire,

with wings raised and firm, sail through the air,
    borne on to their sweet nest by their will alone,   84

so those spirits moved from the band where Dido is,
    coming to us through the malignant air,
    so responsive were they to my affectionate cry.

*Now Francesca speaks, and her first words are an implied prayer to
God whose mysterious justice has condemned her beyond remission, an
unselfish prayer for this living soul who has shown them pity. It is
a prayer for the "peace" which romantic and illicit love can never
know. In her heart's response to Dante's simple words, she treats
him already as "gracious" and "benign" and exaggerates her own
misdoing. Her story is a mere outline, told partly in terms of the
maxims of courtly love. With ladylike reticence she does not name
herself or Paolo, her brother-in-law and lover, or even the city where
she was born. Death itself would not have been so tragic: one moment
for repentance might have permitted her to be saved; it was the
suddenness of her and Paolo's death that was so cruel. Caïna, at
the bottom of Hell, where traitors to kindred are punished, awaits
her husband who surprised and killed them.*

"O living creature, gracious and benign,
    going through the dark air
    visiting us who stained the earth with blood,

if the King of the universe were friendly to us
    we would pray to Him for your peace,
    since you pity our perverse evil.

Whatever you are pleased to hear from us or say
    we will relate and listen to,
    while the wind, as now, is silent.   96

The city [Ravenna] where I was born
    lies on the shore where the Po descends
    with all its tributaries to find peace.

Love which flames quickly in noble hearts
    was kindled in this soul by the fair body
    taken from me; the manner [of that taking] still offends.

Love that exempts no one beloved from loving
    caught me so strongly with his charm
    that, as you see, it still does not leave me.

Love led us to one death together.
    Caïna waits for him who quenched our lives."
    These words were borne from them to us.   108

On hearing this delicate outline of the tragedy, Dante bows his head, perhaps recalling who the speaker is, and then naming Francesca, he asks, in words as respectful and delicate as her own, about the immediate cause and occasion of her sin. Although she dislikes to recall the intimate details, she speaks, unable to refuse an affectionate appeal. There was no premeditation in her sin. She and Paolo had been reading a love story without suspecting the effect it might have. One moment of weakness overcame them, a moment which ended their reading and their lives and which stands now in contrast to eternity.

When I heard those afflicted souls
    I bent down my face, and held it low so long
    that the poet said, "Of what are you thinking?"

When I answered I began, "Alas!
    how many sweet thoughts, what desire
    led them to the woeful pass!"

Then I turned to them and said,
    "Francesca, your suffering
    makes me weep with sorrow and with pity,

ut tell me, at the time of the sweet sighs,
    by what means and how love permitted you
    to know the dubious desires."   120

And she to me, "There is no greater pain
    than to recall a happy time in misery
    and this your teacher knows;

but if to learn the first root of our love
    you have such desire, I will answer
    like one who speaks and weeps.

One day for our delight we were reading
    about Lancelot, how love constrained him;
    alone we were and without any suspicion.

Several times that reading made our glances meet
    and changed the color of our faces;
    but one moment alone overcame us.   132

When we read how the fond smile [of Guinevere]
  was kissed by such a lover,
  he, who never will be separated from me,

kissed me, on my lips, all trembling.
  A Gallehaut [pander] was the book and he who wrote it.
  That day we read no farther."

While one spirit was saying this
  the other wept, so that from pity
  I fainted, as if I had been dying,

and I fell, as a dead body falls.

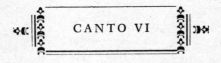

CANTO VI

The Gluttons

On recovering my senses, which were stunned
  by pity for the two kinsfolk
  who overwhelmed me with sadness,

new torments and new tormented shades
  I see around me, wherever I move
  and wherever I turn to gaze.

*The poets are now among the gluttons who are lying like pigs in a
sty under a constant, unvarying rain. Although the punishments here
are relatively mild, they are particularly distasteful to the luxury-loving.
All the senses are afflicted: sight by the dismal setting, touch by the
cold rain, smell and taste by the stench, and hearing by the loud
barking of Cerberus, the three-headed dog, the bestial guardian of
this circle. Cerberus is appeased, not by a honey cake, as in the
Aeneid, but by dirt, to emphasize further the filthiness of gluttony.*

I am in the third circle of the rain,
  eternal, accursed, cold, and heavy;
  its amount and kind never change.

Large hailstones, dirty water, and snow
   pour down through the dark air;
   the ground that receives them stinks.

Cerberus, the fierce and cruel beast,
   barks doglike with three throats
   over those submerged there.

His eyes are red, his beard greasy and black,
   his belly large, his paws armed with claws;
   grasping the spirits, he flays and tears them.

The rain makes them howl like dogs;
   they use one side to shelter the other;
   often they turn, the profane wretches.

When Cerberus, the monster, saw us,
   he opened his mouths and showed his teeth,
   trembling in all his limbs.

And my leader, opening his hands,
   took some earth and threw handfuls
   into the ravenous gullets.

As a barking dog, longing for food,
   grows quiet after he has seized it,
   since he thinks only of eating,

so did those filthy heads of the demon Cerberus
   who thunders over the shades,
   making them wish they were deaf.

*A soul nicknamed "Ciacco" (the pig) recognizes Dante but is himself
unrecognizable since the bestial vice of gluttony disfigures. To spare
the feelings of this shade Dante suggests that perhaps Ciacco's pain
prevented the recognition.*

We passed over the spirits subdued
   by the heavy rain, placing our feet
   on their nothingness which appears as flesh.

They were all lying on the ground
   except one who sat up quickly
   as soon as he saw us pass in front of him.

"O you, led through this Hell,"
   he said to me, "recognize me if you can;
   you were made [born] before I was unmade [died]."

And I to him, "The anguish that you feel
        perhaps takes you from my memory
        so that I do not seem ever to have seen you,

but tell me who you are, placed here
        in such punishment that, if others
        are greater, none is so displeasing."   48

And he to me, "Your city [Florence] so full of envy
        that it can hold no more
        kept me in the bright life.

The citizens called me Ciacco;
        for the damning sin of gluttony,
        as you see, I lie helpless in the rain.

And I, sad spirit, am not alone,
        for all of these are in similar pain
        for a like sin,"—and he said no more.

I answered, "Ciacco, your distress weighs upon me
        so that it moves to tears;
        but tell me, if you can, the fate   60

of the citizens of the divided city;
        if any one of them is just, and tell me
        why such discord has assailed it."

Then he to me, "After long dispute
        they will come to blows, and the rustic party [the Whites]
        will drive out the other with much offense.

Afterward that faction will fall
        within three suns [years], and the other rise
        through one [Boniface VIII] who now is moving carefully.

For a long time it will hold high its head,
        keeping the other under heavy burdens,
        however much it may weep and be put to shame.   72

Two men are just, but are not listened to.
        Pride, envy, and avarice are the sparks
        which have enflamed all hearts."

Here he put an end to his sad words,
        and I said to him, "I wish to learn more,
        and beg you to grant me the gift of further speech.

Farinata and Tegghiaio, who were so worthy,
    Jacopo Rusticucci, Arrigo, and Mosca,
      and the others who set their minds to doing good,

tell me where they are, let me know about them,
    for a great desire urges me to find out
      if Heaven soothes or Hell embitters them."   84

And he, "They are among the blackest spirits;
    different sins weigh them to the bottom;
      if you go down so far, you will see them.

But when you are again in the sweet world,
    I beg you to recall me to the memory of others.
      More I will not say; this is all I answer."

He twisted his straight eyes asquint,
    looked at me a little, then bent his head,
      and fell to the level of the other blind ones.

My guide said to me, "No more will he awaken
    until the angelic trumpet sounds [on Judgment Day]
      when the hostile Power [hostile to sinners] will come.   96

Each then will find his sad tomb,
    will resume his flesh and form,
      and will hear what resounds to all eternity."

Thus we passed over the filthy mixture of the shades
    and of the rain, with slow steps,
      touching a little on the future life.

I asked, "Master, will these torments increase
    after the great judgment,
      or will they be less or equally painful?"

He answered, "Recall your science
    which maintains that the more perfect a thing is,
      the more bliss or pain it feels.   108

Although these accursed people
    never come to true perfection,
      they will be more complete after than before."

We bent our course along that way,
    saying much more than I relate,
      and came to a place for descending.

There we found Plutus, the great enemy.

CANTO VII

The Avaricious and the Prodigal

Plutus, the ancient god of wealth and here the guardian of the circle of the avaricious and the prodigal, is represented as an inflated monster. He speaks in a high voice, like certain fat men, and his words are not clearly comprehensible. A reference to the Power through which the archangel Michael defeated the revolt of Satan easily deflates this weak, unhealthy, and puffy creature, who collapses suddenly, without resistance.

"Papè Satàn, Papè Satàn, aleppe,"[1]
    Plutus began with a clucking voice,
    and that noble sage [Virgil], who understood,

said to comfort me, "Do not fear,
    for whatever power he may have,
    he cannot prevent our descending this rock."

Then he turned to that inflated visage
    and said, "Keep still, accursed wolf;
    consume yourself inwardly with your rage.

Not without reason is our going to the depth.
    It is decreed on high where Michael
    took vengeance for the proud revolt."   12

As sails swelled by the wind
    fall entangled when the mast breaks,
    so the cruel monster fell to the ground.

The avaricious on one side and the prodigal on the other push great weights around their respective semicircles. At the two points where they clash, like the waves between Scylla and Charybdis, they exchange insults and turn, going to the opposite point. Thus they work hard, like the avaricious on earth, but uselessly, missing the spiritual

---

[1] These words are not clearly understandable; perhaps a threat and a warning to Satan.

pleasures which make this life and the next worth while. All are
alike, without distinction, and unrecognizable as individuals.

Thus we descended into the fourth cavity,
    taking in more of the dismal bank
    which holds all the evil of the universe.

Ah, Justice of God! Who can combine
    so many new pains and torments,
    and why does our sin so waste us?

As the waves above Charybdis break
    against each other as they meet,
    so in this place the souls must clash.   24

Here I saw more people than elsewhere
    on one side and the other, shouting loudly
    and pushing weights with their chests.

They bump against each other and then all turn,
    pushing back the load and crying,
    "Why do you hoard?" or "Why do you squander?"

Thus they go on each side
    of the dark circle to the opposite point,
    shouting their insulting refrains.

When they reach that place, they turn again
    through their half circles to the other clash.
    And I, my heart oppressed, said,   36

"Master, now tell me who these are
    and if all the tonsured ones
    on the left are of the clergy?"

And he to me, "In the first life
    all were so twisted mentally
    that they could not spend with moderation.

Quite clearly their voices bark this out
    when they come to the two points of the circle
    where contrary faults divide them.

Those whose heads are tonsured, as you see,
    were clerics and popes and cardinals
    in whom avarice shows its strength."   48

And I, "Master, among such as these

I must surely recognize some
   who were defiled by these vices."

And he to me, "You conceive a vain thought;
   the undiscerning life which made them sordid
   now leaves them too obscure for recognition.

Throughout eternity they will clash;
   some will arise from the grave with fists closed,
   and the others [the prodigal] with their hair shorn.

Bad giving and bad keeping have taken from them
   the fair world and placed them in this strife
   which words of mine will not glorify.   60

Wealth, according to Dante, is in the hands of a special divinity,
Fortune, who performs her functions as the angels guide and direct
the various heavens. No reason or moral order is discernible in the
distribution of wealth among individuals, families, and nations. (The
passages enclosed between [. . .] may be omitted by those con-
cerned with only the main course of the journey.)

[Now, my son, you can see how wealth,
   committed to Fortune, and for which
   the human race struggles, mocks us.

All the gold that is under the moon
   or ever was, could not give rest
   to one of these weary souls."

"Master," I asked, "now tell me,
   who is this Fortune
   with the world's riches in her hands?"

And he to me, "Oh foolish creatures,
   how deep is the ignorance that blinds you!
   Now I want you to hear my judgment.   72

He [God] whose understanding transcends all
   made the heavens and gave them guides,
   so that each part shines on all the others,
distributing the light equally.

   Likewise, for mundane splendors,
   He ordained a general minister and guide
to transfer vain wealth in due time
   from people to people, and from one to another family,
   beyond the intervention of human intelligence.

Thus one people rules and another languishes,
 according to her judgment, which is hidden from us,
 like a snake in the grass.   84
Your knowledge is of no avail against her;
 she foresees, judges, and rules her province
 as the other gods [angels] do theirs.
Her activity has no truce;
 necessity makes her quick to act,
 so that changes [in fortune] come often.
She is the one so reviled
 even by those who should praise her
 but who, instead, give her ill repute.
Yet she is blessed and does not hear;
 happy with the other primal [angelic] creatures
 she rules her sphere and rejoices in her bliss.] 96

*It is now a little after midnight of Good Friday. In a swamp the poets
see the bemired souls of the angry and the bubbles made by the sullen
beneath the surface. The travelers make a long detour to the left,
which indicates an approach to worse things.*

Now let us descend to greater misery;
 already each star that was rising when I started
 is falling, and staying too long is forbidden."
We crossed the circle to the inner bank
 along a stream which bubbled and flowed
 through a channel it had formed.
The water was darker than purplish-black;
 and, accompanying the murky waves,
 on a rough path, we reached the place below.
This dreary stream forms a marsh, the Styx,
 when it has reached the foot
 of the gray, malignant banks.   108
And I, who remained intent on looking,
 saw muddy people in that bog,
 naked, and with angry looks.
They struck each other not only with their hands,
 but with their heads, chests, and feet,
 and tore each other with their teeth, bit by bit.

My good master said, "Son, now see
        the souls of those whom anger overcame;
        I wish you to believe also

that under the water there are people sighing
        and making bubbles on the surface
        as your eyes tell you wherever you look.   120

Fixed in the slime they say, 'Sullen were we
        in the sweet air gladdened by the sun,
        keeping within us the fumes of spite;

now we are sullen in the black mire.'
        This hymn is gurgled in their throats,
        for they cannot speak in clear words."

Thus we covered a wide arc around the filthy slough
        between the dry bank and the swamp,
        with eyes turned to those swallowing the mire.

At last we came to the foot of a tower.

CANTO VIII

The Angry and the Sullen

*Continuing the account of the fifth circle, Dante anxiously inquires
about the meaning of certain signals. These are explained by the
coming of a boat guided by Phlegyas, the guardian of this round.*

I say, continuing, that long before we reached
        the foot of the high tower
        our eyes were drawn to its top

by two little flames placed there;
        and another gave back a signal from so far
        that our eyes could hardly catch it.

Turning to the sea of all wisdom, I asked,
        "What does this mean? what does the other flame
        answer? and who are they who light it?"

And he to me, "Over the foul waters
    already you can see what is expected
    if the mist of the marsh does not hide it from you."   12

Never did a bowstring drive an arrow
    which sped so quickly through the air
    as a little boat I saw then

coming through the water toward us
    under the guidance of a single boatman
    who cried, "Now you are caught, fell spirit!"

"Phlegyas, Phlegyas, this time you cry out
    in vain," said my lord, "you will keep us
    only while crossing the slough."

As one who learns of a great trick
    played on him and who resents it,
    so Phlegyas became in his pent-up rage.   24

My guide stepped down into the boat,
    making me get in after him,
    and only then did it appear burdened.

As soon as my master and I had embarked,
    the ancient prow moved on,
    cleaving more of the water than it does with others.

*Dante becomes angry at one of the shades, apparently incurring the
very sin punished here, but is commended for it by Virgil. The episode
is intended to show that righteous indignation is permissible. We
cannot love gentleness and politeness intensely without disliking
arrogance and incivility with equal intensity.*

While we were going through the stagnant channel,
    a shade covered with mud rose up, saying [insolently],
    "Who are you, coming before your time?"

I answered, "If I come, I do not stay,
    but who are you, now so dirty?"
    And he, "You see I am one who weeps."   36

Then I to him, "With tears and grief
    stay here, damned spirit,
    for I recognize you for all your filth."

Then the shade stretched both hands toward the boat,

but my wary master pushed him off, saying,
"Get over there with the other dogs!"

And embracing me with both arms
he kissed my face and said, "Indignant soul,
may she be blessed who bore you!

In the world he was an arrogant person;
no kindness adorned his memory,
so his shade is furious here.   48

How many think themselves great kings
who will lie like swine in the mire,
leaving behind horrible censure."

And I, "Master, I would be glad
to see him soused in this soup [muddy water]
before we leave the pond."

He answered, "Before you see the shore
you will be satisfied;
it is proper that such a wish be granted."

In a little while I saw the muddy crowd
wreak such havoc on him
that I still praise and thank God for it.   60

All cried, "At Filippo Argenti!"
and the raging Florentine spirit
turned with his teeth upon himself.

Here we left him, and of him I say no more.
A wailing now struck my ears,
so that I looked ahead intently.

My good master said, "Now son,
the City of Dis [Satan] draws near,
with its grave citizens, its great garrison."

And I, "Master, already I discern its mosques
clearly there within the valley,
red, as if they had come out of fire."   72

He continued, "The eternal flames
enkindling them make them glow
as you see in this lower Hell."

We now arrived within the moats

which surround the disconsolate city,
the walls of which seemed of iron.

Not without making a wide circuit [to the left]
did we come to where the boatman loudly cried,
"Get out, here is the entrance!"

Above the gates more than a thousand [rebellious angels],
rained down from Heaven, cried angrily,
"Who is this one, without death,   84

going through the kingdom of the dead?"
And my wise master signaled
that he wished to speak with them secretly.

Then they held back their great anger
and said, "You come alone and let him go
who so boldly entered this kingdom.

Let him return by himself on the mad path;
let him see if he can; for you will stay here,
you who have led him through so dark a country."

*Threatened with the loss of Virgil (Reason), Dante begs not to be
left alone. His guide tries to reassure him, but, as an intellectual
rather than a suggestive force, he can do that only imperfectly. As
Virgil leaves, Dante wonders whether the answer to a question about
the success of the mission will be "yes," or "no." Virgil also is not
sure, but, on returning, tries to comfort Dante by passing off his doubt
and dismay as anger. He hopes, with the limited confidence reason
gives, that an angel will bring divine aid.*

Think, Reader, if I was frightened
at the sound of the accursed words,
for I did not believe I could ever return.   96

"O my dear guide, you who many times
have made me safe and drawn me
through deep peril confronting me,

do not leave me so undone," I said,
"and if going farther is denied us,
let us retrace our steps together rapidly."

Then that lord who had brought me there replied,
"Do not fear, for no one can prevent our journey;
by Such a One it has been granted.

Wait for me here, and with good hope
 comfort and feed your weary spirit,
 for I will not leave you in the lower world."   **108**

Thus my dear father went away
 and abandoned me, and I remained in doubt,
 for "yes" and "no" struggled within my mind.

I could not hear what he said to our adversaries,
 but he did not stay long with them
 before each of them raced back.

They closed the gates in the face
 of my lord, who remained outside
 and then came toward me with slow steps,

his eyes upon the ground and with a face
 shorn of all boldness. He asked, sighing,
 "Who has denied us the abode of woe?"   **120**

Then to me he said, "Although I may get angry,
 do not fear, for I will win the fight,
 whatever is contrived within.

This insolence of theirs is not new;
 they showed it once at a less secret gate
 which is now without a fastening.

Over it you saw the deadly inscription;
 and already on this side of it,
 passing through the circles without escort,

someone descends who will open the city for us."

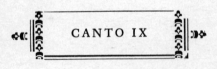

CANTO IX

The City of Dis

The hue that cowardice put on my face
 when I saw my guide come back
 made him repress more quickly his dismay.

He stopped, attentive, like a man listening;
    for sight could not go far
    through the dark air and thick mist.

"Still we must win the fight," he began,
    "if nòt . . . such help was offered us;
    oh, how I long for someone to come!"

I noticed how he covered up
    his first words with those that followed
    which expressed a different thought,   12

and his remark made me afraid
    because I drew the words cut off
    into a meaning perhaps worse than he intended.

Dante asks indirectly if Virgil really knows the way.

"To this depth of the dismal hole
    does any ever descend from the first circle
    where hope cut off is the only punishment?"

This question I asked, and he answered,
    "It seldom happens that one of us
    makes the journey on which I am going.

It is true that I was down here once before,
    conjured by that cruel Erichtho [a sorceress],
    who brought shades back to their bodies.   24

Not for long had my flesh been without me
    when she made me go within those walls
    to bring out a spirit from Judas' circle.

That is the lowest and darkest place, the one
    farthest removed from the heaven that encircles all.
    I know the road well; therefore be reassured

This swamp exhaling the great stench
    surrounds the woeful city
    which we cannot enter now peacefully."

Three Furies, handmaidens of Hecate, the ancient queen of Hell,
symbols of madness or remorseful terror, rise up, citing their error
in letting Theseus enter their region to rescue Persephone. Dante
clings to Virgil with desperation. The Furies then call upon the

Gorgon (Medusa, Despair) to turn the intruder to stone. Virgil warns his charge with great urgency not to look at her.

The allegorical meaning is perhaps as follows: the reforming Christian (Dante), when confronted by remorseful terror (the Furies) may lose his reason (Virgil), but as long as hope remains, he can appeal for divine aid. Only despair (Medusa) cuts off irremediably the path to salvation.

And more he said, but I do not recall it
    because my eyes drew all my thoughts
    to the glowing summit of the high tower   36

where suddenly three infernal Furies,
    with the shape and features of women,
    and stained with blood, stood upright.

They were girded with green hydras
    and had serpents and horned snakes for hair
    with which their wild heads were bound.

And he who knew well the handmaidens
    of the Queen of eternal lamentation
    said to me, "Behold! the fierce Erinyes [Furies].

The one on the left is Megaera;
    she on the right, weeping, is Alecto;
    Tisiphone is in the middle,"—and with that he was silent. 48

They were tearing their breasts with their nails,
    beating themselves with their hands, and shouting
    so loudly that in fear I drew close to my master.

"Let Medusa come, and we will change him to stone,"
    they all said, looking down,
    "badly did we avenge the assault of Theseus."

"Turn back and keep your eyes closed,
    for if the Gorgon [Medusa] shows herself
    and you see her, there will be no returning."

Thus my master spoke, and he himself
    turned me around, not trusting my hands,
    but with his also covered my eyes.   60

O you who have sound understanding,
    observe the meaning hidden
    beneath the veil of the strange verses.

And now over the turbid waters
> came a crash full of terror
> at which both the shores trembled,

a sound like that of a whirlwind
> made violent by conflicting currents
> which hits the forest without restraint,

shatters, beats down, and sweeps away the boughs.
> Behind a cloud of dust it moves on fiercely,
> and makes the beasts and shepherds flee.   72

My master freed my eyes and said,
> "Now direct your sight over that ancient foam
> to where the mist is thickest."

As frogs before their enemy the snake
> scatter through the water
> until each squats on the bottom,

so I saw more than a thousand ruined spirits
> fleeing before one [an angel] who,
> with dry feet, passed over the Styx.

From his face he fanned that gross air,
> moving his left hand in front of it,
> and only with that effort seemed weary.   84

I saw at once that he was sent from Heaven,
> and I turned to my master, who made a sign
> that I should keep quiet and bow to him.

How full of scorn he seemed to me!
> Coming to the gate, he opened it
> with a wand, for there was no resistance.

"O outcasts from Heaven, despised creatures!"
> he began, on the horrible threshold,
> "why do you harbor this insolence?

Why do you oppose that will
> whose purpose can never be hindered,
> and which has several times increased your pain?   96

Of what use is it to butt against fate?
> Your Cerberus [chained by Hercules] because of this
> still has a chin and throat without hair."

Then he turned back over the filthy road.

and said no word to us, but seemed
like one intent on other cares

than those of the people near him;
and we moved on toward the city,
safe, after the holy words.

On entering, Dante sees open tombs, hotter than iron in a black-
smith's forge. Each contains the leader of a heretical sect with his
followers. Here, contrary to their custom, the travelers turn to the
right, perhaps to indicate that heresy can be incurred honestly,
although persistence in it is a sin of pride.

We entered without any strife,
and I, wanting to see what punishments
such a fortress enclosed,   108

as soon as within glanced around
and saw on every side a great plain
full of grief and torment.

As at Arles where the Rhone spreads out
or at Pola near [the bay of] Quarnero
which encloses Italy and bathes her boundaries,

the tombs make the land uneven,
so they did here, on all sides,
except that these graves were more terrible;

for among the tombs flames spread
by which they were so heated
that no trade needs iron hotter.   120

All their lids were open,
and such harsh laments came from them
as from the wretched and the suffering.

And I, "Master, who are the people
buried within the tombs,
making themselves heard by their painful sighs?"

And he to me, "Here are the archheretics
with their followers of every sect;
and the tombs are laden much more than you think.

Like with like is buried,

and the monuments are more and less hot."
Then, after we had turned to the right,   132
we passed between the torments and the high battlements.

Farinata degli Uberti

Now along a solitary path
    between the city wall and the torments,
    my master makes his way, and I behind him.

"O supreme genius, you who through the impious circles
    turn me [to the left or right] as you please," I began,
    "speak to me and satisfy my wishes.

The people lying in the sepulchres,
    might they be seen?—all the lids
    are raised and no one guards them."

And he to me, "All will be locked in
    when they return from Jehoshaphat [on Judgment Day]
    with the bodies they have left above.   12

*Epicurus is with the heretics of Christian times since he, almost alone
among ancient philosophers, denied the immortality of the soul.*

*Still hesitant about asking questions, Dante represses his desire to
see certain Florentines.*

On this side is the burial place
    of Epicurus and of all his followers
    who hold that the soul dies with the body.

But concerning the question you ask
    you will soon be satisfied,
    and also as to the wish you keep silent."

And I, "Good guide, I hide my thought
    only to speak little; not long ago
    you disposed me to do that."

A deep voice sounds amid the silence of the graves. It is that of Farinata degli Uberti, a Ghibelline leader who, in 1260, won the bloody battle of Montaperti over the Florentine Guelfs, to which party Dante's family belonged. In recalling the bloodshed, Farinata has a moment of spontaneous repentance. Dante timidly draws closer to his guide who then directs him toward this proud, towering figure.

"O Tuscan, you who through the city of fire
    go alive, speaking thus modestly,
    may it please you to remain in this place.   **24**

Your speech shows you a native
    of that noble fatherland
    to which, perhaps, I was too harmful."

Suddenly this sound came
    from one of the tombs, so that, startled,
    I drew closer to my guide.

He said to me, "Turn around! what are you doing?
    See Farinata, who has stood erect;
    from the waist upward, wholly, you can see him!"

I had already fixed my eyes on his,
    and he lifted up his chest and head,
    as if he had scorn for Hell,   **36**

and the bold and ready hands of my guide
    pushed me among the sepulchres to him,
    saying, "Let your words be well chosen."

Disappointed in not seeing someone of his own generation, Farinata asks about Dante's ancestors. On hearing the names of these former enemies, he tells angrily how he had scattered them. Now Dante's partisan spirit is aroused. He points out that his party has been able to return to Florence, whereas Farinata's has not learned the art of getting back. Dante's remark is an unexpected blow for the Ghibelline captain, who is unaware of all the events and who remains silent, trying to recover and to collect his thoughts.

When I was at the foot of his tomb
    he looked at me a little; then, almost disdainfully,
    he asked, "Who were your ancestors?"

I, desirous to obey, did not hide them,

but revealed them all,
whereupon he raised his brows a little

and said, "Fiercely were they adverse
to me and to my ancestors and to my party,
so that twice I scattered them."   48

"If they were driven out, they came back from every side,"
I answered him, "both the first and the second time,
but yours did not learn well that art!"

*Now the shade of the father of Guido Cavalcanti, the latter a leading
poet and Dante's best friend, rises beside the great Ghibelline leader.
He too is not interested in Dante. He assumes that our poet is allowed
to visit Hell because of some peculiar merit, and since he cannot
conceive of greater nobility of mind than that of his son, he wonders
why Guido is not there also. Dante is perplexed, not knowing that the
shades are ignorant of immediate happenings on earth, and replies
ambiguously, implying lack of devotion on Guido's part to Virgil.
The important point, however, is the past tense of the verb he uses.
Cavalcante assumes from it that his son is dead, and from the embar-
rassed tone of Dante's remarks, suspects that Guido may have had
a fate somewhat like his own. Dante's delay in answering confirms
his fear, and he falls back into his tomb.*

Now beside him there arose to sight
a shade visible down to his chin;
I believe he had risen on his knees.

He looked around me as if anxious
to see if someone else were with me,
but when this expectation was wholly spent,

weeping he said, "If through this blind prison
you go because of the greatness of your mind,
where is my son? why is he not with you?"   60

And I to him, "By myself I do not come;
Virgil, waiting there, guides me,
whom perhaps your Guido held in disdain."

His words and the manner of his punishment
had already revealed his name to me;
therefore my reply was so complete.

Rising suddenly he cried, "What did you say?

he *held?* Does he not live still?
    Does not the sweet light strike his eyes?"

When he was aware of some delay
    before I answered, he fell back supine
    and showed himself no more.   **72**

*Meanwhile Farinata has been pondering over Dante's remark and,
without transition, oblivious to the drama enacted at his feet, he
returns the verbal blow by predicting the poet's exile within four
years. Relieved by this aggression, he asks in a more kindly tone why
the Florentines have persecuted his family, and he points out proudly
how, after the battle, when the Ghibelline leaders proposed razing
Florence to the ground, he alone defended and saved her. Now Dante's
partisan spirit is likewise softened, and in the conversation that follows
he learns that the shades remember the past and can predict the future,
but, like farsighted people, cannot see what is close at hand. This
accounts for the misunderstanding between him and Cavalcante, and
he asks to have his error corrected.*

But that other magnanimous one, at whose instance
    I had stopped, did not change his expression,
    nor move his head, nor bend his body.

"And if," he said, continuing his first remark,
    "they have badly learned that art,
    it torments me more than this bed.

But not fifty times will be rekindled
    the face of her [Hecate, the moon] who rules here
    before you will know the hardness of that art!

And—so may you return sometime to the sweet world—
    tell me why the people are so fierce
    against my kindred in all their laws."   **84**

Then I to him, "The slaughter and havoc
    which dyed the [river] Arbia red
    cause such prayers to rise in our temple."

Sighing he shook his head and said,
    "In that I was not alone, nor certainly
    would I and the others have moved without cause,

but I was alone when all the rest

agreed to wipe out Florence:
    I defended her openly before all."

"So may your descendants sometime have rest,"
    I replied, "please solve for me this puzzle
    which has now entangled my judgment.   96

It seems that you see, if I hear rightly,
    what the future brings,
    but for the present have a different vision."

"Like those with imperfect sight,
    we see things far from us," he said,
    "so much light the Supreme Ruler still allows,

but when they come close, or exist, our minds
    do not perceive them, and, without news from others,
    we know nothing of your human state.

Therefore you can understand that our knowledge [gained
        from others]
    will be wholly dead after that moment [Judgment Day]
    when the gates of the future are closed."   108

Then, as if sorry for my fault,
    I said, "Now please tell that fallen one
    that his son is still joined with the living,

and if I was silent at his question,
    let him know it was because my thoughts
    were confused by the error you have corrected."

*Before moving on, Virgil declares emphatically that Beatrice will
reveal to Dante the course of his life. This is a mistake on Virgil's
part: Cacciaguida, not Beatrice, makes the prophecy.*

*(The treatment of the heretics is a comedy of errors which illustrates
the fallibility of human reason. The Epicureans, in their tombs, erred
in thinking that the grave ended all; Farinata is deceived in several
ways; Cavalcante makes a series of false assumptions; Dante likewise
is bewildered. Finally Virgil [Reason itself] is emphatically wrong.)*

Already my master was calling me back,
    so that I begged the spirit more hastily
    to tell me who was with him.

He said, "With more than a thousand I lie:

here is the second Frederick [of Sicily]
and the Cardinal [Ubaldino]; of the others I am silent."   120

Then he hid himself, and toward the ancient poet
I turned my steps, meditating
about the prophecy hostile to me.

My guide moved on and, as we were going,
he said to me, "Why are you so bewildered?"
and I satisfied his request.

"Let your mind retain what you have heard
against you," that sage commanded me,
"and now listen to this," and he raised his finger:

"When you face the sweet light
of her [Beatrice] whose fair eyes see everything
you will learn from her the journey of your life."   132

Then he turned his steps to the left;
we went from the wall toward the center
along a path which goes into a valley

which even up there stifled us with its stench.

CANTO XI

The Classification of Sins

*As the poets proceed toward the inner edge of the sixth circle, they
observe a tomb inscribed with the name of Anastasius. There was
confusion in Dante's time between a pope and a heretical Byzantine
emperor of that name.*

*While waiting to become accustomed to the smell which rises from
a river of hot blood below, Virgil explains the various divisions of Hell.
These are shown in the outline on pages 3–5.*

*To explain why usurers are classed with blasphemers and sodomites
as doing violence to God, Virgil points out that Nature, which offers
man its bounty, derives from God; that man's art (industry) gives*

further value to the products of Nature and, in a sense, derives also
from God; that man was intended to earn his living through the bounty
of Nature and by the sweat of his brow, and that usurers violate this
divine plan.

At the end of the canto we learn by the position of the stars that it
is about three hours after midnight, Saturday, April 9, 1300.

[On the edge of a high bank
    formed by a circle of broken rocks
    we stood above a more cruel pack;
and here because of the horrible stench
    which the deep abyss exhales
    we approached behind the cover of a great tomb
on which I saw an inscription saying,
    "I hold Anastasius, the pope,
    whom Photinus drew from the straight path."
"Our descent must be slow, so that our sense of smell
    may get used to the foul breath,
    and then we will not heed it."   12
Thus my master spoke, and I, "Please find compensation,
    so that time will not be wasted."
    And he, "That is what I have been thinking of.
My son," he then continued,
    "below us are three smaller circles
    like those you are leaving,
full of accursed spirits. In order
    that sight alone may suffice henceforth,
    observe how and why they are confined.
The malice which Heaven reproves
    causes injury and grief to others
    either by violence or by fraud,   24
but because fraud is peculiar to man
    it displeases God more; therefore
    the fraudulent are placed lower and have more pain.
The next circle [seventh] is for the violent,
    and, since force can be used
    against God, oneself, and one's fellow men—
I mean against them or their property—
    it is divided into three bands
    as you will clearly hear.

Death and painful wounds may be inflicted
    on one's fellows, and plunder, arson,
    and extortion on their property.   36
Thus the first round torments, in various groups,
    assassins, plunderers, and robbers,
    and all who strike maliciously.
A man may commit violence against himself
    and against his property; therefore, in the second round,
    all who deprive themselves of your world
or gamble and dissipate their wealth
    must unavailingly repent
    and weep instead of being happy.
Violence is committed against the Deity
    by cursing Him and denying Him in one's heart;
    and by scorning Nature and her bounty;   48
therefore the smallest band stamps with its seal
    both Sodom [the sodomites] and Cahors [the usurers]
    and those [the blasphemers] who speak disdaining God.
Fraud which hurts man's conscience
    can be used against those who trust
    and against those who have no special confidence.
In the latter case, only the love that Nature makes
    [the natural brotherhood of man] is violated;
    thus, in the following [eighth] circle are nested
hypocrisy, flattery, sorcery,
    falsifying, theft, and simony,
    panders, barrators, and similar filth.   60
The other fraud violates
    both the love Nature creates and that
    which implies a special trust.
Therefore, in the smallest circle
    at the center of the universe where Dis [Satan] holds
        forth
    whoever betrays is eternally consumed."
And I, "Master, your account proceeds clearly
    and makes plain the division
    of this abyss and those who are in it,
but tell me, the souls [above] in the slimy bog,
    those whom the wind blows, and those the rain beats,
    and those who meet with such sharp tongues,   72

why are they not inside the ruddy city
    if God is angry with them,
    and if not, why are they in such a plight?"
He answered, "Why does your mind
    go astray more than usual?
    or are you thinking of something else?
Do you not remember those words
    with which your *Ethics* [of Aristotle] treats
    the three dispositions Heaven does not admit—
incontinence, malice, and mad bestiality—
    and how incontinence offends God less
    and incurs less blame?   84
If you consider this teaching
    and recall who is being punished
    outside of the city,
you will see why they are separated
    from these and why, less angrily,
    Divine Justice torments them."
"O Sun, you who heal every troubled vision,
    I am so glad to hear you explain
    that to question pleases me no less than knowing;
but go back a little," I said,
    "to where you say that usury offends
    divine goodness, and solve the puzzle."   96
"Philosophy," he said,
    "states in more than one place
    that Nature takes her course
from the Divine Intellect and from Its operation,
    and if you note well your *Physics*,
    you will find after not many pages
that your activity follows the divine plan,
    as the pupil does his master, so that your art [industry]
    is, as it were, a grandchild of God.
From these two [Nature and Industry], if you recall
    the early part of Genesis,
    man should earn his living and prosper.   108
And because the usurer takes another way,
    he scorns Nature in itself and in its follower [Industry],
    since he places his hope in something else.
But follow me now, for I wish to go.

The Fishes [Pisces] are quivering on the horizon
    and the Chariot [Big Dipper] lies wholly over Caurus
        [the northwest],
and the cliff we descend is far over there.]

CANTO XII

The Violent

*Near a break in the cliff, a landslide caused by the revulsion of the
earth at the Crucifixion, is the Minotaur, a creature with a man's body
and a bull's head, the bestial guardian of the circle of the violent.
To get around this monster, Virgil puts him in a blind rage by men-
tioning the circumstances of his death, how his half sister, Ariadne,
had guided Theseus through the labyrinth to him.*

The place where we came to descend the bank
    was craggy and, because of what was there [the
        Minotaur],
    such that every eye would shun it.

As the landslide which, on this side of Trento,
    struck the Adige, either because of an earthquake
    or from being undermined—

for, from the top of the mountain
    to the plain, the cliff has so fallen
    that it provides a path for one above—

such was the descent into this ravine;
    and on the edge of the broken chasm,
    the infamy of Crete [the Minotaur], conceived   12

in the false [wooden] cow, was stretched out.
    On seeing us the monster bit himself
    like one subdued by anger.

My sage cried to him, "Perhaps you think
    the Duke of Athens [Theseus] is here
    who killed you in the world.

Get away, beast, for this man does not come
  instructed by your sister,
  but journeys on to see your punishments."

As a bull that breaks loose at the moment
  when it receives a mortal blow
  and cannot go straight, but plunges here and there, 24

so I saw the Minotaur stagger,
  and my wary guide shouted, "Run to the pass;
  while he is raging it is well for you to go down."

Thus we made our way over the loose rocks
  which often moved under my feet
  because of the unusual burden.

As I went on, thinking, my guide said,
  "Perhaps you are wondering about this landslide
  guarded by the bestial wrath I outwitted.

Now I want you to know that the other time
  I went down here into deep Hell
  this cliff had not yet been broken, 36

but, if I discern correctly, shortly before
  He [Christ] came to the first circle
  to remove the great prey from Dis [at the "harrowing"]

the loathsome pit trembled on all sides
  so that I thought the universe felt love
  because of which some [philosophers] believed

the world has many times reverted to chaos [a fusion
  of the elements]; and at that moment these old rocks
  here and elsewhere fell down.

But look below, for the river of blood
  is near, in which are boiled
  those who through violence harm others." 48

*On the banks of the river are centaurs, creatures with horses' bodies,
but whose heads (unlike that of the Minotaur) are human.*

O blind greed, wicked and foolish,
  which so spurs us in the brief life,
  and in the eternal condemns to such pain!

I saw a wide moat making a bend

surrounding the level ground [of the circle]
　　like the one my escort had mentioned,

and between the foot of the bank and the ditch
　　centaurs, armed with arrows, were running, in single file,
　　as they used to go hunting in our world.

Seeing us descend all stopped,
　　and three came from the band,
　　having armed themselves with bows and arrows.　　　　**60**

One shouted from afar, "To what punishment
　　are you coming? Tell us from there;
　　if not, I'll draw the bow!"

My master answered, "We will reply
　　to Chiron over there; unfortunately,
　　you were always quick to act."

Then he touched me and said, "That is Nessus
　　who died for the beautiful Dejanira
　　and by himself took vengeance for himself.

The one in the middle, looking at his breast,
　　is the great Chiron, the teacher of Achilles,
　　and the other is Pholus, who was so full of rage.　　**72**

Around the ditch they go by thousands
　　shooting shades that rise from the blood
　　farther than their sins allow."

As we drew near those rapid beasts
　　Chiron took an arrow, and with the notch
　　combed back the beard on his jaws,

and when he had uncovered his great mouth
　　he said to his companions, "Did you notice
　　that the one behind moves what he touches?

The feet of the dead do not do this."
　　And my good guide, already close to the breast
　　where the two natures were joined, answered,　　　　**84**

"He is indeed alive, and thus alone
　　I must show him the dark valley.
　　Necessity brings him here, not pleasure.

A lady [Beatrice] who came from singing hallelujah

entrusted this mission to me;
   he is no robber nor am I a thief.

Therefore, by that power through which
   I move my feet over so rough a road,
   give us one of your band to be with us,

to show us where the ford is, and to carry
   this man on his back, for he is not a spirit
   that can go through the air."   96

Chiron, turning to his better side, appoints Nessus as the leader. The party see first various Greek and Italian tyrants, sunk to their eyebrows in the blood; then assassins, among whom, shunned by the others, is the first Englishman mentioned, Guy of Montfort who in a church at Viterbo killed Prince Henry. Henry's heart, it was said, was placed in a golden urn in Westminster Abbey.

Chiron turned to his right
   and said to Nessus, "Go back and guide them,
   and if you meet another band, make it give way."

We started with our trusted escort
   along the bank of the vermilion stream
   in which those boiled uttered loud cries.

I saw shades in it up to their eyebrows;
   and the great centaur said, "These are tyrants
   who engaged in bloodshed and in plunder.

Now they weep for their pitiless crimes.
   Here are Alexander and fierce Dionysius
   who gave Italy years of woe,   108

and that head with such black hair
   is Azzolino; and the blond one,
   Opizzo da Este, who, in truth,

was killed by his stepson in the world above."
   Then I turned to the poet, who said,
   "Let him go first now and me second."

A little farther on the centaur stopped
   above a group who down to their throats
   appeared above the boiling stream.

Then he showed us a shade to one side, alone, saying,

"That one, in God's bosom, pierced the heart
   that still is honored on the Thames."   120

Afterward I saw some who kept their heads
   and chests out of the stream,
   and of those I recognized many.

Thus, little by little, the blood grew shallow
   until it cooked only the feet,
   and there was our passage over the moat.

"As on this side you see the boiling river
   grow shallow," said the centaur,
   "so I wish you to believe

that on the other its bottom gets deeper
   until it reaches the place
   where tyrants must groan.   132

There Divine Justice torments
   that Attila who was a scourge on earth,
   and Pyrrhus and Sextus; and eternally it milks

the tears, which the boiling releases,
   from Rinieri da Corneto and Rinieri Pazzo
   who waged such warfare on the highways."

Then Nessus turned back and repassed the ford.

CANTO XIII

Pier delle Vigne

*The poets enter the wood of the Christian suicides. This wild forest
represents the world as it would be if all revolted against life. It is
infested by the Harpies, loathsome creatures, half human, half birds,
which stand for the storm winds of human passions.*

*In every way the suicides, now changed into trees or saplings, are
frustrated. They have used their power of movement to deprive them-
selves of what distinguished them from plants; but they have not*

*found death. The Harpies they tried to escape go with them, and the
old agony is pent up in their new embodiments.*

Nessus had not yet reached the other side
    when we entered a wood
    that was marked by no path.

No green foliage was there, but of a dark color,
    no smooth branches, but knotty and twisted,
    no fruit, but poisonous thorns.

The wild beasts that shun cultivated places
    do not have such dense and tangled thickets
    [in the Maremma] between Cecina and Corneto.

Here the ugly Harpies make their nests
    who with sad predictions of future harm
    drove the Trojans from the Strophades.   12

They have wide wings and human necks and faces,
    feet with claws, and great feathered bellies;
    they utter laments on the strange trees.

My good master began to speak, saying,
    "Before you go any farther, know
    that you are in the second round and will be

until you come to the horrible sand.
    Therefore look closely and you will see
    what would seem incredible in my speech."

I heard moans on every side
    and saw no one to make them,
    so that I stopped, all bewildered.   24

I believe he believed that I believed
    that so many voices came from people
    hidden from us among the trees;

therefore he said, "If you break
    a twig of one of these woody plants
    the thoughts you have will be corrected."

Then I stretched forth my hand
    and plucked a small branch from a great thorn tree,
    and its trunk cried, "Why do you break me?"

After it had grown dark with blood,

it began again to lament, "Why do you tear me?
have you no trace of pity?   36

We were men, and now are turned to wood;
    your hand should have been more merciful
    if we had been the souls of serpents."

As a green log, burning at one end,
    drips from the other and hisses
    with the steam that escapes,

so from the broken branch words and blood
    came out together; and I let the twig fall
    and stood like one afraid.

*The tree whose branch Dante has broken is that of Pier delle Vigne,
a famous statesman, scholar, and poet at the court of Frederick II of
Sicily. (In several curious, repetitious lines Dante imitates the style of
the Frederician poets.) Frederick accused him of treason, had him
blinded and led in derision on an ass from town to town. To escape
this dishonor, Pier is said to have beaten his head against the walls
of his prison. Dante presents him as innocent, as the model of a
devoted public servant. He is proud of the office he once held and
still loyal to the king who could do no wrong. It was Envy, he says,
the harlot at every court, who caused his death. And he swears by
his new body that he was never unfaithful.*

"If he [Dante] could have believed, offended soul,"
    my master answered,
    "what he has seen only in my verse,   48

he would not have raised his hand against you,
    but the incredible thing made me prompt him
    to do what grieves me.

Now tell him who you were, so that
    to make amends, he may refresh your fame
    in the world above to which he is permitted to return."

Then the tree, "You so allure me with kind words
    that I cannot keep silent, and may you
    not be wearied if I grow sticky talking.

I am the one who held both keys [of consent and denial]
    to Frederick's heart, and who turned them,
    locking and unlocking so softly

that I kept almost everyone from his secrets.
   Such trust I bore to the glorious office
   that I lost sleep and strength.

The harlot [Envy] who never from Caesar's dwelling
   has turned aside her shameless eyes,
   the common bane and vice of courts,

inflamed all minds against me,
   and the inflamed so inflamed Augustus [Frederick]
   that my joyous honors changed to dismal sorrow.

My soul with disgust and scorn,
   hoping to escape disdain,
   made me unjust to my just self.   72

By the new roots of this tree, I swear to you
   that I never broke faith with my lord
   who was so worthy of honor.

And if either of you return to the world,
   comfort my memory which still lies crushed
   by the blow that Envy gave it."

Pier tells how the souls fall and become trees and bushes.

*After Judgment Day, the bodies the suicides could not endure for
a few brief years will hang on their branches forever. This is the
final frustration.*

The poet waited a little and then said,
   "Since he is silent, do not lose the chance,
   but question him if you want to hear more."

And I answered, *"You* ask what you think
   will satisfy me, for I could not;
   such pity saddens me."   84

Then he began, "So may this man
   do freely for you what you ask,
   please tell us, imprisoned spirit,

how the soul becomes bound in these branches,
   and let us know if you can
   if any ever frees himself from them."

The tree blew loudly, and soon

the wind changed into these sounds:
"Briefly will you be answered.

When the fierce soul leaves the body
from which it has torn itself,
Minos sends it to the seventh depth. 96

It falls into the wood; no place is chosen for it,
but where chance throws it
it sprouts, like a grain of wheat.

It grows into a sapling and a wild tree;
the Harpies, feeding then upon its leaves,
give pain and to the pain an outlet.

Like the others we will come for our bodies,
but not to be clothed again with them,
for it is not right to get back what is rejected.

Here we will drag them, and
in the sad wood our bodies will be hung
on the branches of our injurious souls." 108

Two spirits rush by, chased by the hounds of ruin and crying for a
second death they can never have. These are souls of reckless
squanderers, destroyers of their estates and indirectly of themselves.
One, Lano, in desperate circumstances, allowed himself to be killed
in the battle of Toppo.

We were still attentive to the tree,
believing that it wished to say more,
when a loud sound startled us

as it does the hunter who sees the boar and chase
approach his post and who hears the beast
and the crash of the branches.

And behold! two on the left,
naked and scratched, fleeing so fast
that they broke the brambles of the wood.

The one in the front cried, "Now come, now come, O Death!"
and the other who saw himself outdistanced, called,
"Lano, your legs were not so nimble 120

at the tournament of Toppo " And, perhaps
because his breath had failed, he plunged
into a bush, making a tangle of it and of himself.

Behind them the wood was full of black bitches,
    ravenous and running fast,
      like greyhounds just freed from the leash.

They fixed their teeth in the one who squatted
    and tore him to pieces,
      then carried off the suffering members.

My guide then took me by the hand
    and led me to the bush, which lamented vainly
      through its bleeding wounds.

"O Giacomo da Sant'Andrea," it cried,   132
    "what do you gain by making me a screen?
      what blame have I for your wicked life?"

My master had stopped beside it and asked,
    "Who were you, you who through so many breaks
      blow forth your woeful blood and words?"

*The soul in the bush deplores the situation in Florence where martial
virtue has been sacrificed for money-making (represented by John the
Baptist whose image was stamped on Florentine coins); then he iden-
tifies himself briefly, not by a name but by an act: he desecrated his
own home by making a gallows in it.*

And the bush to us, "O souls coming
    to see the shameful ravage
      that has so separated my leaves from me,

gather them together at the foot of the poor plant.
    I was of the city which changed its first patron [Mars]
      for the Baptist, because of which   144

that god will always sadden it with his art,
    and if, at the bridge over the Arno
      there did not remain a trace of him [the ruins of a statue],

those citizens who rebuilt the city
    on the ashes left by Attila
      would have done their work in vain.

I made a gibbet for myself of my own house."

CANTO XIV

The Violent against God

The round of the violent against God or Nature is characterized by sterility. On the hot sand the blasphemers are lying supine, the sodomites are running, the usurers sitting. Over all is falling a rain of fire which, here and elsewhere, symbolizes the direct wrath of God.

Because love for my native city moved me,
    I gathered the scattered leaves and gave them back
    to him whose voice was already faint.

Then we came to where the second round [the wood]
    is divided from the third [the plain]
    and where is seen a fearful kind of justice.

To make the new place manifest,
    I say that we reached a desert
    which repels every plant from its bed.

The doleful wood forms a garland around it,
    just as the dismal moat does to the wood.
    Here, at the very edge, we stopped.   12

The ground was of dry, thick sand,
    not different from that [of the Libyan desert]
    once trod by Cato's feet.

O how greatly the vengeance of God
    should be feared by everyone who reads
    what was apparent to my eyes!

I saw many groups of naked souls,
    all of whom wept miserably,
    but different positions were imposed on them.

Some were lying supine upon the ground,
    some were sitting, bent over,
    and others were running continually.   24

Those that kept moving were most numerous

and those fewest who were lying in the torment,
    but their tongues were loosened by greater pain.

Over all the plain, falling slowly,
    dilated flakes of fire came down,
    like snow in Alps without a wind.

As Alexander in those hot parts
    of India saw flames fall on his host
    intact as far as to the ground,

and made his legions trample
    on the soil, since the fire
    could be extinguished better before it spread;   36

so fell the eternal heat
    by which the sand was kindled
    like tinder under flint, to double the pain.

Ever without rest was the dance
    of the miserable hands, now here, now there,
    brushing off the fresh burning.

*Dante notices a shade still untamed, bold, indomitable, defying Jove
and the thunderbolts which defeated the giants. Virgil has more
contempt for this apparent superman than for anyone else in Hell.
Flat on his back, feeling hour after hour eternally the power of the
God he is defying, his attitude seems stupid rather than courageous,
and is peculiarly disgusting to Reason.*

I began, "Master, you who have overcome everything
    except the fierce demons who rushed out against us
    at the entrance to the City,

who is that great shade not heeding the fire,
    lying scornful and contorted,
    whom the rain does not seem to ripen?"   48

And he, aware that I was asking my guide
    about him, shouted loudly,
    "As I was alive, so am I dead.

Though Jove exhaust his smith from whom,
    angrily, he took the sharp thunderbolt
    by which I was struck on my last day,

and though he weary the others [the Cyclops] one by one

in Mongibello [Mt. Etna] at the black forge,
crying, 'Help, help, good Vulcan!'—

as he did in the battle of Phlegra [against the giants]—
and hit me with all his strength,
he could not have the joy of vengeance."   60

Then my guide spoke with such feeling
that I had never heard his voice so loud,
"O Capaneus, since your pride

remains untamed you are punished more.
No torture except your rage itself
would be adequate for your fury."

Then he turned to me with a better look, saying,
"This was one of the seven kings
who besieged Thebes; he held and still seems

to hold God in contempt, and to fear Him little;
but, as I told him, his blasphemy
is a fitting ornament for his breast.   72

*The travelers come to where the overflow from Phlegethon, the river
of blood, crosses the plain. The water of this little stream is like the
Bulicame, a hot spring near Viterbo, where special bathhouses were
provided for prostitutes. Its sterile banks offer a passageway, since over
the blood-stained water the fire is quenched, a confirmation or symbol
of atonement, the appeasing of God's wrath by human suffering.*

Now follow me and be careful
not to put your feet on the burning sand,
but always keep them close to the wood."

In silence we came to where, out of
the forest, a little rivulet gushes,
the redness of which still makes me shudder.

As from the Bulicame a stream flows
which sinful women share among themselves,
so this one flowed across the sand.

Its bottom and both its sides
were made of stone and also the banks
on which I perceived that our way led.   84

"Among all the things I have shown you

since we entered the gate
        whose threshold is denied to none,

nothing has been seen by your eyes
        as notable as the present stream
        which quenches all the flames above it."

These words were spoken by my guide,
        and I asked him to grant the food
        for which he had given me an appetite.

With elaborate symbolism, Virgil now tells of man's fall from grace and the consequences. On Mount Ida, in Crete, the center of the ancient world and the supposed cradle of the human race, there is a statue which represents the history of mankind. Its back is turned toward the East, its face in the direction of the course of empire. Its head, representing the Golden Age of the Ancients or the period of the Garden of Eden, is of gold; other parts, according to the various ages, are of different metals. One foot is of iron (the Roman Empire), the other of clay (the Papacy), and the weight of the statue bears too heavily on the latter, the cause, in Dante's view, of much of the anarchy and disorder in the world. The whole statue except the head has been cracked by man's sin. From this fissure tears drip. They flow down to Hell, form the waters of the Acheron, the Styx, the Phlegethon, and ultimately the frozen Cocytus. Thus, by a kind of conservation of sorrow, the tears shed through cruelty are not lost, but flow down to punish those who cause them.

Another river, the Lethe, descends to Hell from Purgatory carrying with it the last trace, that is, the very memory, of sin.

["In the middle of the sea," he said then,
        "lies a waste land, called Crete,
        under whose kings the world once was chaste.   96

A mountain there, named Ida,
        was joyous with water and with leaves;
        now it is deserted, like a thing worn out.

Rhea chose it for the safe cradle
        of her son [Jupiter]; and to hide him better
        when he cried, she had a clamor made.

On the mountain stands a great old man [a statue]
        with back turned toward Damietta [in the East]
        and looking toward Rome as in a mirror.

His head is formed of fine gold,
    his arms and breast are of pure silver;
    then he is of brass as far as to the fork.   108
From there down he is made of fine iron,
    except that the right foot is of baked clay,
    and he stands on that more than on the other.
Every part except the gold is broken
    by a fissure which drips tears
    and these, joining, cut through that bank,
flow down to this pit, and form the Acheron,
    the Styx, and the Phlegethon;
    then, moving on through this narrow channel,
go down to where there can be no further descent.
    They form Cocytus; and since you will see
    how that lake is, I do not describe it."   120
And I to him, "If the present stream
    comes thus from our world,
    why does it appear only here?"
And he, "You know that the place is round,
    and, although you have come far
    always descending to the left,
you have not yet completed the circle;
    therefore, if something new appears,
    it should not cause marveling."
Then I asked, "Master, where are the Phlegethon
    and Lethe, for you are silent about one [Lethe]
    and say that this rain forms the other."   132
"In all your questions you please me,"
    he replied, "but the boiling red water
    ought to answer one [about the Phlegethon].
You will see Lethe outside of this pit
    where souls go to wash themselves
    when guilt, repented, is removed.
Now it is time to leave the wood;
    see that you come behind me;
    the banks, not burned, offer a way,
and over them all fire is extinguished."]

CANTO XV

Brunetto Latini

The banks of the rivulet are like the dikes built by the Flemings or those made along the Brenta before the snow melts in the Chiarentana mountains. As the poets pass, they are eyed intently by a band of sodomites. Dante recognizes one as Brunetto Latini, a famous author and scholar, some of whose lectures Dante evidently heard. Dante extends his hand with reverence and, using the polite (voi) form of address, tells of his surprise at meeting him in this place.

Now one of the hard banks offers us a way,
    and the vapor of the stream makes a shelter
    which protects the shores and water from the fire.

As the Flemings between Wissant and Bruges,
    fearing the flood which rushes toward them,
    make a bulwark to repel the sea,

and as the Paduans do along the Brenta
    to defend their cities and their castles,
    before Chiarentana feels the heat,

in such a manner those banks were formed,
    although their builder, whoever he was,
    made them not so high nor so thick.   **12**

Already we were so far from the wood
    that I could not have seen where it was
    if I had turned back

when we met a band of spirits
    coming along the bank, and each gazed at us
    as, at dusk, under a new moon,

men are wont to look at each other,
    sharpening their eyes at us
    as an old tailor does at his needle's eye.

Thus gazed at by such a group,

I was recognized by one who grasped my skirt
    and cried, "What a marvel!"   24

And as he held out his arm toward me
    I fixed my glance on his baked aspect
    so that his burned face did not prevent

the recognition of him by my memory.
    Lowering my hand toward his face,
    I asked, "Are *you* here, *ser* Brunetto?"

Brunetto proposes to accompany Dante by walking along below him.
He must keep moving: restlessness is common to the punishment of
all sexual sinners. Dante shows the greatest affection for his old
master, a feeling reciprocated by Brunetto, who prophesies Dante's
quarrel with the Florentines. They, according to legend, represent
a fusion of the descendants of a Roman colony and of the rough hill
people from Fiesole. Dante wishes that Brunetto had not been
banished in a double sense from human nature, and pays him the
supreme tribute to a teacher: he taught, not the minutiae of scholarship
and pedantry, but the important things, how man, through fame, can
make himself eternal.

And he, "O my son, may it not displease you
    if Brunetto Latini goes back with you a little,
    letting his company move on."

I said to him, "As much as I can I beg you to,
    and if you want me to sit down with you,
    I will do so, if he with whom I go permits."   36

"O son," he said, "whoever of this flock
    stops one instant, lies afterward a hundred years
    without brushing off the fire that strikes him;

therefore, go on; I will follow at your skirts
    and then I will rejoin my band
    which goes lamenting its eternal punishment."

I did not dare go down from the path
    to be with him, but I held my head low
    like one who walks with reverence.

He began, "What chance or destiny
    brings you here before your last day,
    and who is this one showing you the road?"   48

"Up there in the serene life," I answered,
  "I went astray in a valley,
  before my allotted time was spent.

Yesterday morning I turned my back on it;
  then, as I was falling into it again, this shade appeared
  who is taking me home by this road."

And he to me, "If you follow your star
  you cannot fail to reach a glorious port
  if I discerned rightly in the fair life.

And if I had not died so early,
  seeing the heavens so gracious to you,
  I would have cheered you in your work.   60

That ungrateful, malignant people who of old
  came down from Fiesole and still keep
  the roughness of the mountains and the rocks

will become your enemies because of your good deeds.
  And that is right, for among the bitter sorb trees
  it is not fitting that the sweet fig bear fruit.

Old report in the world calls them blind,
  an avaricious, envious, haughty people:
  see that you cleanse yourself from their ways.

Your fate reserves such honor
  that both parties will be hungry for you;
  but far from the goat will be the grass!   72

Let the beasts of Fiesole make fodder
  of themselves and not touch the plant
  if one grows on their dung heap

in whom the holy virtues are revived
  of those Romans who remained there
  when it was made the nest of such wickedness."

"If my request could be fully granted,"
  I answered him, "you would not yet
  be exiled from human nature;

for in my mind is fixed and my heart knows
  the dear and kindly image of you
  as a father when, from hour to hour,   84

you taught how man makes himself eternal;

and, while I am alive, it is fitting
    that my tongue show how grateful I am.

What you say about my life I write down
    and keep to be explained with another text
    by a lady [Beatrice] who can do this if I see her.

This much I would have plain to you—
    so may my conscience not chide me—
    I am prepared for Fortune as she wills.

Such warnings are not new to my ears;
    therefore, as they please, 'Let Fortune
    turn her wheel, and the churl his mattock.'"   96

My master turned to the right
    and looked at me, then said,
    "He listens well who notes what is told."

*Among the many famous and infamous men guilty of sodomy was
Dante's bishop, whom Boniface VIII, instead of punishing severely,
merely transferred to another see. Thus the two men whose duty was
to teach Dante how to become eternal on earth and in Heaven are
together.*

*Brunetto hurriedly commends his work, The Treasury, to Dante and
then leaves, running fast, his loss of dignity showing the effect of
one vice on an otherwise venerable character.*

Nonetheless I continued talking
    to *ser* Brunetto, and I asked
    who were his most noted companions.

And he to me, "It is well to know of some;
    of the others it is more laudable to keep silent,
    for time would be short for so much speech.

Know briefly that all were clerks
    and scholars and of great fame,
    by the same sin defiled on earth.   108

Priscian goes with that wretched crowd,
    and Francesco d'Accorso; moreover,
    if you had a hankering for such filth,

you might see him who by the Servant of the Servants
    was transferred from the Arno to the Bacchiglione,
    where he left his ill-strained muscles.

I would say more, but my going and my speech
  must not continue longer, since I see new smoke
  rising over there from the sand.

People are coming with whom I must not be.
  Let my *Treasury,* in which I live
  be commended to you; more I do not ask."   120

Then he turned, and seemed like one of those
  who, at Verona, through the fields, run races
  for a green cloth; and of these he appeared to move
like the one who wins, and not like the one who loses.

CANTO XVI

The Waterfall

Already I had reached a place where the roar
  of the water falling into the next circle
  could be heard, like the hum of a beehive,

when three shades running together
  left a troop passing through the rain
  of the fiery torment.

They came toward us and each cried,
  "Stop, you who by your dress seem to us
  to come from our perverse city!"

Ah! what wounds I saw on their bodies,
  old and recent, burnt in by the flames!
  I still grieve whenever I recall it.   12

My teacher listened to their cries,
  then turned his face toward me and said,
  "Now wait, to these we must be courteous,

and if it were not for the fire
  which the nature of this place lets fall,
  I should say that haste befitted you more than them."

*Since the edge of the precipice is not far off, the shades propose to
keep moving by circling around one spot.*

As we stopped they began again their old lament,
    and when they had reached us
    all three made of themselves a circle,

as wrestlers, naked and oiled, are wont to do,
    watching for a hold and an advantage,
    before the tugs and blows begin.   24

Thus circling, all kept their eyes on me,
    so that their heads and necks,
    together with their feet, moved continually.

And one of them began, "If the misery of this sandy place
    and our scorched and burned faces
    cause scorn for us and for our prayers,

may our fame incline you to tell us
    who you are, you who move so securely
    your living feet through Hell.

The man in whose footsteps you see me tread,
    although he goes now bare and hairless,
    was of a higher rank than you might believe.   36

He was a grandson of the good Gualdrada;
    Guido Guerra was his name, and in his life
    he did much with counsel and with sword.

The other who treads the sand behind me
    is Tegghiaio Aldobrandi, whose voice
    should have been heeded in the world.

And I, placed on the cross with them,
    am Jacopo Rusticucci; and certainly my fierce wife
    troubles me more than anything else."

If I had been sheltered from the fire,
    I would have thrown myself down among them,
    and I believe my master would have permitted;   48

but since I would have been burned and cooked,
    fear overcame the good will
    which made me eager to embrace them.

Then I began, "Not contempt, but such grief

as will not soon leave me,
    your condition caused in me

as soon as my lord spoke words
    through which I inferred
    that people like you were coming.

I am from your city; and always
    I have heard and told with affection
    of your honored deeds and names.   60

I leave the gall and go for the sweet fruit
    promised me by my truthful guide,
    but first I must descend to the center."

"So may your soul long guide your body,"
    he answered then,
    "and so may your fame shine after you,

tell us if courtesy and valor dwell
    in our city as they were wont
    or whether they have gone entirely,

for Guglielmo Borsiere who has suffered with us
    only a little while and is over there with his companions
    grieves us much with his remarks."   72

"New people and sudden gains, O Florence,
    have generated pride and excess in you
    so that already you are weeping!"

This I cried with my face raised, and the three
    who understood my words as a reply, glanced at each other
    as people do when the truth is spoken.

"If, at other times, it costs you so little
    to satisfy others," they all replied,
    "you are fortunate, speaking thus at will;

therefore, if you escape from this dark place
    and return to see the beautiful stars,
    when you can delight in saying 'I was there . . .'   84

see that you speak to others about us."
    Then they broke the wheel, and in their flight
    their nimble legs seemed wings.

An "amen" could not have been said

so quickly as they disappeared;
  whereupon my master thought it best to go on.

I followed him, and we had not gone far
  before the waterfall was so near
  that we could hardly hear each other speak.

As the river which has its own channel at first
  from Monte Veso toward the east,
  on the left slope of the Apennines—   96

which is called Acquacheta up above
  before it flows to its lower bed,
  and at Forlì loses that name—

resounds there above San Benedetto dell'Alpe,
  because of falling in one single leap
  instead of being broken by a thousand,

so, down from a steep bank
  we found the colored water roaring so loudly
  that it soon would have hurt our ears.

A cord around Dante's waist probably stands for self-confidence, use-
ful in combating incontinence, but worse than useless in dealing with
the fraud ahead. He gives it to Virgil who throws it over the precipice
as a signal. Dante waits anxiously to see what will happen.

I had a cord around my waist
  with which I had thought once
  to catch the leopard with the painted hide.   108

After I had loosened it from my body
  as my leader had ordered me,
  I handed it to him, coiled and knotted.

Then he turned to the right side,
  and threw it far from the bank
  down into that deep abyss.

"Surely," I said within myself, "something strange
  must respond to this new signal
  which my master so follows with his eyes."

Ah, how cautious we must be
  with those who see not only what we do
  but look also within our thoughts!   120

He said to me, "Soon what I am waiting for
    will come up, and what you are thinking about
    will be revealed to your eyes."

To the truth which appears to be a lie
    we should close our lips as long as we can,
    not to incur blamelessly a reproach;

but here I cannot keep silent and, Reader,
    by the notes of this Comedy, I swear to you—
    so may it not lack long favor—

that I saw, through that thick and dark air,
    a form marvelous to every steadfast heart
    come swimming up   132

as a swimmer rises after going down
    to loosen an anchor caught by a rock
    or something else hidden in the sea,

who stretches forth his arms and draws up his feet.

CANTO XVII

Geryon

The monster coming up is Geryon, a symbol of the fraud which is universal and more powerful than arms. His face has an honest look, but his body is reptilelike and covered with devious and intricate patterns, like oriental tapestries. He lies with his head on the bank as beavers were supposed to do when using their tails to throw their prey on the shore.

"Behold the beast with the pointed tail
    that can cross mountains and break through walls;
    behold the one that infects the whole world!"

Thus my guide began to speak to me
    and signaled to the beast to come ashore
    near the end of the stone banks we had walked on;

and that foul image of fraud came up
    and landed his head and breast,
    but did not put his tail upon the bank.

His face was that of an honest man,
    so kind an aspect it had outwardly,
    but all the rest was like a reptile.   12

He had two paws, hairy to the armpits;
    his back and breast and both sides
    were decorated with loops and circles;

never did Tartars nor Turks make cloth
    with more colors in groundwork and in pattern,
    nor did Arachne ever put such webs on her loom.

As skiffs sometimes lie along the shore
    partly in the water and partly on land,
    and as up there among the gluttonous Germans

the beaver sits to carry on his war,
    so that worst of wild beasts lay
    on the edge which binds the sand with stone.   24

He darted his tail in the empty space,
    twisting up its venomous tip
    which was armed like that of a scorpion.

The usurers (the remaining group of the violent against God) are crouching near the edge where it is easy to fall into the circle of fraud below. Dante treats them with the utmost contempt, as he does all mercenary souls. They are unrecognizable except by the coats of arms on their now empty purses.

Virgil has warned Dante not to waste words on them: our poet does not speak at all. The usurers are still competing, quarreling, rivaling, and envying each other, without honor, courage, good manners, artistic or intellectual distinction.

My leader said, "We must now bend our course
    a little as far as to the wicked beast
    that is lying over there."

We descended to the right
    and took ten steps on the extreme edge
    in order to avoid the sand and the flames.

After we had reached the monster,
   I saw a little farther on some people on the sand
   sitting close to the empty space.

My master said, "So that you may take with you
   complete experience of this round,
   go and see their ways.

Let your talk with them be brief;
   until you return I will speak with this one
   so that he may lend us his strong shoulders."

Thus I advanced along the extreme edge
   of the seventh circle all alone
   to where the sad souls were sitting.

Through their eyes their grief burst forth;
   on this side and that they used their hands,
   brushing off the fire and lifting themselves from the hot
      ground;

not otherwise are dogs busy in summer,
   now with their muzzles and now with their paws,
   when bitten by gadflies or fleas.

In looking at the faces of some
   on whom the painful fire was falling,
   I could recognize none, but I noticed

that from the necks of each a purse hung
   which had a certain color and design
   and on which it seemed that their eyes feasted.

As I came looking at them,
   on a yellow purse I saw in azure
   the head and the form of a lion.

Then continuing the course of my glances,
   I saw another, red as blood,
   showing a goose whiter than butter.

And one who had a white sack marked
   with an azure pregnant sow,
   said to me, "What are you doing in this hole?

Now go away and, since you are still alive,
   know that my neighbor Vitaliano
   will sit here on my left side.

With these Florentines I am a Paduan;
    many times they deafen my ears,
    shouting, 'Let the sovereign knight come   72

who will bring the pouch marked by three goats.'"
    Then he twisted his mouth and stuck out his tongue
    as an ox does to lick its nose.

And I, fearing that to stay longer
    might annoy my master, who had admonished me
    to be brief, turned my back on those wearied souls.

*When Dante climbs on Geryon's back over the immense void, he is
so frightened he cannot speak.*

*The transition from violence to deliberate, premeditated fraud is
shown by the long and slow descent.*

I found my leader already mounted
    on the back of the fierce animal.
    He said to me, "Now be strong and bold;

we descend here by such stairs.
    Mount in front, for I wish to be placed
    so that the tail cannot hurt you."   84

As one who has the chill of the quartan fever
    so close that his nails are already blue,
    and who shivers merely at the sight of shade,

so I became on hearing these words,
    but Virgil's admonition caused the shame
    which, in sight of his master, makes a servant strong.

I placed myself on those big shoulders.
    "See that you hold me," I wished to say,
    but my voice did not come out as I thought.

And he who at other times helped me
    in other fears, as soon as I had mounted,
    embraced and held me with his arms;   96

then said, "Geryon, move now;
    let the circles be large and the descent slow;
    think of the new burden that you have."

As a little ship moves from its berth,
    back, back, thus Geryon moved off,
    and when he felt his whole body clear,

he turned his tail to where his breast had been,
    and stretching it out, moved it like an eel,
    and with his paws drew in the air.

I do not believe there was greater fear when Phaëthon
    let loose the reins [of the sun's chariot] so that the sky
    as still appears [by the Milky Way] was scorched,   108

nor when poor Icarus [while flying] felt his loins unfeathered
    because of the melting of the wax,
    his father shouting to him, "The wrong way you're
        taking!"

than was mine when I saw myself in the air
    on every side and with every view hidden
    except that of the beast.

It went on swimming slowly, slowly,
    circled and descended, but I was aware of the movement
    only by the wind blowing in my face and from below.

Already I heard the torrent on the right
    roaring horribly beneath us,
    so that I stretched out my head to look down.   120

Then I was still more afraid,
    for I saw fires and heard laments,
    at which I crouched back, all trembling.

I noticed then the descending and the circling
    which I had not seen before
    by the torments drawing near on every side.

As a falcon that has long been on the wing
    without seeing a bird or lure, and that makes the
        falconer cry,
    "Alas, you are coming down!"

descends wearily, after many circles,
    to where it had swiftly started out,
    and lands far from its master, sullen and angry,   132

so Geryon set us down on the bottom,
    at the foot of the jagged rock;
    then freed of the weight of our bodies,

he darted off, like an arrow-notch from the string.

CANTO XVIII

Panders, Seducers, and Flatterers

*The matter-of-fact description of Malebolge contrasts with the devious-
ness of the fraud it harbors. The term means "evil pouches" or "purses,"
perhaps with some reference to the greed which motivates most fraud.
Those who sinned through violence are in the open. The fraudulent,
appropriately, are hidden in dark ditches. Over the moats are "scogli,"
rocky bridges, which come together at the center like spokes of a wheel.*

There is a place in Hell called Malebolge,
    all of stone and of an iron color
    like the bank which surrounds it.

Right in the middle of the baleful space
    a well, rather wide and deep, opens up
    whose features I will describe in their place.

The belt that remains, then,
    between the well and the high, hard bank,
    has its bottom divided into ten valleys.

As the ground appears
    where several moats surround a castle
    as a protection for the walls,   12

such was the design these made.
    And, as from the thresholds of fortresses
    little bridges extend to the outer banks,

so from the bottom of the wall, rough spans
    crossed the ditches and the banks down to the well
    which brings them all together and cuts them off.

In this place, shaken from the back of Geryon,
    we found ourselves, and the poet started
    to the left, and I moved on behind him.

*The souls in the first bolgia or ditch are guided by traffic regulations as
was the crowd at the jubilee in Rome in 1300, the panders on the
outside going to the right, the seducers on the inside to the left.*

We now meet the first devils. These, appropriately, wear the horns associated with adultery. We find also the first shade who is ashamed. When recognized, he tells how he sold his sister to the Marquis of Este. He confesses also for the other Bolognese panders, more numerous than the little children learning the dialect word for "yes" within the boundaries of their province.

Here, as elsewhere, movement characterizes punishments for sins related to sexuality. Where the activity was natural, the agent of punishment is wind, a natural force; where unnatural, as on the plain, a supernatural fire is falling. Here, among the fraudulent, a devil plies the whip.

On the right I saw new misery,
>> new torments, and new tormentors
>> with which the first ditch was filled.   24

The sinners along the bottom of the ditch were naked,
>> coming on this side facing us, on the other
>> moving with us, but with longer steps.

Thus the Romans because of the great throng
>> in the year of the jubilee, chose a way
>> to divide the traffic on the bridge,

so that on one side all had their faces
>> toward the Castle [of Sant' Angelo], and went to St. Peter's,
>> and on the other side they advanced toward the Mount
>>> [Giordano].

On both sides of the dark rock
>> I saw horned demons with great whips
>> beating the shades fiercely from behind.   36

Ah, how they made them lift their legs
>> at the first stroke! Indeed,
>> none waited for the second or for the third.

While I was going on, my eyes fell on one;
>> whereupon immediately I said,
>> "I am not fasting for the sight of him!"

Therefore I delayed advancing to look;
>> and my dear leader stopped with me
>> and consented that I go back a little.

The whipped shade thought he could hide

by lowering his face, but it availed him little,
    for I said, "You who cast your eyes on the ground,   48

if the features you wear are not false,
    are Venedico Caccianemico;
    but what brings you into such a pickle?"

And he to me, "Unwillingly I say it,
    but I am compelled by your clear speech
    which makes me recall the world.

I am the one who led Ghisolabella [his sister]
    to do the Marquis' [of Este's] will,
    however the vile tale may sound,

and I am not the only Bolognese weeping here;
    on the contrary the place is so full of them
    that as many tongues are not now being taught   60

to say 'sipa' between the Savena and the Reno;
    and if you want assurance of that,
    recall to your mind our avaricious hearts."

While he was speaking thus, a demon struck him
    with his whip, saying, "Away, pander!
    Here are no women to turn into cash!"

*To see the seducers, who have been going to the left, the poets mount
to the top of the bridge. They observe Jason, a dignified figure, but
whipped, like the others. His principal crime, besides robbing the
Colchians of the Golden Fleece and deserting Medea, was the seduc-
tion of Hypsipyle. The latter, according to the legend, had already
shown her weakness by saving her father's life when the disgusted
women of Lemnos tried to kill off all the men.*

I rejoined my escort; then,
    after a few steps, we came
    to where a rough bridge projects from the bank.

Quite easily we climbed it,
    and turning to the right over its ridge
    we moved away from that eternal bank.   72

When we reached the point below which the bridge opens
    to give passage for those whipped,
    my leader said, "Stop, and let your sight

fall on these other ill-born souls
   whose faces you have not yet seen,
   since they have been going with us."

From the old bridge we looked at the file
   coming toward us on the other side
   and whom the whip likewise drove on.

And my good master, without my asking, said,
   "Look at that great one coming,
   who, for his pain, sheds no tears;   84

what a regal bearing he still has!
   That is Jason who through courage and slyness
   deprived the Colchians of their ram [Golden Fleece].

He passed through the island of Lemnos
   after the bold and pitiless women
   had given up to death all their men.

There, with gifts and fine words,
   he deceived Hypsipyle, the young girl
   who first had deceived all the others.

He abandoned her pregnant and forlorn.
   Such guilt condemns him to this punishment;
   and vengeance is taken also for Medea.   96

With him go all those who deceive in this way:
   let this knowledge suffice for the first vale
   and for those it holds in its grip."

*The poets proceed to where they can see the flatterers in the second
ditch. Dante chooses the elegant Thaïs as his ancient example, perhaps
to emphasize the essential filthiness of these sinners who, like dogs,
lick the sores of those they exploit. The contrast is all the more striking
because the charge against her seems trivial. Moreover, Dante had
misread the incident in Cicero; the guilty one was Gnatho, not Thaïs.
But the lesson is clear: even Thaïs could not make flattery clean.*

We had already come to where the narrow road
   crosses the second bank and makes of it
   an abutment for another arch.

Here we heard people moaning in the next ditch
   and puffing with their snouts
   and hitting themselves with their hands.

The banks were encrusted with a mold
    condensed from the vapor from below
    which offends both the eyes and nose.   108

The bottom was so deep it could be seen
    only by mounting to the summit of the arch
    where the bridge stands highest.

We reached that place, and down in the ditch
    I saw people plunged in excrement
    which seemed to have come from human privies.

And while I was searching down there with my eyes,
    I saw one with his head so smeared with filth
    that you could not tell if he were a layman or a clerk.

He bawled to me, "Why are you so eager
    to look at me more than at the other ugly ones?"
    And I to him, "Because, if I remember well,   120

I saw you once with dry hair;
    you are Alessio Interminei da Lucca;
    therefore, I eye you more than all the rest."

Then beating on his pate, he said,
    "The flatteries with which my tongue
    was never cloyed have put me down here."

After that my guide said to me,
    "See that you extend your gaze
    so that your eyes may reach the face

of that filthy and disheveled wench
    who is scratching herself with her dirty nails
    and now squats and now is standing on her feet.   132

Thaïs, she is, the harlot
    who answered her paramour when he said,
    'Have I *great* favor with you?' 'No, *marvelous!*'

And with this let our sight be satisfied."

CANTO XIX

The Simonists

Dante's objectivity ceases when we come to the simonists who by trafficking in church offices and enriching themselves tend to destroy the Church itself. Their fat feeds the fire which now punishes them.

O Simon Magus! O rapacious followers,
    you who should be wedded to righteousness
    and instead prostitute the things of God

for gold and silver, now for you
    it is necessary that the trumpet sound,
    since you are in the third ditch.

Already we had mounted to that part
    of the following bridge
    which hangs over the middle of the moat.

O Supreme Wisdom, how great is the art Thou showest
    in Heaven, on earth, and in the evil world,
    and how justly Thy power rewards!   12

I saw the livid stone covered with holes
    on the sides and on the bottom,
    all round, and of one breadth.

They appeared neither larger nor smaller
    than those in my beautiful San Giovanni
    made for the baptizers to stand in,

one of which, not many years ago, I broke
    to save a drowning child—and let this
    be my seal [on the truth] to undeceive all men.

From the mouth of each a sinner's feet protruded
    and his legs up to the calf,
    and the rest remained within.   24

The soles of the feet of all were on fire,
    and their legs above the joints writhed so sharply
    that they would have broken withes or ropes.

As flames on oily things are wont
  to move only over the outer surface,
  so they did here from heel to toe.

"Who is that one, Master, who writhes so,
  twitching more than the others, his companions,
  and who feeds a ruddier flame?" I asked.

And he to me, "If you want me to carry you down there
  over the [inner] bank which slopes less steeply,
  you will learn from him about himself and his misdeeds."   36

And I, "Whatever you want is good for me;
  you are my lord, and you know that my will
  is like your own, and you know also what I keep silent."

Then we came to the fourth bank
  where we turned and descended on the left
  down into the narrow and pitted bottom.

My kind master still did not put me down,
  but carried me to the hole of the one
  who was so lamenting with his shanks.

*The inverted shade, Pope Nicholas III, mistakes Dante for Boniface
VIII (still living in 1300) who, after outraging the Church (the "Bride
of Christ"), is to follow him here. Nicholas belonged to the Orsini
family (orso, bear), and used his office to advance the cubs. In this
mockery of the apostolic succession, Boniface will be succeeded by
Clement V, who, as the tool of Philip the Fair of France, transferred
the papacy to Avignon. A certain vulgarity characterizes the speech of
all mercenary sinners and the terms used to describe them.*

"O, whoever you are, sad spirit,
  upside down, planted like a stake,"
  I began to say, "if you can, speak."   48

I stood like the friar confessing a treacherous assassin
  who, after being put in the hole [to be buried alive],
  calls the confessor back to delay his death,

and he shouted, "Are you already standing there,
  are you already there, O Boniface?—
  The writing [Book of Fate] lied to me by several years.

Are you so quickly sated with the wealth

for which you were not afraid to seize the beautiful lady
    through guile and then to outrage her?"

I became like those who wonder
    if they are mocked, not understanding the words
    said to them, and who are unable to reply. 60

Then Virgil said, "Tell him quickly
    'I am not, I am not the one you think,'"
    and I answered as I had been bidden.

At that the spirit twisted both his feet,
    then sighing and with a tearful voice
    he said, "What do you ask of me?

If you want so much to learn who I am
    that you have come down the bank to hear,
    know that I was clothed with the great mantle,

and truly I was a son of the she-bear,
    so covetous to advance the cubs
    that on earth I put wealth, and here myself, in a sack. 72

Below, under my head, the others
    who preceded me in simony are compressed,
    squeezed into the fissures of the rock.

Down there I also will be pressed
    when he comes for whom I took you
    when I asked the sudden question.

But I have already been roasted
    and have stood thus upside down longer
    than he will stay planted with reddened feet,

for after him, out of the West, will come
    a shepherd without law, of uglier deed,
    fit to cover both him and me. 84

He will be like the Jason of whom we read in Maccabees,
    and as to Jason a king dealt gently,
    so will the ruler of France treat him."

*Dante addresses Nicholas with intense feeling, restrained only by
reverence for this sinner's past office. He mentions the Scarlet Woman,
as the symbol of the corrupt Church.*

In this bolgia things are generally upside down. The clergy inverted

their duties and are now inverted themselves; Dante, a layman, hears a
confession, like a friar, and then preaches a sermon to an ex-pope.

I do not know if I was now too bold,
    but I answered him in this strain:
    "Alas, now tell me, how much treasure

did our Lord ask of St. Peter
    before he put the keys in his hands?
    Surely he demanded only, 'Follow me!'

Nor did Peter and the others ask Matthias
    for gold or silver when he was chosen
    for the place the guilty soul [Judas] had lost.   96

Therefore, stay there, for you are well punished,
    and keep securely the ill-got money
    which made you so bold against Charles [of Anjou].

And if I were still not prevented
    by reverence for the holy keys
    which you kept in the happy life,

I would use words still heavier;
    for your avarice afflicts the world,
    crushing the good and lifting up the bad.

The Evangelist [St. John] had shepherds like you in mind
    when she [the Scarlet Woman] that sitteth upon many
        waters
    was seen by him fornicating with kings,   108

she who was born with seven heads [virtues]
    and from ten horns [commandments] gained strength
    as long as virtue pleased the bridegroom [the papacy].

You have made a god of gold and silver,
    and how do you differ from the idolater,
    except that he worships one thing of gold, and you a
        hundred?

The papal claims to temporal power were based in part on the sup-
posed gift of the Western Empire to St. Sylvester by Constantine. The
document confirming this transfer was not recognized as a forgery until
after Dante's time, but our poet held that the emperor had no power
to make such a gift nor the pope to receive it.

Virgil, as the representative of the Roman Empire in the political allegory, is so delighted with Dante's sermon that he carries his pupil out of the ditch and to the top of the next bridge.

Ah, Constantine, to how much ill gave birth
  not your conversion, but that dowry
  which the first rich father took from you!"

While I sang these notes to him,
  whether anger or conscience stung him,
  he kicked hard with both his feet.   120

I believe my leader was pleased,
  with such a contented look he listened
  to the true words I had expressed.

With both arms he took hold of me,
  and when he had me quite upon his breast,
  he remounted by the way we had come down,

nor did he tire of holding me tightly,
  but carried me to the top of the arch
  which crosses from the fourth to the fifth bank.

There, softly, he put down his burden—
  softly because of the rough and steep rocks
  which would have been a hard road even for goats.   132

From there another valley was disclosed.

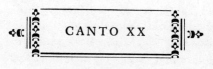

CANTO XX

The Diviners

The sight of the soothsayers, diviners, and magicians, with their heads twisted around and walking backward, makes Dante weep. He had previously shown pity for the victims of our human defects, but now he is sorry for the punishment itself. This is a kind of protest against the divine order, and he is severely rebuked by Virgil. The scolding is more striking since Virgil had been considered a diviner, a master of magic art, and the sin punished here often tempted men of learning like Dante himself.

For new punishments I must make verses
    and provide matter for the twentieth canto
    of the first book, which is about the damned.

I was already placed where I could see
    into the uncovered depth
    which was bathed with tears of anguish,

and I saw people move silent and weeping
    through the circular valley, at the pace of those
    who chant litanies in this world.

When my eyes saw them more clearly
    each appeared to be twisted marvelously
    between the chin and the beginning of the chest,   12

for their faces were turned to the rear,
    and each was obliged to move backward,
    since seeing ahead was denied them.

Perhaps by the force of paralysis
    someone might be wholly twisted thus,
    but I have never seen the case nor believe it exists.

Reader, so may God let you profit
    by your reading, now think for yourself
    how I could keep my face dry

when I saw our [human] image, close at hand,
    so twisted that the tears from the eyes
    bathed the buttocks along the cleft.   24

Certainly I wept, leaning on a rock
    of the hard bridge, so that my escort said to me,
    "Are you, too, like the other fools?

Here pity lives when it is completely dead.
    Who is more impious than that one
    who feels sorrow for God's judgment?

Virgil now points out certain soothsayers of antiquity, characters chosen from various epic poems. The accounts of them are incorrect in some respects, perhaps to show once more the fallibility of men's minds. In discussing Manto, Virgil gives an account of the founding of Mantua

different from one in the Aeneid. Moreover, in the Purgatory, Manto
*is mentioned as in a different circle. The digression interests even
Dante only slightly.*

[Lift up your head and see him [an augur] for whom
    the earth opened in the sight of the Thebans
    so that they cried, 'Where are you falling,
O Amphiaraus? why are you giving up the war?'
    and he did not stop rushing headlong
    down to Minos who seizes everyone;   36
observe how he has made a breast of his shoulders;
    because he wished to see too far ahead,
    he looks behind, and goes backward.
See Tiresias [a soothsayer] who changed his semblance
    when he became from man, a woman,
    transforming all his members,
and before he could regain his manly hair
    it was necessary for him to strike again
    the two entwined serpents with his wand.
The one backing up to his belly
    is Aruns who, in the Luni mountains
    beneath which the Carrarese live and plow,   48
had a cave in the white marble for a dwelling
    from which no obstacle cut off
    a view of the sea or of the stars.
And she who covers her breasts
    which you do not see, with her loose tresses,
    and has on the other side all hairy skin,
was Manto, who sought through many lands
    before she settled where I was born
    and of her I would like for you to hear.
After her father had given up his life
    and Bacchus' city [Thebes] was enslaved
    she wandered a long time through the world.   60
In beautiful Italy, above the Tyrol,
    at the foot of the Alps which enclose Germany,
    lies a lake named Benaco.
A thousand brooks and more bathe the Apennino
    from Guarda to Val Canonica
    whose waters come to rest in this lake.

In the middle is a point where the pastors
 of Trento, Brescia, and Verona
 could give a blessing if they went that way.
Peschiera lies as a fair and powerful rampart
 to face the Brescians and the Bergamese
 where the shore is lowest.   **72**
There, all that the lap of Benaco
 cannot hold must overflow
 through green pastures and make a river.
When the water begins to flow,
 it is no longer called Benaco, but Mincio
 as far as Governo, where it falls into the Po.
After a short course it finds a flat region
 over which it spreads and forms a marsh
 which in summer is wont to be noisome.
While passing there, the cruel virgin
 saw land in the middle of the fen
 uncultivated and devoid of inhabitants. **84**
There, to shun all human intercourse,
 she, with her servants, stayed to practice her
  art,
 and lived, and left there her empty body.
Later the people scattered around
 gathered in that place which was strong
 because of the marsh on all sides.
They built the city on her bones
 and for her who first chose the place
 they called it Mantua, without other augury.
Once its people were more numerous
 before the madness of Casalodi [its ruler]
 was deceived by Pinamonte.   **96**
Therefore I warn you, that if you ever hear
 of another origin for my city,
 let no falsehood defraud the truth."
And I, "Master, your account is so certain
 and takes such hold on my belief
 that others would be like dead coals.
But tell me about the people passing by,
 whether you see any worthy of note,
 for to that alone my mind reverts."]

The account of Eurypylus at the time of the Trojan wars differs also from its source in Virgil, a slip all the more striking since Dante implies that he knew the Aeneid by heart.

Among the modern soothsayers is Michael Scott who lived at the court of Frederick II of Sicily. His legend survived in Scotland down to modern times. Other minor figures include Guido Bonatti, an astrologer of Forlì, Asdente, the cobbler of Parma, and various fortune-tellers and witches.

In Italian folklore, the Man in the Moon is Cain. He is mentioned in indicating the time. It is about six o'clock on Saturday morning, April 9, 1300.

Then he said, "That one who from his cheeks
    lets his beard fall on his dark shoulders
      was an augur [during the Trojan War] when Greece
        was so empty of males   108

that scarcely any remained for the cradles,
    and in Aulis, together with Calchas,
    he set the time for setting sail for Troy.

Eurypylus was his name, and my lofty tragedy
    sings of him in one place,
    as you know well, since you know it all.

The other, so slender in the flanks,
    was Michael Scott, who really knew
    the game of magic frauds.

See also Guido Bonatti, see Asdente
    who now wishes he had attended
    to his leather and his thread, but too late repents.   120

See the poor women who left the needle,
    the shuttle, and the spindle, and became fortunetellers;
    they wrought magic with herbs and images.

But come now, for Cain with his thorns
    is already on the confines of both hemispheres
    and below Seville is sinking in the sea,

and last night the moon was round;
    you must remember, since it was not unwelcome
     at times in the deep wood."

Thus he spoke as we moved on.

CANTO XXI

The Barrators (Grafters)

Thus we went from bridge to bridge, talking of things
    my Comedy does not care to mention,
    and reached the top of the next arch

where we stopped to see the ditch
    and to hear the other vain laments;
    and I found it marvelously dark.

As in the shipyards of the Venetians,
    in winter, the tenacious pitch boils
    to calk their damaged ships,

since the sailors cannot navigate, and instead
    some build new boats, some strengthen the ribs
    of one that has made many voyages;   12

some hammer at the prow and some at the stern;
    some make oars, and some twist ropes;
    some mend the jib and mainsail,

so, not by fire, but through divine art
    a dense tar boils down there
    which coats the banks on each side.

I saw the pitch, but did not see in it
    anything except the bubbles which rise,
    swell up, and then collapse.

While I was looking fixedly down there
    my guide drew me from where I was,
    saying, "Look! look!"   24

Then I turned like one suddenly dismayed,
    striving to see something
    from which he must escape

and who, to see, does not delay his start;
    and I noticed behind us a black devil
    coming at a run over the bridge.

Ah, how fierce he was in aspect,
    and how ferocious he seemed in act,
    with wings open, and light upon his feet!

His shoulders which were high and sharp
    were burdened by the haunches of a sinner
    the sinews of whose feet he clutched.   36

From our bridge he cried, "O Malebranche [devils],
    here is one of the elders of Santa Zita [Lucca],
    put him under while I go back for more

to that city I have so well furnished with them.
    Everyone is a barrator there, except Bonturo;
    there, for money, a 'no' becomes a 'yes.'"

Down he hurled him, and turned back
    over the rough bridge, and never was a mastiff
    in such haste to follow a thief.

The sinner plunged in, then rose doubled up,
    but the demons hiding under the bridge shouted,
    "Here there is no Holy Face [as at Lucca] to pray to!   48

Here you do not swim as in the Serchio!
    So, unless you want to feel our hooks,
    don't show yourself above the pitch!"

Then they struck him with more than a hundred prongs,
    saying, "Here you must dance under cover
    and pilfer secretly if you can!"

Not otherwise do cooks have their scullions
    dip the meat in the middle of the boiler
    with forks, so that it will not float.

Virgil holds a parley with the demons below the bridge. Then Dante rejoins his master, keeping as close to him (Reason) as he can, but using his eyes as well. The entire episode with the devils beginning here (a concession to the popular spirit of the Middle Ages) symbolizes incidentally Dante's narrow escape from Florence, where one of the false charges against him was barratry.

My good master said, "So that it may not appear
    that you are here, crouch down
    behind a rock and remain hidden,   60

and whatever outrage is done to me
    do not be afraid, for I know about this business;
    once before I was in a like affray."

Then he went to the head of the bridge,
    and as he arrived on the sixth bank
    he needed a steadfast heart.

With that fury and that uproar
    with which dogs run out at a beggar
    who suddenly stops and begs from where he is,

those devils rushed out from under the bridge,
    turning against him all their hooks.
    But he cried, "Let none of you be headstrong.   **72**

Before your grapples touch me,
    let one of you come forward to hear me
    and then decide about hooking me."

All shouted, "Let Malacoda go"; whereupon one
    stepped forward while the others stood firm,
    and came to him saying, "What good will it do him?"

"Do you think, Malacoda,
    that you see me here," my master said,
    "safe from all your opposition,

without divine will and propitious fate?
    Let me go on, for it is willed in Heaven
    that I should show another this wild way."   **84**

Then Malacoda's pride collapsed so suddenly
    that he let his hook fall at his feet
    and said to the others, "Do not strike him."

And my guide called to me, "O you, crouching quietly
    behind the rocks of the bridge,
    you may come now securely."

I started out and went quickly to him,
    and all the devils pressed forward,
    so that I feared they might not keep their pact.

Thus I once saw foot soldiers afraid
    on leaving Caprona under safe conduct,
    when they saw themselves among so many enemies.   **96**

I drew close to my guide with my whole body,
    but did not take my eyes
    from the devils' looks, which were not good.

They lowered their hooks, one saying to another,
    "Should I nick him on the rump?"
    and being answered, "Yes, let him have it!"

But the demon who had held the parley
    with my leader turned instantly,
    and said, "Quiet, quiet, Scarmiglione!"

Malacoda proposes that a squad accompany the travelers to the next "unbroken" bridge. Since all the bridges over the next bolgia are broken, the devils understand that a trick is to be played on Virgil. To be more convincing in his fraud, Malacoda cites some statistics to show how much time has passed since the Crucifixion and the resultant earthquake. Dante, using his senses and intuition, would prefer to go on alone, but Virgil (Reason), taken in, tries to reassure him; and the grotesque company moves on.

Then he said to us, "You cannot go farther
    on this bridge, since the sixth arch
    lies all broken on the bottom,   108

but if you still want to go ahead,
    keep advancing along this bank;
    nearby is another bridge that provides a way.

Yesterday, five hours later than this hour,
    a thousand two hundred and sixty-six years
    were completed since the bridge here was broken.

I am sending some of my men over there
    to see if any are airing themselves;
    go with them, since they won't be harmful.

Step forward, Alichino and Calcabrina,"
    he then began to say, "and Cagnazzo,
    and you, Barbariccia, guide the squad.   120

Let Libicocco come and Draghignazzo,
    Ciriatto with his tusks, and Graffiacane,
    and Farfarello, and mad Rubicante.

Look around the boiling glue;

let these be safe as far as to the bridge
which *all unbroken* passes over the dens."

"Oh, Master, what is this I see?"
I exclaimed. "Ah, without escort, let us go alone
if you know the way; as for me, I ask for none.

If you are as wary as usual,
don't you see that they are gnashing their teeth,
and with their frowns threaten grief to us?"   132

And he to me, "Do not be afraid,
let them grind away as they like,
because they do that for the wretches in the pitch."

The devils turned to the left on the bank,
but first each pressed his tongue between his teeth,
as a signal to their leader,

and he, for a trumpet, used his rump.

CANTO XXII

Ciampolo of Navarre

I have seen horsemen move camp
and launch an attack, and hold their muster,
and sometimes turn back to escape;

I have seen scouting parties in your land,
O Aretines! and foragers start out,
tournaments begin and races run,

sometimes at the sound of trumpets or of bells,
with drums and with castle signals,
and with familiar and strange devices,

but never yet did I see horse or footmen move
to so strange a bugle call,
or a ship at a sign on land or in the sky.   12

We went along with the ten demons;

ah, fierce company! but "in church with saints,
   and in the tavern with the gluttons!"

I was attentive to the pitch
   to see what the bolgia contained
   and the people burning in it.

As dolphins make signs to sailors
   by the arching of their backs
   to prepare to save their ship,

so now and then, to relieve the pain,
   some of the sinners showed their backs
   and hid again as fast as lightning flashes;

and, as at the edge of the water of a ditch,
   frogs lie with just their muzzles out,
   hiding their feet and bodies,

so, on every side, the sinners lay;
   but when Barbariccia came near,
   they withdrew within the boiling.

I saw, and still my heart shudders at it,
   a soul waiting thus, just as it happens
   that one frog may remain when the others dart away,

and Graffiacane who was closest to him
   hooked his pitchy locks, and pulled him out
   so that he looked like an otter.

I already knew the names of all the demons
   so well did I note them when they were chosen,
   and as they called each other I noticed how.

"O Rubicante, see that you get your claws
   on him and skin him alive,"
   the accursed ones shouted all together,

and I, "Master, find out if you can
   who the unfortunate wretch is
   that has fallen into the hands of his enemies."

My guide went close to him and asked
   whence he came, and he replied,
   "I was born in the kingdom of Navarre.

My mother placed me as a servant to a lord,

24

36

48

for she had borne me to a spendthrift,
a destroyer of himself and of his property.

Then I was in the service of good King Thibault;
there I began to commit barratry
for which I give reckoning in this heat."

And Ciriatto from each side of whose mouth
a tusk issued, as from a boar's,
made him feel how one of them could rip.

The mouse had fallen among vicious cats;
but Barbariccia took him in his arms
and said, "Stand over there while I grip him."   60

And turning his face to my master,
"Ask, if you want to hear more about him,"
he said, "before the others mangle him."

My guide then said, "Now tell me, do you know
any others under the pitch who are Italians?"
And he answered, "A little while ago

I left one from a nearby island—
(might I still be covered with him,
for then I would fear neither claw nor hook!").

And Libicocco cried, "Too much have we endured,"
and with his prong seized his arm
and tearing it, carried off a sinew.   72

Draghignazzo also tried to lay hold
of his legs, whereupon their corporal
turned around with wicked looks.

When they were somewhat pacified
my guide without delay addressed the sinner
who was still looking at his wounds.

"Who is the one you say you left
unluckily in order to come ashore?"
and he replied, "It was Friar Gomita,

from Gallura, a vessel of every fraud
who had his master's enemies in his hands
and dealt with them so [gently] that all praise him.   84

Money he took, and let them off quietly

as he says; and in other offices also
  he was not a little barrator, but a supreme one.

With him Don Michel Zanche of Logodoro
  keeps company, and their tongues
  are never tired of talking about Sardinia.

O me! see that one grinding his teeth;
  I would say more, but I am afraid
  he is getting ready to scratch my sticky coat!"

And their commander in chief, turning to Farfarello,
  who was rolling his eyes on the point of striking,
  said, "Get over there, vile bird!"   96

"If you wish to see or hear,"
  the frightened one [Ciampolo] then began,
  "some Tuscans or Lombards, I will have some come,

but let the Malebranche stand back a little
  so that their vengeance will not be feared,
  and I, sitting in this very place,

for one that I am, will make many come
  when I whistle, as it is our custom
  to do when any of us gets out."

Cagnazzo at these words raised his snout,
  shaking his head, and said, "Listen to the trick
  he has thought of to plunge down."   108

Then he [Ciampolo], who had a wealth of guile,
  answered, "I am too tricky indeed
  when I get greater sorrow for my friends!"

Alichino could hold back no longer
  and contrary to the others said,
  "If you plunge, I'll not gallop after you,

but will beat my wings above the pitch!
  Let the ridge be left and the bank made a screen
  to see if you can get the best of us."

O you who read will now hear new sport.
  All turned their eyes to the other side,
  and he first who had been most unwilling.   120

The Navarese chose well his time,

steadied his feet upon the ground, and in an instant
leaped, and from the marshal freed himself.

At that each was stung with guilt, and that one most
who had been the cause of the mistake.
He, swooping down, cried, "You're caught!"

but it availed little, for wings
could not outstrip terror. The sinner went under,
and his pursuer, flying, turned up his breast.

Not otherwise does the wild duck plunge
when the falcon comes near
which, defeated and angry, flies up again.   132

Calcabrina, furious at the trick,
also went after him, eager for the sinner to escape
so that he could start a quarrel.

And when the barrator had disappeared,
he turned his claws on his companion
and grappled with him above the ditch.

But Alichino was a full-grown hawk
for clawing him back, and both fell
into the middle of the boiling pond.

The heat at once broke their grip,
but there was no way for them to rise,
since their wings were so beglued.   144

Barbariccia, complaining with the rest,
had four fly to the other bank
with all their hooks, and quickly

on this side and that they went to their places
and reached with their grapples to those stuck
and already partly cooked within the crust;

and while they were embarrassed in this way we left them.

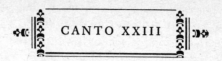

CANTO XXIII

The Hypocrites

The devils' fight over the pitch has reminded Dante of a fable which tells how a frog offers to tow a mouse tied to himself over a stream, intending to pull the rodent under. A kite, seeing their struggle, swoops down and carries off both.

Silent, alone, and without company
    we went on, one in front of the other,
    as minor friars go along their way.

My thought was turned to Aesop's fable
    by the present quarrel, where he speaks
    of the frog and of the mouse;

for "mo" and "issa" [synonyms for "now"] are not more alike
    if one compares with close attention
    the beginning and the end of each case.

And, as one thought bursts from another,
    there arose from that one a second
    which caused my first fear to be doubled.   12

I reflected thus: "Those devils through us
    are mocked with such scorn and damage
    as, I believe, must enrage them.

If anger is added to ill will,
    they will rush after us more fiercely
    than a hound after the rabbit he snaps up."

Already I felt my hair stand on end from fear,
    and I looked back intently and said,
    "Master, if you do not quickly hide

yourself and me, I fear the Malebranche;
    we already have them right behind us,
    I so imagine it that I can feel them now."   24

And he, "If I were leaded glass [a mirror]

I would not reflect your outer image
    more quickly than I do your inner feelings.

Just now your thoughts were coming among mine
    similar to them in force and in meaning,
    so that of them all I made one resolve.

If it happens that the right bank lies
    so that we can go into the next ditch,
    we will escape the dreaded chase."

He had not finished giving this counsel
    when I saw the demons not far away
    coming with wings extended to seize us.   36

My guide suddenly took hold of me and,
    as a mother who is awakened by a noise
    and sees close to her the burning flames,

who takes her son and flees, caring more for him
    than for herself, and who does not stop
    even long enough to put on any clothes,

so, down from the edge of the hard bank,
    lying on his back, my guide slid over the rock
    which walls one side of the ditch.

Water never ran so fast through a sluice
    to turn a millwheel, at the moment
    when it is closest to the paddles,   48

as my master went down over that bank,
    carrying me upon his breast,
    not as a companion, but as a son.

Scarcely had his feet touched the bottom
    when the devils reached the height above us,
    but there was nothing to fear,

for High Providence, which wished to put them
    as ministers of the fifth ditch,
    took from all of them the power to leave.

The hypocrites whom the travelers now see wear gowns brilliant out-
wardly but of lead, like those Frederick II was supposed to have had
melted on the backs of offenders against the throne. Like all who affect
a pose, they must carry the weight of it forever. They move slowly,
watching their steps. A kind of whining reproach sounds in their

affected reference to Dante's and Virgil's clothes and to their "run-
ning." Not willing to commit themselves, they qualify the slightest
promise with a "perhaps."

Down there we found a painted people
    who moved around the circle with slow steps,
    weeping, and, in countenance, wearied and overcome.   60

They wore capes with low hoods coming down
    in front of their eyes, cut in the style
    of those worn by the monks of Cluny,

outwardly gilded, so that they dazzled,
    but within of lead, and so heavy
    that [in comparison] those Frederick used were of straw.

O mantle eternally tiring! We turned once more
    to the left, moving with the sinners
    and listening to their sad lament;

but, because of their loads, those weary people
    came so slowly that at every step we took
    we found ourselves in new company.   72

Therefore I said to my guide, "Try to find someone
    who by name or deed might be recognized,
    and look around as we move on."

And one who understood the Tuscan speech
    shouted from behind us, "Stay your steps,
    you who are running so through the dark air;

perhaps you will hear from me what you ask for."
    My guide turned around and said,
    "Wait, and then come on at his pace."

I stopped and saw two showing by their looks
    great eagerness to be with me,
    but their burden and the narrow way delayed them.   84

When they came up, with sidelong glances
    they looked at me, without saying a word,
    then turned to each other and remarked,

"This man, by the movement of his throat, seems alive,
    and if they are both dead, by what privilege
    do they go divested of the heavy gown?"

Then they addressed me, "O Tuscan, you who have come
    to the college of the sad hypocrites,
    do not disdain to tell us who you are."

And I to them, "I was born and grew up
    by the beautiful Arno river, in the great city,
    and I am in the body I have always had.   96

But who are you whose distilled grief
    drips down over your cheeks,
    and what punishment glitters so on you?"

*The two shades had been chosen as arbiters in the party strife of
Florence instead of the usual one man. Far from being neutral, they
favored the Guelfs. As a result certain houses of Ghibelline leaders
near the old Gardingo fortress were destroyed and the site was made
into a public square.*

*One shade, new to Virgil, naked, like Christ at the Crucifixion, is
lying on the ground. This is Caiaphas, the high priest who, with
others of the council of the Jews, favored sacrificing Christ.*

And one answered, "The orange-colored mantles
    are of lead, so thick that their weight
    would make any scales creak.

We were Jolly Friars, and Bolognese,
    I Catalano, and he, Loderingo,
    appointed together by your city

(as a single man usually is taken)
    to preserve the peace, and what we did
    can still be seen around the Gardingo.   108

I began, "O Brothers, your evil . . ."
    but I said no more, for the sight of a shade on the ground,
    crucified with three stakes, caught my eye.

When he saw me he writhed all his body,
    breathing into his beard with sighs,
    and Friar Catalano who noticed that

said to me, "The transfixed one at whom you are looking
    counseled the Pharisees that it was fitting
    to torture one man for the people.

Now he is lying crosswise and naked on the road,

as you see; and he must feel
    the weight of each one who passes.   120

In a similar way his father-in-law is tortured
    in this ditch, and the others of the Council
    which was a seed of evil for the Jews."

Then I saw Virgil marveling
    over the one stretched out so basely,
    like a cross, in the eternal exile.

*Virgil learns of the humiliating trick played on him by the devils of
the fifth bolgia. The hypocrites are more expert in perceiving this
deception than Reason itself. In his usual indirect manner, not com-
mitting himself, Catalano points out that the Devil tells lies. Virgil,
angry at the trick and disgusted with Catalano, moves on con-
temptuously, without a word.*

Afterward he addressed to the friar these words,
    "Please tell us, if you can,
    whether there is a gap on the right side

by which we two can get out of here
    without constraining the black angels
    to come and extricate us from this bottom."   132

He answered, "Nearer than you expect
    is a bridge which begins at the outer circle
    and covers all the cruel valleys,

except that over this one it is broken.
    You will be able to climb up on its ruins
    which slope down the side and pile up on the bottom."

My guide stood a moment with his head lowered,
    then said, "Falsely did the one up there
    who hooks the sinners explain the matter."

And the friar added, "I once heard someone say at Bologna
    that the Devil has many vices, among which I heard
    that he is a liar and the father of lies."   144

Then with long steps my guide went on,
    a little disturbed in his looks by anger,
    and I also departed from the burdened ones,

following the imprints of the beloved feet.

CANTO XXIV

Vanni Fucci

*A dainty comparison takes us for a moment into the fresh air of late
winter when the nights are beginning to get shorter and when the frost
resembles for a while the snow.*

The poets struggle laboriously to get out of the ditch of hypocrisy.

In that part of the young year
    when the sun warms his locks beneath Aquarius
    and the long nights are moving toward the south,

when the frost copies on the ground
    the image of her white sister
    although the point of her pen lasts but little,

the poor peasant whose fodder is getting low
    rises, looks out, and sees the fields all white;
    whereupon he strikes his thigh,

turns back and, lamenting, walks up and down
    like a wretch who does not know what to do.
    Later he looks out again and recovers hope   12

on seeing that the world, in a little while,
    has changed appearance; and he takes his crook
    and drives forth the lambs to feed.

Thus my master made me disheartened
    when I saw his face so troubled,
    and thus quickly to the sore the plaster came.

For, when we reached the ruins of the bridge
    my guide turned to me with that pleasant look
    which I saw first at the foot of the mountain.

He opened his arms, after having made a plan
    within his mind, and looking carefully
    at the rocks he took hold of me,   24

and like one who calculates while working,

who always seems to provide ahead of time,
  on lifting me toward the top of one rock

he examined another crag, saying,
  "Afterward catch hold of that,
  but see first if it will bear your weight."

It was not a way for one clothed in a leaden cloak,
  for we, he a shade and I pushed,
  could hardly mount from jag to jag.

And were it not that on this side
  the slope was shorter than on the other,
  I do not know about him, but I would have been ex-
    hausted;

but, since Malebolge slopes wholly
  toward the edge of the lowest well,
  the position of each ditch demands

that one side be higher than the other.
  We came finally to the place
  where the last stone is broken off.

The breath had been so pumped from my lungs
  as I went up that at the top
  I could go no farther, and sat down at once.

"Now you must free yourself from sloth,"
  my master said, "for, sitting on down
  or lying under covers, no one comes to fame,

without which whoever consumes his life
  leaves such vestige of himself on earth
  as smoke in air or foam on water.

Therefore get up, overcome your panting
  with the spirit which wins every battle
  if it does not sink with its heavy body.

A longer stairs must be climbed;
  it is not enough to have left this one;
  if you understand, act so that it may profit you."

I then got up showing myself better furnished
  with breath than I was, and I said,
  "Go on, for I am strong and bold."

36

48

60

The travelers now come to the ditch of the thieves.

We made our way up over the bridge
    which was rocky, narrow, and difficult,
    and much steeper than the previous ones.

I kept talking in order not to appear faint;
    whereupon from the next ditch a voice issued
    unsuited for forming words.

I do not know what it said, although I was already
    on the top of the arch that crosses there,
    but whoever spoke seemed moved to anger.

I had turned to look down, but my living eyes
    could not penetrate to the bottom
    through the darkness; therefore I said,   72

"Master, let us try to reach the next bank,
    for, just as I hear, but do not understand,
    so I look, and can distinguish nothing."

"No reply do I make except by an act,"
    he said, "for a modest request
    should be followed silently by the deed."

We went down the bridge to the place
    where it joins the eighth bank,
    and then the ditch was revealed to me.

I saw in it a terrible pack of serpents
    of such diverse appearance
    that the memory of it still chills my blood.   84

Let Libya with its sands boast no longer,
    for if it produced chelydri, jaculi, and phareae,
    and cencri with amphisbaena [fabulous snakes],

it has never shown so many plagues
    or such bad ones, together with all of Ethiopia
    and the land [Arabia] which lies above the Red Sea.

Amid this cruel and dismal swarm, I saw people running,
    naked and terrified, without hope of hiding place
    or of heliotrope [to make themselves invisible].

Their hands were tied behind them by serpents

which stuck their heads and tails through their backs,
and were knotted together in front.   96

And behold! at one that was near our bank
a serpent sprang and transfixed him
right where the neck meets the shoulders.

Neither I nor O was ever written so quickly
as he took fire and burned and fell
like a cinder to the ground.

Then when he was thus destroyed
the ashes came together of themselves
and took on instantly the previous form.

Thus it is maintained by great sages
that the Phoenix dies and then is reborn
when the five-hundredth year approaches.   108

During its life it feeds on neither grain
nor herb, but on incense and amomum,
and nard and myrrh make up its shroud.

And like one [an epileptic] who falls not knowing how,
through the force of a demon pulling him to the ground
or through some obstruction that paralyzes him,

and who, when he gets up, looks around, all bewildered
by the great anguish he has suffered,
and while looking sighs,

such was the sinner after he arose.
O Power of God, how severe it is
in showering down such blows of vengeance!   120

*The stricken soul is Vanni Fucci, one of Dante's former political
enemies, whom the poet had known, not as a thief, but only as hot-
headed and violent. Vanni predicts obscurely and maliciously certain
events which will lead to the defeat of the Florentine Whites.*

My guide then asked the sinner who he was;
whereupon he answered, "I rained down from
Tuscany into this gullet a little while ago.

A bestial, not human life, I liked,
mule [of irregular birth] that I was; I am **Vanni Fucci**,
a beast, and Pistoia was a den worthy of me."

I said to my guide, "Tell him not to slip away
    and ask what sin thrusts him down here,
    for I saw him once a man of blood and rage."

And the soul, having heard, did not dissemble,
    but directed toward me his face
    and his attention with a look of dismal shame.   132

Then he said, "It grieves me more
    that you have caught me in this misery
    than when I was taken from the other world.

I cannot deny what you ask for;
    I have been put down this far for the theft
    of the fine ornaments of the sacristy,

for which another was falsely accused.
    But to keep you from enjoying this sight,
    if you ever get out of this dark place,

open your ears to my prophecy and hear:
    Pistoia first is thinned of Blacks,
    then Florence renews her masters and her ways;   144

Mars draws a fiery vapor [thunderbolt] from Val di Magra
    which is wrapped in turbid clouds,
    and in an impetuous and angry storm

a battle will be fought on the Piceno field;
    then the blast will pierce the mist
    so that every White will be wounded by it.

And I have told you this so that you may grieve."

CANTO XXV

The Metamorphosis of Thieves

At the end of his remarks the thief
    raised both hands, making the [obscene] sign of the fig,
    and shouting, "Take that, God, for at Thee I point them!"

From then on the serpents were my friends,
    for one coiled around his neck, as if saying,
    "I will not have you speak any more,"

and another encircled his arms and bound them,
    so clinching itself in front
    that he could not make a move with those members.

Ah, Pistoia, why do you not resolve to burn
    so that you will last no longer, since you surpass
    your own founders [followers of Catiline] in wickedness?   12

Through all the dark circles of Hell
    I saw no spirit so bold against God,
    not even him [Capaneus] who fell from the walls of
        Thebes.

The thief fled, saying nothing further.
    Then I saw a centaur, full of wrath, come calling,
    "Where is he? Where is the impious one?"

I do not believe Maremma has as many snakes
    as the centaur had on its back
    up to where our human form begins.

Upon his shoulders, behind his neck,
    a dragon was lying with open wings
    which set on fire all it met.   24

My master said, "That is Cacus [a fire-breathing monster]
    who, under the rocks of Mount Aventine,
    many times made a lake of blood.

He does not go on the same road as his brothers [the other
        centaurs]
    because of the theft he slyly made
    of the great herd [of cattle] kept near him,

which led to the end of his wicked life
    under the club of Hercules, who gave him
    perhaps a hundred blows, although hardly ten were felt."

While Virgil was saying this, the centaur ran off,
    and three spirits [Agnello, Buoso, and Puccio] came
        below us
    whom neither my master nor I had noticed   36

until they cried, "Who are you?"

Whereupon our talking ceased,
and we gave heed to them alone.

I did not recognize them, but it happened
as sometimes occurs by chance
that one needed to name the other,

saying, "Where can Cianfa [now a serpent] have remained?"
In order to make my guide attentive,
I held my finger against my mouth from chin to nose.

If you are slow, Reader, to believe
what I am to relate, it will be no wonder,
for I who saw it scarcely admit it to myself.   48

As I kept my eyes on them, a serpent [Cianfa]
with six legs darted in front of one
and fastened itself wholly to him.

With its middle feet it clasped his belly
and with those in front seized his arms;
then it set its fangs in both his cheeks.

It spread its hind feet over his thighs
and thrust its tail between them
drawing it up along his back.

Ivy never clung to a tree so tightly
as the horrible beast
entwined the other's members in its own;   60

then they grew together and exchanged their color
as if they had been hot wax,
nor did either one or the other appear as before.

Thus a dark hue moves ahead of a flame
over a sheet of paper, as the whiteness
dies away before it becomes black.

The other two [Buoso and Puccio] watched and shouted,
"O me, Agnello, how you are changing!
Behold! You are now neither two nor one."

The two heads had already fused into one,
and the shapes of two faces appeared blended
in the one in which the others had disappeared.   72

The two arms were formed of four strips;

the thighs with the legs, the belly and the chest,
became such members as were never seen.

All the former features were blotted out;
the perverse image seemed two and none,
and thus went away with slow steps.

As a lizard, under the great scourge
of the dog days, passing from hedge to hedge,
seems a flash as it crosses the path,

so appeared, making for the bellies
of the remaining two, a small, fiery serpent,
livid and black as a peppercorn,   84

and pierced that part in one of them
where we first receive our nourishment;
then fell, stretched out, in front of him.

The one transfixed [Buoso] looked at it, silently,
and with feet motionless, yawned,
as if sleep or a fever had come upon him.

He eyed the reptile, and the reptile him;
from the wound of one and mouth of the other
thick smoke issued and combined.

Let Lucan be silent now where he tells
of poor Sabellus and of Nasidius [transformed by serpents],
and wait to hear what is announced.   96

Let Ovid keep still concerning Cadmus and Arethusa,
for if he changes one into a serpent in his verse
and the other into a spring, I do not envy him,

since he never changed two natures
face to face so that both forms
were ready to exchange their substance.

The two responded to each other in such a way
that the serpent made a fork of its tail,
and the wounded shade drew its feet together.

The legs and the thighs united,
so that in a little while there was no sign
you could see of the joining.   108

The split tail took on the shape

lost in the other; the skin of one became soft
and that of the other hard.

I saw the arms withdraw through the armpits
and the short legs of the reptile
lengthen as much as the other's arms were shortened.

Then the hind feet, twisted together,
became the member man hides,
and the shade from his made two legs project.

As the smoke covered both with a new color
it brought out hair on one
and removed it from the other.   120

One got up and the other fell,
neither, however, turning aside his gaze
under which each had changed faces.

The one standing drew his snout toward his temples,
and with the flesh left over
ears were formed on the smooth cheeks.

What was not drawn back and remained
in excess made a nose for the face
and thickened the lips to a fit size.

The one on the ground stretched forth his nose,
withdrew his ears within his head,
as a snail does its horns,   132

and his tongue which had been undivided
and apt for speech, split; and the forked tongue
united; then the smoke stopped.

The soul that had become a brute
fled hissing through the ditch,
and after it the other, talking and sputtering.

Then he turned his new back to the reptile
and said, "I want Buoso to run
as I have, crawling over the way."

Thus I saw the seventh ballast change
and interchange, and let the strangeness of it
be my excuse if my pen has gone astray.   144

Although my eyes were somewhat confused

and my mind bewildered, those shades
    could not slip away so secretly

that I did not recognize easily
    Puccio Sciancato, who was the only one
    of the three companions left unchanged.

The unidentified figure (originally the second snake) was Francesco de' Cavalcanti, killed by the people of Gaville. The town mourns because of the vengeance taken for him.

The other was he because of whom you, Gaville, weep.

CANTO XXVI

Ulysses

The bitter tone of the beginning lines of an apostrophe to Florence ends quickly when Dante thinks of the misfortune certain to come to his city, a disaster wished for by neighboring towns, like Prato, not to mention enemies. Here, as elsewhere, the invective expresses deep concern, a kind of inverted love.

Rejoice, Florence, since you are so great
    that over land and over sea you beat your wings,
    and your name is famous in Hell!

Among the thieves I found five citizens of yours,
    such that shame comes over me;
    and you do not rise through them to great honor.

But if the truth is dreamed of near the morning,
    you will soon feel what Prato,
    not to mention others, craves for you.

And if that had already happened, it would not be
    too soon; so were it, since it has to be!
    for it will weigh heavier on me as I grow older.

The poets reach the summit of the bridge over the bolgia where evil counseling is punished. This sin, incurred mainly by those of superior intelligence, offered constant temptations to Dante, an exile dependent upon patronage.

In the ditch below, lights appear, like fireflies at dusk on a summer evening. And just as Elisha saw Elijah rise up, enveloped in a cloud of flame, so here the fire concealed the spirits. Dante asks about a double flame, like that on the funeral pyre of Eteocles and Polynices, two brothers who had killed each other.

We departed, and over the steps
    which stones had made for our descent,
    my guide remounted, and drew me up,

and continuing our solitary way
    over the stones and rocks of the bridge,
    feet did not advance without help from hands.

I grieved then, and now I grieve again
    when I direct my thought to what I saw,
    and I control my mind more than usual

so that virtue alone may guide it.
    Thus, if a kindly star or something better [Divine Grace]
    has given an advantage, it may not be harmful through
        abuse.   24

As a peasant who is resting on a slope
    in the season when the sun that lights the world
    keeps his face least hidden from us—

at the hour when gnats take the place of flies—
    sees fireflies down below in the valley,
    perhaps where he gathers grapes or plows;

so, with as many flames the eighth bolgia
    was all resplendent, as I noticed
    when I came to where I could see the bottom.

And, as he [Elisha] who avenged himself with the bears
    saw the chariot of Elijah depart
    when the horses rose erect to Heaven—   36

for he could not follow so closely with his eyes
    that he could see anything except the flame itself,
    like a little cloud rising upward—

so each light moved through the ditch,

none revealing what it hid,
and yet each concealed a sinner.

I was standing on the bridge leaning out to see,
so that if I had not held to a rock,
without being pushed I would have fallen,

and my guide, who saw me so attentive, said, *Virgil.*
"Within the fires are the spirits; *tells him*
each is wrapped in what is burning him."
48

"Master," I answered, "through hearing you
I am more certain, but already I was aware
that this was so, and wished to ask

who is in the fire which comes so divided at the top
that it seems to rise from the pyre
on which Eteocles was placed with his brother."

*Ulysses and Diomed, in the double flame, are guilty on three counts:
(1) the trick of the Trojan horse, which led to the destruction of Troy
and the founding of Rome; (2) enticing Achilles to abandon Deidamia
and to leave for the Trojan wars, and (3) the theft of the Palladium, a
statue of Pallas on which the fate of Troy depended.*

He answered, "In that flame Ulysses and Diomed
are tortured, and thus they go together
in punishment as in their battles.

They groan within their flame for the ambush
of the horse which was the portal
through which came the noble ancestors of the Romans.
60

Also they weep for the art on account of which
Deidamia still grieves for Achilles,
and they suffer too for the Palladium."

"If they can speak within those fires," I said,
"Master, I beg you earnestly, and beg again
(and may my prayer be worth a thousand),

that you do not deny our waiting
until the horned flame comes here;
you see how my desire bends me toward it!"

And he to me, "Your request is worthy
of praise; therefore I grant it,
but see that your tongue keeps silent.
72

Let me speak, for I have conceived
    what you want to know. Since they were Greeks,
    they might shy away from your words."

*When Virgil, who had celebrated Ulysses in the Aeneid, asks about
his death, the latter, the representative of the spirit of adventure and
of scientific discovery, answers with great dignity and relevance,
pointing out how compelling was his desire for knowledge of the
two worlds of things and of men. In the story Dante invents, instead
of returning to Penelope and the comforts of home, Ulysses sails
westward through the Mediterranean, then past Gibraltar, and out on
the vast and terrifying Atlantic. His course, like that of Columbus
almost two centuries after Dante, is west-southwest. Five months pass;
the crew of old men see the constellations of the other hemisphere;
then land (probably the island of Purgatory) appears. But a storm
arises, and Ulysses ends his life in the glory of a last adventure.*

When the flame had come to where
    time and place seemed best to my guide,
    I heard him speak in these terms:
"O you two within one fire,
    if I merited thanks from you while I lived,
    if I deserved much or little

when in the world I wrote the lofty verses,
    do not move, but let one of you tell
    where, lost, he went to die."   84

The greater horn of the ancient flame
    began to shake, murmuring like a fire
    struggling in the wind,

then moving the tip here and there,
    as if it were a tongue speaking,
    it formed words, and said:

"When I left Circe who detained me
    more than a year near Gaeta
    before Aeneas had named it thus,

neither fondness for my son, nor pity
    for an old father, nor the love for Penelope
    which should have made her happy,   96

could overcome in me the desire I had

to gain experience of the world
and of the vices and the worth of men.

I set out on the high, open sea,
with only one ship, and with that little company
by which I was not deserted.

Both coasts I saw as far as Spain,
down to Morocco and the island of Sardinia,
and the others that are bathed in that sea.

I and my companions were old and slow
when we came to that narrow pass [Gibraltar]
where Hercules set up his landmarks 108

so that men should not venture beyond.
On the right I left Seville,
and on the other side had already passed Ceuta.

'O brothers,' I said, 'you who
through a thousand perils have come to the West,
to the brief vigil of our senses

which is left, do not deny
experience of the unpeopled world
to be discovered by following the sun.

Consider what origin you had;
you were not created to live like brutes,
but to seek virtue and knowledge.' 120

With this little speech I made my companions
so eager for the journey
that scarcely then could I have held them back,

and, having turned our stern to the morning,
we made wings of our oars for the mad flight,
always gaining on the left.

The night already saw the stars
of the other pole, and ours [the North Star] so low
it did not rise from the ocean floor.

Five times the light upon the moon
had shone and been extinguished
since we started on the deep way, 132

when a mount appeared to us,

dim in the distance, and which seemed
    higher than any I had ever seen.

We rejoiced; but soon our joy changed to sorrow,
    for, from the new land a whirlwind arose
    which struck the prow of our ship.

Three times it made it whirl with all the water;
    the fourth time it lifted high the stern
    and made the prow go down, as pleased Another [God],

until at last the sea closed over us."

CANTO XXVII

Guido da Montefeltro

*A second flame roars like the brass statue of a bull in which prisoners
were burned alive. This instrument of torture was made for a tyrant
of Agrigentum and was tried out first on its inventor. The flame con-
tains the soul of Guido da Montefeltro, a famous Ghibelline leader
referred to in the* Convivio *as "our most noble Italian." Guido enquires
about Romagna, and Dante outlines briefly the conditions in that
region, designating the various rulers by their armorial bearings.*

Already the flame was erect and quiet,
    having ended its speech, and was going from us
    with the leave of the dear Poet,

when another flame that came behind it
    made us turn our eyes to its tip
    because of a confused sound issuing from it.

As the Sicilian bull which roared first
    with the groans of the one who made it
    with his tools (and that was right)

bellowed with the voice of the tortured
    in such a way that, although it was of brass,
    it seemed transfixed with pain,

so, not having any opening or outlet
    from their source in the fire,
    the doleful words were transformed into its language.

After they had found their way
    up through the tip, giving it the vibration
    the tongue had imparted to them,

we heard it say, "O you to whom I direct my voice,
    and who were speaking Lombard just now,
    saying, 'Now go, further I do not urge you,'

although I have perhaps arrived somewhat late,
    do not be displeased to speak with me;
    you see it does not irk me, and I burn!   24

If you have just now fallen into this blind world
    from that sweet Latin land
    from which I bring all my sin,

tell me if the Romagnuols have peace or war,
    for I was from the mountains there
    between Urbino and the peak from which the Tiber
        comes."

I was still attentive and bent down
    when my leader nudged me, saying,
    "*You* speak, this is an Italian."

And I, having already prepared my reply,
    began without delay, "O soul,
    you who are hidden down there,   36

your Romagna is not and never was
    without strife in the hearts of its tyrants,
    but no open warfare did I leave there just now.

Ravenna stands as it has for many years,
    the eagle of Polenta brooding over it,
    and covering Cervia with its pinions.

The city [Forlì] which once bore the long siege,
    and made a bloody heap of the French,
    finds itself under the green claws [the Ordelaffi family].

The old and young mastiffs of Verrucchio [the Malatestas]
    who disposed badly of Mantagna [their prisoner],
    as usual, make an auger of their teeth.   48

The cities on the Lamone and the Santerno
>   are ruled by the young lion in the white lair [Maghinardo
>   da Susinana]
>   who, from summer to winter, changes party.

And the city [Cesena] whose side the Savio bathes,
>   as it lies between the mountain and the plain,
>   lives [under party bosses] between tyranny and freedom.

Now I beg you to tell us who you are;
>   do not be more reluctant than another has been;
>   so may your name stay proudly in the world."

After a successful military career, Guido da Montefeltro withdrew from
the world and joined the Franciscan order, hoping to make amends
for the sins inseparable from military life and to prepare securely for
the future world. His plan might have succeeded except for the pope,
Boniface VIII, who asked him by what faithless stratagem he might
defeat his enemies, offering absolution in advance for the evil counsel.
Obliged either to comply or to disobey his superior, Guido chose what
seemed (to a soldier) the lesser evil, and told how the pope might,
through treachery, secure Palestrina, the stronghold of his enemies.

After the flame had roared a while in its manner,
>   the sharp tip moved to and fro,
>   and breathed forth this sound: 60

"If I believed that my reply were to anyone
>   who would ever return to the world,
>   this flame would remain quiet,

but since no one from this ditch
>   has ever returned alive, if I hear the truth,
>   I will answer without fear of infamy.

I was a man of arms, and then a Cordelier,
>   believing, thus girt, to make amends;
>   and certainly my intent would have been realized

except for the Great Priest (may ill befall him!)
>   who put me back into my former sins;
>   and how and why I want you to hear.   72

While I had the form of the flesh and bones
>   my mother gave me, my deeds
>   were not lionlike, but those of a fox.

The tricks and the secret ways,
    I knew them all, and so carried on their art
    that my fame spread to the ends of the earth.

When I saw that I had reached
    that point in life when everyone
    should lower sail and coil his ropes,

what first had pleased me became repugnant
    and, having repented and confessed, I gave myself to God,
    and, alas! that should have availed.   84

The Prince of the new Pharisees [Boniface VIII],
    waging war close to the Lateran—
    and not with Saracens or with Jews,

for every enemy of his was a Christian,
    and none had been a renegade at Acre
    or a merchant in the Sultan's land—

considered neither his high office
    and sacred orders, nor in me that cord I wore
    which used to make those bound with it thinner.

But, as Constantine called upon Sylvester
    in Soracte to cure him of his leprosy,
    so he called me, as his physician,   96

to cure the fever of his pride.
    He asked advice of me, and I kept silent,
    because his words seemed drunken,

and then he said, "Do not let your heart mistrust,
    right now I absolve you; let me know
    how to cast Palestrina to the ground.

I can open and close Heaven,
    as you know, since two are the keys
    that my predecessor [Celestine V] did not hold dear."

The heavy arguments brought me to where
    silence seemed worse to me than complying,
    and I said, 'Father, since you wash away   108

the sin into which I now must fall,
    long promise with short fulfillment
    will make you triumph on your lofty seat.'

*At Guido's death, St. Francis came for him, but a "black Cherub"
from the eighth circle of Hell, the counterpart of those of the eighth
heaven who likewise operate through intelligence, objected, and
pointed out the impossibility of absolution in advance.*

*Dante uses this extreme example to emphasize the point that salvation
depends on the state of the soul at the moment of death. A similar
contest, related in Purgatory, occurs in the case of Guido's son, but
in almost exactly opposite circumstances.*

When I was dead, Francis came for me,
    but one of the black Cherubim said to him,
    'Don't take him, don't wrong me.

He must come down among my minions
    because he gave the fraudulent advice,
    since when I have been lurking to grasp his hair.

For one who does not repent cannot be absolved,
    nor can *repenting* and *willing* go together
    because the contradiction does not allow it.'   **120**

Ah, wretched me, how I shuddered
    when he seized me, saying,
    'Perhaps you did not think I was a logician!'

To Minos he brought me, who twisted his tail
    eight times around his stiff back,
    and after he had bitten it in his rage, he said,

'This is one for the thievish fire.'
    Therefore I am lost here as you see,
    and while moving, clothed in fire, I grieve."

When he had finished speaking
    the sorrowing spirit went on
    twisting and shaking his sharp flame.   **132**

My guide and I passed over the bridge
    to the top of the next arch
    which crosses the ditch in which a fee is paid

by those who get a burden by dividing [sowing discord].

CANTO XXVIII

The Sowers of Discord

*If it were possible to bring together the wounded on the battlegrounds
of southern Italy in the long series of wars from ancient times down
to the Norman invasions and the wars of Charles of Anjou against
Manfred, the scene would be similar to that of the ninth bolgia.*

Who even in unrhymed words [prose]
    could ever fully tell in many narrations
    of the blood and of the wounds I now saw?

Every tongue certainly would fail
    because our language and our memories
    are insufficient to contain so much.

If all the soldiers were assembled
    who, on the stormy fields of Apulia,
    have groaned for their blood

shed by Trojans, and in the long [Punic] war
    which made so vast a spoil of rings [from fingers of dead
          Romans],
    as Livy writes, who does not err,   12

together with those who suffered painful wounds
    by opposing Robert Guiscard [the Norman conqueror]
    and others whose bones are still piled up

at Ceperano, where every Apulian [allied with Manfred]
    was a traitor, and at Tagliacozzo
    where old Alardo conquered without arms [by strategy],

and were one to show his limbs pierced,
    another his cut off, the view would not equal
    the awful sight of the ninth ditch.

*Mahomet, the first shade recognized, had been considered as originally
a Christian and as the deliberate cause of the separation of the world
into two monotheistic faiths. Mahomet mentions prophetically and*

*with malicious pleasure Fra Dolcino, the leader of a heretical sect
who, beseiged in 1306, was forced by hunger to surrender.*

Indeed, a cask without a stave or endboard
    looks less mutilated than one I saw
    split from his chin down to where wind is broken.   24

His entrails hung between his legs,
    the vital parts appeared with the foul sack
    which makes excrement of what is swallowed.

While I was intently looking at him,
    he gazed at me, and with his hands opened his breast,
    saying, "Now see how I tear myself,

see how mangled Mahomet is!
    In front of me Ali [a son-in-law] goes weeping,
    his head split from chin to forelock;

and all the others you see here
    while alive were sowers of scandal and of schism
    and therefore are split like this.   36

A devil is here behind us who cuts us
    thus cruelly with the edge of his sword,
    reopening all the wounds

when we have gone around the doleful road,
    since they are healed
    before we come again before him.

But who are you, dallying on the bridge,
    perhaps to delay going to your punishment
    decreed upon your own confession?"

"Not yet has death come to him, nor does guilt
    bring him to torment," my master said,
    "but to give him complete experience,   48

I, who am dead, must take him
    down here from round to round, and this
    is as true as that I am speaking to you."

More than a hundred in the ditch,
    when they heard this, stopped to look at me,
    forgetting their pain in their marveling.

"Now tell Fra Dolcino, you who perhaps

will soon see the sun again, that unless he wants
    to follow me he had better provide himself

with food, so that the snow
    will not bring victory to the Novarese,
    which otherwise would be hard for them to gain."   60

After he had lifted one foot to go
    Mahomet said these words to me,
    then placed it on the ground, moving on.

*Pier da Medicina, another schismatic of whom little is known, adds
the prophecy of the death of two citizens of Fano who will be called
to a parley and treacherously thrown overboard. They will not need
the usual protection from the squalls of Focara, since they will never
reach that place. Then Curio is mentioned who from private motives
urged Caesar to cross the Rubicon and begin the civil war. He wishes
now he had never seen the town of Rimini near that river. Another
sower of discord, Mosca, according to tradition advised the killing of
an opponent to settle a feud rather than a milder punishment, since
that, he thought, would end the matter. Instead, the murder led to
the first conflict between the Guelfs and Ghibellines in Florence. On
seeing Mosca, Dante's Florentine spirit flares up, and he tells him of
the banishment of his family, the Lamberti, from the city.*

Another who had his throat cut
    and his nose severed up to his eyebrows,
    and who had only a single ear,

having stopped to look with wonder,
    before the others cleared his windpipe
    which was all red outside, and said,

"O you whom sin does not condemn
    and whom I have seen in the Latin land,
    if too much resemblance does not deceive me,   72

recall to mind Pier da Medicina
    if ever you go back to see the sweet plain
    which from Vercelli slopes to Marcabò,

and make known to the two best men of Fano,
    to Messer Guido and to Angiolello,
    that, unless foresight here is vain,

they will be thrown from their ship

and drowned near La Cattolica
through the treachery of a base tyrant.

Between the islands of Cyprus and Majorca,
Neptune has never seen so great a crime
of pirates or of Argolic people [Greeks].   84

That traitor who sees with one eye only [Malatestino]
and holds the city [Rimini] which someone here [Curio]
would wish never to have seen,

will have them come for a parley with him,
and will act so that to allay Focara's wind,
they will need neither vow nor prayer."

And I to him, "Point out and tell me
if you want me to take news of you above,
who found the sight of that city bitter?"

Then he laid his hand on the jaw
of one of his companions, and opened his mouth,
saying, "This is he, and he does not speak.   96

While exiled, he quieted Caesar's fears,
affirming that a man well prepared
always loses by any delay."

Oh, how dismayed he seemed to me
with his tongue cut in his throat,
Curio, who before spoke so boldly!

And one who had both hands cut off,
lifting the stumps in the dark air
so that the blood dirtied his face,

cried, "Remember also Mosca
who said, alas, 'A thing done has an end,'
which was a seed of evil for the Tuscans."   108

And I added, "And death to your kindred,"
whereupon he, heaping grief on grief,
went off like one maddened by sorrow.

*The last example is that of the Provençal poet, Bertran de Born who,
Dante believed, had fomented a quarrel between Henry, the "young
English king," and his father.*

But I remained to look at the throng,

and I saw a thing I would fear
  to tell about without more proof,

except that conscience reassures me,
    the good companion which emboldens man
    under the breastplate of conscious innocence.

I saw certainly, and I still seem to see
    a body without a head, going on
    like the others of the sad troop.   **120**

It held by the hair its severed head
    dangling from its hand like a lantern,
    which looked at us and said, "Woe is me!"

Of itself it made a lamp for itself,
    and they were two in one and one in two;
    how this can be He knows who so ordains.

When it was at the foot of the bridge,
    it lifted the head high with its arm
    to bring the words closer to me,

which were, "Now see my terrible penalty,
    you who, breathing, are visiting the dead;
    judge if any is as great as this.   **132**

And, that you may take news of me,
    know that I am Bertran de Born, the one
    who gave the young king the evil encouragement.

I made father and son rebellious to each other;
    Ahithophel did not do worse to Absalom
    and to David with his wicked plots.

Because I separated persons thus joined,
    I now carry my brain, alas,
    detached from its source in this body.

Thus retribution is observed in me."

CANTO XXIX

The Falsifiers

Fascinated by the sight of the horrible wounds, Dante keeps looking
at them and incurs a reproach. He excuses himself (he is growing up
in his relationship with his master) by mentioning that he believed
that a relative was there, Geri del Bello, whose violent death had not
been avenged. Dante pities Geri, perhaps for the latter's obvious
adherence even here to the code of family vengeance.

The time, as usual in Hell, is indicated by the position of the moon:
it is now shortly after noon on Saturday.

The great crowd and the diverse wounds
    had made my eyes so inebriated
    that they were eager to remain and weep.

But Virgil said, "What are you looking at?
    Why does your sight still rest down there
    on the sad, mutilated shades?

You have not done so at the other ditches.
    Consider, if you wish to count them,
    that the valley circles for twenty-two miles;

already the moon is under our feet;
    the time granted to us now is short,
    and there is much more to see."   12

"If you had taken note," I answered then,
    "of the cause that made me look,
    perhaps you would have granted me a longer stay."

Meanwhile my guide kept going on
    and I followed, making my reply
    and adding, "Within that hollow

on which I kept my eyes fixed so closely
    I believe a spirit of my own blood
    laments the sin that costs so much down here."

Then my master said, "From now on

do not let your thoughts be distracted by him;
　　attend to something else and let him stay there,　24

for I saw him at the foot of the little bridge
　　pointing you out and threatening you with his finger,
　　and I heard him called Geri del Bello.

You were then so completely occupied
　　with him [Bertran de Born] who once held Altaforte
　　that you did not look over there, and he departed."

"O my guide, his death by violence
　　which has not yet been avenged," I said,
　　"by [relatives] the partners of his shame,

made him indignant; therefore he went off
　　without speaking to me, as I judge,
　　and by that he has made me pity him the more."　36

The shades in the tenth bolgia are divided into four groups: falsifiers
(1) of metals (alchemists), punished by leprosy and paralysis; (2) of
persons (impersonators), punished by delirium or madness; (3) of coins
(counterfeiters), afflicted with dropsy; and (4) of words (liars), suffering
from high fever. Dante treats them with mild and amused contempt.

Thus we talked as far as to the point
　　which would have shown the next ditch
　　to the bottom if there had been more light.

Then, when we were above
　　the last cloister of Malebolge, so that
　　its lay brothers could be observed by us,

diverse laments kept striking me
　　which had their arrows barbed with such pity
　　that I covered my ears with my hands.

Such suffering as there would be if the sick
　　in the hospitals of Valdichiana, Maremma, and Sardinia
　　[malarious regions] between July and September　48

were all together in one ditch,
　　was here; and such stench issued
　　as comes from festered limbs.

We descended to the last bank of the long bridge,
　　still keeping to the left,
　　and then my sight was clearer

down toward the bottom, where the minister
    of the Supreme Lord, Infallible Justice,
    punishes the falsifiers registered here.

I do not believe there was greater sadness
    to see all the people of Aegina sick
    when the air was so full of pestilence   60

that the animals, even to the little worm,
    fell dead—and then the ancient people,
    as the poets hold as true,

were restored by the seed of ants—
    than it was to see in the dark ditch
    the spirits languish in diverse heaps.

One lay upon the belly and one upon the shoulders
    of another, and one on all fours
    was crawling along the dismal path.

Step by step we went without speaking,
    observing and listening to the sick,
    who could not lift their bodies.   72

I saw two sitting, leaning on each other
    as stewpan is propped against stewpan to warm,
    spotted with scabs from head to foot,

and never have I seen a currycomb handled so quickly
    by a stableboy whose master was waiting for him
    or by one staying up against his will

as each of these plied the clawing of his nails
    on himself, because of the great rage
    of itching that had no other help;

and the nails scraped off the scabs
    as a knife does the scales from bream
    or some other fish that has them larger.   84

"O you who disarm yourself with your fingers,
    at times making pincers of them,"
    my guide began to say to one of them,

"tell us if any Latin is among those
    who are here; so may your nails
    suffice eternally for this work!"

"We are both Latins whom you see
    so disfigured here," one answered, weeping,
    "but who are you, asking about us?"

My guide replied, "I am one descending
    with this *live* man from ledge to ledge,
    and I intend to show Hell to him."

96

Then the mutual support broke,
    and each of them, trembling, turned to me,
    with others who had overheard the words.

My good master drew close to me, saying,
    "Ask them what you want to know."
    And I began to speak as he desired:

"So may your memory not fade
    from human minds in the first world,
    but may it live on for many suns,

tell me who you are, and of what people;
    let not your ugly and annoying punishment
    make you afraid to reveal yourselves to me."

1o8

*Griffolino, a fraudulent alchemist, tells how he was burned by the
presumptive father of the simple-minded Albero da Siena, who had
taken seriously his remarks about flying. This prompts Dante to speak
of the Sienese whose sometimes aristocratic folly was a standing joke
in the bourgeois atmosphere of Florence. Dante is helped in his gibes
by Capocchio, who mentions ironically the notorious spendthrift
Stricca and the "Spendthrifts' Club," a group of young Sienese who
deliberately ruined themselves by extravagance.*

"I was of Arezzo," one answered,
    "and Albero da Siena had me burned at the stake;
    but what I died for does not bring me here.

It is true that I told him, speaking in jest,
    that I could rise in the air in flight,
    and he who had the desire but little sense

wanted me to show him the art, and because
    I did not make him a Daedalus [a flyer], he had me burned
    by one who considered him as a son.

But to the last ditch of the ten,

Minos, who cannot err, condemned me
for the alchemy that I practiced in the world.' 120

And I said to the poet, "Now was there ever
a people as silly as the Sienese?
Certainly the French are not so by far."

Thereupon the other leper who heard me
answered my question and said, "Except Stricca
who knew how to spend with moderation,

and Niccolò who first discovered
the expensive use of the clove
in the garden where such seed takes root,

and except the company in which
Caccia d'Ascian squandered vineyard and forest
and the Abbagliato displayed his wit. 132

But that you may know who seconds your remarks
against the Sienese, sharpen your eyes toward me,
so that my face may give the right response.

Then you will see that I am the shade of Capocchio
who falsified the metals by alchemy,
and you must recall, if I see you correctly,

how good an ape of nature I became."

CANTO XXX

Master Adam and the False Greek

*Two terrible examples of insanity are cited at the beginning of this
canto, the hallucination of Athamas and the hysterical grief of Hecuba.
Two impersonators show a similar mania. One, Gianni Schicchi, had
been engaged by Buoso Donati's son to impersonate his father and
dictate a more favorable will. The commission was well performed
except that the testator included himself in the legacy as the heir
of the "queen of the herd," a valuable mare. The other example is
that of Myrrha.*

At the time when Juno because of Semele
    was angry at the Theban royal family,
    as she had shown already more than once,

Athamas was stricken with such madness
    that on seeing his wife coming
    burdened with two sons, one on either hand,

he shouted, "Let us spread the net, so that I
    may catch the lioness and cubs as they pass";
    then he stretched out his pitiless claws,

and seizing one, whose name was Learchus,
    whirled him around and dashed him on a rock;
    and she, with her other burden, drowned herself   12

And when Fortune had brought low
    the bold pride of the Trojans
    so that both king and kingdom were blotted out,

sad Hecuba, miserable and captive,
    after she had seen her [daughter] Polyxena slain
    and, forlorn, recognized the body of [her son] Polydorus

on the shore of the sea, in her madness
    barked like a dog, so greatly
    had grief wrenched her mind.

But neither Theban nor Trojan Furies
    were ever seen anywhere so cruel
    in goading beasts, much less human bodies,   24

as those I saw in two spirits, pale and naked,
    who ran biting as a hungry boar does
    when just released from the sty.

One rushed on Capocchio and seized him
    by the neck, then dragging him,
    made his belly scrape on the hard bottom.

And the Aretine [Griffolino], who remained trembling,
    said to me, "That mad one is Gianni Schicchi,
    and he goes thus tearing others."

"Oh," I said to him, "so may the other
    not bite you, please tell us
    who it is before it gets away."   36

And he to me, "That is the ancient spirit
    of wicked Myrrha, who was devoted to her father
    beyond the bounds of lawful love.

She came thus to sin with him,
    changing herself into another's form,
    just as the other who is running off

undertook, to gain the mistress of the herd,
    to impersonate Buoso Donati,
    making a will and giving it a legal form."

After the two mad ones on whom
    I had kept my eyes had passed,
    I turned to look at the other ill-born shades.   48

The counterfeiters are swollen with dropsy. One, a master of the art, had served the counts of Romena in one of the coolest, best watered of mountain regions, and the image of the place where he had worked increases the torture of his thirst. Amused at the size of Master Adam's belly, Dante asks about two shades on his boundaries. One, Sinon, suffering now from high fever, had pretended to be a fugitive from the Greeks, and had persuaded the Trojans to take in the wooden horse. The other liar is Potiphar's wife. Sinon objects to being called a "Greek from Troy," and we have a quarrel, the pot calling the kettle black. Sinon, considering each counterfeit coin as a separate indictment, charges Master Adam with the commission of more sins than any other demon. His opponent, in rebuttal, mentions the infamous notoriety Sinon has gained through the works of Homer and Virgil. Dante is scolded for listening to the quarrel. He tries to reply, but is so ashamed that he cannot, and excuses himself by this embarrassment more effectively than if he had been able to speak.

I saw one who would have looked like a lute
    if only he had had his legs cut off
    at the groin, where they join the body.

The heavy dropsy, disproportioning him thus
    with humors badly absorbed,
    left his head too small for his belly,

and made him hold his lips apart
    as the hectic does who, for thirst,
    has one turned up, the other down.

"O you who are without any punishment
    in this wretched world, and I don't know why,"
    he said to us, "see and take note   60

of the misery of Master Adam!
    When alive I had enough of what I wanted,
    and now, alas! I long for a little drop of water.

The streams which from the green hills
    of Casentino flow down to the Arno,
    making their beds cool and soft,

always stand before my eyes and not in vain,
    for the vision of them dries me up
    more than the disease which wastes my features.

The rigid Justice which goads me
    takes advantage of the place where I sinned
    to put my sighs to quicker flight.   72

There is Romena where I counterfeited
    the [Florentine] currency sealed with the Baptist's image,
    for which I left my body burned above.

But if I could see the miserable soul
    of Guido or of Alessandro or their brother [his employers]
    I would not trade the sight for Fonte Branda [a spring].

One is already in, if the mad shades
    that move around tell the truth,
    but of what avail is it, if my limbs are tied?

Yet, if I were still nimble enough
    to make an inch in a hundred years,
    I would already have started out   84

to find them among these disgusting people,
    although the ditch circles for eleven miles,
    and is not less than half a mile across.

Because of them I am in such a household;
    they induced me to stamp the florins
    which had indeed *three* carats of alloy!"

And I to him, "Who are the two wretches,
    steaming like wet hands in winter,
    lying close to your right frontier?"

"Here I found them on raining down in this ditch,"
    he answered, "since when they have not turned over,
    nor will they, I believe, in eternity.   96

One is the lying woman who accused Joseph;
    the other is false Sinon, the Greek from Troy;
    because of their fever they emit such stench."

And one of them [Sinon] who perhaps
    took badly being named thus darkly,
    with his fist struck the vile belly

which sounded like a drum, and Master Adam
    struck him back in the face with his arm
    which did not seem less hard,

saying to him, "Although locomotion is impossible
    because of my heavy limbs,
    I have an arm free for such business!"   108

Whereupon the other answered, "When you went
    to the fire, you were not so quick,
    but you were still quicker when you made the coins."

And he of the dropsy, "You tell the truth about this,
    but you were not so good a witness
    at Troy when the truth was asked of you."

"If I spoke falsely, you falsified the coins,"
    said Sinon, "and I am here for one fault,
    and you for more than any other demon."

"Remember, perjurer, the horse!" he of the swollen belly
    answered, "and let it be a plague to you
    that the whole world knows of it."   120

"And may the thirst that cracks your tongue
    be a curse to you," said the Greek, "and the foul water
    which makes a hedge before your eyes."

Then the counterfeiter, "Thus your mouth
    still opens to your harm, as usual,
    for, if I am thirsty and humor stuffs me up,

you have the burning and the headache,
    and to lick the mirror of Narcissus
    you would not need a second invitation."

I was wholly intent on listening to them
    when my master said to me, "Now keep on gazing!
      a little more, and I will quarrel with you." 132

When I heard him speak to me with anger,
    I turned to him with such shame
      that the memory of it still haunts me.

As one who dreams of a misfortune
    and, while dreaming, hopes it is a dream,
      so that he longs for what is as if it were not,

so I became, not being able to speak
    although I wanted to excuse myself and did so,
      without knowing that I was doing it.

"Less shame washes away a greater fault,"
    said my master, "than yours has been;
      therefore, free yourself of all sadness 144

and take note that I am at your side
    if it happens again that chance catches you
      where people are in a similar wrangle,

for wishing to overhear it is a low desire."

CANTO XXXI

The Giants

Titans against God

The same tongue first stung me
    so that it tinted both my cheeks,
      then offered me its cure.

Thus I hear that the lance of Achilles
    and of his father was wont first
      to wound and then to heal.

We turned our backs on the miserable ditch,
    going up without speaking
      over the bank which surrounds it.

Here it was less than night and less than day,
    so that my sight did not go far;
    but I heard a horn sound so loudly   12

that it would have made any thunder faint;
    and retracing the course the sound took
    I directed my eyes to one spot.

After the doleful rout,
    when Charlemagne lost his holy company,
    Roland did not blow so terribly.

Only a short while did my eyes look toward the sound
    when I seemed to see many high towers,
    and I asked, "Master, tell me, what city is this?"

And he to me, "Since you are looking
    through the darkness from too far off
    your imagination leads you astray.   24

You will see when you arrive there
    how the senses are deceived by distance;
    therefore move a little faster."

Then he took me tenderly by the hand
    and said, "Before we go farther,
    to make the event seem less strange,

know that these are not towers, but giants,
    and they are in the well around the bank
    from the navel down, all of them."

As, when a mist has cleared somewhat,
    our eyes little by little make out
    what the vapor in the air had hidden,   36

so, piercing through the thick gloom
    on approaching closer and closer to the bank,
    my error fled, and my fear increased.

As, on the circle of its walls,
    Montereggione [a fortress] is crowned with towers,
    so, above the bank which surrounds the pit,

the horrible giants, whom Jove still threatens
    when he thunders in the heavens,
    towered above us with half their bodies.

Already I saw the face, shoulders, and chest
    of one, and a large part of his belly,
    and both his arms down by his side.   48

Certainly when Nature gave up the art
    of producing these creatures she did well
    to deprive Mars of such agents;

and if she does not repent for elephants
    and whales, whoever looks closely
    will hold her more discreet and just,

for where the force of intellect [as in the giants]
    is added to ill will and strength,
    mankind can have no defense.

His face seemed to me as long and wide
    as the pine cone at St. Peter's in Rome,
    and his other features were in proportion.   60

Thus the bank which was an apron
    from his middle down, showed so much of him
    that three Frieslanders [tall men] would have boasted

in vain to reach up to his hair.
    I saw, indeed, thirty great spans of him
    down from [the neck] where a man buckles on his cloak.

Nimrod, the builder of the Tower of Babel, a "mighty hunter before the Lord," is with the giants who revolted against Jove. His words are meaningless. Virgil apostrophizes him for Dante's benefit. Then the travelers come to Antaeus, who was not present at the battle of the giants against the gods, and therefore is not bound like the others. Flattered by Virgil, who understands his fatuous character, Antaeus extends his hand and places the two poets on the bottom of the pit in the ninth and last circle.

"Raphèl maỳ amèch zabì almì"[1]
    the savage mouth for which sweeter
    hymns were unfitting began to say.

And my guide to him, "Stupid soul,
    keep to your horn, and with it express yourself
    when anger or some other passion moves you.   72

---

[1] These are meaningless words.

Search around your neck and you will find the strap
    which holds it, O confused spirit;
    see it curving across your great chest."

Then he said to me, "He accuses himself.
    This is Nimrod, through whose evil thought
    a single tongue is not used in the world.

Let us leave him and not speak in vain,
    for, as the language of others is to him,
    so is his to them, and is understood by none."

We kept on still to the left
    and at the distance of a crossbow shot
    we found another giant larger and fiercer.   **84**

Who the master was to bind him
    I cannot say, but his right arm
    at his back and the other in front

were bound by a chain, which held him tied
    from the neck down, so that over his exposed part
    it encircled him five times.

"This haughty creature wished to make trial
    of his power against supreme Jove,"
    said my master; "therefore, he has such a reward.

Ephialtes is his name; he fought in the great battle
    when the giants frightened the gods:
    the arms he used once, he never moves."   **96**

Then I to my guide, "If possible
    I should like for my eyes
    to gain experience of the immense Briareus."

Whereupon he answered, "You will see Antaeus
    nearby, who speaks and is unbound
    and who will put us in the lowest depth of guilt.

The one you wish to see is farther on
    and is bound and built like this one
    except that he looks more ferocious."

Never did an earthquake jar
    so violently a massive tower
    as Ephialtes suddenly shook himself.   **108**

Then I feared death more than ever,
    and fright alone would have caused it,
    if I had not seen the chains.

We went on then and came to Antaeus
    who protruded above the bank
    fully five ells, not counting his head.

"O you who in the fateful valley
    which made Scipio an heir of glory,
    when Hannibal and his army turned back,

you who once brought a thousand lions as prey—
    and, if you had fought in the great war,
    with your brothers, it seems that some believe   120

the sons of Earth [the giants] might have conquered-
    put us down, do not disdain to do so,
    to where cold locks up Cocytus.

Do not make us go to Tityus or to Typhon;
    this man can give what is longed for here;
    therefore bend over and do not scornfully refuse.

He can revive your fame in the world,
    for he lives and expects a long life, if Divine Grace
    does not call him to herself ahead of time."

Thus my master spoke, and Antaeus
    hurriedly held out the hand whose grip
    Hercules once felt, and took hold of my master.   132

When Virgil felt himself grasped,
    he said to me, "Come, let me take hold of you."
    Then, of himself and me he made one bundle.

As the Garisenda tower seems to fall
    if looked at under its leaning side
    when a cloud passes over it in the opposite direction,

so Antaeus appeared to me as I watched
    while he bent over; and he was such
    that I would have wished to go by another way.

But lightly in the depth which swallows
    Lucifer with Judas he placed us,
    nor did he delay long bent over   144

but rose like a mast set in a ship.

The Traitors

*The tone of the Comedy now becomes harsh, scornful, vindictive.
Dante again calls upon the Muses, but this time on those who helped
to build <u>Thebes</u>, "<u>the ancient home of crime</u>."*

If I had rhymes rough and harsh enough
    to be fitting for the dismal hole
    on which all the other circles weigh,

I would press out the substance of my conception
    more fully; but since I do not have them,
    not without fear do I bring myself to speak.

For, to describe the bottom of the whole universe
    is not an enterprise to take up in jest,
    nor for a tongue that still cries "mamma" and "papa."

But may those ladies who helped Amphion
    to enclose Thebes aid my verse,
    so that words and facts will not differ.

O rabble, miscreated above all others,
    in this place to speak of which is hard,
    here [on earth] you would better have been sheep or goats!

When we were down in the dark well
    beyond the feet of the giant and much lower,
    and as I was still looking at the high wall,

I heard someone say, "Watch how you step!
    Move so you won't trample with your feet
    on the heads of the weary, miserable brothers."

Then I turned and saw a lake in front of me
    and under my feet which, frozen,
    had the appearance of glass and not of water.   **24**

The Danube in Austria never made in winter
    so thick a veil for its current,
    nor the Don up there under its cold skies,

as this did; for if Tambernicchi [a mountain]
    had fallen on it, or Pietrapana,
    it would not have given a creak even at the edge.

And as a frog lies croaking
    with just its muzzle out, in the season
    when the peasant woman thinks of gleaning,

so the shades were lying in the ice,
    livid up to where shame appears,
    their teeth chattering like storks' bills.   36

Each held his face down; their mouths
    gave evidence of the cold,
    and their eyes of their sad hearts.

Caïna, the first division of the ninth circle, contains traitors to kindred,
*among whom are the counts of Mangona, who killed each other in a
quarrel over an inheritance. Other minor figures also are mentioned.*

When I had looked around a little,
    I glanced at my feet and saw two so bound together
    that the hair on their heads was intermingled.

"Tell me, you who press your chests so close together,
    who you are," I asked, and they bent their necks,
    and after they had lifted their faces to me,

their eyes, which previously were wet only within,
    gushed through the lids, and the cold
    froze their tears and locked them up again.   48

A clamp never bound wood to wood so strongly.
    Then they, like two goats,
    butted each other, such anger overcame them.

And one who had lost both ears from the cold,
    with his face still downward, said,
    "Why do you look at us so much?

If you want to know who these two are,
    the valley from which the Bisenzio flows
    belonged to them and to their father, Albert.

They came from one body, and you might search
    through all Caïna without finding a shade
    more worthy to be preserved in ice,   60

not him [Mordred] whose breast and shadow
   were laid open by a single blow from Arthur's hand,
   not Focaccia; not this one who covers me

with his head, so that I cannot see beyond
   and whose name was Sassol Mascheroni,—
   if you are a Tuscan you know now who he was.

And, so that you will not put me to further speech,
   know that I was Camicion de' Pazzi, and am waiting
   for Carlino to make me [by comparison] seem innocent."

Afterward I saw a thousand faces made doglike
   by the cold; so that a shudder comes to me
   and always will at the sight of frozen pools.   72

*Passing on to Antenora, the second division of the ninth circle, where
traitors to party and country are kept, Dante accidentally kicks one
shade who mentions Montaperti, the scene of a defeat of the
Florentine Guelfs. Dante's suspicion is immediately aroused, and he
tries by force to make the shade name himself. Another, however,
treacherously gives him away as Bocca degli Abati who, at a critical
moment in the battle, cut off the hand of the Florentine standard-
bearer, an act which was thought to have caused the defeat. Dante's
violence incurs no reproach: the implication is that ordinary rules of
conduct are inapplicable to the completely depraved: one must keep
away from them or act according to the code they establish. This is
the realistic Gresham's law of competitive behavior. Bocca in turn
mentions others, including Buoso da Duera, who had been bribed by
Charles of Anjou, and Ganelon, the traitor in the Song of Roland.*

And while we were moving toward the center
   to which all weights are drawn
   and I was shivering in the eternal chill,

whether it was destiny or chance, I know not,
   but while walking among the heads
   my foot struck hard against the face of one.

Weeping it cried, "Why do you kick me?
   Unless you come to increase the vengeance
   for Montaperti, why do you molest me?"

And I, "Master, now wait for me here
   until this one relieves me of a doubt,
   then you can make me hurry as you wish."   84

My guide stood still, and I said to the shade
    who was still cursing loudly,
    "Who are you complaining thus of others?"

"Now who are you, going through Antenora
    kicking others' cheeks," he answered,
    "harder than if you were alive?"

"I am alive," was my response,
    "and it may be dear to you, if you want fame,
    that I should include your name in my notes."

And he to me, "The contrary is what I want,
    get away from here; do not bother me,
    for you know badly how to flatter in this bottom."   96

Then I seized him by the scalp and said,
    "You will name yourself
    or not a hair will be left on your head."

And he to me, "Even if you tear it out
    and fall on my head a thousand times,
    I will not tell or show you who I am."

I had already twisted his hair in my hand
    and had pulled out more than one tuft,
    he howling with eyes cast down,

when another shouted, "What's the matter with you, Bocca?
    Isn't it enough to chatter with your jaws
    but you must bark?—What devil is after you?"   108

"Now," I said, "I do not want you to speak,
    damned traitor, for to your shame
    I will carry off true news of you."

"Go," he answered, "and tell what you want,
    but if you get out of here, don't keep silent
    about him who has his tongue so ready.

He is weeping here for the money of the French.
    'I saw,' you can say, 'him of Duera,
    down there where sinners are put to cool.'

If any one asks about the others here,
    you have beside you the one of Beccheria
    whose throat was cut by Florence.   120

Gianni de' Soldanier, I believe,

is farther on, with Ganelon, and Tebaldello
who opened Faenza while it was sleeping."

We now see a bestial example of hatred. One shade is gnawing the
head of another, as Tydeus, after being mortally wounded by Mena-
lippus whom he in turn killed, called for the head of his enemy and
chewed on it. Aghast at such a sight, Dante wonders what could
motivate such hatred and offers to help in the vengeance by making
the reason for it known in case there is just cause.

We had already departed from him
    when I saw two frozen in one hole,
    so that the head of one was a hood for the other,

and as bread is chewed from hunger,
    so the one on top set his teeth in the other
    where the brain joins the neck.

Not otherwise did Tydeus gnaw
    in his rage the temples of Menalippus
    than he did this one's skull and flesh.   132

"O you who show by such bestial signs
    hatred of him whom you are chewing,
    tell me why," I said, "on this condition

that if you rightfully complain of him,
    knowing who you are and his sin,
    I may repay you up in the world

if that [tongue] with which I speak is not dried up [by
        death]."

CANTO XXXIII

Count Ugolino

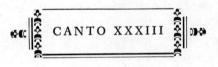

Count Ugolino, a Pisan, had allied himself with the Florentine Guelfs
and in 1285 was in control of his city. Perhaps he is among the
traitors because of this change of party and because of the transfer of

certain castles. In that year the Ghibellines, led by the Archbishop Ruggieri, revolted. Ugolino was called treacherously to a parley, then imprisoned with two sons and two grandsons in what was later known as the "Tower of Hunger." After some months the door of the prison was nailed shut, and the five were left to die of starvation. The bodies, on their removal, appeared mutilated, perhaps rat-bitten. Ugolino recognizes Dante as a Florentine, therefore a Guelf, and explains why he is violating so terribly the obligations of a neighbor.

The sinner raised his mouth from his fierce repast,
　　wiping it on the hair of the head
　　the back of which he had despoiled,

and then began, "You wish that I renew
　　desperate grief, which wrings my heart,
　　merely in thinking of it, before I speak.

But if my words can be seeds to bear infamy
　　to the traitor I am gnawing,
　　you will see me both speak and weep.

I do not know who you are, nor by what means
　　you have come down here, but certainly
　　you seem a Florentine when I hear you.

You must understand that I was Count Ugolino,
　　and this is the Archbishop Ruggieri;
　　now I will tell you why I am such a neighbor.

How, as the result of his evil thoughts,
　　I was seized, trusting in him,
　　and put to death, there is no need to tell,

but what you cannot have learned, that is,
　　how cruel my death was, you will hear
　　and know if he has offended me.

12

As in the Francesca episode, so here Dante reconstructs what could not be known, that is, the lonely, unwitnessed death of the five in prison. In the tower (compared to a "mew" in which falcons were kept while molting) several months had passed when a symbolic and prophetic dream revealed to the prisoners their fate. In describing it, Ugolino's fierce memory gets ahead of his words: the wolf becomes "a father" and the whelps, "sons," and he turns on Dante, reproaching the poet for lack of feeling before he has told what happened.

A little loophole in the mew which
 because of me was called the 'Tower of Hunger'
 and in which others will be imprisoned   24

had shown through its opening several moons already
 when I had the evil dream
 which tore away the veil of the future.

This one seemed the lord and master of the hunt,
 chasing the wolf and whelps on the mountain
 which prevents the Pisans from seeing Lucca.

With lean, eager, and well-trained hounds [the mob],
 he had placed the Gualandi, Sismondi,
 and Lanfranchi [as leaders] in front of him.

After a short course, the father and the sons
 seemed to me weary, and I thought I saw
 their bodies torn by the sharp teeth.   36

When I had awakened before the dawn
 I heard my children who were with me
 weeping in their sleep and asking for bread.

You are cruel indeed not to grieve already
 in thinking of what my heart forboded;
 and if you do not weep now, by what are you ever moved?

The drama passes in silence: almost nothing is said. On the first day Anselm, the smallest, showed concern for his father. On the second, Ugolino bit his hands from grief. That and the third day passed in complete silence. On the fourth, Gaddo weakened and died, and on the fifth and sixth, the others. On the seventh, Ugolino crawled over the bodies, and on the eighth, he succumbed, hunger having accomplished what grief could not do.

The hatred of Ugolino is communicated to Dante who bursts out in an invective against Pisa.

They were now awake, and the hour drew near
 when our food used to be brought to us,
 and each was afraid because of his dream;

and below I heard the door of the horrible tower
 nailed up; whereupon, without saying a word,
 I looked into the faces of my sons.   48

I did not weep, so stony did I become within.

They cried, and my little Anselm said,
  'You look so [hard], father, what ails you?'

Still I shed no tears nor did I answer
  during all that day and the night after,
  until another sun came forth upon the world.

When a little light had entered
  the awful prison, and I saw
  on four faces my own aspect,

I bit both my hands from grief,
  and they, thinking I did it from hunger,
  suddenly got up and said,   60

'Father, it will be much less painful
  if you eat of us; you clothed us
  with this poor flesh; may you take it from us!'

I became quiet then not to make them more sad.
  That day and the next we all remained mute.
  Ah, hard earth, why did you not open!

After we had reached the fourth day,
  Gaddo fell stretched out at my feet, saying,
  'Father, why don't you help me?'

There he died; and as you see me
  I saw the three of them fall one by one
  between the fifth day and the sixth; then I began,   72

already blind, to crawl over each, and for two days
  I called them after they were dead.
  Then fasting did more than grief."

When he had said this, with eyes awry,
  he seized again the wretched head with his teeth
  which gnawed upon the bone, like a dog's.

Ah, Pisa! shame of the people,
  of the beautiful land [Italy] where "sì" ["yes"] is heard,
  since your neighbors are slow to punish you,

may the Capraia and Gorgona [islands] move
  and make a dam for the Arno at its mouth,
  so that it may drown everyone in you;   84

for if Count Ugolino was reputed
  to have betrayed you of the castle,
  you should not have put his sons on such a cross.

Their young age made Uguccione
    and Brigata innocent, you modern Thebes!
    and the other two named by my song.

*The poets move on to Tolomea, the third division, where traitors
to guests are punished. The heads of these sinners are thrown back,
so that the tears, freezing in the cups of their eyes, cause a painful
pressure.*

We went farther on to where the frost
    roughly binds another people
    with faces thrown back, not turned down.

Weeping there prevents them from weeping:
    the tears which find a barrier in the eyes
    turn inward to increase the pain,   96

since they form a solid mass,
    and like visors of crystal fill
    the whole cavity beneath the eyebrows.

And, although, as in a callused spot,
    every feeling had gone from my face
    because of the intense cold,

already I seemed to notice a wind,
    so that I said, "Master, what causes this?
    Is not all vapor [atmospheric change] absent down here?"

And he to me, "Soon you will be
    where your eyes will see the cause
    of the blast and will give you the answer."   108

And one of the wretches in the cold crust
    shouted at us, "O souls so cruel
    that the last place is assigned to you,

take from my eyes the hard veils,
    so that I may relieve the pain a little
    that stuffs my heart before the tears freeze again."

*To induce this soul to speak, Dante makes a promise with false intent,
that is, he commits fraud, as previously in this circle he had com-
mitted violence. Our poet is emphasizing again, in opposition to certain
idealists, that golden rules and codes of honor presuppose a certain
uniformity in the social group. To apply them without discrimination*

*is merely to favor and give superior survival value to the fraudulent
and dishonorable.*

*The soul whom Dante has tricked had had guests murdered at a
banquet, the signal for the execution being, "Bring on the fruit."
He is now getting expensive dates for cheap figs, that is, being repaid
with interest. His soul, apparently, has descended "quick" into Hell,
and is replaced in his body by a demon.*

And I to him, "If you want me to help you,
    tell me who you are, and if I do not relieve you,
    may I go to the bottom of the ice!"

He answered then, "I am Friar Alberigo,
    he of the fruit of the evil garden,
    and am getting here dates for my figs."   120

"Oh," I said to him, "are you dead already?"
    And he to me, "How my body fares
    in the world above, I have no knowledge.

Such an advantage this Tolomea has
    that often a soul falls into it
    before Atropos [a Fate] has thrust it forth.

And—so may you remove more willingly
    the frozen tears from my face—
    know that when a soul betrays as I did,

its body is taken from it by a demon
    who afterward controls the flesh
    until its allotted years have passed.   132

It falls into such a cistern as this,
    and perhaps the body of the shade
    wintering behind me appears on earth.

You must know him if you have just come down;
    He is Ser Branca d'Oria [a Genoese], and many years
    have passed since he was thus locked up."

"I believe that you are deceiving me,"
    I said to him, "for Branca d'Oria has not died,
    but eats and sleeps and puts on clothes."

"In the ditch of the Malebranche above,"
    he said, "where the tenacious pitch is boiling,
    Michel Zanche [his victim] had not yet arrived   144

when a devil took over his body
  and that of a close relative
  who did the treacherous act with him.

But reach out your hand, open my eyes";
  and I did not open them for him;
  and to be rude to him was fitting.

Ah, Genoese, men who are estranged
  from all good ways and full of all corruption,
  why are you not scattered from the earth,

for, with the worst spirit of Romagna [Alberigo],
  I found one of you whose soul
  for his deeds already bathes in Cocytus,   156

and in body seems still alive on earth!

CANTO XXXIV

Satan

*To the first words of a Latin hymn to the cross, "The banners of the
Lord come forth, . . ." Dante adds the word* inferni, *applying them
thus to Satan, the lord of Hell. Dante is now in Giudecca where
traitors to benefactors are completely submerged in the ice.*

*Satan is represented as the counterpart of the Trinity, with heads of
three colors, yellow, black, and red, standing for impotence, ignorance,
and hate, and corresponding to the divine power, wisdom, and love.
His three pairs of wings send forth a threefold blast which freezes
Cocytus. In the mouths of Lucifer are Judas, the traitor to Christ,
and Brutus and Cassius, traitors to the Roman Empire. The poets
reach Satan at six o'clock on Saturday evening, having spent twenty-
four hours on the journey.*

"*Vexilla Regis prodeunt inferni*[1]
  toward us, therefore, look ahead,"
  my master said, "and try to discern him."

---
[1] This sentence is translated in the explanation immediately above.

As, when a thick mist covers the land
    or when night darkens our hemisphere,
    a windmill, turning, appears from afar,

so now I seemed to see such a structure;
    then because of the wind, I drew back
    behind my guide, for there was no other protection.

Already—and with fear I put it into verse—
    I was where the shades are covered in the ice
    and show through like bits of straw in glass.   12

Some were lying, some standing erect,
    some on their heads, others on their feet,
    still others like a bow bent face to toes.

When we had gone so far ahead
    that my master was pleased to show me
    the creature [Lucifer] that once had been so fair,

he stood from in front of me, and made me stop,
    saying, "Behold, Dis! Here is the place
    where you must arm yourself with courage."

How faint and frozen I then became,
    do not ask, Reader, for I do not write it down,
    since all words would be inadequate.   24

I did not die and did not stay alive:
    think now for yourself, if you have the wit,
    how I became, without life or death.

The emperor of the dolorous realm
    from mid-breast protruded from the ice,
    and I compare better in size

with the giants than they do with his arms.
    Consider how big the whole must be,
    proportioned as it is to such a part.

If he were once as handsome as he is ugly now,
    and still presumed to lift his hand against his Maker,
    all affliction must indeed come from him.   36

Oh, how great a marvel appeared to me
    when I saw three faces on his head!
    The one in front [hatred] was fiery red;

the two others which were joined to it

over the middle of each shoulder
were fused together at the top.

The right one [impotence] seemed between white and yellow;
the left [ignorance] was in color like those
who come from where the Nile rises.

Under each two great wings spread
of a size fitting to such a bird;
I have never seen such sails on the sea.   48

They had no feathers, and seemed
like those of a bat, and they flapped,
so that three blasts came from them.

Thence all Cocytus was frozen.
With six eyes he wept, and over his three chins
he let tears drip and bloody foam.

In each mouth he chewed a sinner with his teeth
in the manner of a hemp brake,
so that he kept three in pain.

To the one in front the biting was nothing
compared to the scratching, for at times,
his back was stripped of skin.   60

"The soul up there with the greatest punishment,"
said my master, "is Judas Iscariot. His head
is inside the mouth, and he kicks with his legs.

Of the other two whose heads are down,
the one hanging from the black face is Brutus;
see how he twists and says nothing.

The other who seems so heavy set is Cassius.
But night is rising again now,
and it is time to leave, for we have seen all."

*At the center of the earth, also the center of gravity, the poets turn
and begin climbing laboriously, the effort symbolizing the difficulty of
getting rid of bad habits even when their ugliness is known. Lucifer
now appears upside down, and the time changes to Saturday morning,
since the travelers gain twelve hours in passing from Jerusalem time
to that of Purgatory, directly opposite.*

*Through the passage made by Lucifer as he fell, the poets reach the
foot of Purgatory just before dawn on Easter Sunday.*

Each part of the Comedy ends with the word "stars" which stand for

*the goal of the journey, the objects farthest removed from Satan and
the materialism of the earth, and whose beauty is most ethereal.*

When my guide was ready, I embraced his neck,
    and he took advantage of the time and place
    so that when the wings were wide open   72

he caught hold of the shaggy sides
    and descended from tuft to tuft
    between the tangled hair and the frozen crust.

When we were at the place where the thigh
    revolves on the swelling of the haunches,
    my guide, with effort and with difficulty,

turned his head to where he had had his feet,
    and grappled the hair, like one mounting,
    so that I thought he was returning into Hell.

"Hold fast, for by such stairs,"
    my master said, panting like one weary,
    "we must depart from so much evil."   84

Then he came through the opening in a rock
    and put me on its edge, sitting,
    and climbed toward me with wary steps.

I raised my eyes and thought
    that I would find Lucifer as I had left him,
    but saw him holding up his legs,

and if I then became perplexed,
    let dull people imagine who do not see
    what the point was that I had passed.

"Get up on your feet," said my master,
    "the road is long and the path rough, and already
    the sun has returned to mid-tierce [at 7:30 A.M.]."   96

The place where we were
    was no palace hall, but a natural dungeon,
    dark and with an uneven floor.

"Before I uproot myself from the abyss, Master,"
    I said when I was standing,
    "speak to me a little to dispel my error.

Where is the ice? and how is Satan planted

so upside down? and how in such a short time
has the sun made its way from evening to morning?"

And he to me, "You still imagine you are
on the other side of the center where I grasped the hair
of the wicked monster that pierces the world.   108

You were over there as long as I descended;
when I turned, you passed the point
to which all weights are drawn.

Now you have arrived in the hemisphere
opposite that which dry land covers
and at whose summit [Jerusalem] was consumed

the man [Christ] who was born and lived without sin.
You have your feet on a little circle
which forms the other face of Giudecca.

Here it is morning when it is evening there,
and Satan who made a ladder for us
with his hair is still as he was before.   120

On this side he fell from Heaven, and the earth here,
through fear, made a veil for itself
of the sea, and came to our hemisphere,

and perhaps the land [Purgatory] which shows on this side,
to flee from him, rushed up
and left this passageway empty."

There is a place as remote
from Beelzebub as his tomb extends,
not known by sight, but by the sound

of a little stream which descends in it
along the hollow of a rock which it has eaten out
with a slow and winding course."   132

My guide and I started on that hidden way
to return to the bright world,
and, without caring for any rest,

we climbed, he first and I second,
until I saw, through a round opening,
the beautiful things that heaven bears,

and came forth to see again the stars.

PURGATORY

❖❰❖❰❖❰❖❰❖❰❖❰❖

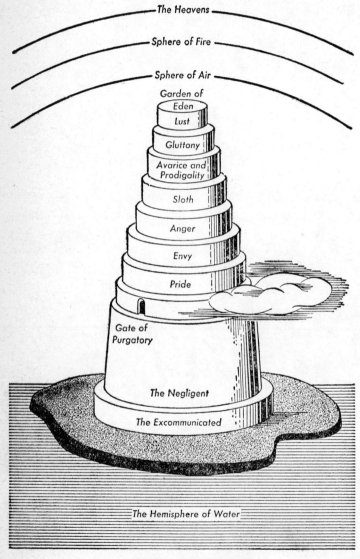

A DIAGRAM OF PURGATORY

OUTLINE OF PURGATORY

NOTE: The suggestive treatment consists of constant contemplation of the "goads" and "checks," that is, beautiful examples of the opposite virtue and repulsive illustrations of the vice itself.

The first three vices are due to love of a bad object, the fourth to insufficient love, and the last three to disproportionate love.

Region	Vices	Method of Suggestion	Disciplines
Shore	[Excommunicated]		
Below gate	[Negligent]		
Ledge 1	Pride	Sculptures	Bending necks under heavy weights
Ledge 2	Envy	Voices	Practice in using other senses besides sight
Ledge 3	Anger	Visual and auditory imagery	Satiation with blindness of wrath
Ledge 4	Sloth	Recitation	Developing habit of speedy activity
Ledge 5	Avarice and Prodigality	Recitation	Satiation with living close to the ground
Ledge 6	Gluttony	Voices	Practice in abnegation
Ledge 7	Lust	Recitation	Purification by fire

The Earthly Paradise (Garden of Eden).

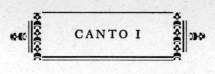

CANTO I

Cato

Dante indicates his new subject and invokes the "holy" Muses, especially Calliope, the inspirer of epic poetry whom the daughters of King Pieros once challenged in song, for which boldness they were changed into magpies. It is just before sunrise on Easter, April 10, 1300. The morning star, Venus, is obscuring with its light the constellation of the Fishes. In the new sky are four stars representing the cardinal virtues—Prudence, Temperance, Fortitude, and Justice—previously seen only by Adam and Eve.

To move over better waters now hoists sail
    the little vessel of my mind
    which leaves behind so rough a sea;

and I will sing of the second realm
    where the human spirit is cleansed
    and becomes worthy to rise to Heaven.

Here, O holy Muses, since I am yours,
    let dead poetry be revived
    and let Calliope arise a while,

accompanying my song with the music
    which struck the ears of the wretched magpies
    so that they despaired of pardon.   12

A sweet color of oriental sapphire
    which was forming in the clear sky,
    pure from the zenith to the horizon,

restored delight to my eyes
    as soon as I came out of the dead air
    that had afflicted both my eyes and lungs.

The beautiful planet which prompts to love
    made the whole east smile,
    veiling the Fishes that escorted her.

I turned to the right and set my mind
    on the other pole, and I noticed four stars
    never seen except by the first people.   24

The heavens seemed to rejoice in their light.
    O region of the north, widowed!
    since you are denied that view.

Cato, Dante's favorite hero of antiquity and the symbol of Free Will,
appears, his face shining with the light of the four virtues. Rather than
submit to Caesar, he had committed suicide, a Christian but not a
pagan sin. For this devotion to freedom and for other merits he is made
the guardian of Purgatory and will be saved on Judgment Day.

When I had withdrawn my eyes from them,
    turning for a moment to the north
    where the Great Bear [Dipper] had already disappeared,

I saw a solitary old man near me,
    in semblance worthy of so much reverence
    that no son owes more to his father.

The beard he wore was long
    and streaked with white, like his hair
    of which two tresses fell upon his breast.   36

The rays of the four holy lights
    so brightened his face that he appeared
    as if the sun were shining on him.

"Who are you who, moving up the dark stream,
    have fled from the eternal prison?"
    he asked, shaking his plumelike beard.

"Who has guided you or given you a light
    to issue from the black night
    which darkens the infernal depth?

Are the laws of the abyss thus broken,
    or have decrees been changed in Heaven
    so that the damned may come to my cliffs?"   48

My guide then took hold of me,
    and with words and hands and gestures
    made reverent my knees and brow.

Then he answered, "By myself I do not come;
    a lady descended from Heaven, at whose prayers
    I helped this man with my companionship.

But, since it is your will that more

of our present condition be explained,
  my will is not able to refuse you.

This man has not seen his last hour,
  but through his folly was so close to it
  that there was little time left.   60

I was sent to him, as I said,
  to rescue him, and there was no other way
  than this one on which I have started.

I have shown him all the wicked people
  and now propose to reveal those spirits
  who are purging themselves under your charge.

How I have brought him here would take long to tell;
  a Power from above has helped me
  to bring him to see and to hear you.

May it please you to welcome his coming;
  he is seeking freedom, which is precious,
  as one who gives up life for it knows.   72

You understand, since death for you was not bitter
  in Utica where you left the clothing of your flesh
  which, on the great day, will be so bright.

The eternal laws are not broken by us,
  for this man lives, and Minos does not condemn me.
  I am from the circle where the chaste eyes

of your Marcia still seem to supplicate,
  O holy breast! that you hold her for your own.
  For love of her, then, incline toward us;

let us go through your seven kingdoms;
  I will tell her of your grace
  if you deign to be mentioned down there."   84

Cato states plainly his indifference to the fate of his wife, Marcia: the
felicity of Heaven would be impaired if earthly relationships were not
ended and if sorrow could be felt for the damned. He directs Virgil
to gird Dante with a reed (Humility) and to wash his face, so that
he can appear properly before the guardians of the ledges of Purgatory.
The sun (Righteous Choice, Enlightenment) must be their guide
henceforth.

The two poets descend to the sea which Ulysses alone had sailed.
There, the reed which Virgil plucks for Dante replaces itself. Humility
cannot be defeated: the more it is crushed the more it grows.

"Marcia pleased my eyes so much
      while I was yonder," he said then,
      "that I granted all the favors she asked.

Now that she dwells beyond the evil stream
      she cannot move me because of the law
      which was made when I came from there.

But if a lady from Heaven sends and commands you,
      as you say, there is no need for coaxing;
      it is enough that you ask me for her sake.

Go then and see that you gird this man
      with a slender rush, and that you bathe his face,
      so that all stains are washed from it,   96

for it would not be fitting that eyes
      darkened by any mist should meet
      the first minister of those in Paradise.

This little island, around its very base,
      where the waves beat upon it,
      bears reeds upon the soft mud.

No other plant which brings forth leaves
      or grows hard could exist there,
      since it would not yield to the waves.

Afterward do not return along here;
      the sun which is rising now will show you
      the easiest way to climb the mount."   108

Then he disappeared, and I got up
      without speaking and drew close
      to my guide, my eyes fixed on him.

He began, "My son, follow my steps,
      let us turn back, for from here
      the plain slopes down to its low bounds."

The dawn was dispelling the morning hour
      which fled before it, so that from afar
      I recognized the trembling of the sea.

We went over the solitary plain
   like men returning to the road they have lost
   who, until they get there, seem to walk in vain.   120

When we reached the place where the dew
   contends with the sun and
   in shaded spots has dried but little,

my master softly placed both hands
   spread out on the wet grass,
   and I, aware of his purpose,

held toward him my tear-stained cheeks
   on which he wholly restored the color
   which the smoke of Hell had hidden.

We came then to the deserted shore
   whose waters had never been sailed
   by anyone who afterward was able to return.   132

There he girded me, as another [Cato] wished.
   O marvel! for, as he plucked the humble plant,
   it was suddenly reborn as it was

in the place from which he had torn it.

CANTO II

The Arrival of the Blessed

*As the sun reaches Gibraltar, the horizon of Purgatory, Night is con-
ceived as rising in India opposite to it, in the constellation of the
Scales, where it continues to rise until, after the equinox of autumn,
the nights are longer than the days. A light seen coming over the sea
is that of an angel with white wings and dress, bringing a boatload of
souls who sing of their deliverance.*

Already the sun had reached the horizon
   whose meridian covers Jerusalem;
   and Night, which circles opposite,

was issuing from the Ganges with the Scales
    which fall from her hands when her length
    exceeds that of the day,

so that where I was, the cheeks
    of beautiful Aurora, first white
    and then rosy, soon changed to orange.

We were still near the seashore
    like persons thinking of their way
    who move in spirit but in body linger,   **12**

and behold! as at the approach of morning
    Mars shines red through the thick mist,
    low in the west over the ocean floor,

so there appeared to me (may I see it again!),
    a light coming so rapidly over the sea
    that no flight could equal its speed.

After I had withdrawn my eyes from it
    to ask a question of my guide,
    I saw it again brighter and larger.

Then on each side of it there appeared
    something white, and underneath,
    little by little, another whiteness.   **24**

My master did not say a word
    until the first brightness appeared as wings;
    then, when he discerned the pilot,

he shouted, "Bend, bend your knees;
    here is the angel of God; fold your hands!
    from now on you will see such ministers.

See how he disdains human means,
    so that he needs no other oar or sail
    than his wings between such distant shores.

See how he has them raised toward the sky,
    fanning the air with eternal feathers
    which are not molted like mortal plumage."   **36**

Then, as the divine bird approached,
    he became brighter, so that close at hand
    my eyes could not endure the light.

I looked down, and he came to the shore
    with a vessel so slender and light
    that it skimmed the surface of the water.

On the stern stood the celestial boatman,
    seeming to have "blessed" inscribed on him,
    and more than a hundred spirits sat within.

In exitu Israel de Aegypto[1]
    they all sang together in one voice
    with the remaining words of that psalm.   48

Then he made the sign of the Holy Cross,
    whereupon all threw themselves on the shore,
    and he left as rapidly as he had come.

The new arrivals stand unworried but bewildered in their strange surroundings and ask Dante and Virgil about the way. They notice that the former is alive, and with dreamy, childlike simplicity crowd curiously around him. One recognizes him and advances with signs of affection, whereupon our poet tries to embrace him. The friendly spirit is that of Casella, a musician of Florence. Since he had died several months before Easter of 1300, Dante wonders why he is just arriving. Casella accepts without complaint the mysterious working of Divine Providence which has delayed his departure for Purgatory and refers incidentally to the plenary indulgence (remission of penance) granted pilgrims to Rome during this year of the jubilee. He sings one of Dante's own poems.

The crowd that remained there
    seemed strange to the place, looking around,
    like persons experiencing new sights.

On all sides the sun was shooting forth the day,
    having driven Capricorn from the middle of the sky
    with his unfailing rays,

when the new people lifted their heads,
    saying to us, "If you can,
    show us the way to the mountain."   60

And Virgil answered, "You believe perhaps
    that we know this place,
    but we are pilgrims, just as you are.

---

[1] "When Israel went out of Egypt."

We came a little while before you
    by another way, so rough and hard
    that climbing now will seem play for us."

The souls who had noticed by my breathing
    that I was still alive,
    in their marveling grew pale,

and, as around a messenger with an olive branch,
    people gather to hear the news
    and none shows himself shy about crowding,   72

so these souls, fortunate all of them,
    gazed fixedly at my face, as if forgetting
    to go and beautify themselves.

I saw one of them draw forward to embrace me
    with such great affection
    that he moved me to do the same.

O shades, empty except in semblance!
    Three times behind him I clasped my hands
    and as often drew them back to my breast.

My face showed, I believe, my marveling,
    whereupon the spirit smiled and drew back,
    and I, following, pressed forward.   84

Gently he told me to desist;
    then I recognized who he was and begged him
    to stay and speak with me a while.

He answered, "Just as I loved you in my mortal body
    so I love you released from it;
    therefore I stop; but why are you going this way?"

"My Casella, to return here another time
    I make this journey," I said,
    "but why have you been robbed of so many months?"

And he to me, "No wrong was done
    if the angel who takes when he chooses and whom,
    has several times denied me this journey,   96

for his will is guided by justice.
    For three months, he has received
    in all peace whoever has wished to come,

so that I, having arrived at the seashore
    where the Tiber becomes salty,
    was benignly taken in by him.

He has already directed his wings
    to that point, since there all assemble
    who do not go to the Acheron."

And I, "If your new condition does not take away
    the memory and the art of songs of love
    which used to quiet all my desires,   108

may it please you to console my spirit
    which, in coming here
    with its body, has become so weary."

Love that converses with me in my mind
    he then began to sing so sweetly
    that the sweetness still resounds in me.

*The suggestible, unhurried shades listen, forgetting the task they have
to accomplish, and are scolded by Cato. The group breaks up, moving
rapidly, as in a daze, toward the mount.*

My master and I and the people
    who were with him seemed happy,
    as if mindful of nothing else,

when, behold! as we were all attentive
    to the notes, the venerable old man came
    shouting, "What is this, laggard spirits?   120

What negligence, what delay is this?
    Run to the mountain and get rid of the slough
    which keeps you from seeing God."

As doves assembled for their food,
    and plucking wheat or tares,
    are quiet, without their accustomed pride,

but suddenly give up their eating
    if something frightens them,
    since they are assailed by a greater care,

so I saw that new troop end their singing
    and move toward the slope
    like men who go without knowing where,   132

and our leaving was not less sudden.

CANTO III

The Excommunicated

*To console Virgil for his shame in permitting the delay, Dante draws
close to him and points out affectionately his need for Reason's
guidance.*

*As the poets proceed toward the mountain, Virgil describes certain
characteristics of the shades. He takes occasion also to point out once
more that Reason cannot understand the mystery of the world.*

While sudden flight scattered
    those shades over the plain, on their way
    to the mount toward which Justice drives us,

I drew close to my trusted companion.
    How could I have gone on without him?
    Who would have brought me up the mountain?

He seemed stung by self-reproach.
    O pure and noble conscience,
    how bitter a little fault is for you!

When his feet gave up the haste
    which takes dignity from every act,
    my mind, at first preoccupied,   12

broadened its range, as if curious,
    and I looked at the mountain
    which rises highest toward Heaven from the sea.

The rays of the sun which flamed red
    behind me were broken in front of me
    in the form that my body cut them off.

I turned to one side with fear
    that I had been abandoned when I saw the earth
    dark in front of me alone.

But my comfort, turning toward me,

said, "Why do you still distrust?
Do you not know that I am here to guide you?   24

It is already evening where the body is buried
in which I cast a shadow.
Naples has it; it was removed from Brindisi.

If no shadow appears in front of me,
do not marvel any more than at the heavens
which do not obscure each other's rays.

To suffer torments, heat and cold,
bodies like ours are disposed by a Power
that does not want Its ways revealed.

Mad is he who hopes that our reason
can explore the infinite working
of One Substance in Three Persons.   36

Be content, O human race, with the *quia* [the facts],
for if you could have understood all,
Mary would not have needed to give birth.

You saw, longing hopelessly and eternally
in their sorrow, men [in Limbo] whose desires
otherwise would have been quieted—

I mean Aristotle and Plato
and many others." And here he bent his brow
and said no more, and remained disturbed.

*On reaching the foot of the mountain, Virgil tries to discover, by
thinking, the way to ascend. Dante uses his eyes, and proposes (to
Reason's relief) that they ask some shades coming slowly along the
bank. To reach the group, Dante and Virgil turn to the left, the
wrong way. The quiet, trusting souls shrink back at this irregularity.*

Meanwhile we came to the foot of the mountain.
There we found the bank so steep
that the nimblest legs would be useless.   48

Between Lerici and Turbia the most solitary,
the most deserted path is a stairway
wide and easy compared with that.

"Now who knows where the cliff is broken,"

said my master, stopping, "so that
    it can be climbed by someone without wings?"

And while he held his face low
    and thought within his mind about the way,
    I looked up, and along the rock

on our left a crowd of souls appeared
    moving toward us, but not seeming to,
    so slowly did they come.   60

"Lift your eyes, Master," I said,
    "over here are some who will give us counsel
    if you cannot find it by yourself."

He looked then, and with an air of relief answered,
    "Let us go to them, since they are coming too slowly;
    and you, my son, be steadfast in your hope."

Those people were still as far off—
    I mean after a thousand steps of ours—
    as a good slinger could throw,

when all drew back against the high bank
    and remained motionless and close together,
    as men, when startled, stop to look.   72

"O spirits elect, you who *ended* well,"
    Virgil began, "by that peace
    which, I believe, awaits all of you,

tell us where the mountain slopes
    so that going up is possible;
    for the wisest dislike most to lose time."

*The shades, suggestible and sheeplike, move forward. They are
through with the competition and struggles of our world and can safely
indulge this dreamy passivity.*

As sheep issue from the fold, by ones,
    by twos, by threes, and the others stand,
    timidly bending eyes and noses to the ground,

and what the first one does, the others do,
    huddling against it if it stops,
    simple and quiet, without knowing why,   84

so I saw coming forward then

the head of that fortunate flock,
  modest in countenance, in movement dignified.

When those in front saw the light
  broken on the ground at my right side,
  and my shadow falling on the bank,

they stopped and drew back a little
  and all the others who came after them,
  not knowing why, did the same.

"Without your asking, I declare to you
  that this is a human body that you see
  by which the sun's light is broken.

96

Do not marvel, but believe
  that not without strength from Heaven
  he tries to scale this wall."

Thus my master spoke, and those worthy people,
  making a sign with the back of their hands,
  said, "Turn, then go ahead."

Among the shades is Manfred, the natural son of Frederick II of Sicily and the former excommunicated head of the Ghibellines, whom Dante modestly disclaims knowing. He had been slain in the battle of Benevento and buried under a mound of stones. The pope, Clement IV, later ordered the bishop of Cosenza to have the body disinterred and, in a ceremony for the excommunicated, "with tapers quenched," thrown outside the kingdom of Naples which Manfred had lost. Dante points out that salvation depends only on the state of the soul at the moment of death. The excommunicated are penalized, however, by being forced to delay their purgation.

And one of them began to speak,
  "Whoever you are, while going on,
  glance back to see if you ever knew me."

I turned and looked fixedly at him.
  He was blond and handsome, of a noble presence,
  but a blow had cleft one of his eyebrows.

108

When I had disclaimed humbly
  ever to have seen him, he said, "Now, look,"
  and showed me a wound high on his breast.

Then, smiling, he added, "I am Manfred,
    the grandson of Constance, the Empress,
    and I pray that when you return

you see my beautiful daughter, the mother
    of the honor [kings] of Sicily and of Aragon,
    and, whatever may be related, tell her the truth.

After my body had been pierced
    by two mortal blows, weeping I surrendered
    to Him who pardons willingly.   **120**

Horrible were my sins, but Infinite Goodness
    has such wide open arms
    that It embraces all that turn to It.

If the shepherd of Cosenza,
    sent by Clement to hunt me down,
    had read well that page of God's book,

the bones of my body would still be
    at the head of the bridge near Benevento
    under the weight of the heavy stones.

Now the rain bathes and the wind moves them
    outside of the Kingdom, close to the Verde,
    where he transferred them with tapers quenched.   **132**

Through their [the clergy's] curse no one is so lost
    that eternal love cannot come to him
    as long as hope bears a leaf that is green.

True it is that whoever dies in contumacy
    of Holy Church, although he may repent at last,
    must remain outside of this bank

thirty times the period he lived
    in his presumption, if such a decree
    is not shortened by holy prayers.

You see now how happy you can make me
    by revealing to my good [daughter] Constance
    how you have seen me, and also this ban,   **144**

for much is gained here through [the prayers of] those on
        earth."

CANTO IV

The Indolent

When through delight or pain
    experienced by one of our senses
    the mind concentrates on the impression,

it seems to make use of no other faculty;
    and this is counter to the error
    which maintains that several souls are in us.

Therefore, when something is heard or seen
    which keeps the mind attentive,
    the time passes without being noticed,

for it is one faculty [the sensitive] that listens
    and another [the intellective] that keeps the soul intact,
    the latter bound [concentrating], the former free.   12

Of that I had true experience
    listening to that spirit and admiring,
    for the sun had risen fully fifty degrees

without my being aware of it
    when we came to where those shades
    shouted all together, "Here is what you asked for."

In the season when the grapes are darkening,
    a peasant with a forkful of his thorns
    often fills a larger opening in his hedge

than the path my leader began to climb,
    with me following him, we alone,
    when the flock [of shades] had left us.   24

You can go to San Leo and descend to Noli
    or mount Bismantova to its summit
    with feet alone, but here you must fly—

I mean with the swift wings and feathers
    of great desire, following that guidance
    that gave me light and hope.

We climbed within the cleft rock where,
    on either side, the banks touched us,
    and the ground beneath required both feet and hands.

After we had reached the upper edge
    of the high cliff, on the open hillside,
    "Master," I said, "which way shall we take?"   36

And he to me, "Let none of your steps fall back;
    make your way behind me up the mount
    until some guide appears to us."

The summit was so high it surpassed my sight,
    and the slope much steeper than a line
    from mid-quadrant to the center [45 degrees].

I was weary when I began to speak,
    saying, "O father, turn, and see
    how I must remain alone if you do not stop."

"My son," he said, "pull yourself up there,"
    and he pointed to a ledge a little higher
    which on that side encircled the hill.   48

His words so spurred me that I forced myself
    to crawl up after him
    until the shelf was under my feet.

Then both of us sat down
    facing the direction from which we had climbed,
    since looking back is wont to console.

*While facing east just before noon, Dante notices that the sun shines
on his left side. He learns that Jerusalem and Purgatory are on
opposite sides of the earth, and that the sun's path lies between these
points. He learns also that Purgatory becomes easier to climb toward
the top.*

[I cast my eyes first on the low shores;
    then I lifted them to the sun, and wondered
    that it shone on my left side.
The poet noticed my bewilderment
    on seeing the chariot of the light
    move between us and the north.   60
He said to me, "If Castor and Pollux [as in June]

accompanied that mirror which sheds its light
   on both sides of the equator,
you would see the ruddy zodiac [the sun's path]
   still closer to the Great Dipper [in the north]
   unless it abandoned its old path.
If you wish to see how that is,
   concentrating, imagine Zion [Jerusalem]
   in such relation to this mountain
that they have a single horizon
   and different hemispheres. Then you will see
   that the path Phaëthon could not follow   72
must pass this place on one side
   when it passes Zion on the other,
   if your mind thinks clearly."
"Certainly, master," I said,
   "never did I see so clearly
   what before my mind failed to grasp,
that the middle circle of the supernal motion,
   called 'equator' in a certain science,
   which always remains between the sun and winter,
for the reason that you say
   is as far from here to the north
   as the Hebrews saw it toward the hot regions.   84
But if you care to tell, I would willingly learn
   how far we have to go, for the hill
   rises farther than my eyes can reach."
And he to me, "This mountain is such
   that at the bottom it is hard to climb,
   and the higher one goes, the easier it becomes.
Therefore, when it seems to you so pleasant
   that going up will be as easy
   as floating in a boat down a stream,
then you will be at the end of this road;
   there expect to rest from your weariness.
   I have nothing more to answer: this I know is true."]   96

One of the negligent, the lazy Belacqua, has been listening idly to this
conversation. Although approving of energy in others, he is conscious
principally of the need for rest. With his head between his knees,
too lazy even to lift it, he glances at the strangers as they come up,

moving only his eyes. Like all the negligent, he must remain a certain
time outside the gate of Purgatory proper, and he sees no use in
making an attempt to get in. Even the prayers of those on earth for
his advancement are not worth the effort, he says (in his unenterpris-
ing way), unless offered by those who are favored with divine
grace.

When he had spoken, a voice nearby
    observed, "Perhaps first
    you will have need of sitting down."

At the sound each of us turned,
    and we saw on the left a great rock
    which we had not noticed before.

We went to it, and saw persons there
    resting in the shade it made
    as men are wont to do through indolence.

And one of them who seemed weary to me
    was sitting, holding his knees with his arms,
    and keeping his head low between them.   108

"O my lord," I said, "look at that one
    who shows himself more negligent
    than if laziness were his sister."

Then the shade turned and looked at us,
    casting his glance just along his thigh,
    and said, "Now go ahead, you who are strong."

I knew then who he was, and that weariness
    which still quickened my breath a little
    did not prevent my going to him,

and after I had reached him, scarcely did he lift his head,
    saying, "So you have seen how the sun
    drives his chariot on your left!"   120

His lazy movements and brief words
    moved my lips to smile a little.
    Then I began, "Belacqua, I grieve for you no more,

but tell me why you are seated here.
    Are you waiting for an escort,
    or have you just resumed your accustomed ways?"

And he, "Brother, what's the use of going up?
    The angel of God sitting at the gate
    would not admit me to the torments.

First the heavens must circle around me
    as many times as during my life
    because I delayed my good sighs to the end,   132

unless prayers meanwhile should help me
    which arise in hearts that live in grace;
    of what use are the others, unheard in Heaven?"

It is now noon in Purgatory and night covers the hemisphere of land.

Already the poet was climbing
    in front of me, saying, "Come now, you see
    that the meridian is touched by the sun,

and Night already sets her foot on Morocco's shore."

CANTO V

The Late Repentant

I had already left those shades
    and was following the footprints of my leader
    when someone behind me, pointing his finger, cried,

"Look! the sun's rays do not seem to shine
    on the left of the one behind;
    he goes along as if he were still alive!"

I turned my eyes at the sound of these words,
    and I saw shades gazing in astonishment
    at me, at me alone, and at my shadow.

"Why is your mind so entangled,"
    my master said, "that you slacken your steps?
    What does it matter what is whispered here?   12

Come behind me, and let the people talk;

stand like a tower the top of which does not shake
  because of the blowing of the winds,

for always a man in whom thought sprouts upon thought
    puts his goal farther from him
    because one reflection weakens another."

What could I answer except, "I come"?
    I said it suffused somewhat with the color
    that often makes one deserve to be pardoned.

*A new group approaches, those who died violent deaths and who
repented only with their last breath. They are eager for the prayers
on earth that can shorten the time of their waiting.*

And meanwhile across the slope
    a little ahead of us, people were coming
    singing *Miserere*[1] verse by verse.   24

When they saw that my body gave no place
    for the passage of the rays,
    their song changed into an 'Oh!,' long and hoarse,

and two of them as messengers
    ran toward us and asked,
    "Let us know of your condition!"

My master said, "You can go back
    and tell those who sent you
    that the body of this man is really flesh.

If they stopped because they saw his shadow,
    as I believe, enough is answered them;
    let them do him honor and he may help them."   36

I have never seen kindled vapors [meteors or lightning]
    cleave so quickly the clear air
    of early night or August clouds at sunset

as they returned to their companions
    and then came back with the others
    like a troop running at full speed.

"That crowd of people who press around us
    has come to ask a favor of you," said the poet,
    "but keep on and, while walking, listen."

---

1 "Have mercy [upon me, O God.]"

"O soul, you who go on to be happy
    with those members with which you were born,"
    they shouted, "stay your steps a while;   48

observe if you have ever seen any of us,
    so that you may take news of us yonder.
    Alas! why do you go on? why do you not stop?

We were all killed by violence
    and were sinners until the last hour;
    then light from Heaven made us understand,

so that repenting and pardoning, we came forth
    from life at peace with God
    who now saddens us with the desire to see Him."

And I, "Although I look into your faces,
    I recognize none of you, but,
    if I can do anything for you, O well-born spirits,   60

tell me, and I will do it, by that Peace which,
    following the footsteps of such a guide,
    I am made to seek from world to world."

*The first to speak is Jacopo del Cassero of Fano. Then Buonconte da
Montefeltro, the son of Guido, the evil counselor whose story is told
in the Inferno, gives an account of his death. Unlike his father, no one
ever cared for him, so that even in this company he hangs his head.
He was killed in the battle of Campaldino in which Dante probably
took part, but his body was never found. Now he tells how he fled,
mortally wounded, and managed to gasp out Mary's name as he fell
and died. As in the case of his father, an angel and a devil dispute for
his soul, and this time the angel prevails. Dante uses these extreme
examples to illustrate the doctrine that salvation is determined by the
condition of the soul at the moment of death.*

And one of them began, "Each of us
    trusts you without an oath
    if your will is not thwarted by lack of power;

therefore I, speaking ahead of the others,
    beg you, if you ever see that country [Ancona]
    which lies between Romagna and the land of Charles,

that you be charitable to me in Fano

by requesting prayers for me,
     so that I may purge away my heavy offenses.   72

I came from there; but the deep wounds
     from which issued my blood and life
     were given me in the bosom of the Antenors [near Padua]

where I thought myself most secure.
     He of Este, who was angry with me
     far more than right demanded, had me killed.

But if I had fled toward La Mira
     when surprised by the assassins at Oriaco
     I would still be among those who breathe.

I ran to the swamp, and the reeds and mire
     so entangled me that I fell, and there
     I saw a pool form from my veins."   84

Then another said, "Alas, so may the wish
     that brings you up the high mountain be fulfilled,
     help my desire with your pity.

I was from Montefeltro, I am Buonconte:
     neither [my wife] Giovanna nor anyone else cares for me,
     so that among these I hang my head."

And I to him, "What force or what chance
     led you so far from Campaldino
     that your burial place has never been found?"

"Oh," he answered, "at the foot of the Casentino
     a stream, called the Archiano, flows,
     which rises in the Apennines above the Hermitage.   96

At its mouth where it loses its name
     I arrived with my throat cut, fleeing
     on foot, and bloodying the plain.

There, already blind, I ended my words
     with the name of Mary, and there I fell,
     and my flesh alone remained.

I tell the truth; relate it among the living.
     The angel of God took me, and a devil from Hell
     cried, 'O you from Heaven, why do you rob me?

You carry off the eternal part of this man,

depriving me of him for one little tear!
But I will dispose of the other part [the body].'   108

You know how the air collects
   the vapor which turns to water
   when it rises to where cold condenses it.

The devil, desirous of evil, combined ill will
   with intelligence, and moved the mists and winds
   through a power given him by his nature.

When day was spent he covered the valley
   from Pratomagno to the great mountain range
   with clouds and made the sky above dark,

so that the saturated air turned to water.
   The rain fell, and what the land
   could not absorb ran to the ditches,   120

and as the water formed great streams
   it rushed in such a torrent to the royal river [the Arno]
   that nothing could hold it back.

The raging Archiano found my cold body
   at its mouth, carried it into the Arno,
   and loosened the cross on my breast

that I had made when pain overcame me.
   It rolled me along its banks and over its bottom;
   then covered and bound me with its sediment."

Now La Pia, with ladylike delicacy and politeness, asks to be re-
membered. She was born in Siena and died in a castle of the
Maremma, as her husband knows, who, after having married her with
solemn rites and promises still vivid in her memory, murdered her.

"Alas, when you have returned to the earth
   and are rested from your long journey,"
   a third spirit continued after the second,   132

"remember me, La Pia. Siena made me,
   Maremma unmade me, as he knows who,
   with the gem set in the ring,

before that day had taken me to be his wife."

CANTO VI

Sordello

Dante frees himself from the eager crowd. In it is Benincasa, the jurist, killed in court by Ghin di Tacco, whose brother he had condemned. Others are mentioned, among them Marzucco's son whose murderer was pardoned by Marzucco himself. Also Pierre de la Brosse, the chamberlain of Philip III of France, whom Dante considered an innocent victim of Philip's wife, Mary of Brabant.

When the game of dice breaks up
    the loser stays behind, grieving,
    recalling the throws, and sadly learns.

The crowd goes off with the winner;
    one seizes him in front and one behind;
    another at his side gains his attention.

He does not stop but listens to them;
    those whom he rewards insist no longer,
    and thus he saves himself from the crowd.

So, surrounded by that thick throng,
    I turned my face here and there,
    and by promising, I freed myself.   **12**

There I saw the Aretine who received death
    from the hands of fierce Ghin di Tacco,
    and the other [Aretine] who was drowned while fleeing.

There, with hands stretched forth,
    Federigo Novello prayed, and the Pisan
    who made good Marzucco seem strong.

I saw Count Orso and the soul
    divided from its body by spite and envy,
    they say, not for any crime committed.

Pierre de la Brosse, I mean; and here
    let the Lady of Brabant see to it, while she is yonder,
    that she does not come to a worse flock.   **24**

When I was free from all these shades
   who pray only that others pray
   to make them blessed more quickly,

I began, "O light of mine, it seems
   that in one passage [of the *Aeneid*] you deny expressly
   that prayer can change a decree of Heaven,

yet these people ask only for that.
   Could their hope, then, be vain,
   or are your words not clear to me?"

*Dante learns that Divine Justice is not thwarted if certain souls are
helped in their atonement. When Virgil denied the efficacy of prayer,
it was in the case of a pagan who did not live in grace. But this deep
matter can hardly be understood except through revelation.*

And he to me, "My writing is plain,
   and the hope here is not misplaced
   if you consider the matter with sound mind.   36

For the lofty height of Justice is not lowered
   even if love fulfills in a moment
   the satisfaction due [to God] from those here.

And where I stated the contrary,
   defects were not made good by prayer
   because the prayers were disjoined from God.

Still, in such great questions do not conclude
   unless she informs you who will be
   a light between truth and comprehension.

I do not know if you understand: I mean Beatrice;
   you will see her above at the summit
   of this mountain, smiling and happy."   48

And I, "My lord, let us go with greater haste,
   for already I am not tired as before
   and you see that the mountain now casts a shadow."

"We will keep on our way today,"
   he answered, "as far as we can,
   but the journey is not as you imagine.

Before you are up there you will see the sun return
   which now covers itself with the slope
   so that you do not stop its rays.

Sordello, who now appears in dignified isolation, was a wandering poet, born near Mantua, whom Dante presents as a patriotic critic of corrupt government. When Virgil names Mantua as the place of his own birth, Sordello's proud indifference disappears, and he rushes to embrace his fellow citizen.

But see over there a shade who is seated
    all alone and is looking at us;
    he will show us the quickest way."   60

We went to him. O Lombard soul!
    how proud and disdainful was your bearing,
    and your glances, how dignified and slow!

He said no word to us,
    but let us go on, merely gazing at us
    like a lion when lying at rest.

Virgil went up to him, asking that he show us
    the best way, but he did not reply.
    Instead, he enquired

about our city and our condition.
    My gentle leader began his answer:
    "Mantua . . ." and the shade who had been lost   72

in his thoughts, sprang toward him, saying,
    "O Mantuan, I am Sordello, from your own city!"
    And the two embraced each other.

This show of affection prompts an intense but restrained invective against Italy. Everywhere, Dante says, there is anarchy and dissension, even within the walls of a single city. The shame would not be so great if Italy had not inherited the Roman laws. But the Code of Justinian is useless, since there is no emperor to enforce it and since the clergy has usurped the temporal power. The poet predicts (as of 1300) the misfortunes to befall Albert of Hapsburg for abandoning Italy. He mentions the constant changes in Florentine laws, and finally, he compares his city to an old woman, sick, and tossing on her bed.

Ah, servile Italy, hostelry of woe!
    ship without a pilot in a great storm,
    no longer mistress of provinces, but a brothel!

That noble soul was eager
merely at the sweet name of his city
to welcome here his fellow citizen;

and now those living in you cannot remain
without war; and one gnaws the other,
even those whom a single wall and moat enclose.   84

Search, miserable one, around your shores
and then look within your boundaries
to see if any part of you enjoys peace.

Of what use was it that Justinian
should refit your bridle, if the saddle is empty?—
without that the shame would be less.

O you [the clergy] who should be devout
and let Caesar sit in the saddle
if you understand what God has written,

see how vicious this beast has become
through not being corrected by the spurs
since you put your hands on the reins!   96

O German Albert, you who have abandoned her
so that she has become untamed and wild—
and should bestride her saddle—

may just judgment from the stars
fall on you and may it be notable
so that your successor may have more fear;

for you and your father, through greed
for things far off [in Germany], have permitted
the garden of the Empire to become desolate.

Come and see the Montecchi and the Cappelletti,
the Monaldi and Filippeschi, man without care,
those already sad and these in dread.   108

Come, cruel one, come, and see the distress
of your nobles, and heal their wounds;
and you will see how dark [oppressed] is Santafior!

Come and see your Rome that weeps
widowed and alone, crying day and night,
"My Caesar, why are you not with me?"

Come and see the people, how they love each other;
  and if no pity for us moves you,
  come and be ashamed for your repute.

If it is permissible, O supreme Jove,
  Thou who wert crucified for us on earth,
  are Thy just eyes turned elsewhere,   120

or is it some preparation which is made
  in the abyss of Thy counsel for a good
  wholly hidden from our understanding?

For the cities of Italy are all full
  of tyrants, and every villain
  that joins a party becomes a Marcellus [a hero].

My Florence, you can indeed be content
  with this digression, which does not concern you,
  thanks to your people who manage so well.

Many have justice in their hearts, but are slow to act,
  not wanting to shoot the arrow without thought;
  but your people have justice always on their tongues.   132

Many refuse the public offices, but not your people
  who answer without being called
  and shout, "Let me take on the burden."

Now rejoice, for you have good cause,
  you rich, you at peace, you with judgment!
  The facts will not hide the truth I am telling.

Athens and Sparta which made
  the ancient laws and were so civilized
  gave few signs of good living

compared with you, who make such shrewd provisions
  that the thread you spin in October
  does not last beyond the middle of November.   144

How often in the time you remember
  you have changed laws, coins, offices, and customs,
  and renewed your citizenship!

If you consider this and note the light,
  you will see yourself like a sick woman
  who cannot find rest on her bed,

and who, by tossing, struggles to allay her pain.

CANTO VII

The Valley of Princes

*On hearing which Mantuan he has been embracing, Sordello receives
a second shock, and clasps Virgil once more, this time "where the
inferior lays hold." The ancient poet explains that he is with the
pagans who were endowed with the cardinal virtues (Prudence,
Temperance, Fortitude, and Justice) but lacked the Christian virtues
(Faith, Hope, and Charity). Sordello proposes to lead the travelers to
the Valley of Princes—reserved for rulers whose cares of state led to
neglect of religious duties—to pass the night, since advance (reform)
is impossible without the Sun's guidance.*

After the dignified and glad greetings
    had been repeated three or four times,
    Sordello drew back and asked, "Who are you?"

"Before souls worthy of rising to God
    had come to this mountain,
    my bones were buried by Octavian.

I am Virgil, and for no other fault
    did I lose Heaven except not having Faith."
    Thus my leader then answered him.

As one who suddenly sees something at which
    he marvels, who believes and does not believe,
    saying, "It is," and "No, it is not,"   12

so Sordello appeared; and he then bent his head,
    returned, and embraced Virgil again
    where the inferior lays hold.

"Oh glory of the Latins," he said, "through whom
    our language showed what power it has,
    Oh eternal honor of the place from which I came,

what merit or what grace shows you to me?
    If I am worthy of hearing your words,
    tell me if you come from Hell and from what cloister."

"Through all the circles of the fearful kingdom,"
    my leader answered, "I have come here.
    A power from Heaven moved me, and with it I proceed.   24

Not for doing, but for not doing have I lost
    the sight of the Sun for which you long
    and which was known by me too late.

There is a place down there not sad through torment,
    but from darkness only, where the laments
    sound, not as groans, but as sighs.

There I stay with the little innocents
    bitten by the teeth of Death
    before they were exempt from human sin.

There I stay with those not clothed
    with the three holy virtues, but who, without vice,
    knew the others and observed them all.   36

But if you can, give us counsel,
    so that we can come more quickly to the gate
    where Purgatory has its real beginning."

Sordello answered, "No fixed place
    is assigned to us; I am free to go up and around.
    As far as I can I will join you as a guide.

But see how the day already is declining.
    Going up by night is impossible;
    therefore, it will be well to think of a resting place.

Not far from here, to the right, are some souls;
    if you wish, I will take you to them,
    and not without pleasure will they be known to you."   48

"How is that?" was the reply. "If someone wanted
    to climb at night, would he be prevented
    or would he lack the strength to do so?"

The good Sordello drew his finger
    along the ground, saying, "Look, you could not cross
    this line after the sun has disappeared;

not that anything would prevent going up
    except the darkness of the night
    which makes the will powerless.

One can, however, go down
    and wander around the hillside
      while the horizon holds the day shut off."   60

Then my master, as if wondering,
    "Take us," he said, "where you say
      we can have delight in tarrying."

We had gone a short distance from there
    when I noticed that the mount was hollowed out
      as valleys cut into them on earth.

"We shall go over there," Sordello said,
    "where the slope makes a lap of itself,
      and there we shall await the new day."

A slanting path, neither steep nor level,
    led us to the edge of the dell
      where the bank was more than half gone.   72

Gold and fine silver, crimson and white lead,
    indigo, bright and clear,
      fresh emerald, at the moment it is split

would be surpassed in color by the grass
    and by the flowers within the hollow
      as the lesser is by the greater.

Not only had Nature painted there,
    but with the sweetness of a thousand odors
      made one fragrance, undefinable and unknown.

I saw souls sitting on the grass
    and on the flowers, until then concealed
      by the hollow, singing *Salve Regina.*[1]   84

"Do not ask me to guide you among them
    until the little remaining sun has gone to rest,"
      said the Mantuan who had brought us,

"for, from this place you will see
    their faces and expressions
      better than down among them.

*Sordello points out the rulers of Dante's time, and delivers judgments
on them.*

---

[1] "Hail, Queen," is an antiphon recited for the last service of the day.

[The one on the highest seat with the look
    of having neglected what he should have done
    and who does not move his lips to the others' song,
was Rudolph the Emperor, who might have healed
    the wounds that have so destroyed Italy
    that it will be too late now to revive her.   96
The other who seems to comfort him ruled the land
       [Bohemia]
    from which the water comes which the Moldau
    carries to the Elbe, and the Elbe to the sea.
Ottocar was his name, and in swaddling clothes
    he was better than his son as a bearded man
    whom idleness and lust consume.
And that one with the small nose [Philip the Bold] in close
       counsel
    with him of the kindly face [Henry the Fat],
    died fleeing and deflowering the lilies [of France].
See how he beats his breast!
    Look at the other [Henry] who has made a pillow
    for his cheek with his hand.   108
They are the father and son-in-law of the plague
    of France [Philip the Fair]; they know his vicious and
       filthy life;
    thence comes the grief that so assails them.
The one who appears so robust [Peter IV of Aragon], and
       who harmonizes
    his singing with him of the virile nose [Charles of
       Anjou],
    was girded with the cord of every worth.
And if the young man who sits behind him
    had remained king after him,
    worth would have passed from vessel to vessel,
which cannot be said of the other heirs.
    These, James and Frederick, have the kingdoms [Aragon
       and Sicily];
    neither possesses the better heritage.   120
Seldom does human goodness pass on
    from father to son, and this is willed
    by Him who grants it, so that He may be asked for it.
My words apply also to the big-nosed one [Charles of Anjou]

not less than to Peter [of Aragon] who sings with him,
  on account of whom Apulia and Provence already grieve.
The plant [Charles II] is as much inferior
  to its seed [Charles I] as Constance [the wife of Peter]
  more than Beatrice and Margaret [wives of Charles II]
       can boast of her husband.
See the king of the simple life,
  Henry [III] of England, sitting there alone;
  he has better issue in his branches.   132
That one on the ground lowest among them
  and looking up, is William the Marquis
  because of whom Alessandria and its war
make Monferrato and the Cavanese weep."]

CANTO VIII

The Allegory of the Snake

*The opening lines, re-echoed in Gray's elegy, tell of parting day. When
darkness comes, an allegorical pageant is enacted. Two angels, armed
with the pointless swords of defense, descend to protect the trusting
shades. Their raiment is green, the color of Hope. At the mention of
the serpent of temptation, Dante, still vulnerable, draws close to Virgil
(Reason).*

It was now the hour that turns homeward the longing
  of those at sea, and softens their hearts
  on the day when they have said good-by to their friends,
and which pierces the new pilgrim's heart
  with love, when he hears the distant bells
  which seem to mourn for the dying day.
I stopped listening and began
  to watch one of the spirits
  who, risen, with signs, asked for quiet.
He clasped and lifted both his hands,

fixing his gaze on the east, as if saying to God.
"For nothing else do I care."   12

Te lucis ante[1] came so devoutly from his lips
and with such sweet notes
that I was unconscious of all else,

and then the others, sweetly and devoutly,
followed through the entire hymn,
keeping their eyes fixed on the revolving stars.

Reader, here sharpen your eyes for the truth,
for the veil [of allegory] now certainly is so thin
that seeing through it is not hard.

Afterward I saw that noble host
looking up in silence, pale
and humble, as if expectant.   24

And I saw coming from on high
two angels with fiery swords
broken off and deprived of their points.

Their raiment, green as newborn leaves,
trailing behind them, was touched
and fanned by green feathers.

One placed himself a little above us
and the other on the opposite bank,
so that the company was in between.

Well did I discern their blond heads,
but my eyes were dazzled by their faces,
like a faculty deadened by excess.   36

"Both come from Mary's bosom,"
Sordello said, "to guard the valley,
because of the serpent which will soon come."

And I, not knowing what way it would take
turned around, all chilled,
and drew close to the trusted shoulders.

Then Sordello spoke: "Let us go down
among the great shades and speak to them;
it will be a pleasure for them to see you."

---

1 "Before the close of light . . ." is a hymn sung at evening prayer.

Dante now recognizes his old friend Nino Visconti, a judge of Gallura and later captain general of the Guelf league, in one of whose campaigns Dante took part. Nino's wife has remarried into the family of the Milanese Visconti, but not to her advantage.

When Dante reveals that he is still alive, Sordello, who has paid slight attention to him, has a third shock of surprise.

I went down three steps, I believe,
    and when below I saw someone looking at me
    as if he were trying to recognize me.   48

It was the time of day when the air grows dim,
    but not so dark that the space between us
    could conceal what at first was hidden.

He advanced toward me and I toward him.
    Noble Judge Nino, how pleased I was
    when I saw you, not among the damned!

No fine greeting was left unsaid; then he asked,
    "How long has it been since you came
    to the mount over the distant waters?"

"Oh," I answered, "from the home of pain
    I came this morning, and am in my first life,
    although I gain the other by this journey."   60

And when my reply was heard
    Sordello and he drew back
    like persons suddenly dismayed.

One turned to Virgil, the other to a spirit
    sitting nearby, shouting, "Get up, Conrad!
    Come and see what God through his grace has willed!"

Then turning to me, "By that special gratitude
    you owe to Him who so hides his purpose
    that there is no ford to it,

when you are beyond the wide waters
    tell my [daughter] Giovanna to pray for me
    [in church] where the innocent are heard.   72

I do not believe her mother loves me any more,
    since she changed her white [widow's] veils,
    which, unfortunate, she must long for again.

Through her one understands easily
    how long the fire of love lasts in women
    if eye and touch do not often rekindle it.

The viper emblazoned in the Milanese coat-of-arms
    will not decorate her tomb as well
    as Gallura's cock would have done."

Thus he spoke, his face marked
    by the stamp of that upright zeal
    which glows in due measure in his breast.   84

My eager eyes next turned upward
    to the pole where the stars move slowest,
    like a wheel closest to its axle.

My leader asked, "Son, at what are you gazing?"
    and I, "At those three lights [the Christian virtues]
    with which this pole is all aflame."

And he to me, "The four clear stars
    which you saw this morning have gone down,
    and these have risen where they were."

Now the serpent comes, turning back its head in a deceptively innocent
gesture. The protecting angels swoop down, and the snake flees.
Conrad then asks for news about his state. In 1306 (later than the
supposed date of the journey), Dante enjoyed the patronage of
Conrad's descendants, and pays a debt of gratitude here by praising
them.

As Virgil spoke, Sordello drew him
    to himself, saying, "Behold our adversary,"
    and pointed with his finger for him to look.   96

On the side of the valley which has no barrier
    was a serpent, perhaps like the one
    that gave Eve the bitter food.

The evil creature came through the grass and flowers,
    turning its head to its back now and then,
    licking, like an animal sleeking itself.

I did not see and therefore cannot say
    how the celestial falcons started,
    but I saw both of them in motion.

Hearing the green wings cleave the air,

the serpent fled, and the angels turned back,
    flying abreast up to their posts.

The shade who had joined the judge
    when he called, through all that attack
    did not stop looking at me.

"So may the light which leads you up
    find in your free will the fuel needed
    to reach the garden on the summit,"

he began, "if you have news of Val di Magra,
    or of the neighboring regions, tell me,
    because once I was powerful there.

I was called Conrad Malaspina;
    I am not the elder, but descended from him.
    For my family I bore the love that here is purified."   120

"Oh," I said to him, "I have never been
    in your country, but where in all Europe
    does anyone live to whom it is unknown?

The fame which honors your house
    proclaims its lords and proclaims the country,
    so that those who have never been there know of them,

and I swear to you, as I hope to go above,
    that your honored family does not deprive itself
    of the glory of the purse and of the sword.

Custom and nature so favor it
    that although the guilty head [Rome] leads the world
        astray,
    alone it goes straight and scorns the evil path."   132

*Conrad predicts that within seven years Dante's good opinion of the
Malaspinas will be confirmed by their actions, their hospitality.*

And he, "Now go, for the sun will not lie seven times
    in the bed which the Ram [Aries] covers
    and bestrides with his four feet,

before this courteous opinion
    will be nailed firmly in your head
    with better nails than mere words,

if the course of judgment is not stayed."

CANTO IX

St. Peter's Gate

Dante falls asleep, and near morning, when dreams are prophetic, an eagle seems to carry him up, just as Ganymede had been taken to be cupbearer to the gods. As he passes in his dream through the sphere of fire above that of the air, he awakens, and is bewildered by the strange surroundings in which he finds himself. He is now at the gate of Purgatory, having been carried up in his sleep by Lucia (Divine Grace).

The concubine of ancient Tithonus [the moonrise]
    already was growing white on the terrace of the east,
    having risen from the arms of her sweet lover.

Her face was shining with the gems [stars]
    set in the shape of the cold creature [Scorpio]
    which stings people with its tail,

and of the steps [hours] with which Night rises
    two had been taken where we were
    and a third was nearly finished,

when I, having in me something of Adam [the flesh],
    overcome by sleep, lay upon the grass
    where all five of us had been seated.   **12**

At the hour close to the morning
    when the swallow [Philomela] begins her sad lays,
    perhaps in memory of her first misfortunes,

and when our mind, wandering farthest
    from the flesh and least bound by thought,
    is almost divine in its visions,

in a dream I seemed to see an eagle
    with golden feathers and wings outspread
    poised in the sky, intent on coming down.

I seemed to be where the people

were abandoned by Ganymede
when he was snatched up to the high consistory.

I thought, "Perhaps it strikes
only here, and disdains to take any
in its claws from another place."

Then it seemed to me that, circling a little,
it came down, terrible as a thunderbolt,
and lifted me up as far as to the fire.

There both it and I seemed to burn,
and so did the imagined fire scorch
that my sleep forcibly was broken.

Not otherwise was Achilles startled,
casting around his awakened eyes,
not knowing where he was,

36

when his mother carried him in her arms
while he slept from Chiron to Scyros
whence the Greeks [Ulysses and Diomed] took him
away,

than I started when sleep fled
from my eyes; and I became pale
like one chilled by terror.

My comfort was alone beside me,
the sun already more than two hours high,
and I had turned my face to the sea.

"Do not be afraid," my lord said;
"be reassured, for we have come to a good place;
do not relax, but put out all your strength.

48

You have now arrived at Purgatory;
see the rampart that encloses it;
see the cleft where the entrance is.

A while ago, in the dawn that precedes the day,
while your soul was asleep within you
on the flowers which adorn the place below,

a lady came and said, 'I am Lucia;
permit me to take this sleeping man,
and I will help him on his way.'

Sordello and the other shades remained.
  She took you, and when the day was clear
  came up, I following her footsteps.   60

Here she put you down, but first her fair eyes
  had shown me that open entrance;
  then she and your sleep together went away."

*Dante, now reassured, moves on to the symbolically narrow entrance.
An angel, the representative of ecclesiastical authority, guards the gate.
The three steps may represent the three stages in the history of
mankind: innocence, sin, and redemption. The last is the foundation
of the angel's authority. The adamant threshold represents the strength
of ecclesiastical power.*

Like a man who is reassured in his doubt
  and who changes fear to comfort
  after the truth has been disclosed to him,

so I changed, and when my leader
  saw me without dismay he moved on
  toward the height, I following.

Reader, you see how I elevate
  my theme; therefore do not marvel
  if I sustain it with greater art.   72

We moved on to a place
  where a break appeared in the rampart,
  like a fissure dividing a wall.

I saw a gate and three steps beneath it
  rising to it, of different colors,
  and a keeper who, as yet, said nothing.

As I looked more intently at him I saw him
  sitting on the top step, so dazzling in countenance
  that I could not endure the brightness.

He held a naked sword in his hand
  which reflected such rays toward us
  that I looked at it often in vain.   84

"Tell from there, what do you wish?"
  he began to say. "Where is the escort?
  See that coming up does not harm you!"

A lady from Heaven, aware of these things,"
   my master answered, "said to us
   a little while ago, 'Go on, there is the gate.'"

The courteous keeper began again to speak, saying,
   "May she speed your steps toward the good:
   come ahead then to our stairs."

The first step which we reached
   was of white marble, so polished and smooth
   that my true image was mirrored in it.   96

The second was darker than purplish black,
   of a rough and burned stone,
   cracked through its length and across.

The third which rises on top
   seemed of porphyry, as flaming red
   as blood that spurts from a vein.

On this the angel of God kept both feet,
   and sat firmly on the threshold,
   which seemed to me of adamant.

Over the three steps with good will
   my guide drew me, saying to me,
   "Ask humbly that the lock be opened."   108

*Dante strikes three times on his breast in symbolic penance for sins
of thought, word, and deed. Then seven P's (standing for peccata,
sins) are inscribed on his forehead. They represent the capital vices
(Pride, Envy, Anger, Sloth, Avarice or Prodigality, Gluttony, and
Lust) which Dante (and mankind) must remove through the disciplines
of Purgatory. The angel's dress symbolizes the humility of the priest,
God's servant. Both the golden key of power and the silver key of
discernment are necessary for opening the gate. The first is more
precious, since bought with Christ's blood. The angel errs on the side
of leniency, provided the soul asking for admittance is contrite. In
beginning reform, there must be no mental reservations, no looking
back.*

Devoutly I threw myself at the holy feet,
   asking through mercy that the door be opened,
   but first I struck three times on my breast.

Seven P's the angel inscribed on my forehead

with the point of his sword, and said,
"When within, see that you wash away these marks."

Ashes or earth that has dried
are of the same color as his raiment;
and, from under it, he drew two keys.

One was of gold, the other of silver.
First the white and then the yellow
he applied to the gate, so that I was gratified.　　　120

"Whenever one of these keys fails,
so that it does not turn rightly in the lock,"
he said, "this entrance is not opened.

One is more precious, but the other demands
much art and wit before it works,
since it is the one which frees the bolt.

From Peter I hold them, and he told me to err
in opening rather than in keeping closed
if the souls throw themselves at my feet."

Then he pushed the door of the holy portal
saying, "Enter," but be warned
that whoever looks back must remain outside.　　　132

*Apparently the gate is seldom opened. The sound it made was like that
of the door of the Roman treasury at the foot of the Tarpeian rock when
Caesar removed the guard, Metellus, and robbed it. As Dante enters,
he hears a hymn of rejoicing and of praise.*

And as the pivots of the sacred door
which are of metal, resonant and strong,
began to turn on their hinges,

Tarpeia did not roar so loudly or show itself
so stubborn when good Metellus was taken
from it, after which it remained bare.

I turned, attentive to the first sound within,
and *Te Deum laudamus*[1] I seemed to hear
in a voice accompanied by sweet music.

---

[1] "We praise Thee, O Lord."

What I heard gave precisely such an impression
    as we sometimes have when people are singing
    with an organ, so that now the words   144
are understood, and now are not.

CANTO X

The Burden of the Proud

*The poets climb to a ledge which encircles the mountain. Here the
fundamental vice of pride is purged. Part of the discipline consists in
contemplating examples of the opposite virtue (the "goad"), and of the
vice itself (the "check"). The first example is always from the life of
the Virgin. Here a carving shows her in her humility at the Annuncia-
tion. Next is portrayed the story of David dancing before the ark:
"less than a king" in decorum, "more than a king" in his humility.
There is a reference also to Uzzah, who touched the Ark and was
killed for his presumption. Usually Christian and pagan examples alter-
nate. Here Trajan, whose salvation was due to the intercession of
Gregory the Great, is shown, not too proud to hear and grant the
petition of a poor widow.*

When we were within the threshold of the gate
    seldom opened because of the perverse love
    which makes the crooked way seem straight,

I knew by sound that it was closed again;
    and if I had looked back at it, what valid excuse
    could there have been for the fault?

We climbed through a cleft in the rock
    which zigzagged back and forth
    like waves that come and go.

Here we must use a little skill,"
    my guide began, "to avoid the bank
    on one side and the other."

and this made our steps so short
    that the moon, which now was waning,
    went down to regain its bed

before we were out of that needle's eye;
    but when we were free and in the open,
    in a place where the mountain recedes,

I weary, and both of us uncertain
    about our way, we stopped on a ledge
    as solitary as a road in the desert.

From the edge where the void begins,
    to the foot of the inner bank which rises sheer,
    a human body would reach three times,   24

and, as far as my eyes could see
    on the right and on the left,
    the ledge seemed to be the same.

Our feet had not yet reached
    the encircling bank which, because perpendicular,
    could not be climbed, when I noticed

that it was of white marble, and so adorned
    with carving that not only Polycletus
    but Nature herself would have been put to shame.

The angel [Gabriel] that brought the decree of peace
    wept for during so many years
    and that opened Heaven from its long interdict   36

appeared engraved there in front of us
    in so gracious an attitude
    that the image did not seem silent.

You would have sworn that he was saying *"Ave,"*[1]
    for shown there also was she [Mary]
    who turned the key to open the exalted love,

and in her attitudes the words
    ecce ancilla Dei[2] were as clearly written
    as a figure stamped in wax.

"Do not pay attention only to one place,"

---

1 "Hail!"
2 "Behold the handmaid of the Lord."

said my gentle leader, who had me
on that side of him where the heart lies.

Therefore I turned my face and saw,
beyond the form of Mary, on the side
where he was who led me,

another story portrayed on the rock.
I went past Virgil and came to where
my eyes might see it better.

There, carved in the very marble,
were the cart and oxen drawing the sacred ark
because of which men fear to be officious.

In front people appeared divided
into seven choirs who made one sense [hearing]
say "no," the other [sight], "yes, they sing."   60

Likewise at the smoke of the incense
shown there, the eyes and nose
disputed between "yes" and "no."

There the humble psalmist [David], girt up and dancing,
went in front of the sacred vessel,
and seemed both more and less than king.

Opposite, portrayed at the window
of a great palace, Michal [his wife] looked on,
like one who is angry and scornful.

I moved from the place where I was
to look closely at another story
which, behind Michal, glistened in my eyes.   72

There was depicted the great glory
of the Roman prince whose justice
moved Gregory to his great victory:

I am speaking of Trajan, the emperor;
and a poor widow was at his bridle
seeming to shed tears in her grief.

The ground around him appeared trampled
by a throng of horsemen, and, above,
the golden eagles moved visibly in the wind.

The poor woman among all of these

seemed to say, "Lord, avenge me for my dead son
   because of whom I am brokenhearted,"   84

and he answered her, "Now wait
   until I return," and she,
   like one whose grief is urgent,

"My lord, suppose you do not come back?" And he,
   "Whoever takes my place will do it." She, "Of what use
   is another's virtue, if you forget your own?"

Whereupon he: "Now be comforted;
   I must do my duty before I leave.
   Justice demands it, and pity makes me stay."

He [God] who has never seen anything strange
   produced this visible speech,
   new to us, because not found on earth.   96

While I took delight in looking
   at the images of such humility,
   precious also because of their Maker,

the poet murmured, "Behold, over there
   are some people, taking slow steps;
   they will guide us to the stairs."

My eyes, which were delighted
   to look at new things, were not slow
   to turn toward those pointed out.

I do not wish, Reader, that you be diverted
   from good resolve through hearing
   how God wants us to pay our debts.   108

Do not dwell on the form of the punishment;
   think of what follows, and that, at its worst,
   it cannot go beyond the Great Judgment.

*The proud who in our life held their heads too high are now getting
practice in lowering them. They carry burdens heavy in proportion to
their previous pride, and those with the smallest loads are so weighed
down that they seem at the limit of endurance.*

I began, "Master, these things I see
   moving toward us do not look like persons;
   yet I know not what they are, so confused is my sight."

And he to me, "Their heavy torment
    bends them to the ground, so that at first
    my eyes also debated about them.

But look closely and observe those
    under the stones; already you can see
    how each one beats himself."   120

O proud Christians, miserable and weary,
    who, sick in your mental vision,
    keep faith in backward steps,

do you not see that you are insects
    born to form the angelic butterfly
    which flies without defense to judgment?

Why does your vain pride soar so high,
    since you are imperfect and incomplete,
    like worms in which development is lacking?

As, to support a roof or ceiling,
    a statue is sometimes seen as a corbel,
    its knees pressing against its breast,   132

which from an unreal, causes a real pain
    in the person who sees it,
    so I saw the shades when I looked closely.

It is true that they were more or less bent over
    according as they had more or less on their backs;
    yet the one who seemed least burdened,

weeping, appeared to say, "I can endure no more!"

CANTO XI

Pride of Birth, Artistic Talent, and Power

The burdened souls recite a paraphrase of the Lord's Prayer.

"Our Father who art in Heaven,
    not restricted there, but through greater love
    for the first of Thy creatures [the angels],

hallowed be Thy name and Thy power
    by everyone, since it is meet
    to give thanks for Thy sweet effluence.

May the peace of Thy kingdom come to us,
    for we can do nothing by ourselves
    with all our thought, unless it comes.

Just as the angels sacrifice their will
    to Thee, singing hosannas,
    so may men do with theirs.   **12**

Give us this day our daily manna [spiritual food]
    without which, in this bitter desert,
    he goes backward who struggles most to advance.

As we pardon others for the evil we have endured,
    may Thou benignly forgive us
    and not consider our just deserts.

Tempt not our strength, so easily subdued,
    with the old adversary who so spurs us
    toward evil, but deliver us from him.

This last petition, dear Lord, we make
    not for ourselves, for we do not need it,
    but for those who remain behind us."   **24**

Thus those shades, praying for good speed
    for themselves and us, went on under weights
    like those of which we sometimes dream,

circling around the first ledge,
    weary and unequally distressed,
    purging away the foul vapors of the world.

If up there they pray for us
    what can be said and done for them here [on earth]
    by those who have good roots for their will?

We should help them wash away the stains
    they bring from here, so that pure and light
    they can go forth to the stars.   **36**

"So may Justice and Pity unburden you quickly
    and let you move the wings
    which will lift you as you desire,

show which is the shortest road to the stairs,
    and if there is more than one way up,
    tell us which is the least steep;

for my companion who is clothed
    and burdened with the flesh of Adam
    is slow in climbing, in spite of his desire."

It was not clear from whom the words
    came which were spoken in answer
    to those of my guide,   48

but someone said, "To the right along the ledge,
    come with us, and you will find the opening
    through which a live person can climb.

And if I were not hindered by the rock
    which subdues my proud neck
    so that I must hold my face down,

I should look at the one of you still living,
    not naming himself, to see if I know him,
    and to make him have pity for this load.

*The first shade, Omberto Aldobrandesco, represents the pride of birth,
although he is now almost cured of that vice. Disdaining his enemies
in his presumption, he had been killed by the Sienese at Cam-
pagnatico. Oderisi of Gubbio, an illustrator of manuscripts, likewise
reforming, stands for the pride of artistic excellence. He knows now
the vanity of fame, how those who excel are almost certain to be
surpassed unless normal progress is interrupted by a decline in
civilization.*

I was an Italian, born of a great Tuscan.
    Guglielmo Aldobrandesco was my father—
    I do not know if his name was ever known to you.   60

My ancient family and the noble deeds
    of my ancestors made me so arrogant
    that, unmindful of our common mother,

I held everyone in disdain, to such an extent
    that I died on account of it, how, the Sienese know,
    and every child in Campagnatico.

I am Omberto, and pride troubles

not only me, but it has drawn
all my relatives with it into evil ways.

And here among the dead I must bear this weight
until God is satisfied,
since I did not bear it among the living."   72

While listening I bent down my face
and one of them (not he who was speaking)
twisted under the weight encumbering him

and saw me and recognized me and called to me,
with effort keeping his eyes on me
as I went along bent down [sharing in the penance].

"Oh," I said to him, "are you not Oderisi,
the honor of Gubbio and of that art
which in Paris is called 'illuminating'?"

"Brother," he answered, "the pages
that Franco Bolognese paints smile more brightly;
the honor is mainly his now, and mine in part.   84

I would certainly not have been so courteous
while I was living, because of the great desire
for excellence on which my heart was bent.

For such pride the fee here is paid,
and I should not even be here except that
while still able to sin I turned to God.

Oh, the vainglory of human talent!
how short a time the greenness of its leaves
lasts, unless barbarous ages follow!

Cimabue thought to hold the field in painting,
and now Giotto has the acclaim,
so that the other's fame is dim.   96

Thus one Guido [Cavalcanti] has taken from the other
[Guinizelli]
the glory of our tongue, and perhaps a man is born
who will drive both of them from the nest.

Worldly fame is nothing but a breath of wind
which moves this way and that,
and changes name when it changes its direction.

What greater repute would you have,
    despoiled of flesh in old age,
    than if you had died before giving up baby talk,

after a thousand years, a shorter time
    in relation to eternity than the twinkling of an eye
    to the revolution of the slowest heaven."   108

*A third example is that of Provenzan Salvani, a Ghibelline leader,
haughty once because of power, who would be among the late re-
pentant except for one act of humility: to redeem a friend held for
ransom by Charles of Anjou, he once humbly solicited alms in the
public square, trembling like a beggar. Dante, in his exile, will
understand how he felt.*

All Tuscany once resounded with the name
    of him who moves slowly in front of me,
    and now scarcely is it whispered in Siena

where he was a lord, when the rage
    of Florence, then proud,
    as she is now a prostitute, was destroyed.

Our fame is like the color of the grass
    which comes and goes, and He
    who causes it to sprout withers it."

And I, "Your true speech puts humility in my heart
    and reduces a large tumor;
    but who is he of whom you just spoke?"   120

"That," he answered, "is Provenzan Salvani,
    and he is here for presuming
    to bring all Siena into his grasp.

He goes and has been going thus without rest
    since he died; such coin must be paid
    by those who are too daring over there."

And I to him, "If those who wait
    until they reach the end of life
    before repenting stay below,

unless good prayers help them,
    until as much time passes as they lived,
    why was he allowed to come?"   132

"While living most gloriously," he answered,
  "in the market place of Siena,
  devoid of shame, he freely placed himself,

and there to relieve a friend of the pain
  endured in Charles' prison,
  he allowed himself to tremble.

More I will not say, although I know I speak darkly,
  but little time will pass before your neighbors
  will act so that you can comment on this trembling.

This humiliation released him from those bounds."

CANTO XII

The Check on Pride

*After sharing in the penance, Dante is relieved of the first and
fundamental vice.*

Side by side, like oxen under the yoke,
  that burdened soul and I went on
  as long as my kind teacher allowed it;

but when he said, "Leave them,
  for here with sail and oar
  we must speed our bark with all our might,"

I stood erect in body, as a man
  should walk, although my thoughts
  remained bent down and smaller.

Willingly I followed the steps
  of my master, and both of us
  showed already how light we were,

when he said to me, "Look down,
  it will do you good, as a solace on the way,
  to see the ground beneath your feet."

12

As, to preserve the memory of the dead,
　　tombstones on their graves bear images
　　to show how they were before,

which often make us weep again
　　because of the sting of remembrance
　　that spurs only the compassionate;

so I noticed sculptures there,
　　but of superior workmanship, covering the ledge
　　that projects from the bank.

　　　　　　　　　　　　　　　　　24

On the floor of the ledge the travelers see examples of pride to serve as the "check." Among the pagan figures are Briareus, one of the giants who attacked the gods, and Niobe, who was punished for excessive pride in her seven sons and seven daughters. Likewise Arachne appears, who challenged Pallas to a contest in weaving and became a spider for her presumption. Cyrus is mentioned whose severed head was put in a sack of blood by the Scythian queen, Thamyris; and Alcmaeon, whose mother, bribed by a necklace, had betrayed his father, for which crime Alcmaeon killed her.

I saw on one side that one [Satan]
　　who was created nobler than any other creature
　　falling like lightning down from Heaven.

I saw Briareus pierced by the celestial bolt,
　　lying on the other side,
　　heavy on the ground in the chill of death.

I saw Apollo, I saw Pallas, and Mars,
　　still armed around their father [Jove],
　　looking at the scattered limbs of the giants.

I saw Nimrod at the foot of his great structure
　　as if bewildered and looking at the people
　　who, in Shinar, were proud with him.

　　　　　　　　　　　　　　　　　36

O Niobe! with what sorrowing eyes
　　I saw you engraved on the road
　　between seven and seven dead children!

O Saul! how dead you appeared
　　on your own sword in Gilboa
　　which afterward felt neither rain nor dew.

O mad Arachne! I saw you already half a spider,
    sorrowing on the shreds of the embroidery
    you made unfortunately for yourself.

O Rehoboam! your image there no longer seems to threaten,
    but full of terror, a chariot carries you away
    without your waiting to be driven out.   48

It [the hard pavement] showed also
    how Alcmaeon made the fatal ornament
    seem costly to his mother.

It showed how Sennacherib's sons
    fell upon him in the temple
    and how they left him dead.

It showed the destruction and cruel slaughter
    which Thamyris wrought when she said to Cyrus,
    "You thirst for blood, and I fill you with it."

It showed how the Assyrians fled in rout
    after Holofernes had been slain [by Judith],
    and the remains of the slaughtered one.   60

I saw Troy in ashes and in ruins.
    O Ilion! how base and vile
    the image I discerned there showed you!

What master of brush or chisel
    could have portrayed the lights and shadows
    amazing even to a subtle mind?

Dead were the dead, and the living seemed living.
    The real does not appear more vividly
    than what I trod upon as I walked bent over.

Now be proud, and hold your heads high,
    children of Eve, and do not bend your faces down
    so that you can see your evil path!   72

*The travelers come to the stairs which lead to the next ledge. In the
description of the steps there is an ironic reference to Florence and to
certain local scandals, the removal of a sheet from the municipal
record and the use of a dishonest measure by a salt commissioner.
Dante feels lighter, and is surprised to discover that one "P" (for
pride) has been removed.*

We circled more of the mount,
    and more of the sun's course was spent
    than my busy mind had realized,

when he who advanced attentively
    said, "Lift up your head,
    there is no more time for walking so engrossed.

See over there an angel getting ready
    to come toward us; see how the sixth handmaiden [noon]
    is returning from her service to the day.

Let your face and bearing show reverence,
    so that he will gladly send us up.
    Consider that this day will never dawn again!"   84

I was accustomed to the warning
    not to lose time, so that on this point
    he could not speak obscurely to me.

The fair creature came toward us,
    dressed in white and in countenance
    like the trembling morning star.

He opened his arms and then his wings,
    saying, "Advance, here are the steps,
    and climbing is easy now."

To this announcement people rarely come.
    O human race, born to fly,
    why do you fall at such a breath of wind?   96

He led us to where the rock was cleft,
    then touched my forehead with his wings
    and promised me a safe passage.

As in climbing the mountain on the right
    where the church [San Miniato] stands
    which dominates the well-governed city [Florence]

above the Rubaconte [bridge], the bold ascent
    is broken by steps made at the time
    when registers and measures were safe,

so here the steep decline
    from the other ledge is relieved,
    although the banks press on either side.   108

On turning there we heard voices singing
    Beati pauperes spiritu[1]
    in a way that speech cannot tell.

Oh, how different these passages are
    from those in Hell, for here with songs
    you enter, and down there with fierce laments.

Already we were mounting the sacred stairs
    and I seemed much lighter
    than I had been on the level ground

so that I said, "Master, tell me what heavy thing
    has been taken from me; in climbing
    I feel almost no effort."   120

He answered, "When the P's remaining
    on your face, almost extinct, are all gone
    like the first which is wholly wiped out,

your feet will be so overcome by good will
    that not only will they feel no effort
    but will delight in being urged upward."

I then became like persons
    with something on their heads unknown to them,
    although others' signs make them suspect;

whereupon they use their hands
    and feel and find, accomplishing
    in that way what sight cannot do;   132

and with the fingers of my right hand
    I found only six of the letters
    inscribed on my temples by the keeper of the keys,

observing which my leader smiled.

---

[1] "Blessed are the poor in spirit."

CANTO XIII

The Envious Sapia

On arriving at the ledge of the envious, Virgil apostrophizes the Sun of Divine Enlightenment.

The "goads" (examples of love, the opposite of envy) are heard as voices. The first case of loving solicitude recalls the wedding feast in Cana. Next Orestes is mentioned whose friend Pylades tried to impersonate him when Orestes was condemned to death.

We were at the top of the stairs
    where the mountain which cures
        by being climbed is cut back a second time.

There, likewise, a terrace
    curves around it, similar to the first,
        although in a smaller arc.

No shades or carvings can be seen;
    the bank and road are smooth
        and of the livid color of the stone.

"If we wait here to question someone,"
    the poet said, "I fear the choice of our way
        will be delayed too long." 12

Then he looked steadily at the sun,
    made a pivot of his right side
        and turned the left.

"O sweet light, trusting in which
    I start upon the new road, lead us,"
        he said, "since here we must be led.

Thou givest warmth to the world, and shinest upon it.
    If some reason does not oppose,
        Thy beams should always be our guide."

We had already gone the distance
    on earth counted as a mile,
        quickly, because of our ready will. 24

when we heard spirits flying toward us
    unseen, but giving courteous invitations
    to the feast of love.

The first voice in passing loudly said,
    "Vinum non habent,"[1] and went on,
    repeating the words behind us.

And before it was inaudible
    through distance, another passed,
    shouting, "I am Orestes."

"Oh," said I, "Father, what sounds are these?"
    and behold! as I asked, the third, saying,
    "Love him through whom you have suffered."   36

Then the good master, "This ledge punishes
    the vice of envy; therefore
    the lashes of the goad come from love.

The check demands contrary examples;
    I believe you will hear them
    before you reach the pass of pardoning.

But look closely in front of you
    and you will see people ahead of us
    sitting along the bank."

I opened my eyes wider then and,
    looking ahead, saw shades with cloaks
    not different in color from the stone.   48

And after we had gone a little farther
    I heard someone cry, "Mary, pray for us,"
    and invoke Michael, Peter, and all saints.

I do not believe a man lives today
    so hard that he would not be touched
    by pity for what I then saw,

for when I had arrived so close to them
    that their features became clear,
    grief brought tears to my eyes.

The souls here, correcting their earthly habits, support and help each

---

[1] "They have no wine."

other. Their eyes, the sense organ most involved in envy, are sewed up, so that Dante feels embarrassed, as if invading their privacy.

Since envy is a vice of petty souls, Virgil admonishes his pupil to be brief in his questioning.

They appeared to be covered with haircloth,
　and one supported the other with his shoulders,
　and all were leaning on the bank.   60

Thus the blind, when destitute,
　lie at Pardons to beg,
　and one leans his head against another

so that people may pity more quickly,
　not only because of the words,
　but because of sight which moves no less.

And, as the sun does not help the blind,
　so to the shades of whom I speak,
　the light of heaven was denied;

for a wire pierced all their eyelids
　and sewed them up, like those of a falcon
　when it will not keep still.   72

As I walked on, looking and not being seen,
　I seemed to give offense,
　⁻so that I turned to my wise counselor.

Knowing what my silence meant,
　he did not wait for my question
　but said, "Speak, and be brief and to the point."

He was on that side of the ledge
　from which one can fall,
　since there is no parapet around it.

The devout shades were on the other side,
　forcing tears which bathed their cheeks
　through the horrible stitches.   84

I turned to them and began,
　"O people, certain to see the light
　which alone is the object of your desire,

so may grace clear away the scum

from your conscience and let
    the river of memory flow undefiled,

tell me, for it will be gracious,
    if any Italian is here among you;
    perhaps it will be well for you if I know."

"Oh, my brother, each of us is a citizen
    of the true city [of God], but you mean one
    who lived as a pilgrim in Italy."   96

This I seemed to hear as a reply
    spoken farther on from where I was;
    therefore I advanced to make myself heard.

Among the others I saw a shade apparently expectant;
    and if someone should ask "How?"
    [I would say] "By raising its chin like a blind man."

"Spirit," I said, "you who subdue yourself
    only to rise, if you are the one who answered,
    make yourself known by name or country."

"I was a Sienese, and with these others
    I am cleansing my wicked life," was the reply,
    "praying in tears that God lend Himself to us.   108

Sapient I was not, though named Sapia.
    I was much happier at others' harm
    than at my own good fortune.

And so that you may know I do not deceive you,
    hear whether I was as foolish as I say,
    the arch of my years already descending.

Near Colle, my fellow citizens
    were joined in battle with their enemies,
    and I prayed God for what He brought about.

They were defeated there and turned back
    in the bitter steps of flight, and I felt a joy
    above all others in seeing the rout;   120

so that I turned up my bold face,
    crying out to God, 'Now I fear Thee no longer,'
    as the blackbird does for a little clear weather.

At the very end of my life, repentant,

I asked for peace with God,
    and still my debt would not be paid

except that Piero the comb-seller,
    who felt sorry for me,
    remembered me in his holy prayers.

But who are you, asking about our condition
    with eyes free to see, I believe,
    and speaking with your breath?"   132

"My eyes will be taken from me here
    but only for a little while, for slight
    is their offense in gazing with envy.

Much greater is the fear that besets my soul
    of the torment [of pride] below, for already
    the burden from down there weighs upon me."

And she to me, "Who then has led you
    here among us, if you expect to return below?"
    And I, "He who is with me and says nothing.

I am alive; therefore, ask me, spirit elect,
    if you wish that I move
    my mortal feet for you on earth."   144

Sapia rejoices now on hearing the favor Dante has been granted. She repeats, however, one of the many gibes at Siena. This town had wished to become a maritime power and secured a little port, Talamone. The project failed, like the attempts to reach a river, the Diana, which was supposed to flow under the city.

"Oh, this is so strange a thing," she answered,
    "that it is a sign that God loves you;
    therefore help me now and then with your prayers.

And I ask by what you long for most,
    if ever you tread the land of Tuscany,
    that you restore my good name to my kindred.

You will see them among those vain people
    who put hope in Talamone and who
    will waste more there than in finding the Diana,

although the chief losers will be the [expectant] admirals."

CANTO XIV

Guido del Duca

Two souls from Romagna, Guido del Duca and Rinieri da Calboli, who have overheard Dante, begin to talk about him. Dante identifies himself modestly as a Tuscan born near the Arno River. This leads to a satirical picture of the regions through which the Arno flows.

"Who is this man circling our mount
    before death has given wings for his flight,
    and who opens and closes his eyes at will?"

"I do not know who he is, but I am sure
    he is not alone. Ask him, you are closer,
    and greet him so that he will speak."

Thus two spirits on the right,
    leaning on each other, spoke about me,
    then turned up their faces to address me.

And one said, "O soul going to heaven
    still contained in a body,
    console us with your charity and tell us   12

whence you come and who you are,
    for you make us marvel at such grace
    as never before has been seen."

And I, "Through the center of Tuscany
    a little stream flows that rises in Falterona,
    and a hundred miles are not enough for its course.

From its banks I bring this body.
    To tell you who I am would be to speak in vain,
    for my name is not yet well known."

"If I understand your meaning,"
    the first speaker then replied,
    "you are referring to the Arno."   24

And the other said, "Why did he hide

the name of the river
as that of something disgraceful?"

The shade who was questioned
acquitted himself thus, "I do not know,
but the word for that stream ought to perish.

For, from its source in the rugged range which has
such abundant water that few places have more,
and from which Mt. Pelorus [in Sicily] is cut off,

down to [its mouth] where it gives back
what the sky takes from the sea
so that rivers can flow,

virtue like a snake is avoided,
either through the misfortune of the place
or through bad habits which goad people,

so that the inhabitants of the miserable valley
have changed their natures
as if Circe had them in her pasture.

Among ugly swine, more worthy of acorns
than of food for human use,
the river first directs its feeble course.

Coming down [at Arezzo] it finds curs next
snarling more than their strength warrants,
and disdainful, it turns its snout from them.

On it goes descending, and the larger it becomes
the more the accursed and ill-fated ditch
finds dogs [at Florence] making wolves of themselves.

Having passed then through many deep pools
it finds foxes [at Pisa] so full of fraud
that they fear no trap to catch them.

I will not stop speaking because another [Dante] hears me,
and it will help him if he remembers
what true inspiration reveals to me.

*A grandson of Rinieri (to whom Guido del Duca is speaking), while
mayor of Florence, tortured and executed many Florentines, especially
members of Dante's party.*

I see your grandson becoming a hunter

of these wolves on the shore of the fierce river
and terrifying them all.   60

He sells their flesh while they are still living
and slaughters them like old cattle;
many he deprives of life and himself of honor.

Bloody he comes out of the sad wood
and leaves it such that in a thousand years
it will not be forested as it was before."

As, at the announcing of painful ills,
the face of the listener is troubled,
from whatever source the peril comes,

so I saw the other soul who had turned to hear
become troubled and sad
after he had understood the words.   72

The remarks of one and the appearance of the other
made me want to know their names,
and with entreaties I asked.

The spirit who spoke first began,
"You wish me to do for you
what you will not do for me,

but since God has willed that so much of his mercy
shine in you, I will not be grudging.
Therefore, know that I am Guido del Duca.

My blood was so on fire with envy
that if I had seen a man becoming happy
you would have observed my face grow pale   84

Of my sowing I reap this straw.
O human race, why do you put your hearts
on [material] things that lead to exclusion of common
    sharing?

*Guido del Duca now introduces Rinieri and a satire on Romagna like
that on Tuscany, but in terms of the fortunes of the old families
and the decline from the days of chivalry.*

[This is Rinieri; he is the pride and honor
of the house of Calboli, in which none since him
has been an heir of his worth,

and not only his family has become destitute
  of truth and chivalry within the Po,
  the mountains, the shore, and the Reno;
for the land [Romagna] inside these boundaries
  is full of poisonous shoots
  so that only long tillage would destroy them.   96
Where are good Lizio and Arrigo Manardi,
  Pier Traversaro and Guido di Carpigna,
  O Romagnols, turned to bastards?
When will a Fabbro take root again in Bologna?
  When in Faenza a Bernardin di Fosco,
  a noble scion of a small plant?
Do not marvel if I weep, Tuscan,
  when I recall Guido da Prata
  and Ugolin d'Azzo who lived with us,
Federico Tignoso and his company,
  the Traversara family, and the Anastagi,
  both now without an heir, and also   108
the ladies and the knights, the toil and sports
  which love and courtesy made dear to us
  where hearts now have become so wicked.
O Brettinoro, why do you not flee,
  since your family has gone
  with many others to escape corruption?
Bagnacaval is fortunate to have no sons,
  while Castrocaro does badly and Conio worse
  to take the trouble to breed such counts.
The Pagani will do well when the demon
      [Maghinardo]
  in their family disappears, but not so well
  that it will ever leave a clear record.   120
O Ugolin de Fantolin, your name is safe,
  since no longer is a descendant expected
  who, by going astray, can darken it.
But go now, Tuscan, since I much prefer
  to weep than to speak, so painfully
  has our conversation wrung my heart."]

As the "check," a voice thunders out the first example of envy, a line
from Genesis referring to Cain. A second example is that of Aglauros

of Athens, who was changed to a statue because of envy for her
sister, loved by Mercury.

We knew that those dear souls heard us go on;
　　therefore, by their saying nothing,
　　we had confidence in the direction we took.

When we had moved on alone a voice
　　like lightning cleaving the air
　　crashed toward us, saying,　　　　　　　　　　132

"Whoever finds me shall slay me!"
　　And it fled, like thunder dying away
　　after suddenly piercing a cloud.

When our hearing had respite from it
　　behold! another crash like thunder
　　that follows the lightning instantly.

"I am Aglauros who was turned to stone."
　　Then, to draw closer to the poet,
　　I took a step to the right instead of forward.

Already the air was quiet on every side,
　　and he said, "That was the hard bit [check]
　　which should keep mankind within bounds;　　144

but you mortals take the bait, so that the hook
　　of the ancient adversary pulls you to him,
　　and checks and lures avail little.

The heavens call you and circle around,
　　showing you their eternal beauties,
　　and still your eyes gaze at the ground,

so that He, who sees all, beats you!"

CANTO XV

Material and Spiritual Good

The ecliptic, in Dante's fancy, plays like a child by skipping from
one side to the other of the celestial equator. It is now about 3:00 P.M.

in Purgatory, midnight in Italy. The brightness of an angel, added to
the light of the sun, blinds our poet.

As much of the circle which plays like a child
      as is visible between the end of the third hour
      and the beginning of the day

now appeared to be left of the sun's course;
      it was vespers there
      and midnight here,

and the rays were striking us full in the face,
      since, in circling the mountain,
      we were now going toward the west.

I felt my brow oppressed by a splendor
      much greater than before,
      and the strangeness of it left me dazed.   12

Therefore I put my hands to my eyes
      to make myself a visor
      and to reduce the excess of light.

As a ray from above the water
      or a mirror, reflected by them,
      rises in the opposite direction

from which it descends and at the same distance
      from the perpendicular,
      as science and experiment show,

thus I seemed to be struck there
      by a reflected light
      so that my sight was quickly lost.   24

"What is it, dear father, from which I cannot
      screen my eyes," I asked,
      "and which seems to come toward us?"

"Do not marvel," he replied, "if those from Heaven
      still blind you; this is a messenger
      coming to invite us to ascend.

Soon, seeing these things
      will not be painful, but a delight
      as great as nature has fitted you to feel."

Then when we reached him, with a joyous voice

  the holy angel said, "Enter here
  on a stairway less steep than the others."   36

As we were climbing, having left that place,
  Beati misericordes[1] was sung behind us,
  and "Rejoice, O Thou that conquerest."

As the poets climb to the next ledge, Virgil explains the difference between material and spiritual pleasures and possessions. Envy is due to excessive desire for the material "good," which is decreased by fellowship or sharing. In the case of spiritual (or intellectual, or artistic) good, on the other hand, the more it is shared, the greater the total and the part of each individual.

My master and I went up, we two alone,
  and I thought while climbing
  to gain advantage from his words.

I addressed him saying,
  "What did the shade from Romagna [Guido del Duca]
    mean
  by mentioning 'exclusion' and 'common sharing'?"

And he to me, "He knows the cost
  of man's greatest defect; therefore do not wonder
  if he blames it so that you may weep less.   48

Because your desires are directed
  toward things diminished by sharing,
  envy moves the bellows of your sighs;

but if the love of the highest sphere
  lifted up your desires
  that fear would not be in your hearts,

for the more up there who say 'our,'
  the greater the good each possesses
  and the brighter love glows in that cloister."

"I am still hungrier for understanding," I said,
  "than if I had at first kept silent,
  and I burden my mind with further doubt.   60

How can it be that a good thing

---

[1] "Blessed are the merciful."

divided among many makes each richer
than if possessed only by a few?"

And he to me, "Because you still
set your mind on earthly things,
you gain darkness from the light itself.

The infinite and ineffable good above
runs toward love for itself
as a ray of light to a bright surface.

As much brightness as it finds, so much it gives,
so that the more widely love extends
the more eternal goodness grows upon it,

72

and the greater the number who comprehend
and love each other, the more love there is,
since one gives to another, like a mirror.

And if my words do not quiet your hunger,
you will see Beatrice who will fully requite
this and every other desire.

Try to remove quickly, like the two already erased,
the five remaining wounds [marks]
which are healed by being painful."

*The poets now come to the ledge of the wrathful. Here visual and
auditory hallucinations present the "goads" and "checks." The first
example is that of Mary speaking to the child Jesus in the Temple;
the next that of Pisistratus, a lord of Athens whose wife wanted him
to kill a youth who had publicly kissed their daughter. The last
example of gentleness is that of St. Stephen.*

As I was about to say, "You satisfy me,"
I saw that we had reached the next ledge,
so that my eager eyes kept me silent.

84

I seemed, in an ecstatic vision,
to be suddenly carried away
and to see many people in a temple,

and a lady at the entrance
in the sweet attitude of a mother,
saying, "My son, why have you dealt thus with us?

Behold! your father and I, sorrowing,

were looking for you," and when she was silent
  what appeared at first vanished.

Then I saw another woman with tears
  running down her cheeks
  which grief due to resentment distills,   96

saying, "If you are lord of the city [Athens]
  for whose name there was such strife among the gods
  and from which all knowledge shines forth,

avenge yourself on those bold arms
  that embraced our daughter, O Pisistratus!"
  And her lord seemed to answer her gently

and graciously, with a mild look,
  "What shall we do to those who wish us harm
  if we condemn those who love us?"

Then I saw people burning with rage,
  slaying a youth with stones,
  shouting loudly to each other, "Kill! kill!"   108

And I saw him whom death already burdened
  sink to the earth with eyes
  which still gazed on Heaven,

praying to God in his agony
  and with a look which unlocks pity
  that He might pardon his persecutors.

When my mind turned again
  to real things outside of it,
  I recognized my not wholly false errors.

My guide who saw me walk
  like one awakening from deep sleep, said,
  "What is the matter that you cannot stand erect?   120

You have come more than half a league
  with eyes covered and with a stumbling gait,
  as if oppressed by sleep or wine."

"O my kind father, if you listen,
  I will tell you what appeared to me," I said,
  "when my legs were taken from me."

And he, "If you had a hundred masks

on your face, your slightest thoughts
would not be hidden from me.

What you saw was to leave you no excuse
for not opening your heart to the waters of **peace**
poured forth from the eternal spring.

I did not ask 'What is the matter?' as one does
who sees only with the eyes
which are blind when the body is dead,

but I asked to give strength to your feet.
Thus one must spur the slow and slothful
to use their waking hours."

We were walking in the evening looking ahead
attentively as far as our eyes could reach
against the sun's bright beams,

when, behold! little by little
smoke came toward us, black as night,
nor was there room to escape it.

It took from us our sight and the pure air.

132

144

CANTO XVI

Mark the Lombard

The gloom of Hell and of a night
deprived of every star, under a low sky
darkened by clouds as much as can be,

never made so thick a veil for my eyes
nor of so harsh a texture
as the smoke which there covered us.

It did not let me keep my eyes open,
so that my trusted leader drew close
and offered me his shoulder to direct me.

As a blind man goes behind his guide

to avoid getting lost or hitting something
    which might injure or kill him,   12

so I went through the bitter and foul air,
    listening to my master [Reason] who kept saying,
    "See that you are not separated from me."

I heard voices, each seeming to pray
    for peace and mercy to the Lamb of God
    who takes away our sins.

The first words were always *Agnus Dei;*
    all spoke alike, in the same measure,
    so that complete harmony appeared among them.

"Master, are those spirits that I hear?" I asked;
    and he to me, "You infer correctly;
    they are loosening the knot of anger."   24

"Now who are you cleaving our smoke
    and speaking of us as if
    you still divided time by calends?"

Thus a voice spoke to me; whereupon
    my master said, "Answer, and ask
    if one can go up along here."

And I, "O creature, cleansing yourself
    to return fair to Him who made you,
    you will hear something marvelous if you come with me."

"I will follow as far as I can," he answered,
    "and if the smoke does not let us see each other,
    hearing will keep us together instead."   36

Then I began, "I go up with that body
    that death dissolves, and I came here
    through the anguish of Hell,

and if God has included me so completely
    in His grace that He is willing for me
    to see His court, alone in modern times,

do not conceal who you were before your death,
    but tell me, and let me know the right way;
    your words will be our escort."

"I was a Lombard; my name was Mark. I learned

the ways of the world and loved the good
  at which few now aim their bows.

You are on the right path to go up."
  Thus he answered and added, "I beg you,
  please pray for me when you get there."

*Dante is eager to know whether the corruption of the world is due
to the stars (providence, predestination) or to man. He learns that
the fault is in man and in the guidance (suggestion, conditioning) he
receives. The situation is made worse because the papacy, which
should be concerned with spiritual guidance only, has usurped the
functions of the emperor who should direct men toward earthly
felicity. The pope "may chew the cud but lacks the cloven foot"
that is, does not meet the requirements of the double office.*

And I to him, "I bind myself by my word
  to do what you ask of me,
  but I will burst from a doubt if it is not resolved.

At first it was simple, but now is double
  because of your statement which confirms
  what here and elsewhere [from Guido del Duca] I have
      added to it.

The world is indeed as completely deserted
  by every virtue as you proclaim,
  and covered and heavy with wickedness,   60

but I beg you to point out the cause
  so that I may understand it and teach others,
  for some people place it in the stars and others below."

A deep sigh, which grief articulated as "O . . . ,"
  he uttered first and then began,
  "Brother, the world is blind and you come from it.

You who are living consider every cause
  as originating in the heavens
  as if they determined all, of necessity.

If this were so, free will would be destroyed,
  and there would be no justice,
  no joy for good nor sorrow for evil.   72

The heavens initiate your impulses—

I do not say all, but granting I did say so,
  a light is given to you to distinguish good from evil,

and free will which, if it is severely tested
  in its first battles with the heavens,
  afterward, rightly nurtured, conquers all.

You are subject in your freedom
  to a greater force [than the heavens] and to a better nature
  which create minds not controlled by the stars.

Therefore, if the world goes astray,
  the cause is in yourselves,
  and to prove this, I will be a spy [for the truth].   84

The soul issues from the hands of Him,
  who loves it even before it is created,
  like a little child, weeping and smiling.

The simple spirit which knows nothing
  except that it is animated by a happy Maker
  turns willingly toward whatever delights it.

At first it has a taste of a trivial pleasure
  which deceives it, and it rushes after it,
  unless a guide or check turns its desire aside.

Therefore laws are necessary to impose restraint;
  a ruler is needed who can discern
  at least the tower of the true city.   96

The laws exist, but who enforces them?
  No one, because the shepherd who takes the lead
  may chew the cud but lacks the cloven foot.

Therefore the people who see their guide
  strive only for material things for which he is greedy,
  feed on them also, and ask for nothing more.

You can see that bad leadership
  is the cause of the world's disorder,
  and not Nature which has been corrupted in you.

Rome which made the world good used to have
  two suns [pope and emperor] to point out both paths,
  that of the world and that of God.   108

One has suppressed the other, and the sword

is joined with the shepherd's crook,
and of necessity they go badly together
since, combined, one cannot check the other.
If you do not believe me, consider the result,
for every plant is known by its fruit.

In the land [Italy] watered by the Adige and the Po,
courtesy and valor were found once
before Frederick had his dispute [with the popes].

Now it can be safely traversed
by anyone who would be embarrassed
at speaking to the good or being close to them.   120

There are three old men still in whom
the ancient times rebuke the new, but they long
for God to remove them to a better life.

Currado da Palazzo and the good Gherardo
and Guido da Castel, who is better named,
in the French fashion, the simple Lombard.

So tell now how the Church of Rome
by combining in itself two sovereignties
falls into the mire and soils itself and its burden."

"O my Mark," I said, "you argue well,
and now I see why the sons of Levi
were excluded from inheriting.   132

But which Gherardo has remained,
as you say, an example of those extinct
and a reproach to the barbarous age?"

"Either your speech deceives or tests me,"
he answered, "for although speaking Tuscan,
you seem to have heard nothing of good Gherardo.

I know him by no other name, unless I should identify him
by his [notorious] daughter Gaia.
May God be with you; I can come no farther.

See the light shining white
through the smoke. The angel is there;
I must leave before he sees me."   144

Then he turned and did not wish to hear me further.

CANTO XVII

The Rise to the Slothful

Reader, if ever in the mountains a mist
    has caught you, through which your sight
    was like a mole's, through a membrane,

and if you remember how, when the thick vapors
    began to lighten, you could see faintly
    from within them the sphere of the sun,

it will be easy for you to imagine
    how I saw that planet which already
    was on the point of setting.

So, keeping step with my trusted master,
    I issued from the cloud into the sun's rays
    which were already dead on the shore below.   12

Among the checks on anger is the example of Procne who, to avenge
a wrong done by her husband to her sister, made him eat, unsuspecting,
the flesh of his own child. Later she was changed into a nightingale.
Another example is that of the mother of Lavinia who committed
suicide at the false report of the death of Turnus to whom her
daughter had been betrothed. She feared that the victorious Aeneas
would take Lavinia from her.

O fantasy which at times steals us
    from ourselves, so that we are not aware
    if a thousand trumpets sound around us,

who creates you, since the senses give no impressions?
    A light formed in heaven moves you
    either by itself or by a will that directs it down.

A trace of the impiety of her [Procne]
    who changed into the bird that delights most
    to sing, appeared in my imagination,

and my mind was so intent

within itself, that from without
no impressions were received by it.   24

Then fell within my soaring fantasy
one [Haman] crucified, scornful and fierce
in looks even as he died.

Around him were the great Ahasuerus,
Esther his wife, and the just Mordecai
who was so honest in word and deed.

And as this vision broke of itself,
like a bubble as the water fails
of which it is formed,

so there arose in my vision a maiden
weeping loudly and saying, "O queen,
why in your anger did you wish to be nothing?   36

You killed yourself for fear of losing Lavinia,
yet you have lost her. I must mourn for you
before mourning for another."

As sleep is broken when suddenly
a light strikes the closed eyes,
and being broken, wavers before it quite dies away,

so my imagining ended as soon as a light
greater than any known here
had struck my face.

I was turning to see where I was when a voice,
banishing every other thought,
said, "Here you mount."   48

It made my will so eager to see
who was speaking that it could not rest
until confronted with what it wanted.

But as the sun burdens our sight
and with its excess veils its form,
so here my powers failed.

"This is a divine spirit, directing us
on our way without our asking,
and with his light he hides himself.

He acts as a man should; for whoever

sees help needed and waits to be asked,
　　may prompt an unkind refusal.　　　　　　　　　60

Now let our feet accept such an invitation;
　　let us try to rise before dark,
　　for afterward we cannot, until day returns.

Thus my master spoke, and with him
　　I turned toward the stairway;
　　and as soon as I was on the first step

I felt near my face the motion
　　and the fanning of a wing, and heard the words,
　　Beati pacifici[1] who are without sinful anger.

Already the last rays followed
　　by the night were so high above us
　　that stars appeared in several places.　　　　　72

"O my strength! why do you melt away?"
　　I said to myself, for I felt [as the sun set]
　　the power of my legs suspended.

We were at the top, where the stairs
　　could not be climbed further,
　　and were stranded, like a grounded ship.

I waited a while to see if I might hear
　　some sound on the new ledge;
　　then I turned to my master and said,

"My dear father, tell me what offense
　　is purged on the round where we are;
　　if our feet are stayed, do not end your words."　　84

And he to me, "Love of good,
　　when insufficient, is here restored;
　　here the slackened oars are plied again.

But, in order to understand more clearly,
　　direct your mind to me
　　and you will gain good fruit for our tarrying."

*Virgil now classifies the various vices by relating them all to love
(desire). Instinctive desires are primarily innocent, but acquired love
may involve a bad object or be devoted to a legitimate one without*

---

[1] "Blessed are the peacemakers."

moderation. *A bad object implies injury to our fellow men, since all creatures are free from self-hatred or hatred of God. Proud men wish to dominate others; the envious wish for their decline; the angry are eager for vengeance. These vices are reformed on the first three ledges. Insufficient love for spiritual good (sloth) is punished on the fourth ledge. On the last three, disproportionate love for an object not bad in itself (avarice or prodigality, gluttony, and lust) is cured. (The classification is shown in the outline on page 169.)*

[Neither Creator nor creature, my son," he began
    'was ever without love [desire] either instinctive
    or dependent upon the will [acquired], as you know.
The instinctive is always without error,
    but the other can err through a bad object
    or through too little or too much vigor.   96
While it is directed to primal [spiritual] good
    and is moderate in other things,
    it cannot be a cause of sinful pleasure.
But when it turns to evil or to legitimate pleasures
    with too much or too little care,
    the creature works against his Creator.
Hence you can understand that love
    must be the seed of every virtue in you
    and of every act that deserves punishment.
Now, since love can never turn
    from the welfare of its possessor,
    all things are free from self-hatred.   108
And because no one can be conceived
    as separate from the First [God] and existing by himself,
    every desire is cut off from hating Him.
It follows, if I distinguish rightly,
    that the evil we love is our neighbors',
    and this arises in three ways in our mortal clay.
Some [the proud] hoping to excel
    through their neighbors' decline
    long only to reduce their greatness.
Others [the envious] fear losing power,
    honor, and fame if another rises,
    and wish for the contrary.   120
Still others [the angry] feel so disgraced

by injuries received that they long
    for vengeance and plan suffering for others.
This threefold love is wept for down below.
    Now I want you to hear about that love
    which seeks the good with wrong intensity.
Everyone conceives confusedly
    some ultimate [spiritual] good that will quiet
    all longing, and everyone desires it.
If insufficient love impels us
    toward it, this ledge,
    after due repentance, torments us.   132
There are other good things which do not make us happy;
    they do not give felicity, are not
    the essence and root of every good fruit.
Love which abandons itself too much to them
    is wept for above us in three rounds,
    but why it is described as threefold, I do not say,
so that you can discover it for yourself.]

CANTO XVIII

Moral Responsibility—The Slothful

*Dante is troubled by still another problem. He wants to understand
better what "love" is, to which all vices and virtues are related. He
learns that natural, instinctive desire is innocent. Love acquired
through indulgence, however, may be sinful and deserving of punish-
ment, since man possesses innate ideas of right and wrong, and a will
which makes choice possible. But the question of moral responsibility
is too deep for Reason alone. Beatrice (Revelation) must give the
final answer.*

[The eminent teacher had ended his explanation,
    and looked attentively in my face
    to see if I appeared content,

and I, tormented by a new thirst,
    outwardly kept silent, but inwardly said,
    "Perhaps too much questioning will bother him.
But that true father who knew
    of my timid, unexpressed wish
    gave me the boldness to ask.
Therefore I said, "Master, my sight is so quickened
    in your light that I discern clearly
    all that your explanations contain or describe;   12
so I beg you, dear father,
    to explain 'love' to me, to which you reduce
    every good action and its contrary."
"Direct toward me," he said, "the sharp eyes
    of your mind, and the errors of the blind
    who try to lead will be apparent to you.
The soul created ready to love
    is susceptible to everything that pleases
    as soon as it is awakened into activity.
Your perception of an object
    creates an impression in you
    which makes the soul turn toward it,   24
and if, so turned, it inclines in that direction,
    that inclination is love. It is a natural feeling
    reinforced in you through pleasure experienced.
Then as fire rises because of its form
    which makes it ascend
    to where it can remain in its element,
so the soul, captivated by a desire,
    a spiritual force, never rests
    until the thing loved makes it rejoice.
Now you know the truth
    hidden from those who maintain
    that every love is praiseworthy in itself,   36
because, although it may *appear* good,
    not every seal has worth
    even if impressed on good wax."
"Your words and my attentive mind," I answered,
    "have revealed to me what love is,
    but that has made me doubt still more
for, if love comes from without

and the soul acts on no other basis,
    whether it goes straight or not, it has no merit."
And he to me, "Whatever reason can see in this
    I can tell you; expect to hear the rest
    only from Beatrice, since it requires faith.   48
Every substantial form [soul] distinct
    from body and united with it
    has in itself a specific virtue
which is imperceptible except in operation
    and demonstrated only by its results,
    as life in plants is shown by their green leaves.
Therefore, whence comes understanding
    of axiomatic truths, man does not know,
    nor his liking for the primal objects of desire
which is in you like the instinct in bees
    to make honey; and this first love
    does not admit of praise or blame.   60
Now, to make every desire conform,
    there is, innate in you, the virtue that counsels
    and which must defend the threshold of consent.
This is the source from which
    merit derives, according as good and bad loves
    are accepted or winnowed out.
Those who have gone deeply in philosophy
    have been aware of this innate liberty,
    and therefore have left ethics to the world.
Thus, supposing that every love
    by necessity is kindled in you,
    the power exists in you to resist it.   72
Beatrice understands this noble virtue as free will;
    therefore see that you have it in mind
    if she undertakes to speak to you about it."]

The poets have spent the evening at the edge of the fourth ledge.
Souls, formerly slothful, rush by, citing as the "goad" examples of
haste and diligence and the opposite qualities as a "check."

The moon, delayed almost to midnight,
    looked like a red-hot kettle,
    and made the stars seem fewer.

It proceeded against the sky's movement [backing up]
   on the path [the ecliptic] which the sun enflames
   when from Rome it is seen setting between Sardinia
     and Corsica,

and that noble soul [Virgil], on account of whom
   Pietola [his birthplace] is more famous than any other
     Mantuan city,
   had put down the burden of my loading.   84

So I, having received clear and plain answers
   to my questions, remained
   like one who lets his mind wander.

But this somnolence was dispelled suddenly
   by people who, behind our backs,
   had come around to where we were.

As [the rivers] Ismenus and Asopus once saw a tumult
   and a throng [the Bacchic orgies] at night along their
     banks
   whenever the Thebans had need of Bacchus,

so such a throng, judging by what I saw,
   bent its way around that ledge,
   driven on by good will and love.   96

That great crowd, because all in it
   were running, was soon upon us,
   and two in front, weeping, shouted,

"Mary *ran* in haste to the mountain,"
   and "Caesar, to subdue Lerida,
   attacked Marseilles and then *rushed* to Spain."

"Quickly, quickly, let no time be lost
   through insufficient love," shouted the others,
   "so that our efforts to do good may renew grace."

"O people, you in whom keen fervor now
   makes up perhaps for negligence and delay
   shown previously in well-doing,   108

this man who lives (and certainly I do not lie)
   wishes to go up when the sun shines again;
   therefore, tell us where the nearest opening is."

These were the words of my guide,

and one of those spirits said,
"Come behind us, and you will find the pass.

We are so full of desire to move
   that we cannot stay; therefore pardon us
   if you take our punishment for rudeness.

I was the Abbot of San Zeno at Verona
   under the rule of the good Barbarossa
   of whom Milan still talks with sorrow.   120

And another already has a foot in the grave
   who will weep for having had power
   over that monastery,

because his son, deformed in body
   and worse in mind and a bastard,
   he has installed in place of its true pastor."

I do not know if he said more or was silent,
   so far had he already moved from us,
   but this I heard and gladly retained.

And Virgil, my help in every need,
   said, "Turn around, see two coming,
   giving sloth a curb [check]."   132

Behind the rest they were saying,
   "The people [sluggish Hebrews] for whom the sea
      opened
   were dead before Jordan [the Promised Land] saw its
      heirs," and,

"Those that did not endure toil to the end
   with the son of Anchises [Aeneas]
   gave themselves up to a life without glory."

Then when those shades were so far from us
   that they could no longer be seen,
   a new thought came into my mind,

from which others, different, arose,
   and so much did I ramble from one to another
   that in my wandering I closed my eyes,   144

and transmuted thought into dreams.

CANTO XIX

The Avaricious and the Prodigal

It is now just before dawn. A chill is descending from the cold planet Saturn, and the Fortuna Major *(an arrangement of six stars used by fortune-tellers) is rising. Dante, soon to enter the wards of sins of the flesh, dreams prophetically of a siren. In his vision a lady, representing conscience or the aspirations of the spirit, helps him to see the real character of the temptress.*

At the hour when the day's heat
    overcome by the earth and at times by Saturn
    can no longer temper the cold of the moon;

when the geomancers see their *Fortuna Major*
    rise in the east before dawn
    on a course which is dark only a short time,

a stuttering woman came to me in a dream,
    cross-eyed, with crooked feet,
    maimed hands, and of a sallow color.

I looked at her, and as the sun comforts
    the cold limbs that night benumbs,
    so my gazing at her loosened her tongue,   12

straightened her whole body,
    and in a little while colored her wan face
    with the shade that love desires.

When her tongue was freed, she began to sing,
    so that with difficulty
    could I have turned my attention from her.

"I," she sang, "I am the sweet siren,
    who leads mariners astray far at sea,
    such a delight it is to hear me.

With my song I turned Ulysses from his eager journeying,
    and whoever abides with me
    seldom leaves, so completely do I content him."   24

Her mouth was not yet closed,
  when a lady, holy and alert, appeared
  beside me to confuse her.

"O Virgil, Virgil, who is this?"
  she asked angrily; and he came
  with eyes fixed on the honest one.

He seized the other, and tearing her clothes,
  laid bare her breast and showed her belly
  the stench of which awakened me.

I looked around, and the good master said,
  "At least three times I have called. Get up,
  and let us find the pass through which you can **mount**."   36

When I arose the ledges of the holy mountain
  were already covered with light,
  and we moved on with the sun behind us.

While following my guide I carried my head
  like a person burdened with thought,
  making a half arch of my body.

Then I heard, spoken in a gracious and kindly **manner**
  unheard within our mortal boundaries,
  these words, "Come, here is the pass."

With open swanlike wings, the one
  who spoke directed us
  between two walls of hard stone.   48

He touched and fanned me with his feathers
  affirming that *qui lugent*[1] will be blessed,
  their souls enriched with consolation.

"What is the matter that you still gaze
  on the ground?" my guide said to me
  after both of us had mounted above the **angel**.

And I, "A strange vision which preoccupies **me**
  makes me proceed with such dread
  that I cannot get rid of the thought."

"You saw," he said, "that old witch

---

[1] "[Declaring] them that mourn [to be blessed]."

because of whom those above us weep.
    You saw how one is freed from her.   60

Let that suffice, and spurn the earth,
    turn your eyes to the lure placed
    by the Eternal King in the revolving heavens."

As a falcon which first gazes at its feet,
    then turns at a call and extends its head
    through desire for the food that allures it,

so I leaned forward and, as far as the rock is broken
    to provide a way for one going up,
    I went on to where the arc begins.

*The poets now come to the ledge of the avaricious and the prodigal.
The souls here are lying prone, keeping their heads earthward as
in life, and getting their fill of the view. Among them is the pope
Adrian V, who tells in Latin of his former rank.*

When I was in the open on the fifth ledge
    I saw people on it weeping and lying
    on the ground with their faces down.

"Adhæsit pavimento anima mea!"[2]
    I heard them say with such deep sighs
    that their words were scarcely heard.

"O chosen of God, whose sufferings
    both justice and hope make less hard,
    direct us toward the high ascent."

"If you are just released from lying down
    and wish to find the shortest way,
    let your right hand always be on the outside."

Thus the poet questioned and was answered
    by someone a little ahead of us
    whose face I became aware of by his speech.   84

Then I turned my eyes to my lord
    who, with a gesture, assented gladly
    to what my eager look requested.

Since I was free to do as I wished

---

[2] "My soul cleaveth unto the dust."

I drew near that soul
　　whose words first made me note him,

saying, "Spirit in whom weeping ripens the repentance
　　without which one cannot return to God,
　　suspend for a moment your greater care.

Who were you? and why do you have your backs
　　turned up? and tell me if you want something
　　on earth from which I have come alive."　　　　　　96

And he to me, "Why the heavens turn our backs
　　to them you will learn, but first
　　scias quod ego fui successor Petri.[3]

Between Siestri and Chiaveri [near Genoa]
　　a fair stream [the Lavagna] flows, and from its name
　　the title of my family had its ending [last word].

In one month and a little more I found out how heavy
　　the great mantle [of the papacy] is, when kept from
　　　　the mire:
　　all other burdens seem like feathers.

My conversion, alas! was late,
　　but when I became the Roman pastor,
　　then I discovered how false life is.　　　　　　108

I saw that on earth the heart is never quieted,
　　nor can one rise higher in that life;
　　therefore the love of this was kindled in me.

Until then I had been a soul miserable,
　　deprived of God, and wholly avaricious.
　　Now, as you see, I am punished for it here.

What avarice does is shown
　　by the purgation of the inverted souls;
　　and the mountain has no more bitter penalty.

Just as our eyes, fixed on earthly things,
　　were not lifted on high,
　　so here, justice turns them to the earth.　　　　　　120

Since avarice quenched our love

---

[3] "Know that I was a successor of Peter."

for all that is worthy, and caused our good works
    to cease, justice here holds us bound,

tied hand and foot, and as long
    as the just Lord wishes, so long
    will we remain motionless and stretched out."

*Adrian points out that reverence for him is no longer necessary, since
earthly relationships are not continued in the future world.*

I had kneeled and wanted to speak,
    but as I began he became aware
    of my reverence, merely by listening.

"What reason," he asked, "made you bend down?"
    and I, "Because of your dignity,
    my conscience troubled me while I was standing."   132

"Straighten your legs, get up, brother!" he answered.
    "Do not be mistaken; I am a fellow servant
    with you and with all the others of one Power.

If you ever understood the phrase
    of Holy Gospel which says *neque nubent*[4]
    you can see why I speak thus.

Now go, I do not want you to remain longer,
    for your stay hinders the weeping
    with which I ripen the repentance you mentioned.

I have a niece yonder, named Alagia,
    good in herself, provided our family
    does not make her bad by its example;   144

and she alone has remained to me in that world."

---

[4] "They neither marry . . ." This is a reference to the ending of earthly
relationships in the future world.

CANTO XX

Hugh Capet

A lesser will contends vainly against a better one;
  therefore, to please him [Adrian], contrary to my wish,
  I drew the sponge unfilled from the water.

My leader and I moved on along the clear space
  near the bank, as one goes on a wall
  close to the battlements,

for the people distilling through their eyes, drop by drop,
  the evil [greed] which possesses the whole world,
  on the other side lay too close to the edge.

Be accursed, ancient wolf, you
  who have more prey than any other beast
  because of your endlessly ravenous hunger!   12

O heavens! through whose revolutions people believe
  that conditions here below are changed,
  when will someone come to drive it [the wolf] away?

The shades cite examples of worthy poverty as a goad.

We went on with slow and short steps
  intent upon the shades whom I heard
  weeping piteously and complaining,

and by chance I heard someone ahead of us
  invoke "Sweet Mary" in his tears
  as a woman does in childbirth.

And he continued, "Thou wast so poor!
  as can be seen by that hostelry
  where thou didst lay down thy burden."   24

Afterward I heard, "O good Fabricius,
  you preferred to have virtue in poverty
  rather than great riches with vice!"

These words were so pleasing to me

that I moved on to gain acquaintance
    with the spirit from whom they came.

He spoke next of the gifts bestowed
    by St. Nicholas on the maidens
      so that they might conduct their youth with honor.

"O soul, you who speak of so much good,
    tell me who you were," I asked, "and why,
      alone, you renew this deserved praise.

36

Your words will not be without reward
    if I return to complete the short journey
      of that life which flies to its end."

And he, "I will tell you,
    not for any comfort I expect, but because,
      before your death, such grace shines upon you.

Hugh Capet, the founder of a line of French kings, gives a review of the rule of his descendants, as generally interpreted in Dante's time by Italians. In the list of crimes, connected in the account by the ironic "for amends," is the charge that Charles of Anjou had had St. Thomas Aquinas poisoned, and had caused the death of Corradino, a lad of sixteen, the grandson of the emperor Frederick II. A second Charles (of Valois), armed only with treachery, "the lance of Judas," will betray Florence to the Blacks. Still a third Charles (of Apulia) will sell his youngest daughter in marriage to an old man. But the greatest crime will be the attack by Philip the Fair on Boniface VIII, at Anagni. This pope was execrated by Dante, but in this case he was the injured party, and the Church itself was humiliated in the person of its leader. Philip is blamed also for the destruction of the order of the Templars.

I was the root of the evil tree
    that darkens the whole Christian land,
      so that good fruit is seldom plucked from it.

But if Douai, Lille, Ghent, and Bruges
    had the power, there would soon be vengeance;
      and I request it of Him who judges all.

48

Yonder I was called Hugh Capet;
    from me are born the Philips and the Louis's
      by whom France recently has been ruled.

I was the son of a Parisian butcher.

When the ancient kings died out,
   except for one [descendant] who wore a monk's gray
      gown,
I found that I held tightly in my hands
   the reins of the kingdom, and such power
   from new possessions, and so many friends,

that my son was promoted
   to the widowed crown, from whom
   the consecrated line begins.   60

Until the great dowry of Provence
   took shame from my blood,
   it had little power and did little harm.

Then, with violence and deception
   its rapine began, and afterward, for amends,
   it seized Ponthieu, Normandy, and Gascony.

Charles came to Italy, and, for amends,
   made a victim of Corradino, and then,
   for amends, sent Thomas back to Heaven.

I see a time not far from the present
   which will bring another Charles [of Valois] from France
   to make himself and his family better known.   72

He will come alone, armed only with the lance
   with which Judas fought, and he will aim it
   so that the paunch of Florence will burst.

For that he will gain, not land,
   but sin and shame, all the heavier
   the lighter he esteems such crimes.

The other, once a captive on a ship,
   I see selling his daughter and haggling
   over her, as pirates do with slaves.

O avarice, what more can you do
   since you have so drawn my family to yourself
   that it does not care for its own flesh!   84

To make past and future wrongs seem less,
   I see the lilies of France enter Anagni
   and Christ, in His vicar, made captive.

I see him mocked another time;
> I see the vinegar and the gall renewed,
> and I see him slain between living thieves.

I see the new cruel Pilate [Philip the Fair],
> still unsatisfied, without decree
> making his greedy way into the Temple.

O my Lord, when will I be happy
> in observing the vengeance which, hidden,
> makes Thine anger sweet in Thy secret counsel?   96

By night, the souls cite examples of avarice as the check. Among those mentioned as exemplifying this vice are Pygmalion, who killed Dido's husband for his wealth; Midas who, after losing at his own request the power to turn all he touched to gold, received an ass's ears; Achan, stoned to death by Joshua for theft; Ananias and his wife Sapphira who, when rebuked by Peter for fraud, fell dead. Still others are Heliodorus who was kicked half to death by a horse while trying to take possession of the treasure in Jerusalem; Polymnestor who, after robbing and killing Polydorus, had his eyes torn out by the maddened Hecuba; and, finally, Crassus who had molten gold poured down his throat.

What I was saying of the only Bride
> of the Holy Spirit [Mary] which made you
> come to me for comment

is our refrain as long as day lasts,
> but when night comes on
> we repeat, instead, contrary examples.

We tell then of Pygmalion
> whose gluttonous lust for gold
> made him a thief, traitor, and parricide,

and of the misery of avaricious Midas
> which, after his first greedy request,
> made people laugh at him.   108

Each recalls how the foolish Achan
> stole the spoils, so that the wrath of Joshua
> still seems to punish him here.

Then we accuse Sapphira and her husband;

we celebrate the kick Heliodorus got,
    and we encircle the mountain with the infamy

of Polymnestor who killed Polydorus.
    Finally we cry out, 'Crassus, tell us,
    since you know, how gold tastes?'

Now one speaks loudly, another low,
    according as an impulse spurs him
    with greater or with lesser force.   120

Therefore, in talking of goodness as we do
    by day, I was not alone just now,
    but nearby, no other person raised his voice."

We had already departed from him
    and were trying to surmount the way
    as far as our powers permitted,

when I felt the mountain shake like a thing falling,
    so that a chill gripped me,
    as it does someone going to his death.

Certainly [the island of] Delos did not shake so much
    before Latona made a nest on it
    to give birth to the two eyes of heaven [Apollo and
        Diana].   132

Then a shout was heard on all sides,
    and my master came close to me, saying,
    "Do not fear as long as I guide you."

All were singing, *"Gloria in excelsis Deo,"*[1]
    judging from what I grasped from those
    close by, whose voices could be heard.

We stood motionless, in suspense,
    like the shepherds who first heard that song,
    until the trembling ceased and the singing ended.

Then we took up again our holy way,
    looking at the shades lying on the ground
    who had resumed already their usual lament.   144

No ignorance ever waged such war

---

[1] "Glory to God in the highest."

on me, or gave me such eagerness
  to know, if my memory does not err,

as my wonder then [about the earthquake];
  but in our haste I was not bold enough to ask,
  nor could I discover anything by myself.

Thus I went on, timid and full of thought.

CANTO XXI

Statius

The natural thirst which is never quenched
  except with the water [of truth] asked for,
  as a boon, by the woman of Samaria,

tormented me, and haste goaded me
  over the encumbered road, behind my leader;
  and I was sorrowing for the just penance,

when, behold! as Luke tells how Christ,
  already risen from the grave, appeared
  to the two who were on the way,

so a shade appeared to us as we were gazing
  at the crowd at our feet, having come from behind,
  nor were we aware of him until he spoke,   **12**

saying, "Brothers, may God grant you peace!"
  We turned quickly, and Virgil,
  with a suitable gesture, returned his greeting

and began, "May the true court
  which keeps me in eternal exile
  take you into the council of the blessed!"

"What!" he [the newcomer] cried as we proceeded quickly,
  "If you are shades whom God does not allow above,
  who has brought you so far over the stairs?"

And my leader, "If you look at the marks

traced by the angel and borne by this man,
    you will see that he must reign among the good.   24

But because she [the Fate] who spins
    day and night had not exhausted the thread
    prepared for everyone by Clotho,

his soul [*anima,* fem.], the sister of yours and mine,
    could not come up alone,
    since it does not see as we do.

Therefore I was summoned from the wide throat of Hell
    to show him the way, and I will continue
    as far as my knowledge can take him.

But tell us if you can why the mountain
    trembled a little while ago, and why
    to its wet base all the souls seemed to shout?"   36

In asking this, he so threaded
    the needle's eye of my desire that
    with hope alone he made my thirst less burning.

*The soul who has just joined them explains that on Purgatory
meteorological changes and earthquakes from natural causes cannot
happen. A trembling, however, occurs whenever a soul feels free to
rise to Heaven, and a cry from all the ledges celebrates the happy
event. As in Hell, a kind of determinism is at work here: the soul
rises of its own accord when it is light enough to do so. Its "absolute"
will to go up is conditioned previously by a compulsion, the need and
desire to get rid of its vices.*

[He began, "The holy rule of the mountain
    permits nothing that is disorderly
    or that is contrary to custom.
This place is free from variations;
    only what heaven takes into itself
    can cause change, nothing else,
so that no rain, hail, snow, dew, or frost
    falls higher than the stairs
    of the three short steps.   48
No heavy or light clouds appear, nor lightning,
    nor Thaumas' daughter [the rainbow]
    who often changes place on earth.

Dry vapor [lightning] does not rise above the top
    of the three steps of which I spoke
    where the vicar of St. Peter stands.
Perhaps below, the mountain quakes more or less
    from wind compressed in the earth
    (I know not how), but up here never.
It trembles here when a soul
    feels cleansed so that it may go up,
    and such a shout accompanies it.   60
Will alone gives proof of the purity
    which takes the soul by surprise, and helps it
    when it is free to change its cloister.
It wills indeed before, but this desire,
    conditioned by Divine Justice
    as formerly by sin, keeps it in its penance.
And I who have lain in this pain
    five hundred years and more, just now
    felt my will free for a better place.
Therefore you noticed the earthquake,
    and the devout spirits on the mountain gave praise
    to the Lord who, I pray, may soon send them up."   72
Thus he spoke to us, and since we enjoy drinking
    in proportion to our thirst,
    I cannot say how much good he did me.
My wise leader said, "Now I see the net
    which holds you here, and how it is broken,
    why the mountain quakes, and at what you
       rejoice.
Now please let me know who you were
    and let me learn from your words
    why you have lain here so long."]

Statius, the newcomer, a pagan poet, the author of the Thebaid and
the unfinished Achilleid (whom Dante had confused with a Christian
rhetorician of the same name and who stands in the allegory for
Reason illuminated by Christianity) identifies himself, and attributes
his supposed conversion to certain works of Virgil. Virgil signals to
Dante not to reveal his identity, but the latter cannot repress a smile,
which Statius asks him to explain. Virgil finally relieves Dante's em-
barrassment and allows him to speak freely. On learning who Virgil

is, Statius tries to embrace him, adding thus another affectionate tribute to the ancient poet whom Dante must soon leave.

"At the time when good Titus with the help
    of the Supreme King, avenged the wounds
    from which flowed the blood sold by Judas,   84

I lived yonder," that spirit answered, "with the title
    [of poet] which lasts longest and honors most.
    I was famous but as yet did not have faith.

So sweet was the music of my verse that,
    although of Toulouse, Rome drew me to herself
    where I merited the myrtle crown.

People still mention my name, Statius.
    I sang of Thebes, and then of great Achilles,
    but I fell by the way with the second burden

The sparks of the divine flame
    which has inspired more than a thousand
    kindled the fire that I felt in me—   96

I mean the *Aeneid* which was a mother to me
    and the nurse of my poetry;
    without it I would not have been worth a drachma,

and to have lived yonder when Virgil was alive,
    I would have agreed to do a year more
    than I owed before coming out of exile."

At these words, Virgil turned to me
    with a look that said, "Be quiet!"
    but the will cannot do all it wishes,

for laughter and tears are such close followers
    of the passion from which they spring
    that they obey least in those who are most sincere.   108

I merely smiled, making an involuntary sign,
    whereupon Statius was silent and looked
    in my eyes where the soul is most expressive,

and said, "So may you complete your task,
    why did your face just now
    reveal to me the flashing of a smile?"

Now I am caught on one side and the other;

one bids me keep silent, the other asks
　　that I speak; whereupon I sigh and am understood

by my master, who said to me,
　　"Do not be afraid, but speak and tell him
　　what he asks for so earnestly."   120

Then I, "Perhaps, ancient spirit,
　　you are wondering at my smile,
　　but I want you to marvel still more.

He who guides my eyes on high
　　is that Virgil from whom you gained
　　the power to sing of the gods and of men.

If you believe anything else caused my laughter
　　consider it as untrue and that the reason
　　was what you said about him."

Already he was bending to embrace my master's feet
　　when Virgil said, "Brother, do not do it,
　　for you are a shade and are looking at one."   132

And he, on rising, "Now you can understand
　　the greatness of the love that warms me
　　for you when I forget our emptiness

and consider a shade as a solid thing."

CANTO XXII

Statius' Conversion—The Gluttons

*Statius explains that he suffered from prodigality, not avarice, and
that the supposed prediction of Christ's coming in one of Virgil's
bucolics led to his conversion to Christianity.*

*In reply to a question, Virgil mentions some of his companions in
Limbo, including certain mythological characters in Statius' own works.*

[Now the angel who had directed us
    to the sixth ledge was behind us,
    having erased a scar from my face
and having called those who long for righteousness
    "blessed," his words completing
    the beatitude with *sitiunt*[1] alone.
And I, lighter than at the other passes,
    was climbing after my rapid guides
    without effort, when Virgil began,
"Love awakened in another person
    by virtue, when revealed,
    always enflames one's love for that person;   12
therefore, from the time when Juvenal
    who had come to the infernal Limbo
    revealed your affection for me,
my good will toward you was such
    as had never bound me to an unseen person,
    so that now these stairs will seem short to me.
But tell me, speaking as a companion
    and pardoning me if, through friendly confidence,
    I take too great liberties,
how could avarice find a place
    in your heart along with such wisdom
    as you gained by your efforts?"   24
This question first made Statius smile a little,
    then he answered, "Every word of yours
    is a dear token of your love.
Many times things appear to us
    which give rise to wondering
    because their true cause is hidden.
Your question shows your supposition
    that I was avaricious in the other life,
    perhaps because of the round on which I was.
Now be advised that avarice was too remote
    from me, and this lack of moderation [prodigality]
    has been punished by thousands of months,   36
and if I had not corrected my ways

---

1 "Thirst," one word of the beatitude, "Blessed are they which do
hunger and thirst after righteousness."

when I understood the lines in which
you exclaim, as if angry with human nature,
'Why, sacred [temperate] hunger for gold,
  do you not control human appetites?'
  I would have rolled weights and heard wretched cries
    [in Hell].
Then I learned that hands could open too freely
  in spending, and I repented for that
  as well as for other sins.
How many [of the prodigal] will rise with shorn locks
  through ignorance during life and at its end
  which prevents repentance for their sin!   48
And know that the offense of repelling a vice
  through the opposite lack of moderation
  is cured here along with that vice.
Therefore, if to purge myself
  I was with those who weep for avarice,
  the cause was the contrary excess."
"Now, when you sang of the cruel strife
  of Jocasta's twofold affliction [her two sons],"
  said the singer of the bucolics [Virgil],
"by the notes with which Clio [the Muse of History] accom-
    panied you,
  it does not appear that you as yet had faith,
  without which good deeds are insufficient.   60
If that is so, what sun or what candle
  dispelled the darkness, so that afterward
  you set your sails to follow the fisherman [St. Peter]?"
And Statius to him, "First you directed me
  toward Parnassus to drink near its grottoes,
  and then, after God, enlightened me.
You acted like those who at night
  carry a light behind them and help,
  not themselves, but those who follow,
when you said, 'The ages become new again;
  justice returns, and the first years,
  and a new progeny descends from Heaven.'   72
Through you I was a poet and a Christian,
  but to make you see better what I sketch,
  I will fill in the color of the picture.

The world was already pregnant
>   with the new belief, sowed by the messengers
>   of the everlasting kingdom,
and your words, mentioned above,
>   so harmonized with the new preachers
>   that I began to visit them.
At last they seemed so holy to me
>   that when Domitian persecuted them,
>   their cries were not without tears of my own,   84
and while I remained yonder
>   I helped them, and their righteous ways
>   made me despise all other sects.
And before I had brought the Greeks [in my poem]
>   to the river of Thebes, I received baptism,
>   but, through fear, I became a Christian secretly,
pretending paganism for a long time.
>   This lukewarmness made me circle
>   the fourth ledge [of sloth] for more than four
>   centuries.
You then, who lifted the veil
>   which had hidden from me the good
>   I speak of, tell me if you can   96
while we have time, where Terence, Caecilius,
>   Plautus, and Varius are. Let me know
>   if they are damned and in what ward."
"They and Persius and I and many others,"
>   my leader answered, "are with that Greek [Homer]
>   whom the Muses nursed more than any other,
in the first circle of the dark prison.
>   Often we talk about the mountain [Parnassus]
>   that still has our nurses [the Muses] on it.
Euripides is with us and Antiphon,
>   Simonides and Agathon, and many other Greeks
>   who once crowned their brows with laurel.   108
There are seen, of your people,
>   Antigone, Deiphile, Argia,
>   and Ismene, still sad, as she was.
She [Hypsipyle] who pointed out Langia
>   is there and the daughter of Tiresias [Manto]
>   and Thetis and Deidamia with her sisters."]

On the ledge of the gluttons, the poets find a tree with branches that get larger toward the top, and which cannot be climbed, a symbol of the prohibition and denial enforced here. Voices in the tree first cite a warning, then examples of temperance as a goad.

Both the poets were silent again
  and intent on looking around them,
  free from climbing and from the walls,

and already four of the handmaidens [hours] of the day
  had remained behind, and the fifth
  was directing the pole of its chariot upward   120

when my leader said, "I believe
  that we must turn our right side to the edge,
  circling the mountain as we have done before."

Thus, custom there was our guide,
  and we proceeded with less misgiving
  because of the acquiescence of the soul [Statius] with us.

The two poets went ahead and I, alone, behind,
  and I listened to their conversation
  which imparted knowledge of poetry.

But soon a tree with wholesome and sweet fruit
  which we found in the middle of the road
  broke off the pleasant talk.   132

As a fir decreases in size from branch to branch
  going up, so this one did coming down,
  in such a way that no one, I believe, could climb it.

On the side where our path
  was closed in, clear water fell
  from a high rock and sprinkled the leaves.

As the two poets approached the tree,
  a voice within the leaves shouted,
  "You will have a dearth of food!"

Then it said, "Mary thought more of how
  the wedding feast might be honorable and complete
  than of her mouth, which now pleads for you,"   144

and, "The ancient Roman women were content
  with water for their drink," and "Daniel
  despised food and gained wisdom."

"The first age (it was as beautiful as gold)
    through hunger made acorns good to eat
    and through thirst made nectar of every brook."

"Honey and locusts were the viands
    which nourished the Baptist on the desert,
    so that he became glorious and great,

as the Gospel reveals him to you."

CANTO XXIII

Forese Donati

While I was looking closely
    through the leaves, as a man does
    who wastes his life hunting birds,

my more than father said to me,
    "Come now, for the time allotted us
    must be more usefully divided."

I turned my face and eyes at once
    toward the sages who were talking in a way
    that made my going easy,

and behold! *"Labia mea Domine"*[1]
    was heard in song and tears,
    so that it gave both delight and pain.

"O dear father, what do I hear?" I began.
    And he, "Perhaps shades are passing,
    loosening the knot of their duty."

As pilgrims become concerned
    at meeting strangers on the way,
    and turn toward them without stopping,

so, coming behind us with greater speed

12

---

[1] "O Lord [open Thou] my lips."

and passing on, a crowd of spirits,
   silent and devout, looked, wondering, at us.

*The shades on this ledge are as emaciated as Erysichthon who, cursed
with hunger, began to eat himself, or a certain Mary who, during the
siege of Jerusalem, ate her own child. Among them is Forese Donati,
a friend and companion of Dante's youth with whom he had ex-
changed some scurrilous sonnets. The tone of the present passage
serves as an apology for past insults, notably those against Forese's
wife, Nella, whose prayers have advanced her husband above the
negligent.*

Their eyes were dark and hollow; they were pale
      and so emaciated that their skin
      took the shape of their bones.   24

I do not believe that Erysichthon
      when he was most afraid of hunger
      was so withered to the skin.

I said to myself, reflecting,
      "Those must be the people who lost Jerusalem
      when Mary fed on her child."

Their eye pits looked like rings without gems;
      whoever reads OMO [*homo*] in the face of man
      would easily have recognized the M.

Who would believe, not knowing how,
      that the fragrance of an apple or a spring,
      by creating desire, would cause such an effect.   36

I was wondering what so famished them,
      since the reason for their leanness
      and dry skin was not yet apparent to me,

when, behold! out of the depths of his head
      a shade turned his eyes to me and looked closely;
      then shouted loudly, "What favor for me is this?"

Never would I have recognized him
      by his face, but what his aspect hid
      was made clear to me by his voice

which, like a spark, rekindled wholly
      my knowledge of his changed countenance;
      and I saw again the face of Forese.   48

"Alas! do not stare at the dry scabs
     which discolor my skin," he begged,
     "nor at my lack of flesh,

but tell me the truth about yourself
     and who the two souls are who guide you;
     do not delay in speaking to me."

"Your face which in death I once wept for
     gives me not less pain now,"
     I answered, "seeing it so disfigured,

but tell me, in God's name, what withers you so;
     do not make me speak while I am marveling,
     for a mind preoccupied speaks badly."   60

And he to me, "From the eternal counsel
     a power comes to the water, and to the tree
     left behind, which makes me so thin.

All these people who sing while weeping,
     for having cared too much for their stomachs,
     make themselves holy again in hunger and in thirst.

The fragrance which comes from the fruit
     and from the spray on the verdure
     gives a craving to eat and drink,

and not once only in circling this level
     is our pain renewed—I say 'pain,'
     although I should say 'solace'—   72

for that desire [for sacrifice] brings us to the tree
     which made Christ cry gladly 'Eli!'
     when, with his own veins, he freed us."

And I to him, "Forese, from that day
     when you changed worlds for a better life
     until now, not five years have passed.

If power to sin ended in you
     before the hour of holy pain [penance]
     which weds us anew to God,

how did you get up here? I thought
     you would still be found below [among the negligent]
     where time for time is exacted.   84

And he to me, "With her flood of tears,
   my Nella has brought me so soon
   to drink the sweet wormwood of torments.

With devout prayers and with sighs she brought me
   from the slopes below where one waits
   and freed me from the other rounds.

My good widow whom I loved so much
   is dearer and more precious to God
   because she is lonely in doing good,

for the Barbagia of Sardinia [a wild region]
   is more modest in its women
   than the Barbagia in which I left her.   96

O dear brother, what do you want me to say?
   A future time is already in sight
   from which this hour will not be remote

when the pulpit will forbid
   the shameless women of Florence
   to show their nipples and their breasts.

What barbarian, what Saracen women
   ever needed spiritual or other discipline
   to make them go covered!

But if the shameless ones knew
   what the swift heavens store up for them,
   they would already have mouths open to howl,   108

for, if foresight here does not deceive me,
   they will be sad before those
   to whom they sing lullabies have hairy cheeks.

But alas! brother, do not hide your story longer;
   you see that not only I, but all these people,
   notice how you veil the sun."

Then I to him, "If you recall to mind
   what you were with me and I with you
   the memory will be a heavy burden.

He [Virgil] who goes in front turned me from that life
   the other day when [Diana, the moon] the sister
   of him [Apollo] (and I pointed to the sun) was full.   120

He has led me through the deep night
    of those who are truly dead
    with this real flesh that follows him.

His comforting has brought me up,
    climbing and circling the mount
    which straightens what the world makes crooked.

He will bear me company, he says,
    until I am where Beatrice is;
    there I must remain without him.

Virgil is he who tells me this (and I pointed to him),
    and this other is the shade
    for whom just now your kingdom shook   132

in all its slopes, as it freed him from itself."

CANTO XXIV

Bonagiunta da Lucca

Our talking did not slacken our pace
    nor our pace our speech, but, conversing,
    we went on rapidly, like a ship in a fair wind;

and the shades who appeared twice dead,
    aware of my being alive, gained wonder
    through the hollow of their eyes.

And, continuing my discourse, I said,
    "Perhaps this shade [Statius] goes slower
    than he would otherwise to be with Virgil longer,

but tell me if you can where Piccarda is,
    and if I see any to be noted
    among those who gaze so at me."

"My sister, already crowned (and whether her goodness   12
    or beauty is greater, I cannot say),
    triumphs happily on high Olympus [in Heaven]."

Thus he spoke first and then added,
  "Here it is not impolite to name each other,
  since our faces are so shrunk by fasting.

This one—and he pointed with his finger—is Bonagiunta,
  Bonagiunta da Lucca. And the face beyond him
  [of Pope Martin IV] more haggard than the others

had the Holy Church in his arms.
  From Tours he came, and by fasting,
  purges the eels of Bolsena and the Vernaccian wine."   24

Many others he named to me, one by one,
  and all seemed glad at the naming,
  so that I noticed no dark glances.

I saw Ubaldino dalla Pila [a prominent Ghibelline]
  biting the air from hunger, and Boniface
  [a rich prelate] who pastured many flocks.

I saw Messer Marchese who had time to drink
  at Forlì with less thirst than now,
  and yet was such that he never felt full enough.

But, as one person interests more than others,
  so I was concerned as I looked at him of Lucca
  who seemed to want most to know about me.   36

*Bonagiunta mentions a certain Gentucca of his city who later will
befriend Dante, and refers to the "sweet new style" (dolce stil nuovo)
used by Dante in his canzone, "Ladies who have intelligence of love."
Dante explains that the new style depends upon inspiration and
expresses true feeling. That distinguishes it from the work of such
predecessors as Iacopo da Lentini (the Notary) and Guittone d'Arezzo.*

He was muttering; and something like "Gentucca"
  I heard coming from [his mouth] where
  the pang of justice that so wastes them is felt.

"O soul," I said, "you who seem so eager
  to speak to me, try to make me understand
  and let your words satisfy me and yourself."

"A woman is born and does not yet wear
  the married woman's veil," he began, "who will make
      my city
  pleasing to you, however much men may reprove it.

You will leave here with this prophecy;
 if you understand my meaning wrongly,
 the facts will make it clear to you.   48

But tell me if I see in you the one
 who drew forth the new rimes beginning,
 'Ladies who have intelligence of love . . .'"

And I to him, "I am one who,
 when Love inspires me, takes note,
 and as he dictates within, I write."

"O brother, now I see," he said, "the knot
 that held back the Notary, Guittone, and me
 from the sweet new style that I hear.

I see clearly how your pens move
 following closely the one who dictates,
 which certainly was not the case with ours.   60

And whoever examines most closely
 sees no other difference between the styles."
 Then, as if satisfied, he was silent.

As the birds that winter along the Nile
 sometimes form a company in the air,
 then go in file to fly with greater speed,

so all the people there,
 turning their faces, hastened their steps,
 fleet through leanness and desire.

And as a man weary of running
 lets his companions go on and walks
 until he relieves the panting of his chest.   72

so Forese let the holy troop pass by
 and came behind me, asking,
 "When will I see you again?"

"I do not know," I answered, "how long I will live,
 but my return indeed will not occur
 before my desire brings me to the shore,

for the place where I was placed to live
 from day to day is more despoiled of good
 and seems to be doomed to ruin."

Forese predicts that his brother, Corso, a leader of the Blacks and a principal cause of the disorder in Florence, will be killed by being dragged and kicked by a horse.

"Now go," he said, "for the one most at fault
    I see dragged at the tail of a beast
    toward the valley [Hell] where there is no absolving.   84

The animal at each step
    goes faster, until it throws him
    and leaves his body basely defaced.

Those wheels (and he directed his eyes to the sky)
    do not have to turn long before you will see clearly
    what my words cannot explain further.

Now you must remain behind, because time
    is precious in this kingdom,
    and I lose too much by coming at your pace."

As a horseman sometimes advances
    at a gallop ahead of a troop
    to have the honor of the first clash,   96

so he left us with greater strides,
    and I remained on the way with the two [Virgil and
        Statius]
    who were such great marshals in the world.

And when he had advanced so far
    that my eyes only could pursue him,
    as my mind did his words,

the green and laden boughs of another fruit tree
    appeared to me, not far off,
    since I had just then turned toward it.

I saw people under it lifting their hands
    and shouting I know not what to the leaves,
    like eager and thoughtless children   108

begging someone who does not answer
    and who, to make their desires keener,
    holds what they want out of their reach.

Then they left as if disillusioned,
    and we came now to the great tree
    which rejects so many prayers and tears.

A voice refers to the Tree of Law (prohibition) broken by Eve; then other voices cite examples of gluttony as a check, first that of the drunken centaurs, the offspring of Ixion and a cloud, who turned a wedding feast into a brawl; then that of Gideon, who chose only three hundred out of an army of Hebrews because they alone drank without kneeling.

"Pass on without coming close;
    there is a tree higher up
    which was bitten by Eve, and this comes from it."

Thus among the leaves someone spoke,
    whereupon Virgil, Statius, and I,
    close together, continued on near the bank.   120

"Remember," it said, "those accursed ones [the centaurs]
    formed in the clouds, who, when gorged,
    fought Theseus with their double breasts,

and those Hebrews weak in drinking
    whom Gideon would not have as companions
    when he descended the hills toward Midian."

Thus, keeping close to the bank
    we passed on, hearing of the sin of gluttony
    which is rewarded, indeed, by wretched pay.

Then spaced out over the solitary way
    we continued more than a thousand steps,
    each in contemplation, without words.   132

"Of what are you thinking, you three going by yourselves?"
    a voice suddenly cried; whereupon I started,
    like a timid, frightened animal.

I lifted my head to see who it was,
    and never have I seen in a furnace
    glass or metal so red and glowing

as an angel there who said, "If you wish
    to go up you must turn here.
    Here those who want peace ascend."

His face had robbed me of my sight
    and I went on behind my teachers
    like one who must guide himself by listening.   144

And, as the May breeze, the herald
    of the dawn, blows and is fragrant,
      steeped in the odor of grass and flowers,

so I felt a fanning on the middle of my brow
    and the moving of a wing
      which brought the fragrance of ambrosia.

I heard, "Blessed are those whom grace
    so enlightens that the love of taste
      does not kindle excessive desire in their breasts

and who hunger always in right measure."

CANTO XXV

The Lustful

It was the hour [in early afternoon] when climbing
    had no obstacle, for the sun and night [opposite]
      had left to Taurus and to Scorpio their meridians;

and, as men who do not stop,
    but continue on their way,
      whatever appears, if spurred by need,

so we entered the gap one after another,
    ascending the narrow stairs
      which separate the climbers.

And as a young stork lifts its wings to fly,
    but does not dare to abandon the nest,
      and lowers them again,

so was I with the desire
    to ask kindled to the point
      of beginning, and then spent.

My dear father, for all our speed, did not keep silent,
    but said, "Loosen the bow of speech
      which you have drawn to the arrow's tip."

12

Then fearlessly I opened my mouth and began,
    "How can one get thin in that place
    where there is no need for food?"

Virgil points out how unsubstantial bodies can exist like images in a
mirror. Statius then presents the current doctrine concerning genera-
tion. The soul is infused directly by God into the body and draws to
itself the functions already active there. After death the soul takes
on an aerial body and becomes visible, like a rainbow.

["If you recall how Meleager was consumed
    at the burning of a piece of wood," he said,
    "this problem will not be so hard for you.   24
And if you think how at each movement
    your image changes in a mirror
    what appears hard will seem easy.
But to quiet your desire
    here is Statius, and I call upon him
    to heal your wound."
"If I reveal what is seen in God
    in your presence," Statius answered,
    "let my inability to deny you be my excuse."
Then he began, "Son, if your mind receives
    and keeps my words, they will be a light
    on the 'how' that you ask.   36
Perfect blood, which is never drunk
    by thirsty veins and remains [in the body]
    like food removed from the table,
obtains in the heart a power that gives shape
    to all your members, like that
    which circulates in the veins to form them.
Refined further, it descends to a place concerning which
    silence is more seemly than description; and then drips
    over another blood in a natural vessel.
There the two mix together, one designed
    to be passive, the other active
    because of the perfect place [heart] from which it comes,   48
and this latter, so united, begins to operate,
    coagulating first and then quickening
    what, to serve as its material, it has made consistent.

The active force having become a soul
>   like that of a plant, although with this difference
>   that the former unlike the latter is to develop,
operates then so that it moves and feels
>   like a sponge, and then proceeds to organize
>   the powers [of sense] of which it is the seed.
Now the force which is in the heart of the begetter
>   develops and spreads, my son, where nature
>   makes provision for all the members.   60
But how from an animal it becomes a child
>   you do not yet see; this is the point
>   which led astray [Averroës] one wiser than you,
for his doctrine disjoined the potential intellect
>   from the [vegetative and animal] soul,
>   not seeing an organ appropriated by it.
Open your breast to the truth which follows
>   and know that as soon as the articulations
>   of the brain are perfected in the embryo,
the First Mover turns to it, happy
>   at its production, and breathes into it
>   a new spirit replete with powers,   72
which draws into itself what it finds active there,
>   and makes a single soul that lives
>   and feels and exists in itself.
And that you may wonder less at my words,
>   consider the heat of the sun which becomes wine
>   when joined to the juice taken from the vine.
And when Lachesis [a Fate] has no more thread,
>   it [the soul] frees itself and carries off,
>   potentially, faculties both human and divine.
Although some of these are mute,
>   memory, intelligence, and will
>   are much keener than before.   84
Without stopping it falls marvelously
>   by itself to one of the shores
>   where it first learns its course.
As soon as space encloses it there
>   the formative power radiates around
>   in the same way as in shaping the living limbs,
and as the air when it is moist

becomes adorned with diverse colors
through rays reflected in it,
so the air here takes on that form
which the soul that has stopped,
through its power, impresses on it.   96
Then just as the flames
follow the fire wherever it moves,
so the new form follows its spirit.
Since the soul derives its visibility in this way,
it is called a shade, and it develops the organs
of every sense, even that of sight.
Thus we speak and thus we laugh,
shed tears, and breathe the sighs
you have heard on the mountain.
We have the appearance that desires
or other feelings impress on us,
and this is why you wonder."]   108

*The poets now come to the seventh ledge, where lust is removed.
Flames dart from the inner bank, and the travelers must proceed
carefully on a symbolically narrow path along the outer edge and
with eyes under rigid control. Shades in the fire shout examples of
chastity, first that of the Virgin Mary, then of Diana who expelled
the fallen Helice.*

And now we had come to the last turn,
and moving to the right,
were attentive to something else.

There the bank sends out flames
which a current rising at the edge
reflects backward, forming a passage.

Therefore we had to go on the open side
in single file, and I feared the fire
on the one hand and falling on the other.

My leader said, "Along here
we must keep a tight rein on our eyes,
since it is easy to make a mistake."   120

Then *Summa Deus clementia*[1] I heard sung

---

[1] "God of clemency supreme."

from within the great burning,
    which made me want to turn and look.
I saw spirits going through the flames,
    and I gazed at them and at my steps,
    dividing from time to time my glances.
When they had come to the end of the hymn
    they cried loudly, *"Virum non cognosco"*[2]
    then in a softer tone took up again the song.
Having finished it they cried,
    "Diana kept to the wood and drove out Helice
    who had tasted the poison of Venus."   132
They afterward returned to their singing,
    celebrating husbands and wives who were chaste,
    as virtue and marriage require.
And this suffices them, I believe,
    for all the time the fire burns them.
    By such treatment, with such diet,
the last affliction must be healed.

CANTO XXVI

Guido Guinizelli

While we were going thus along the rim,
    one in front of the other, my good master often said,
    "Be careful, and profit by being warned."
The sun, already changing the face
    of the west from blue to white,
    struck on my right shoulder,
so that I made the flames more ruddy
    with my shadow, and merely at this slight sign
    I saw many taking heed as they went on.

---

2 "I know not a man," were the words of Mary at the Annunciation.

This made them wonder about me,
    and they began to say, "He does not seem
    to have the body of a shade."   12

Then some came as close to me
    as they could, always taking care
    not to issue from the fire that burned them.

"O you following the others, not for being slower
    but perhaps from reverence, answer me,
    burning as I am from thirst and fire!

Not I alone need your reply,
    for all of these have more desire for it
    than Indian or Ethiopian for cold water.

Tell us how you make of yourself
    a barrier for the sun, as if
    you were not yet in the net of death?"   24

*The souls here are divided into two bands, those who sinned naturally,
and the others. As they pass they cite examples of lust as a check.*

Thus one of them spoke to me,
    and I already would have presented myself
    if I had not noticed another strange thing,

for, through the middle of the fiery road,
    people came facing opposite
    to those who had made me gaze in suspense.

On either side I saw the shades hasten
    and kiss each other without stopping,
    content with a brief greeting.

Thus within their dark troop
    ants rub noses with each other
    perhaps to enquire about their way or fortune.   36

As soon as they end the friendly greeting,
    before taking the first step to pass on,
    each tries to outshout the other,

the new people saying "Sodom and Gomorrah,"
    and the others, "Pasiphaë enters the cow
    so that the young bull may run to her lust."

Then, as cranes fly, some to the Riphean mountains,

and some to the sands, the former
  afraid of the sun, the latter of the cold,

so one group goes on and the other comes,
  and weeping they resume their former song
  and the cry which suits them best.   48

And those who had entreated me
  drew close to me as before,
  showing themselves intent on listening.

I, having twice understood their desire,
  began, "O souls, certain to have,
  whenever it may be, a state of peace,

my members have not remained over there
  either green or ripe, but are with me
  with their blood and with their joints.

I am going upward to be no longer blind;
  a lady there wins grace for me
  to bring my mortal body through your world.   60

But—so may your greater desire
  soon be satisfied, and the heaven shelter you
  which is full of love and spreads widest—

tell me, that I may write it down,
  who you are and what that crowd is
  that goes along behind your backs."

Not otherwise is the mountaineer confused
  who, dazed, gazes speechless
  when wild and rough he comes to the city,

than those shades seemed to be;
  but after they were unburdened of the wonder
  which in lofty hearts is soon quieted,   72

the spirit that asked about us first began again,
  saying, "Blessed are you who, to die better,
  burden yourself with experience of our realm.

The people who do not come with us committed the offense
  for which Caesar once in his triumph,
  heard 'Regina' [Queen] called out against him.

Therefore they leave us shouting 'Sodom,'

reproaching themselves as you have heard,
and add to the burning with their shame.

Our own sin was heterosexual, but
because we did not observe human restraints,
following our lusts like beasts,   84

we recite when we leave, heaping opprobrium
on ourselves, the name of her [Pasiphaë]
who became a beast in the beastlike wood.

Now you know our deed and of what we were guilty.

*The speaker is Guido Guinizelli, Dante's most famous precursor, who
had developed a new conception of love by fusing courtly devotion
with spiritual or divine love, making the lady a symbol, as Beatrice
was for Dante. Guinizelli gives the honor for excellence in poetry to
the Provençal, Arnaut Daniel, who speaks at the end of the canto
in his native tongue.*

If perhaps you wish to know by name
who we were, there is not time enough to tell,

but I will lessen your desire concerning me.
I am Guido Guinizelli, and I purge myself already
because I repented fully before the end."

As, in the sadness of Lycurgus,
two sons became on seeing their mother,
so was I, although I did not rise so high,   96

when I heard my father name himself,
and the father of others, my betters,
who ever wrote sweet and gracious rhymes of love.

And without hearing or speaking
I went on thoughtful, looking at him,
but because of the fire did not draw closer.

When I was filled with gazing
I offered myself as ready for his service,
with affirmations that inspire trust,

and he said to me, "You leave an impression,
by what I hear, so deep and clear
that Lethe cannot remove or dim it,   108

but if your words now have told the truth,

tell me why you show by word
and glance that you hold me dear."

And I to him, "Your sweet verses which,
as long as our modern tongues shall last,
will make precious their very ink."

"O brother," he replied, "that one [Arnaut Daniel]
(and with his finger he pointed to a soul ahead)
was a better artist in the mother tongue.

In love poetry and prose romances he excelled,
and let the fools talk who believe
that the poet from Limoges [Giraut de Bornelh] surpasses
        him.   120

They attend to rumor rather than to truth,
and thus form their opinion
before they listen either to art or reason.

Thus many of our fathers did with Guittone [d'Arezzo],
from outburst to outburst praising him alone,
until the truth won out with most.

Now, if you have such a great privilege
that you can reach the cloister
where Christ is the abbot of the college,

say a *Pater Noster* to Him for me,
so far as it is needful in this world
where we no longer have the power to sin."   132

Then perhaps to give room to others near him,
he disappeared through the fire,
like a fish going to the bottom.

I advanced a little toward the shade pointed out
and told him that my desire had prepared
a grateful place for his name.

He began willingly to speak:
"Your courteous request so pleases me
that I cannot and will not hide from you.

I am Arnaut, and now I go singing and weeping.
Sadly I regret my past folly
and rejoicing see ahead the joy I hope for.   144

Now I pray you, by the power
    that guides you to the top of the stairs,
    recall, while you have time, my grief."
Then he hid himself in the refining fire.

CANTO XXVII

The Dream of Leah

As this canto begins, the sun is setting in Purgatory and rising in Jerusalem; Spain (Ebro) is under the constellation of Libra, and it is noon in India.

The sun was darting its first beams
    on the place where its Maker shed his blood—
    the Ebro falling beneath the lofty scales,

and the waters of the Ganges made hot by noon—
    and [in Purgatory] day was departing
    when God's glad angel appeared.

Out of the flames he stood on the bank
    and sang, *"Beati mundo corde"*[1]
    in a voice much clearer than ours.

Then, "You cannot go farther, holy souls,
    unless the pain of fire is felt. Enter it
    and do not be deaf to the singing beyond."

This he said to us when we drew close,
    and when I heard his words I became
    like one who is laid in the grave.

I leaned over my clasped hands,
    looking at the fire and recalling vividly
    the burned human bodies I had seen.

The good escorts turned toward me

12

---

[1] "Blessed are the pure in heart."

and Virgil said, "My son,
   here there can be pain, but not death.

Remember! Remember!
   and if I guided you safely on Geryon,
   what will I do now, closer to God?

24

Be assured that if you stayed a thousand years
   in the midst of these flames
   they would not make you lose one hair;

and if perhaps you think that I deceive you,
   go toward them, and with your two hands
   and the hem of your dress gain assurance.

Put aside, put aside all fear;
   turn this way, come, and enter securely."
   But I stood firm despite my conscience.

When he saw me remain still and stubborn,
   somewhat disturbed he said, "Now see, my son,
   this wall is between you and Beatrice!"

36

As Pyramus at the sound of Thisbe's name
   opened his eyes and looked at her
   at the time when the mulberry became red,

so, my stubbornness softened, I turned
   to my wise leader, hearing the name
   which always springs up anew in my mind.

Then he shook his head and said, "What?
   do we want to stay on this side?" then smiled
   as to a child won over by an apple.

He stepped into the fire ahead of me,
   begging Statius to come behind
   who, for a long time, had divided us.

When I was in, I would have plunged
   into boiling glass to cool off,
   so extreme was the burning.

My sweet father, to comfort me,
   kept speaking of Beatrice,
   and adding, "I seem already to see her eyes."

A voice singing beyond guided us,

and attentive only to it,
we came to where the ascent began.

Venite, benedicti patris mei![2] sounded there
within a light which so blinded me
that I could not look at it.   60

The sun is leaving," it added, "and evening
comes; do not stop, but hasten
while the west is still not dark."

The path rose straight within the rock
so that the rays of the sun,
already low, were broken in front of me.

The sages and I had mounted a few steps only
when we noticed by my disappearing shadow
that the sun was setting behind us.

And before the vast expanse
of the horizon had become of one hue,
and before Night held all its domain,   72

each of us made a bed of a step;
for the nature of the mountain overcame,
not our desire, but our strength to rise.

As goats, agile and wanton on the heights
before they have eaten, become tame
when ruminating, lying silent and quiet

in the shade while the sun is hot,
watched over by the herdsman who leans
on his staff, and while leaning guards them;

and as the shepherd who lodges in the open
passes the night beside his flock,
watching lest a wild beast scatter it,   84

so we were, all three of us,
I like the goats and they like the shepherds,
hemmed in on both sides by high walls.

There, little could be seen outside,
but in that little the stars appeared
clearer and larger than usual.

---

2 "Come ye blessed of my Father."

Thus, looking at them and musing,
     sleep came upon me, the sleep which often
     announces events before they occur.

In a dream Dante sees Leah, who represents the innocent active life;
Rachel, her sister, stands for contemplation.

At the hour, I believe, when Cytherea [Venus]
     always burning with the fire of love
     first shines from the east on the mount,   96

in a dream I seemed to see a lady,
     young and beautiful, going over a meadow
     gathering flowers and who while singing said,

"Let whoever asks for my name know
     that I am Leah, and I use my fair hands
     to make myself a garland.

I adorn myself to reflect a pleasant image;
     my sister Rachel never leaves her mirror,
     but sits before it all the day.

She likes to see her beautiful eyes
     as I to beautify myself with my hands;
     for her, seeing; for me, doing, satisfies."   108

And now amid the splendors before dawn
     which are the more welcome to pilgrims
     when, on returning, they spend the night nearer home,

on all sides the darkness fled
     and my sleep with it; and I got up
     seeing my great masters already risen.

After climbing to the top of the mountain, Virgil addresses Dante for
the last time. The ancient poet has revealed all that Reason can
disclose. Under his guidance Dante has freed himself not only of bad
habits, but of the innate vices, the very potentiality for sin. He has
attained a freedom from hereditary limitations and from environmental
conditioning that no one on earth can ever have. The faith in the
goodness of Nature, which later in the Renaissance deluded many, is
appropriate for him. Free from the need for choice or thought or inner
struggle, he can do as he pleases. To symbolize this freedom, this
goal of man's reforming efforts, he is figuratively endowed with a
crown and miter, the symbols of temporal and spiritual power.

"That sweet fruit [happiness] for which,
    on so many branches, mortals search,
    today will satisfy your hunger."

These words Virgil addressed to me,
    and never were there gifts
    that caused such delight.   120

So greatly did desire rush upon desire
    to be above, that at every step
    I felt my wings grow for the flight.

When the stairway was wholly under us
    and we were on the top step,
    Virgil fixed his eyes on me and said,

"The temporal fire [of Purgatory] and the eternal [of Hell]
    you have seen, my son, and have come to a place
    where I, by myself, can discern nothing further.

I have brought you here with reason and with art;
    now take pleasure as your guide;
    you are free from the steep and narrow ways.   132

See the sun shining on your brow;
    see the grass, the flowers, and the shrubs
    which the earth here produces of itself.

Until the fair eyes [of Beatrice], now rejoicing, come—
    which in tears made me go to you—
    you can sit or walk among them.

Expect no further word or sign from me;
    free, upright, and whole is your will;
    it would be wrong not to do as it pleases.

Therefore, over yourself, I crown and miter you."

The Garden of Eden

Eager now to look within and around
    the dense and verdant forest which tempered
    for our eyes the light of the new day,

without delay I left the mountain's edge,
    and went slowly over the plain
    on ground fragrant everywhere.

A sweet, unvarying breeze
    touched my face as lightly
    as a gentle wind

and made the leaves, quick to tremble,
    bend in the direction
    of the holy mountain's morning shadow,   12

not deflecting them, however, so far
    that the birds there
    must give up practicing their art;

but these, singing, full of joy, greeted the first hours
    of the day from within the rustling leaves
    which accompanied their song, just as,

in the pine grove on the shore of Chiassi
    a sound swells from branch to branch
    when Aeolus lets the Sirocco blow.

Already my slow steps had taken me
    so far within the ancient forest
    that I could not see where I entered;   24

and behold! a stream prevented me
    from going farther, which with little waves
    bent leftward the grass growing on its banks.

The clearest waters on earth
    would seem to have some mixture in them
    compared with these which conceal nothing,

although they move darkly
    under perpetual shade never pierced
    by the rays of the sun or of the moon.

I held back my steps, but with my eyes
    I glanced beyond the stream to see
    the great variety of fresh May branches.   36

And over there appeared, like something
    which, through the marveling it causes,
    turns every other thought aside,

a solitary lady who went along singing
    and choosing flowers from the flowers
    with which her path was painted.

"O fair lady, you who warm yourself
    in the rays of love (if I can believe your looks
    which are the witnesses of the heart).

may you be pleased to come forward
    toward this stream," I said to her,
    "so that I can understand what you sing.   48

You make me imagine where and how
    Prosperpine was at the time when her mother
    lost her, and when she lost the Spring."

As a lady when dancing turns
    with feet together and close to the ground,
    hardly moving one ahead of the other,

so she turned on the red and yellow flowers
    toward me, like a virgin,
    lowering her modest eyes.

And she fulfilled all my wishes,
    approaching so that the sweet sound
    of her voice came to me with its meaning.   60

As soon as she reached the place where the grass
    was bathed by the waves of the fair rivulet,
    she delighted me by lifting her eyes.

I do not believe that such light shone
    under the eyelids of Venus
    when she was wounded unintentionally by her son.

She smiled, standing on the other bank,
    carrying in her hands flowers of many colors
    which the high land produces without seed.

The river kept us separated by three steps
    but Hellespont, where Xerxes passed—
    still a check on human pride—   72

was not more hated by Leander
    for flowing between Sestos and Abydos
    than this stream by me for not opening.

"You are strangers here," she began,
    "and perhaps because I smile in this place
    chosen as the nest for human kind,

some wonder keeps you marveling;
    but the psalm *Delectasti*[1] gives light
    which can clear the mist from your minds.

And you in front who spoke to me,
    say if you wish to hear more, for I have come
    ready to satisfy all of your requests."   84

Matilda, the symbol of innocence and the guardian or presiding spirit
of the Earthly Paradise, explains that the breeze is caused by the
revolution of the heavens which communicate their movement to the
sphere of air into which Purgatory projects. All plant life is repre-
sented in the Garden of Eden, and its reproductive power is dispersed
over the earth by the moving air. Two streams, Lethe, which removes
guilty memories, and Eunoè, which restores the recollection of all
good deeds, are replenished by the will of God alone.

Matilda adds, as a corollary, that the Ancients with their imperfect
vision of the Christian truth mistook the Garden of Eden for the
world in their "Golden Age." At this reference to their partial error,
Virgil and Statius smile.

["The water," I said, "and the sound of the forest
    combat in me a belief in something
    that denies the possibility of them."
Then she, "I will explain the cause
    of what makes you wonder
    and dispel the fog that has enveloped you.

---

[1] "[For] Thou [Lord] hast made me glad [through thy work.]"

The Supreme Good which follows only Its own pleasure
    made man good and for good, and gave this place
    to him as a pledge of eternal peace.
Through his fault he stayed here
    only a short time; through his fault he exchanged
    innocent laughter and play for tears and toil.   96
To prevent the vapors caused by the evaporation
    of land and water and which follow the heat
    as much as they can
from doing harm to man, this mountain rose
    so high toward Heaven, and is free
    from the gate upward from atmospheric change.
Now, since the air revolves
    with the primal revolution
    if its circling is not broken anywhere,
on this highest summit which projects
    in the air, such movement strikes
    and makes the dense wood give forth a sound;   108
and the smitten plants have such power
    that they impregnate the breeze with their virtues,
    and the air, revolving, scatters them,
and the land elsewhere, according as it is suited
    in itself and in its climate, conceives
    and produces from different virtues different growths.
Having heard this, it should not appear
    a marvel to you when some plant
    without apparent seed takes root.
And you must know that the sacred land
    where you are is full of every seed
    and has fruit not plucked in your world.   120
The water you see does not come from a spring
    restored by vapor condensed by cold,
    like rivers which rise and fall,
but comes from a stable and certain source,
    since it takes from the will of God
    what is poured forth in two streams.
On this side it descends with the power
    to take away memory of sin, and on the other
    it restores that of all good deeds.
Here it is called Lethe, over there

Eunoè, and it is not effective
    unless drunk both here and there.   132
Its taste excels all other flavors.
    And, although your thirst may be quenched
    without my revealing more,
I will add as a favor a corollary;
    nor do I believe my remarks will be less dear
    if they go beyond my promise.
Those who in ancient times
    sang of the Golden Age and its happy state
    perhaps dreamed of this place on Parnassus.
Here the root of man's race was innocent,
    here is eternal Spring, and here is every fruit;
    this is the 'nectar' of which all sing."   144
I turned to my poets
    and saw that with smiles
    they had heard the last remark.
Then I turned my face to the fair lady.]

CANTO XXIX

The Pageant of the Church Militant

At the end of her words, she [Matilda],
    as if enamored, continued her song,
    Beati quorum tecta sunt peccata.[1]
And, as nymphs used to wander
    alone through the woodland shade, some desiring to see,
    others to flee from the sun,
so she started up the stream, moving
    along the bank, with me abreast of her,
    matching her little steps with mine.
Not a hundred paces had we made together

---

[1] "Blessed are those whose sins are covered [forgiven]."

when the two banks turned equally
so that now I faced the east,   12

nor had our way as yet taken us far
when the lady turned toward me, saying,
"My brother, look and listen."

The church comes out of the east in a magnificent symbolic procession
to present Revelation, and to lead the reformed sinner to Paradise.
Dante again invokes the Muses, mentioning Helicon, the fountain
sacred to them, and Urania, the Muse of the heavens (astronomy).

And behold! a light suddenly flashed
everywhere through the great forest
so that I wondered if it were lightning;

but since lightning stops as quickly as it comes,
and that, lasting, shone more and more,
within my thoughts I questioned, "What is this?"

And a sweet melody ran through the luminous air,
so that good zeal
made me reprove the boldness of Eve   24

who, there, when Heaven and earth obeyed,
the only woman, and just formed, did not endure
to remain under any veil [of ignorance],

under which, if she had been devout,
I would have enjoyed these ineffable delights
before and for a longer time.

While I was going on amid so many first fruits
of the eternal pleasure, all expectant,
and desirous of still further joy,

the air in front of us under the green boughs
became like a flaming fire,
and a sweet sound was heard as a song.   36

O most holy virgins [Muses], if ever for you
I have endured hunger, cold, and vigils,
my need spurs me to ask for my reward!

Now Helicon must pour forth for me
and Urania help me with her choir
to put into verse things hard to conceive.

Seven candlesticks, which represent the gifts of the Holy Spirit (wisdom, understanding, counsel, might, knowledge, piety, and fear of the Lord) appear within the ten steps (commandments) by which they were transmitted.

A little later I thought I saw
    seven golden trees which the distance
    separating me from the objects made me imagine;

but when I was so close to them
    that the common features in different things,
    because of distance, no longer caused confusion,   48

the senses which supply impressions to the mind
    showed that they were candlesticks,
    and that the voices were singing "Hosanna."

Above, the beautiful array flamed
    brighter than the moon at midnight
    in a clear sky in the middle of its month.

I turned full of admiration to Virgil
    who answered me with a look
    not less burdened with amazement.

Then I gazed again at the sublime things
    which advanced toward us so slowly
    that brides at their wedding would go faster.   60

The lady cried to us, "Why are you still
    so eager to see the living lights
    and do not look at what comes behind them?'"

Then I saw men clothed in white
    coming as if behind their leaders;
    and such whiteness never was on earth.

The water shone beside me at my feet
    and reflected my left side
    so that I saw myself as in a mirror.

When I reached a place on the bank
    where the stream alone intervened,
    I stopped to observe more closely;   72

and I saw the flames advance,
    leaving the air painted behind them,
    as if by moving brushes,

so that the space above remained marked
      with seven bands in the colors with which
      the sun makes its rainbow and Delia [the moon] her girdle.

These streamers extended farther back
      than my sight could reach, and, I believe,
      ten steps separated those on the outside.

*Now elders come, representing the books of the Old Testament, dressed
in white, the color of Faith, and after them four creatures (the Gospels)
wearing green, for Hope.*

Under so fair a sky as I describe
      twenty-four elders, two by two,
      came crowned with lilies.   84

All sang, "Blessed art thou
      among the daughters of Adam," and
      "Blessed be thy beauty in all eternity."

When the flowers and fresh grass
      opposite me on the other bank
      were free of these chosen people,

as one star follows another in the heavens,
      four creatures came after them,
      crowned with green leaves.

Each had six wings, their feathers
      were full of eyes; the eyes of Argus,
      if living, would be similar.   96

To describe their form I will not waste rhymes,
      Reader, for another need urges me on,
      so that here I cannot be lavish;

but read Ezekiel, who depicts them
      as he saw them coming from the cold region
      with wind and cloud and fire,

and as you find them in his pages,
      so were they here, except that for the wings,
      John agrees with me, and differs from him.

*The Gospels surround the chariot of the Church Triumphant drawn
by a griffon (a lion with an eagle's head) representing Christ in his
divine and human natures. The height of the griffon's wings indicates*

his divine origin. The wheels probably represent the Dominican and Franciscan orders. Three nymphs (the theological virtues of Faith, Hope, and Love) are at the right wheel, with Love showing a slight pre-eminence. On the left, dressed in the imperial purple, are the four cardinal virtues (Prudence, Temperance, Fortitude, and Justice).

The space within the four contained
    a triumphal chariot on two wheels
    drawn by the neck of a griffon.   108

Its wings enclosed the middle band,
    dividing it from the three on either side,
    so as to do no harm by cleaving any.

The pinions rose so high they were lost to sight.
    The birdlike members were of gold,
    the others white mixed with red.

Africanus or even Augustus never delighted Rome
    with so beautiful a chariot;
    and that of the sun would seem poor beside it,

that of the sun which, going astray,
    was consumed at the prayer of the earth
    when Jove was mysteriously just.   120

Three ladies came dancing in a circle
    by the right wheel, one [Love] so red
    she would hardly have been noted in the fire;

the other [Hope] was as if her flesh
    and bones had been of emerald;
    the third [Faith] appeared like newly fallen snow.

They seemed to be led now by the white,
    now by the red, and from the song of the latter
    they took their measure, slow or quick.

At the left side four [nymphs] dressed in purple
    rejoiced, under the leadership of one [Prudence]
    who had three eyes in her head.   132

Now figures representing the Epistles of Luke (a doctor) and of Paul appear. After them come the minor epistles, and St. John of the Apocalypse. All are crowned with red to represent the charity of the New Testament. Then, at a signal from Heaven, the solemn procession

*of the Church stops before the awed, humble, and remorseful
Christian.*

Following the group described
    I saw two old men, different in dress
    but alike in bearing, venerable and grave.

One showed himself a follower
    of the great Hippocrates whom Nature created
    for the creatures [mankind] she holds most dear.

The other [Paul] with a sword bright and sharp
    showed a contrary care,
    so that across the stream I was frightened.

Then I saw four of humble semblance,
    and behind all a solitary old man
    moving in a trance, with visage keen.   144

And these seven were dressed like the first,
    but the garland around their heads
    was not of lilies, but of roses

and other vermilion flowers;
    at some distance you would have sworn
    they were in flames above their eyes.

And when the chariot came opposite me,
    a thunderclap seemed to forbid
    the advance of those worthy people,

and together with the banners they halted.

CANTO XXX

The Coming of Beatrice (Revelation)

*The candlesticks are compared to the Septentrion, the constellation
that contains the North Star. When they stop, all those in the proces-
sion turn expectantly toward the chariot of the Church which is to
bring Beatrice (Revelation) to Dante (Mankind). At a call, angels*

hover over it, and within a rain of flowers that veil her, Beatrice
appears, dressed in the colors of the three evangelical virtues. At this
climactic moment, Latin phrases occur frequently, among them a line
from the Aeneid *(Manibus o date lilia plenis!), spoken by an angel*
as the last and supreme compliment to Virgil, who must now disappear,
eclipsed. Dante feels the effect of Beatrice's presence as he had on
earth, and in his distress turns to Virgil. But his former guide, denied
the sight of Revelation, has already disappeared, and Dante is left
alone before the overwhelming spectacle to accomplish the painful
but necessary rites of contrition, confession, and satisfaction (penance).

When the Septentrion of the first heaven—
    which never knew rising or setting
    nor the veil of any mist except of sin

and which made everyone there aware
    of his duty, as the lower star does
    him who turns the helm to come to port—

had stopped, the true people who had come
    between it and the griffon
    turned to the chariot as to their peace.

And one of them, as if sent from Heaven,
    cried three times in song *"Veni, sponsa, de Libano,"*[1]
    and all the others sang after him.   12

As the blessed, at the last trumpet call,
    will rise quickly from their graves,
    singing with regained voices "Hallelujah,"

so, above the divine vehicle
    a hundred [angels] rose (*ad vocem tanti senis*)[2]
    the ministers and messengers of eternal life.

All cried, *"Benedictus qui venis,"*[3]
    and scattering flowers above and around,
    "Manibus o date lilia plenis!"[4]

I have often seen at the beginning of the day
    the eastern sky all rosy, the rest
    of the heavens beautifully clear,   24

---

[1] "Come [with me] from Lebanon, my spouse."
[2] "At the voice of so great an elder."
[3] "Blessed are you who come."
[4] "Oh, give lilies with full hands!"

and the sun's face appear veiled,
>so that, through the tempering of the vapors,
>the eyes could look steadily at it.

Thus, within a cloud of flowers,
>thrown by angelic hands, which rose
>and fell on and around the chariot,

underneath a white veil, crowned with olive,
>a lady appeared to me, under a green mantle,
>dressed in the color of living flame.

And my spirit which already had spent
>so long a time without the trembling
>from awe which her presence caused,

36

without seeing her more clearly,
>through a hidden influence which came from her,
>felt the great power of its old love.

As soon as on my eyes the great virtue fell
>which already had pierced me
>before I was out of childhood,

I turned to the left with the expectation
>which a child has who runs to its mother
>when afraid or afflicted,

to say to Virgil, "Not a drop of blood
>unmoved is left in me;
>I recognize the signs of the old love!"

But Virgil had left me without his company,
>Virgil, my beloved father, Virgil,
>to whom I gave myself up for my salvation;

nor could all that our ancient mother lost [Eden]
>keep my cheeks, cleaned with dew,
>from being darkened again by tears.

Now Beatrice speaks, not in her role as a tender friend, but severely, as a minister of the sacraments, calling Dante by his name (which appears here only), since the confession to follow must be personal and, in a manner, signed. Dante is paralyzed by this reception, but when the angels show sympathy for him, his awakened self-pity and his distress grow until he bursts into tears. Thus the first stage of the sacrament is accomplished.

Dante, although Virgil is leaving,
    do not weep yet, do not weep yet,
    for you must cry for another wound!"

As an admiral, at the prow or stern,
    looks at those who man the other ships,
    and heartens them to their work,   60

so—when I turned at the sound of my name,
    which is recorded here from necessity—
    at the left side of the chariot

I saw the lady who at first appeared
    veiled under the angelic shower
    directing her eyes at me from beyond the stream.

although the veil descending from her head,
    wreathed with Minerva's leaves [the olive],
    kept her from being completely manifest.

Queenlike, stern in her bearing,
    she continued, like one who speaks
    while holding back the sharpest words.   72

"Look at me! I am indeed, I am indeed Beatrice.
    How did you dare to approach the mount?
    Did you not know that here man is happy?"

My glances fell down to the clear stream;
    but seeing myself in it, I turned them
    to the grass, such shame burdened my face.

As a mother at times seems cruel
    to her son, so she appeared to me,
    since the taste of stern pity is bitter.

Then she was silent, and the angels sang
    at once, "*In te, Domine, speravi,*"[5]
    but did not go beyond *pedes meos.*[6]   84

As snow on the living rafters [trees]
    of the back of Italy [the Apennines] congeals
    when blown and packed by Slavic winds,

then, melted, trickles down, if a breath comes

---

[5] "In Thee, O Lord, do I put my trust."
[6] "[Thou hast set] my feet [in a large room]."

from the land [Africa] without shadows,
      like fire melting a candle,

so was I without tears or sighs
      before those [angels] whose song is accompanied
      by the melodies of the eternal spheres;

but when I heard in their sweet notes
      their pity for me, more than if they had said,
      "Lady, why do you shame him so?"   96

the frost which had gripped my heart
      became breath and water, and with anguish
      through mouth and eyes came from my breast.

To prepare for the next stage, Beatrice tells how Dante, after her death, had devoted himself to the donna pietosa *of the* Vita Nuova *(profane philosophy), and to worldliness.*

She, still standing at the side
      of the chariot, then turned to address
      the angels who had shown pity for me.

"You watch in the eternal day,
      so that neither night nor sleep hides from you
      a step taken on the ways of the world;

therefore, my answer takes greater care
      that he, weeping over there, should understand,
      and that his sin and sorrow should be equal.   108

Not only by the operation of the great spheres
      which direct each seed to some end,
      according as the stars are conjoined,

but through the bounty of Divine Grace
      which has such high vapors for its rain
      that our sight cannot come close to them,

this man was such, potentially, in his young life
      that every good disposition
      might have come to marvelous fruition;

but the more vigor there is in the soil
      the more malignant and rank it becomes
      if uncultivated or sown with bad seed.   120

For a while I sustained him with my countenance,

and showing my youthful eyes to him,
I led him with me in the right direction.

As soon as I was on the threshold
of my second age, and changed life,
he abandoned me, and gave himself to others.

When I had risen from flesh to spirit
and beauty and virtue had increased in me,
I was less dear to him and less esteemed,

and he turned his steps on an evil path,
following false images of good
which never fulfill their promise.   **132**

Nor did it avail me to invoke inspirations
by which, in dreams and otherwise,
I recalled him, so little did he care.

He fell so low that all means
for his salvation would have been unavailing
except to show him the lost people.

Therefore, I visited the portal of the dead,
and to the one who brought him here,
in sorrow I addressed my request.

The high decrees of God would be broken
if Lethe were crossed and such a draught
were tasted without any payment   **144**

of the penance that causes tears to flow."

CANTO XXXI

Confession and Satisfaction

Beatrice now addresses Dante directly.

"O you beyond the sacred stream,"
she continued without pausing,
directing the point of her speech toward me

which even with the edge had seemed sharp,
   "say, say if this is true; to this accusation
   your confession must be joined."

My senses were so confused
   that my words began and were spent
   before released from their organs.

She waited a moment, then, "What are you thinking?"
   she questioned. "Answer me, for your sad memories
   are not yet impaired by the water [of Lethe]!"   12

Confusion and fear joined together
   sent forth such a "yes" from my mouth,
   that eyes were needed to hear it.

As a crossbow under too great a tension
   breaks both the string and the bow,
   so that the shaft hits its mark with less force,

so I burst under my heavy burden,
   pouring forth tears and sighs,
   and my voice died away on its passage.

Then she said, "In your desires for me [Revelation]
   which led you to love the good
   above which there is none to aspire to,   24

what chains or what hindering pitfalls
   did you find that you should lose
   the hope of going onward?

And what comforts or what advantages
   were displayed in the aspect of another good
   that you should seek it?"

After heaving a bitter sigh,
   scarcely had I voice for an answer,
   and my lips only with effort formed it.

Sobbing I said, "The present things,
   with their false pleasures, turned my steps away
   as soon as your face was hidden."   36

And she, "If you were silent or denied
   what you confess, your sin would not be concealed,
   known as it is by such a judge.

But when confession bursts
    from one's own mouth, the grindstone in our court
    turns back against the edge [of the sword of Justice].

Still to make you bear more shame
    for your error, and to make you stronger
    another time if you hear the sirens,

put aside your sowing of tears and listen,
    and you will hear how, when my flesh was buried,
    I should have led you in the opposite direction.   48

Beatrice refers again to the pargoletta *(young girl). Then, by telling*
Dante to lift his "beard" instead of "chin," she points out indirectly
that he is no child and should know better. Overcome by remorse,
Dante falls in a faint, in this way giving "satisfaction," and ac-
complishing the last stage of the sacrament.

Never did nature or art offer such delight
    as the fair members in which I was once enclosed
    and which are now in dust and scattered,

and if the supreme pleasure failed you
    at my death, what mortal thing
    should have drawn you with desire.

At the first shaft of fallacious things
    you should have lifted yourself up,
    following me, no longer [fallacious] like them.

No young girl or other vanity of such brief use
    should have weighed down your wings
    and exposed you to more blows.   60

A young bird takes two or three chances;
    but before the eyes of a full-grown one,
    the net is spread and the arrow shot in vain."

As children mute from shame stand listening,
    with their eyes on the ground,
    conscience-stricken and repentant,

so I stood; and she continued, "Since by hearing
    you suffer, lift up your beard,
    and you will have greater grief in looking."

With less effort a sturdy oak

is uprooted by a wind of ours
　　or by one from Iarbas' land [Libya]　　　　　　　72

than my chin was lifted at her command;
　　and when by "beard" she meant my chin,
　　I knew the venom of the argument.

Then when my face was raised,
　　I saw the primal creatures [angels]
　　resting from their scattering of flowers.

And my eyes, still insecure,
　　saw Beatrice turned toward the beast
　　which is one in two natures.

Under her veil and beyond the stream
　　she seemed to surpass her former self
　　more than she did others when on earth.　　　　　84

The thorn of repentance so pierced me then
　　that of all things, those that had made me
　　love them most now became most hateful to me.

Such remorse stung my heart
　　that I fell, vanquished; and what became of me,
　　she knows who caused this.

When my heart gave back a sense
　　of outward things, I saw the lady [Matilda]
　　above me, saying, "Hold to me, hold to me!"

She had drawn me into the river up to my throat,
　　and pulling me behind her, moved on
　　as lightly as a little boat over the water.　　　　96

When I was near the sacred shore, *"Asperges me,"*[1]
　　I heard so sweetly that I cannot keep the sound
　　in mind, much less describe it.

The fair lady opened her arms,
　　took my head, and held it down
　　until I swallowed the water.

*Matilda now takes Dante to the four nymphs (Prudence, Temperance,
Fortitude, and Justice). These point out the deeper vision of the
evangelical virtues (Faith, Hope, and Love) and bring Dante to the*

---

[1] "Purge me [with hyssop, and I shall be clean . . .]."

griffon (Christ), which he sees reflected in its twofold unity in the
eyes of Revelation.

Then she drew me forth, and led me, bathed,
    to the dance of the four nymphs,
    each of whom covered me with her arms.

"Here we are nymphs, and in Heaven stars.
    Before Beatrice came to the world
    we were ordained for her as handmaids.   108

We will lead you to her eyes; but the three
    over there who gaze more deeply
    will sharpen yours better for the light in them."

Thus they began to sing, and then took me
    with them to the breast of the griffon
    where Beatrice stood, turned toward us.

They said, "See that you do not spare your eyes;
    we have placed you before the jewels
    from which Love once shot his arrows."

A thousand desires hotter than flames
    bound my sight to the shining eyes
    which still were fixed upon the griffon.   120

As the sun in a mirror, not otherwise
    did the twofold creature shine in them,
    now with one, now with the other nature.

Think, Reader, if I marveled
    when I saw the object remain still
    and yet change in its image.

While full of joy and wonder, my soul
    tasted that [spiritual] food which,
    satisfying, gives hunger for itself,

showing themselves of a higher order
    by their actions, the other three [Virtues] advanced,
    dancing to their angelic measure.   132

"Turn, Beatrice, turn your holy eyes,"
    was their song, "to your faithful one
    who, to see you, has taken so many steps!

Do us the favor of unveiling for him

your smile, so that he may discern
    the second beauty which you conceal."

O splendor of the living, eternal light [of Beatrice]!
    who has become so pale in the shade of Parnassus,
    or drunk so deeply at its well,

that he would not seem to have a clouded mind
    in trying to describe you as you appeared
    when the harmonious heavens alone veiled you,   **144**

and you disclosed yourself in the open air?

CANTO XXXII

The Church and the Law

*Revelation cannot be comprehended directly, that is, without the help
of the Church. Therefore Dante is warned not to gaze too fixedly
on Beatrice.*

So fixed and eager were my eyes
    to satisfy their ten years' thirst [to see Beatrice]
    that other perceptions were suspended,

and on this side and that were walled in
    by indifference, so completely had the holy smile
    drawn me back into the old net!

But my eyes were forced to turn
    toward the left by those goddesses,
    since I heard them say, "Too fixedly!"

And the condition of eyes
    just smitten by the sun
    made me remain a while without vision.   **12**

But after my sight re-formed for what was little—
    I mean "little" compared to something greater [Beatrice]
    from which I was forced to turn—

I saw that the glorious army had wheeled
    to the right, and was returning
    with the sun and the seven flames at its head.

As, under their shields, a troop turns to retreat
    and its banner changes direction
    before what follows can completely turn about,

so that soldiery of the celestial kingdom
    which led the column passed us
    before the pole of the chariot turned.   24

Then the nymphs returned to the wheels,
    and the griffon moved the sacred burden
    without displacing his feathers.

The fair lady who had taken me to the ford,
    Statius, and I followed the wheel
    which turned with the lesser arc.

Thus, while going through the pleasant wood,
    empty because of her who believed in the serpent,
    an angelic music timed our steps.

*The procession advances to a tree which stands for Law (Civil
Authority, or Empire), its unclimbable branches symbolizing prohibi-
tion, the form law usually takes. The divine origin of civil authority
is indicated by the tree's height. In the following symbolic representa-
tion, the tree is despoiled first by Adam and Eve who, like all who
harm it, suffer for their act. Then, after many centuries, Christ
attaches the wooden pole of the chariot to it, and the Church is under
the protection of the state. Then, like Argus, who was killed after
having been put to sleep by Mercury's story of the nymph Syrinx,
Dante falls asleep, his peaceful rest indicating the condition of the
world when the law, revived by the Roman Empire, protected the
Church.*

Perhaps three flights of an arrow
    would cover as much ground
    as we had when Beatrice descended.   36

Then I heard all murmur "Adam!"
    and they circled a tree despoiled of flowers
    and of foliage on every bough.

Its branches which spread wider

as it rose would cause wonder
in the woods of India for their height.

"Blessed art thou, griffon, not to break
with thy beak this wood, sweet to the taste,
since afterwards the belly writhes from it!"

Thus around the sturdy tree the others shouted,
and the twofold animal said, "In this way
the seed of all justice is preserved."   48

And turning to the pole he had drawn
he brought it to the foot of the widowed trunk,
and what came from it [the wooden pole] he left tied
to it.

As in Spring when the great light comes down
mixed with that from the constellation [Aries]
which follows the celestial Carp [Pisces],

plants swell, and each is renewed
in color, before the sun
drives his chariot under other stars,

so, showing a hue less than rose
and more than violet [the imperial purple], the tree
which had had such bare branches was renewed.   60

I did not understand, nor do we sing here,
the hymn those people then intoned,
nor did I grasp completely the melody.

If I could describe how the pitiless eyes
[of Argus] fell asleep, on hearing of Syrinx—
the eyes whose long vigil cost so dear—

like a painter working from a model
I would show how I went to sleep;
but let whoever can depict slumber!

Therefore I pass on to my awakening,
and I declare that a light tore the veil of sleep
and I heard a cry, "Arise! What are you doing?"   72

*On Dante's awakening a change has occurred as wonderful as the
Transfiguration. Christ and the Scriptures have returned to Heaven,
leaving the Church below as their representative with Revelation
[Beatrice], available to the poorest, sitting humbly on the ground.*

As in seeing the flowers [the foretaste] of the tree [Christ]
    which makes the angels eager for its fruit
    and causes perpetual rejoicing in Heaven,

Peter, John, and James were overcome,
    and recovered at the words by which
    the deeper slumbers [of death] had been broken,

and saw their company decreased
    by Moses as well as by Elias,
    and the Master's raiment changed,

so I came to myself and saw, standing over me,
    that compassionate lady [Matilda] who had been
    my guide along the stream;   84

and all perplexed I asked, "Where is Beatrice?"
    And she, "See her sitting on the roots
    beneath the new foliage.

Observe the company that surrounds her;
    the others are mounting after the griffon
    with a sweeter and more profound song."

And if her words continued further, I do not know,
    since before my eyes was Beatrice
    who closed my mind to all other things.

She alone was sitting on the bare ground
    as a guard left there for the chariot
    which I had seen tied by the twofold creature.   96

The seven nymphs, with the lights [candlesticks]
    in their hands, which are safe from winds
    whether north or south, formed a ring around her.

*Dante now sees a symbolic representation of the history of the Church:
first the persecutions by certain Roman emperors, then the early
heresies which attacked the Church from within.*

"You will be for a while a forest dweller [on earth]
    and then you will be with me forever a citizen
    of that Rome in which Christ is a Roman.

Therefore for the good of the badly living world,
    keep your eyes on the chariot, and be careful
    that you write down what you see after your return."

Thus Beatrice; and I, completely devoted,
    at the feet of her commands, directed my eyes
    and mind to what she wished.   108

Never did lightning from a thick cloud
    come down with such speed
    from the highest region

as I saw Jove's bird [the Roman eagle] descend
    through the tree, breaking not only the flowers
    and the new leaves, but the bark as well.

It struck the chariot with all its force,
    which reeled, like a vessel in a storm
    beaten by waves on one side and the other.

Afterward I saw a fox [heresy] which seemed
    to be fasting from all good food
    leap into the body of the triumphal vehicle;   120

but, reproaching it for ugly sins,
    my lady [Revelation] turned it back
    as fast as its fleshless bones permitted.

Temporal possessions (the gift of Constantine) are now mentioned;
also the separation of the Greek church (or perhaps the schism caused
by Mahomet); the corruption due to wealth; and the intrusion of the
seven capital vices, the first three of which (pride, envy, and anger)
have double horns, since they harm others as well as their possessors.

Then from where it had first come, I saw the eagle
    descend again to the body of the car
    and leave it feathered with its plumage [riches].

And as a sound comes from a grieving heart,
    so a voice descended from Heaven, saying,
    "O my little vessel, how badly you are laden!"

Then it seemed to me that the earth opened
    between the wheels, and I saw a dragon come forth
    which drove its tail through the chariot;   132

and, as a wasp withdraws its sting,
    so drawing back its malignant tail,
    the monster wandered off with part of the bottom.

What remained, like fertile soil left to weeds,
    covered itself with the feathers
    offered perhaps [by Constantine] with good intent:

and both wheels and the pole
    were covered so quickly with them
    that a sigh keeps the mouth open longer.

Thus transformed, the holy structure
    put forth heads [vices] over various parts,
    three on the pole and one on each corner.   **144**

The first were armed like an ox, but the four
    had only one horn on their foreheads—
    a similar monster has never been seen.

*Coming down to Dante's time, the French kings are shown beside the
corrupt papacy, the violence and insults against Boniface VIII at
Anagni are referred to, and finally the transfer of the papacy to
Avignon.*

Secure as a fortress on a high peak,
    an ungirt harlot [the corrupt papacy] appeared to me
    sitting on it with eyes quick to glance around.

And to prevent her from being taken from him,
    I saw a giant [the house of France] erect beside her,
    and they sometimes kissed each other.

But because her lustful and vagrant eyes
    were turned toward me, that fierce lover
    whipped her from head to foot [as at Anagni];   **156**

then, full of jealousy and cruel anger,
    he dragged the now monstrous chariot
    so far that he made of the wood a screen

for the harlot and the strange conveyance.

CANTO XXXIII

The Final Preparation

*At the complaint of the Virtues, Beatrice flushes, but predicts that
the Church will someday reveal again its truth. She takes ten steps,*

perhaps to represent the time from the transfer of the papacy to
Avignon to the deaths of those responsible, Clement V and Philip the
Fair. She declares (as of 1305) that the Church has no longer moral
or spiritual existence. She sees a time, however, when a DVX (a dux,
a redeemer, an emperor) will come to reform both Church and state.

"*Deus venerunt gentes,*"[1] the ladies began
    as a sweet psalmody, weeping and alternating,
    now three singing, now four.

And Beatrice, sighing and compassionate,
    listened to them, so changed that Mary
    was altered little more at the cross.

But when the other maidens made way
    for her to speak, she said,
    standing on her feet and glowing like fire,

"*Modicum,*[2] *et vos non videbitis me!*
    et iterum, my dear sisters,
    modicum, et vos videbitis me!"   12

Then she put the seven [Virtues] in front,
    and by beckoning she placed me,
    the lady [Matilda], and the sage [Statius] behind.

She moved on, and I do not believe
    that her tenth step was placed
    on the ground when her eyes met mine,

and with a tranquil look, "Come more quickly,"
    she said to me, "so that when I speak
    you will be well placed to listen."

As soon as I was with her, as duty required,
    she said, "Brother, why do you not venture
    to question me, while coming with me?"   24

I was like those who, when speaking
    before their superiors, are embarrassed
    by too much reverence and cannot pronounce distinctly,

and without enunciating clearly,

---

[1] "O God, the heathen are come. . . ."
[2] "A little while and ye shall not see me: and again, a little while, and
ye shall see me."

I began, "My lady, you know my need
and what is good for it."

And she to me, "From fear and shame
I want you now to free yourself
so that you will not talk like one who dreams.

Know that the chariot the monster broke
was and is not; but let those responsible learn
that God's vengeance fears no nullifying.   36

Not for all time will the eagle [the Roman Empire],
which left its feathers in the car and made it
monstrous and a prey, be without an heir,

for I see clearly and therefore state
that stars already near at hand,
immune to any hindrance, will bring a time

when a five hundred ten and five [DVX]
sent by God, will kill the thievish harlot
with the giant that sins with her.

Beatrice's prophecy is obscure like that of ancient oracles, but the
events will solve the enigma, just as the Naiads guessed the answer
to the riddle of the Sphinx.

And perhaps my prophecy, dark as those of Themis
or of the Sphinx, persuades you less because,
like theirs, it clouds the understanding;   48

but soon events will be the Naiads
who will resolve this deep enigma
without loss to the sheep or to the corn.

Take note, and as the words come from me
so relate them to those who live the life
which is a race to death,

and keep in mind when you write them
not to hide how you saw the tree
which has here been despoiled twice.

Whoever robs it or breaks it,
by his blasphemous act, offends God
who made it holy for His service.   60

For eating it, in pain and in desire for five thousand years

and more the first soul [Adam] longed [in Limbo] for
    Him [Christ]
who punished Himself for the eating.

*The height of the tree indicates its divine origin. If Dante's mind
were not colored, as the mulberry was by the blood of Pyramus, he
could see the moral sense of the prohibition, and of submission to
God's righteousness. In any case, he must report Beatrice's words as
evidence of his journey, just as pilgrims to the Holy Land brought
back palm branches to show they had been there.*

Your mind is dormant if you do not see
    that for a special reason this tree
    is so high and inverted as it rises,

and if your thoughts had not been
    like Elsan [lime-laden] waters to petrify your mind,
    and your delight in them a Pyramus to the mulberry,

by so many circumstances alone
    you would recognize in the tree, in a moral sense,
    the righteousness of God in the interdict [prohibition].   72

But, although I see your mind
    is made of stone, and stony, is darkened,
    so that the light of my words dazzles you,

I still wish that you take them with you, outlined
    if not written down, for the reason
    that the pilgrim's staff is wreathed with palm."

And I, "As wax under the seal
    which does not change the figure printed on it,
    my brain is now marked by you.

But why do your desired words
    fly so far above my sight
    that the more I try, the more I miss them?"   84

"In order that you should know that school
    which you have followed," she said, "and should see
    how badly its doctrines can explain my words,

and so that you may see that your way is as distant
    from God's as the earth from the heaven
    which moves highest and with greatest speed."

Dante has forgotten his devotion to the donna pietosa *(profane philosophy), a proof of his error, since Lethe effaces only the memories of sins. After this explanation, the group moves on to a stream, the Eunoè, which restores the memory of all good deeds, as had been explained by Matilda. Dante comes from the water renewed, pure, without inherited vice or acquired sins or even the memory of them, light enough to mount to the stars.*

Then I answered her, "I do not recall
    that I was ever estranged from you,
    nor do I have a conscience that troubles me."

"And if you cannot remember,"
    she answered, smiling, "now recall
    how you drank this day of Lethe,   96

and if fire is inferred from smoke,
    this forgetting clearly proves a fault
    in your desires which were intent on others.

But truly, hereafter, my words
    will be as simple as necessary
    to make them plain to your dull vision.'

Now brighter and with slower steps the sun
    held the meridian [noonday] circle, which shifts
    from side to side as positions [viewpoints] vary.

As a scout who goes ahead
    to escort people pauses
    if he finds strange things or traces of them,   108

so the seven ladies stopped at a shadow
    like that cast by the green leaves and dark branches
    of the Alps over their cold streams.

In front of them I seemed to see
    the Tigris and the Euphrates flow from one spring
    and, as friends, slowly separate.

"O light, O glory of the human race!
    what water is this which derives
    from one source and divides?"

In answer to my prayer I heard,
    "Ask Matilda," and the fair lady
    replied as one freeing herself from blame: 120

"This and other things were told him,
    and I am certain that Lethe's water
    has not hidden them from him."

And Beatrice, "Perhaps a greater care
    which often dulls one's memory
    has darkened the eyes of his mind,

but see Eunoè which rises there;
    take him to it, and, as your custom is,
    revive his weakened faculty."

As a noble mind offers no excuse
    but makes the desires of another its own
    as soon as they are disclosed,   **132**

so, after she had taken hold of me,
    the fair lady moved on, saying to Statius
    with ladylike courtesy, "Come with him."

If I had, Reader, a longer space in which to write
    I would sing at least in part
    of the sweet draught that would never have sated me,

but because all the pages are full
    planned for this second canticle,
    the curb of art does not let me go farther.

I came back from the most holy waters
    born again, like young plants
    renewed by their new foliage,   **144**

pure and prepared to mount to the stars.

PARADISE

❖❈❖❈❖❈❖❈❖❈❖❈❖

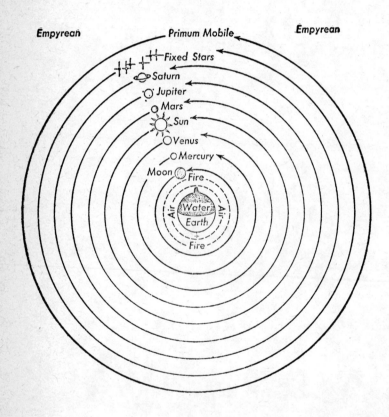

THE HEAVENS

OUTLINE OF PARADISE

The Correspondences

Planets, Heavens	Light	Position	Physical Characteristics	Weakness or Strength
1. Moon	Pearly	Within shadow of earth	Changing phases, spots	Weakness in Faith
2. Mercury	Veiled, eclipsed by sun		Smallness	Weakness in Hope
3. Venus	Color of flame		Double center of motion	Weakness in Love
4. Sun	White	Beyond shadow of earth	Brightness	Strength in Prudence
5. Mars	Red		Redness	Strength in Fortitude
6. Jupiter	Silvery		Temperate quality	Strength in Justice
7. Saturn	Crystal (cold)	Along Golden Ladder	Cold, ascetic	Strength in Temperance
8. Fixed Stars	Various		Variable	
9. Primum Mobile	Diaphanous		Diaphanous	
10. Empyrean				

The Correspondences (Continued)

Planets, Heavens	Souls Represented	Subjects Discussed	Denunciations
1. Moon	Inconstant nuns	Vows	Ill-advised vows
2. Mercury	Lovers of earthly fame	Incarnation, atonement	Guelfs and Ghibellines
3. Venus	Sensual lovers	Heredity	Mercenary ecclesiastics
4. Sun	Theologians	God expounded in his creatures	Mendicant orders
5. Mars	Warriors of Faith	Decay of virility	Effeminacy of Florence
6. Jupiter	Just Rulers	Justice	Unjust rulers
7. Saturn	Monks	Predestination	Luxury and pomp of prelates
8. Fixed Stars	Apostles	Faith, Hope, Love	Unworthy popes
9. Primum Mobile	Angels		Popular preachers
10. Empyrean		[Beatific Vision]	Rejection of Henry VII

330

The Correspondences (Concluded)

Planets, Heavens	Angels	Angelic function	Hierarchies	Earthly Representatives
1. Moon	Angels	Messengers to individuals		
2. Mercury	Archangels	Messengers to nations	Purifying	Deacons
3. Venus	Principalities	Guides of princes		
4. Sun	Powers	Subject to God		
5. Mars	Virtues	Divine motion	Illuminating	Priests
6. Jupiter	Dominations	Dominion		
7. Saturn	Thrones	Stability		
8. Fixed Stars	Cherubim	Knowledge	Perfecting	Bishops
9. Primum Mobile	Seraphim	Love		
10. Empyrean				

CANTO I

The Rise Upward

After suggesting the majestic subject of the Paradiso, *that is, the splendor of the divine idea and its realization in Heaven, Dante invokes Apollo (God) and the Muses (his own talents), the "two peaks" of Parnassus. He hopes he may sing as Apollo did in the contest with Marsyas, who was flayed for his presumption in challenging the god.*

The glory of Him who moves all
    penetrates the universe, and is reflected
    in one place more, in another less.

I have been to the heaven which receives most of His light
    and seen things which one who descends
    has neither power nor knowledge to relate,

for, drawing near to its desire,
    our intellect is lost in such depths
    that memory cannot follow it.

Nevertheless, whatever my mind
    could treasure of the holy kingdom
    will now be the subject of my song.   12

O good Apollo, for the last task
    make me such a vessel of thy worth
    as the beloved laurel crown requires.

Until now one peak of Parnassus
    has been enough for me, but this time
    with both I must enter the arena which remains.

Enter my breast and breathe as thou didst
    when thou drewest Marsyas
    from the sheath of his body.

O divine Power, if Thou lendest Thyself to me,
    so that I may reveal even the shadow
    of the blessed realm imprinted on my mind,   24

Thou shalt see me come to Thy beloved tree [the laurel]
    and crown myself with those leaves
    of which Thou and my subject will make me worthy.

So rarely, Father, are they gathered
    for triumph of Caesar or of poet,—
    the fault and shame of human will—

that the Peneian leaf [the laurel] should bring joy
    to the Delphic deity [Apollo]
    when any is eager for it.

A great flame may follow a little spark;
    perhaps after me, with a better voice,
    prayers will be made to which Cyrrha [Apollo] may
        respond.   36

*The various circles of the heavens, the celestial equator, the ecliptic,
and the colure of the equinoxes, all of which cross the horizon, are
most favorably related on March 21. It is now Wednesday noon, April
13, 1300, not far from this ideal moment, and the sun is still in Aries.*

*Dante rises swiftly from the Garden of Eden, passing through the
sphere of fire which surrounds that of the air. By gazing at Beatrice he
transcends his material self, his humanity.*

The lamp of the world [the sun] rises for mortals
    by various paths, but on that
    which joins four circles with three crosses

it rises on its best course and is conjoined
    with its most propitious star, and tempers and seals
    the world's wax most perfectly.

Such a course had made morning there [in Eden]
    and evening here, and that hemisphere [at noon]
    was all aglow and ours dark

when I saw Beatrice turned to the left
    and gazing upon the sun:
    an eagle never looked at it so intently!   48

And, as a reflected ray
    is wont to rise upward,
    like a pilgrim wishing to return,

so her attitude, imaged in my mind,
    was copied by me, and I fixed my eyes
    on the sun, in a manner unknown here.

Much is possible to our faculties

in the place [Eden] made for the human race
   not granted to us on earth.

I did not endure the sight long
   before I noticed a sparkling [the sphere of fire]
   like molten iron coming from a furnace.   60

Suddenly day seemed joined to day,
   as if He who had power to do so
   had adorned the heaven with another sun.

Beatrice remained with her eyes
   fixed on the eternal revolutions,
   and I turned mine, removed from above, on her.

While gazing at her, I became [transformed] like **Glaucus**
   who tasted the herb which made him,
   in the sea, a companion of the gods.

"Transhumanizing" cannot be expressed in words;
   therefore, let the example suffice those
   for whom Grace reserves this experience.   72

If I were only that part of myself [the soul]
   created last, Thou alone, O Love, knowest,
   Thou that didst lift me with Thy light!

When the revolving [of the heavens] Thou makest eternal
   through desire made me attentive to it
   amid the harmony [of the spheres] Thou didst modulate,

so much of the sky seemed lit up
   by the flames of the sun that never rivers
   or rain ever made so large a lake.

The strangeness of the sound
   and the great light gave me a wish
   never before felt so keenly to know their cause;   84

whereupon she, who saw me as I see myself,
   to quiet my disturbed mind,
   spoke before I asked, and began,

"You become dull through false assumptions,
   so that you do not see
   what you would if you threw them off.

You are not on earth as you believe;

a thunderbolt never fled down from its home
as fast as you are going up to yours."

If I was freed of my first doubt
by these brief words, spoken with a smile,
I was caught more firmly in another.   96

and I said, "Already I was contented
concerning one doubt; but now I wonder
how I can rise through these light bodies."

Then, after a sigh of pity,
she looked at me with that expression
a mother has for a delirious child.

Beatrice explains that all things have certain characteristics or instincts
which enable them to carry out the divine plan as, for example, that
of fire to rise. Likewise men have an instinct that impels them to soar
to Heaven, their true home, although this may be conditioned or
diverted from its goal, just as fire in lightning sometimes descends.
Since all hindrance has been removed, Dante's rise is no more mar-
velous than that water should flow down the side of a mountain.

[She began, "All things have order
in them and this is the Form
which makes the universe similar to God.

In it the exalted creatures see the imprint
of the Eternal Power, the end
for which the rule [order] was created.   108

To the order of which I speak
all natures are obedient, by diverse lots,
as more or less close to their source.

Thus they move to diverse ports
over the great sea of being,
and each with an instinct to lead it on.

This moves the fire upward toward the moon,
this is the motive force in mortal hearts,
this holds together and unites the earth.

Nor do the arrows of this bow
strike only creatures without intelligence,
but also those with understanding and love.   120

The Providence which ordains this
makes serene the heaven [the Empyrean] within which

turns the one [the Primum Mobile] that moves with
    greatest speed.
And now toward it, as to a goal decreed,
    the power of that bow is carrying us
    which aims its shots at a joyful mark.
It is true that, as the form, many times,
    does not realize the intentions of the artisan
    (since the material is slow to respond),
so the creatures thus impelled
    sometimes deviate from their course,
    since they have that power;   132
and as the fire in a cloud [lightning]
    is seen to fall, so the creature's first impetus,
    diverted by false pleasure, brings it to the ground.
If I judge correctly, you should not wonder more
    at our rising than at the falling of a stream
    from a high mountain to its base.
It would be a marvel if, unhindered,
    you should remain seated down below,
    as quietness would be in a living flame."
Then she turned her face again toward Heaven.]

CANTO II

The Heaven of the Moon

*Dante warns those who try to follow with little learning or attention
that they may get lost. Minerva (wisdom), Apollo (God), and the
Muses are showing the poet his way, just as the constellations of the
Big and Little Bears (Dippers) guide sailors on earth.*

*Dante wonders about the spots on the moon which, in Italian folklore,
represent Cain with a bundle of thorns.*

O you who, in a little boat,
    desirous of listening, follow my bark
    which, singing, sails on,

turn to see your shores again;
    do not venture on the deep, for perhaps,
    losing me, you would be lost.

The water on which I move has never been sailed;
    Minerva inspires, and Apollo leads me,
    and the nine Muses show me the Bears.

You other few who, in time, lifted your heads
    for the bread of angels [divine wisdom] on which
    we feed here below without being sated,   12

you can indeed entrust your vessel
    to the high seas, following in my wake
    ahead of the water that becomes smooth again.

Those glorious sailors [the Argonauts] who went to Colchis
    did not wonder as you will
    when they saw Jason become a plowman.

The inborn and perpetual thirst
    for the godlike kingdom carried us on
    almost as fast as a glance through the sky.

Beatrice gazed up and I on her;
    and perhaps in the time an arrow [of a crossbow] takes
    to hit, fly, and be loosened from the catch,   24

I saw myself in a place where something wondrous
    drew my sight to it; and she
    from whom my thoughts could not be hidden

turned toward me as joyous as beautiful.
    "With gratitude, direct your thought to God,"
    she said, "who has united us with the first star [the
        moon]."

It seemed to me that a cloud covered us,
    placid, thick, solid, and polished,
    like a diamond shining in the sun.

Within itself the everlasting pearl
    received us, as water does
    a ray of light, remaining undisturbed.   36

If I were a body (and here it is not conceivable
    how one dimension can support another,
    which must be if one solid enters another),

the desire should be increased
>to see that Essence in which one can observe
>how our nature and God are united.

Then will be seen what we accept through faith,
>not demonstrated, but obvious,
>like the axioms men assume.

I answered, "My lady, as devoutly as I can
>I thank Him who has removed me
>from the mortal world;   48

but tell me, what are the dark spots
>on this body which, on earth,
>make people tell fables about Cain?"

In a typically scholastic manner and with a refutation of contrary
views, Beatrice explains that some parts of the moon are less sensitive
to light than others, which accounts for the inequalities of that body
when viewed from below.

[She smiled a little, and then said,
>"If mortal opinion goes wrong
>when the key of sense does not unlock,

certainly the arrows of wonder
>should not pierce you now, since you see that reason,
>even following the senses, has short wings.

But tell me what you, by yourself, think of it."
>And I, "I believe that the differences up here
>are caused by matter rare or dense."   60

And she, "Certainly you will see your belief
>submerged in error if you listen carefully
>to the argument I will oppose to it.

The eighth sphere shows you
>many lights [stars] which are seen
>to be diverse in kind and in size.

If only rareness or density caused this difference
>a single virtue would be in all,
>more, less, or equally distributed.

Diverse powers [of stars] must result
>from inherent qualities, and all of these except one
>would be excluded by your reasoning.   72

Moreover, if rareness were the cause of that darkness

you ask about, either the planet
     would be deficient in its matter [have holes]
or that matter would be variously distributed
     like fat and lean [not extending through] and
          would be
     like a book with different pages.
The first situation, if true, would be manifest
     in the eclipse of the sun,
     through light shining through the rare matter.
This is not so; therefore the other possibility
     is to be seen, and if it happens that I refute it,
     your opinion will be proved false.   84
If this rarity does not go through,
     there must be a limit beyond which
     its contrary [density] does not let it pass,
and from it the rays would be reflected,
     like color from the back
     of a leaded glass [mirror].
Now you may say that the rays
     show themselves darker in some places
     from being reflected from farther back.
From this objection an experiment
     (the source of the stream of science)
     can free you, if you try it.   96
Take three mirrors and place two
     equally distant from you, and let a third
     farther removed be between the other two.
Turning to them, let a light be placed
     behind your back which the three
     will reflect back toward you.
Although in size the more distant one
     will not be so great, you will see
     that it is equally bright.
Now, as under a shower of warm sunlight
     the ground under snow is left bare,
     stripped of the coldness and color it had,   108
thus you, brought to a like condition,
     I wish to cover with so bright a light
     that it will glitter in your eyes.
Within the heaven of divine peace [the Empyrean]

a body [the *Primum Mobile*] revolves,
    in whose power is all that it envelops.
The next [the starry] heaven, which has so many sights,
    distributes existence in various forms
    different from it, but contained in it.
The other revolutions spread these powers
    with various differences
    according to their own purposes and sowing.   120
These organs of the world operate, as you see now,
    from grade to grade [heaven to heaven], receiving
    from above, and acting on what is beneath.
Now notice how I proceed toward the truth
    you desire, so that afterward
    you may cross the ford alone.
The movement and power of the holy revolutions
    must derive from the blessed movers [angels]
    as the hammer's art from the smith;
and the [starry] heaven, embellished with so many lights,
    takes its stamp from the deep minds [of the Cherubim]
    that turn it and make of it their seal.   132
And, as the soul within your clay
    diffuses itself through differing members
    suited for different functions,
so the intelligence [of the Cherubim]
    spreads its goodness multiplied by the stars,
    itself revolving on [maintaining] its unity.
Different powers make different mixtures
    with the precious [heavenly] bodies they quicken
    and to which they are bound, like life in you.
Because of the happy nature from which it derives,
    the mixed power shines through bodies
    [variously] like joy in a living eye.   144
From this comes the difference in light,
    not from rarity or density; this is
    the formal principle which produces light and dark,
according to [varying] goodness."]

CANTO III

Piccarda and the Empress Constance

In the lowest heaven, that of the moon, a slow-moving, changeable planet within the shadow of the earth, hardly more brilliant with divine light than a pearl, we find the inconstant nuns, their earthly images faintly visible. They serve as examples of the lowest degree of potential beatitude, and represent, perhaps, all weak and inconstant people. Among them are Piccarda, the sister of Dante's friend, Forese Donati, and the great Empress Constance, the two now equal in their rank.

That sun which first had warmed my breast with love
    had unveiled, by proving and refuting,
    the fair face of truth to me

and, to confess myself corrected
    and assured, as was fitting,
    I raised my head to speak,

but a sight attracted
    my attention so closely
    that I forgot to make my confession.

As from transparent and polished glass
    or from clear and quiet water,
    not so deep that the bottom is lost to sight,   12

the outlines of our faces come back
    so faintly that a pearl on a white forehead
    appears as clearly to our eyes,

so I saw several faces ready to speak,
    which led me into the opposite error from that
    which kindled love between the man [Narcissus] and
        the spring;

for, as I became aware of them,
    thinking that the countenances were mirrored,
    I turned to see whose they were

and perceived nothing. Then I looked ahead
    at the light of my sweet guide
    whose holy eyes glowed as she smiled.   24

"Do not marvel if I am amused," she said,
    "at your childish thought,
    since it still does not trust the truth

but turns you as usual toward delusions.
    What you saw are true substances [souls],
    relegated here through failure to keep their vows;

therefore, speak to them, and hear, and believe,
    since the light of the Truth which requites them
    does not let them turn from Itself."

I faced the shade which seemed
    most desirous of speaking, and began
    like one embarrassed by excessive desire,   36

"O well-created spirit, enjoying the rays
    of eternal life, the sweetness of which,
    untasted, can never be understood,

it would be gracious if you contented me
    with your name and your condition."
    Then she, ready and with smiling eyes,

"Our charity does not close the door
    on just wishes, any more than the Love
    which wants all Its court to resemble Itself.

In this world I was a virgin sister,
    and if your memory searches well
    my greater beauty will not hide me from you.   48

You will see that I am Piccarda,
    placed here with these others
    and blessed in the sphere that moves slowest.

Our feelings which are enflamed
    only by the pleasure of the Holy Spirit rejoice
    in being formed according to His plan.

This fate which seems so low
    is given us because we neglected our vows,
    left unfulfilled in some respect."

Then I to her, "In your countenances
    something divine is shining
    which makes you different from before;   60

therefore I was not quick to recall you,
    but what you say helps me now
    so that remembering is easier.

But tell me, while happy here,
    do you desire a higher place
    to see more or to make yourselves dearer?"

With those other spirits she smiled a little,
    then answered me so joyously
    that she seemed to burn in the first flame of love.

"My brother, a charity quiets our wills
    and makes us wish only for what we have,
    and we thirst for nothing else.   72

If we wanted to be higher
    our desires would be discordant
    with the will of Him who places us here,

which, as you will see, cannot happen
    in these spheres if loving is a necessity here
    and if you consider what love implies.

Rather it is essential in this blessed state
    to remain within the divine will
    so that ours can be one with it.

Thus wherever we may be from threshold to threshold
    throughout this kingdom pleases all the realm
    as it does the King who bends our wills to His.   84

And His will is our peace;
    it is that sea to which wholly moves
    what He and Nature create."

I understood then how everywhere in Heaven
    is Paradise, although the grace of the Supreme Good
    does not descend equally on all.

But, as it happens that one food satisfies
    while the craving for another remains,
    which we ask for as we refuse the first,

so by act and word I enquired
 if I might learn what the web [vow] was
 that she had not brought to completion.   96

"A perfect life and great merit place in a higher heaven
 a lady [St. Clare] under whose rule," she said,
 "in your world the veil and dress are worn

so that until death the wearers may wake and sleep
 with that Spouse who accepts every vow
 which love conforms to His pleasure.

To follow her, while a girl, I fled from the world
 and dressed myself in her gown,
 and pledged myself to the ways of her order.

*Both Piccarda and Constance were taken by force from their con-
vents and married against their will. Lethe, however, has effaced the
memory of their submission.*

Afterward men more used to evil than to good
 tore me away from the sweet cloister;
 and God knows what my life then became;   108

and this other splendor which shows itself
 on my right, and which glows
 with all the light of our sphere

applies what I say to herself.
 She also was a sister, and likewise
 the shadow of the sacred veil was taken from her.

But after she had been led back to the world
 against her will and good custom,
 the veil was never loosened from her heart.

This is the light of the great Constance
 who from the second blast of Swabia [Henry VI]
 conceived the third and last power [Frederick II]." 120

Thus she spoke to me; then began to sing *Ave Maria*
 and while singing vanished
 like a heavy body in deep water.

My eyes followed her as far as they could,
 and, when they had lost her,
 turned to the goal of greater longing,

attentive to Beatrice alone
    who flashed so brightly that at first
    my eyes could not endure the light,
and this made me slower in my questioning.

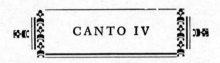

CANTO IV

The Location of the Souls—The Absolute and Conditioned Will

*In the opening lines Dante tells how two questions equally demanded
an answer and left him perplexed. He wonders how Piccarda and
Constance, forced to break their vows, could incur less merit, and
how souls can appear in the various heavens. Beatrice explains that
the true home of all souls is the Empyrean, the tenth and final heaven.
They reflect themselves into the lower spheres merely to illustrate the
degree of beatitude they possess, a beatitude absolute in each case, but
varying between individuals according to unequal potentialities. Then
Beatrice refutes the Platonic view that the soul returns to the star
from which it came, and taking up Dante's first question explains the
difference between the absolute and the conditioned will. The ab-
solute will of Piccarda and Constance was to maintain their vows,
and they might have resisted passively even to the point of death.
They allowed their wills, however, to be modified by the situation into
which they were forced.*

[Between two foods equally distant
    and equally attractive, a free man
    would die of hunger before putting teeth in either.
Thus a lamb would stand, torn by equal fears,
    between the cravings of two fierce wolves;
    thus a dog would remain between two does.
Therefore, if I was silent, I neither reproach
    nor commend myself, since that was necessary,
    torn as I was equally by my doubts.

I kept silent, but my desire was painted
    in my face, and my questions likewise,
    clearer than if put forth in words.   12
Thus Beatrice acted as Daniel did
    in freeing Nebuchadnezzar from the wrath
    that had made him unjustly cruel,
and said, "I see clearly
    how your desires pull you
    so that they bind you and are not expressed.
You reason, 'If good will remains,
    how can another's violence
    diminish the measure of merit?'
The other doubt is caused
    by the souls' apparent return to the stars
    according to Plato's doctrine.   24
These are the questions which equally impel your will;
    wherefore I will treat first
    the one that has most bitterness [heresy] in it.
Of the Seraphim the one
    who lives deepest in God, Moses, Samuel,
    and either John—not even Mary, I say—
have their seats in any other heaven
    than those spirits who just now appeared,
    nor have they more or fewer years for their being;
but all make the first [highest] heaven beautiful
    and live with differing happiness
    through feeling more or less the eternal breath.   36
They show themselves here not because this sphere
    is allotted to them, but to signify
    the degree of heavenly happiness least exalted.
By this means one must speak to your minds,
    since only from sense impressions do you grasp
    what afterward can be understood more abstractly.
Because of this the Scriptures condescend
    to your capacity and attribute hands
    and feet to God while meaning something else;
and Holy Church represents Gabriel
    and Michael with human faces
    and the other [Raphael] by whom Tobit was healed.   48
What [Plato's] Timaeus argues concerning the soul

is not similar to what is seen here
if he feels as he speaks [not allegorically].
He said that the soul returns to its star,
    believing the spirit to have been taken thence
    when nature gave it [to the body] as a form.
But perhaps his meaning is different
    from his words, and may have
    a sense not to be derided.
If he implies that the honor or blame
    for influence [on human souls] belongs to these
        spheres
    perhaps the bow [of his speech] hits some truth.   60
This principle [of stellar influence], badly understood,
    misled once almost all the world
    which spoke of Jove, Mercury, and Mars.
The other doubt which moves you
    has less poison, since its malice
    could not lead you away from me.
For our justice to appear unjust
    in mortal eyes is a proof
    of faith, not of heresy.
But in order that your understanding
    may penetrate to this truth
    as you wish, I will satisfy you.   72
If violence occurs when the sufferer
    contributes nothing to what forces him,
    these souls are still not excused;
for will, unless concurring, cannot be crushed,
    but acts like a [rising] flame even if violence
    turns it from its path a thousand times;
because if it gives in, little or much,
    it abets the violence, and these women did this,
    since they were able to return to the holy place [convent].
If their will had remained intact,
    like that which held St. Lawrence on the gridiron
    and made Mucius cruel to his own hand,   84
it would have put them back on the road
    over which they came, as soon as they were free;
    but such sound will is extremely rare.
Through these words, if you have understood them

as you should, the argument
which kept bothering you is settled.
But now another pass confronts your eyes,
such that alone you would not issue from it,
because you would be exhausted first.
I have certainly established in your mind
that a holy soul would not lie,
since it is always close to the first truth;   96
yet you were able to hear from Piccarda
that Constance did keep her affection for the veil,
so that she seems here to contradict me.
Many times, indeed, my brother, it has happened
that, to avoid peril, things have been done
unwillingly that were not fitting,
as Alcmaeon, urged by his father,
killed his own mother, so that
to comply with filial duty, he became pitiless.
At this point I wish you to believe
that violence can be mixed with the will,
so that the offenses cannot be excused.   108
The absolute will does not commit the evil
except insofar as it fears
by withdrawing to incur greater pain.
Therefore, when Piccarda said this,
she referred to the absolute will, and I
to the other, so that we both speak the truth."
Such was the rippling of the holy stream
that came from the source [Revelation] from which
all truth derives, and quieted both my longings.]

"O beloved of the first Lover, O divine one!"
I said then, "you whose speech overwhelms me
and warms me so that I live more and more,   120
my affection has not sufficient power
to return grace for grace,
but may He who sees, and can, respond for me.
I see clearly how our mind
is never satisfied unless the truth
that includes all illumines it.
Therein it rests, like a beast in its den

when it reaches it, and it can—
otherwise every desire would be in vain.

Therefore at the foot of the truth,
like a sprout, questioning grows, which pushes us on
from peak to peak toward the summit.   132

This invites me, this gives me assurance
to ask you, my lady, with reverence,
whenever something is obscure.

I wish to know if one can make up
for unfulfilled vows with other offerings,
so as not to appear deficient on your scales."

Beatrice looked at me with eyes so divine,
so full of the light of love,
that the power of my eyes was put to flight,

and I became as lost, with downcast gaze.

CANTO V

Compensation for Broken Vows—
The Heaven of Mercury

Beatrice answers Dante's question concerning compensation for broken
vows. Adequate repayment is not possible for the promise itself, since
the vow implies a surrender of free will, man's most precious posses-
sion; but, with church authorization, it is possible to substitute some-
thing for the thing promised, provided what is offered is of greater
value. In the case of monastic vows, nothing can be as precious as
what was sacrificed, and no compensation or remission is possible.

["If I glow in the warmth of love
beyond anything seen on earth,
so that I vanquish the power of your eyes,

do not marvel, for that comes

from perfect vision which turns one
    to the good it perceives.
I see well how the eternal light
    which, merely seen, always kindles love,
    already shines in your mind,
and if anything else seduces your affection,
    it is only because some vestige of this light,
    badly understood, shines in it.   12
You wish to know whether with another service
    one can offer enough for a broken vow
    to save a soul from reproach."
Thus Beatrice began this chant
    and, as one who does not interrupt a speech,
    continued her holy reasoning:
"The greatest gift that God made
    through his liberality in creating
    and most conformable to His goodness
was free will, with which
    intelligent creatures, all and severally,
    were and are alone endowed.   24
Now you will see, if you infer correctly,
    the great value of the vow, if made
    so that God consents when you pledge yourself.
For, in establishing a pact between man and God,
    a sacrifice is made of this treasure
    I speak of, and by its own act.
Therefore, what can one offer as compensation?
    To believe you can use well what you have offered [and
        taken back]
    is to wish to do good with ill-gotten gains.
You are now assured as to the main point;
    but, since Holy Church makes dispensations
    which seem to contradict the truth I have revealed,
you must still sit a while at the table,   36
    since the hard food you have eaten
    demands help for its digestion.
Open your mind to what I make clear,
    and remember it, for to understand
    without retaining does not lead to knowledge.
Two things relate to the essence

of this sacrifice: one is
what is promised, the other the agreement.
This last is never canceled
except through observance, and concerning this
the remarks above are precise.   48
Therefore the Hebrews were obliged
to make offerings, as you know,
although what was offered could be changed.
The matter involved may be such
that no offense is done
when something else is substituted.
But let no one shift the load on his shoulders
by himself, without the turning
of the white and yellow keys [ecclesiastical permission].
And know that every change is vain
unless the thing given up is contained
in that assumed as four in six.   60
Therefore anything that weighs so much
that it turns every scale
cannot be replaced.
Let mortals not take vows lightly;
be loyal and not squint-eyed [unreasonable],
as was Jephthah, who, in his first vow
should have said, 'I did wrong,'
rather than doing worse by keeping it.
Likewise the Greeks' Grand Duke [Agamemnon] was
        stupid,
who made Iphigenia weep for her beautiful face,
and the wise and foolish sorry for her
on hearing of such a sacrifice.   72
Christians, be slower to move;
do not be like a feather in the wind,
and do not believe that every water cleans.
You have the Old and New Testaments
and the shepherd of the Church to guide you;
let this suffice for your salvation.
If evil greed proclaims something else,
be men, not senseless sheep,
lest the Jew [non-Christian] among you scoff.
Do not act like the lamb that leaves

its mother's milk, and, simple and wanton,
    as a pastime, fights against itself.]   84

Beatrice and Dante now enter the heaven of Mercury. The rise from
sphere to sphere is marked, here as elsewhere, by an increase in
Beatrice's light.

Thus Beatrice spoke to me, even as I write.
    Then she turned again full of desire
    to that part [the Empyrean] where the world is most alive.

Her quiet and altered countenance
    imposed silence on my eager mind
    which already had new questions before it.

And as an arrow which hits the target
    before the cord is still,
    so we moved into the second realm.

Here I saw my lady so happy
    as she placed herself in the light of that heaven
    that the planet itself became brighter;   96

and if the star changed and smiled,
    what did I do, who even by nature
    am impressionable in every way?

As in a pond, still and clear,
    the fish come to what is thrown to them
    if they judge it to be their food,

so I saw more than a thousand splendors
    draw toward us, and each was heard to say,
    "Behold! here is one who will increase our love!"

And as each came toward us
    its spirit was seen to be full of joy
    by the bright flash that came from it.   108

Think, Reader, if the story begun here
    did not continue, what desire
    you would have to know more,

and by yourself you will understand how eager I was
    to hear from these about their condition
    when they appeared before my eyes.

"O well-born one, you to whom grace permits

seeing the thrones of the eternal triumph
    before abandoning the warfare of life,

by the light which spreads through all of Heaven
    we are illuminated; therefore if you want
    to be enlightened by us, satisfy yourself at your pleasure." 120

Thus one of those devout spirits spoke to me,
    and Beatrice said, "Speak, speak securely,
    and believe them as if they were gods."

"I see how you nest in your own light
    and display it through your eyes
    because they shine as you smile,

but I do not know who you are, or why,
    worthy soul, you have the grade of the sphere
    which is veiled to mortals by the rays of another [the
        sun]."

This I said, addressing the light
    which first had spoken to me, whereupon
    it became much brighter than it was.   132

As the sun hides itself with too much light
    when the heat has consumed
    the tempering of thick vapors,

so, through greater joy, the holy figure
    hid itself from me within its rays,
    and then, quite concealed, it gave the answer

which the following canto sings.

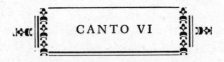

CANTO VI

The Song of Justinian

Justinian, the soul to whom Dante has just spoken, had directed the }
great codification of the Roman laws.

"After Constantine turned the [Roman] eagle eastward,

opposite to the course of the heavens which it had
    followed
behind him [Aeneas] who took Lavinia as a wife,

for twice a hundred years and longer
    the bird of God stayed on the edge of Europe [at
      Byzantium]
    near the mountains [at Troy] from which it came,

and in the shadow of the sacred feathers
    governed the world there from hand to hand
    until, changing, it came into mine.

I was Caesar and am Justinian
    who, through the will of the Holy Spirit,
    removed from the laws what was superfluous and vain.   12

Before I became intent on this work
    I believed there was only one nature in Christ
    and was content in such a faith,

but the blessed Agapetus, who then
    was the supreme pastor, directed me
    with his words to the true faith.

I believed him, and what his doctrine proclaimed
    I see now as clearly as you see [the axiom]
    that contradictory statements contain the false and true.

As soon as my steps conformed with the Church,
    it pleased God, of His grace, to inspire me
    for the great work [the code] to which I was devoted,   24

and I entrusted my arms to my Belisarius
    whom the heavens favored
    as a sign that I should rest.

Now to your first question my answer ends,
    but its implications [concerning the eagle]
    oblige me to add a supplement,

so that you may see with how little reason
    both those [the Ghibellines] who take the holy ensign
    for themselves, and their opponents [the Guelfs] move
      against it.

Justinian now tells of the achievements of the Roman eagle, beginning

with the legendary wars and continuing down to the attempted
revival of the Empire under Charlemagne.

[You see what virtue has made the eagle worthy
    of reverence, beginning from the time
    when Pallas died to give it a kingdom.   36
You know that it dwelt in Alba
    for three hundred years and more until, finally,
    the three [Curiatii] fought against the three [Horatii]
        for it.
You know what it did from the rape of the Sabine women
    down to the woe of Lucretia, under seven kings
    who conquered the neighboring peoples.
You know what it did, borne by the illustrious Romans
    against Brennus, against Pyrrhus,
    and against the other princes and their confederates,
whereby Torquatus and Quinctius [Cincinnatus]
    (named for his neglected locks), the Decii and Fabii
    had the fame which I willingly preserve.   48
It crushed the pride of the Arabs who,
    following Hannibal, crossed the Alpine rocks
    from which you, O Po, descend.
Under it Scipio and Pompey as youths triumphed.
    and it seemed fierce to that hill [of Fiesole]
    under which you were born.
Then near the time when the heavens strove
    to bring the world to their own peace.
    Caesar, by the will of Rome, took it,
and what it did from the Var to the Rhine,
    the Isère, the Loire, and the Seine witnessed,
    and every valley by which the Rhone is filled.   60
What it accomplished [under Caesar] when it issued from
        Ravenna
    and crossed the Rubicon was of such swiftness
    that neither tongue nor pen could follow it.
Toward Spain it turned its host,
    then toward Durazzo, and struck Pharsalia,
    so that on the warm Nile the pain was felt.
Antandros and the Simois from which it came [with Aeneas]
    saw it again, and the place where Hector lies,
    and unluckily for Ptolemy it shook itself.

Then it descended flashing on Juba [in Numidia]
    and turned to the West
    where it heard the Pompeian trumpet.   72
What it did with its following keeper [Augustus],
    Brutus and Cassius bark out in Hell;
    and it made Modena and Perugia wretched.
Sad Cleopatra still weeps because of it
    who, fleeing from it, took
    from an asp sudden and bitter death.
With Augustus it reached the Red Sea;
    with him it put the world in such peace
    that the Temple of Janus [open in time of war] was
        locked.
But what the ensign which makes me speak
    had done before and was yet to do
    in the mortal world subject to it   84
becomes little and obscure when one sees it
    with clear eyes and pure affection
    in the hands of the third Caesar [Tiberius].
For the Living Justice that inspires me
    granted it, in the hands of him I mention,
    the glory of doing vengeance [on Christ] for Its
        wrath.
Now marvel here at what I unfold to you:
    afterward, with Titus, it ran to take vengeance
    for the vengeance against the ancient sin [of Eve].
And when the Lombard teeth bit
    into Holy Church, Charlemagne,
    conquering under its wings, came to her aid.   96
Now you can judge those [Guelfs and Ghibellines]
    whom I accused above and their misdeeds
    which are the cause of all your evils.
One opposes to the universal ensign the yellow lilies [of
        Anjou],
    and the other appropriates it to a party,
    so that it is hard to see who is most at fault.
Let the Ghibellines carry on their business
    under another flag, for the eagle follows badly
    those who separate Justice from it.
And let not this new Charles [II of Apulia] crush it

with his Guelfs, but let him fear its claws
    which have flayed bigger lions.   108
Many times have sons wept for the sins
    of their fathers, and let no one believe
    that God will change his standards for those lilies.]

*In the small, variable planet of Mercury, within the shadow of the
earth and eclipsed by the light of the sun, are souls whose activity
was due to ambition for earthly fame rather than to love for God, and
whose spiritual vision is therefore inferior.*

*Among the shades in this heaven is a certain Romeo whose legend
Dante relates. Here as elsewhere in Heaven we find the great and
small as companions.*

This little star embellishes itself
    with good spirits who have been active
    so that honor and fame could follow them,

and when desires lean on that,
    thus deviating, the rays of true love
    must mount upward less eagerly.

But the proportioning of our reward
    to our merit, so that it is neither too large
    nor too small, is a part of our joy.   120

Hereby the living Justice
    makes our affections so sweet within us
    that they can never be turned toward iniquity.

On earth diverse voices make sweet music;
    so in our life within these wheels,
    different ranks form a sweet harmony.

And within the present pearl shines the light
    of Romeo whose fine and great work
    was so badly rewarded;

but the Provençals who strove against him
    have no cause to laugh, and that proves that he
    who repays good deeds with harm fares badly.   132

Four daughters Raimon Berenguer [of Provence] had,
    and each became a queen; that Romeo brought about,
    a man who came to him humble and as a pilgrim.

Then words of slander moved Raimon
    to demand a reckoning from the honest one
    who had given back seven and five for ten.

And he [Romeo] departed, poor and old,
    and if the world knew the heart he had,
    as he begged for his living bit by bit,

although it extols him much, it would praise still **more.**"

CANTO VII

The Redemption

Justinian, in whom a double light of natural intelligence and illuminating grace shines, moves off with the other changeable, "mercurial," spirits.

Dante wonders how "just vengeance" could be "justly avenged," but, as he raises his head to ask, he is overcome by the awe he had felt on earth even for the mortal Bice (an affectionate shortening of the name Beatrice). She relieves his embarrassment by stating the question for him.

Osanna,[1] *sanctus Deus sabaoth,*
    superillustrans claritate tua
    felices ignes horum malacoth!

Thus, revolving in his song,
    I saw this substance [Justinian] singing,
    in whom a double light shone.

Both it and others moved in their dance
    like rapid sparks veiling themselves
    from me by sudden distances.

---

[1] "Hail, holy God of hosts, doubly illumining with thy brightness the happy fires of these kingdoms."

I wondered, and said within myself,
   "O ask, ask her, ask my lady
   who quenches my thirst so sweetly!"   **12**

But that reverence which masters me completely,
   even for *Be* and *Ice,* again bowed down
   my head, as if I were drowsy.

Only a little while did Beatrice leave me thus,
   then she began to shine with such a smile
   as would make a man in fire happy:

"According to my infallible perception,
   how a just vengeance
   was justly punished has made you wonder;

but I will quickly free your mind
   and do you listen, for my words
   will make you a gift of great doctrine.   **24**

In answer to Dante's question, Beatrice takes up the problem of the Redemption. The vengeance of the Cross was just if we consider the human element in Christ; it was unjust if we consider who assumed that human nature. The two aspects of Christ explain, therefore, how a just vengeance can justly be avenged. Dante now wonders why this particular method for man's redemption was chosen.

Man, created directly by God, was immortal, free, and godlike. The sin of Adam destroyed his dignity wholly, which could be regained only by adequate penance. But man was incapable of sufficient penance by himself, since his presumption was infinite, and his power to compensate for it limited. Only God could enable man to redeem himself. And by showing both justice and mercy, God was more generous than if He had pardoned outright, since His act included both manifestations of His goodness.

Beatrice also clears up another matter. The angels and man were created directly by God and are therefore immortal. Likewise the elements, but the various forms and combinations of these elements are the work of Nature or the stars, a second cause, and therefore undergo transformations and decay. Since man's body as well as his soul was created directly by God, we can assume the resurrection of the flesh.

By not enduring, for his own good, a curb
    on his will, the man never born [Adam],
    by damning himself, damned all his descendants,
so that the human race lay sick down below
    for many centuries, in great error,
    until it pleased the Word of God to descend,
when, by the act of His eternal love,
    He united with Himself
    the nature estranged from its Maker.
Now direct your sight to what is said:
    this [human] nature, united with its Maker,
    when created, was pure and good,   36
but, through its own act, it was banished
    from Paradise, since it turned
    from the way of truth and from its life.
The penalty, therefore, which the cross offered,
    if measured by the nature assumed,
    never struck anyone so justly,
and none ever did such great wrong
    if we consider the Person who suffered
    and by whom that nature was assumed.
Thus from one act different results ensue;
    for the same death which shook the earth
    and opened Heaven pleased God and the Jews.   48
It should not be hard to understand
    any longer that a just vengeance
    was avenged later by a just court.
But I see your mind bound from thought to thought
    in a knot, the loosening of which
    it waits for eagerly.
You say, 'I discern clearly what I hear,
    but why God should choose
    this means for our redemption is hidden from me.'
This decree, my brother, lies buried
    to the eyes of everyone whose mind
    has not matured in the flames of love.   60
Still, since this mark is gazed at much
    and little is discerned,
    I will tell why such a way was most worthy.
The Divine Goodness which spurns all envy,

burning in Itself, so shines
    that It sends forth Its eternal beauty.
Whatever comes directly from It
    has no end, for when It has sealed,
    Its imprint cannot be removed.
What comes directly from It
    is wholly free, because not subject
    to the power of the new things [stars].   72
What is most conformed to It, therefore, pleases It most,
    for the holy ardor which shines on everything
    is brightest on what is most like Itself.
The human creature had all these advantages,
    and if one of them is lacking,
    he must fall from his nobility.
Only sin disqualifies him and makes him
    dissimilar to the Supreme Good,
    so that he is brightened little with Its light;
and he can never regain his dignity
    unless, with penance equal to his wicked pleasures,
    he makes up for the loss.   84
Your nature when it sinned wholly
    in its seed [Adam] was removed
    from this dignity as well as from Paradise.
Nor could man recover it,
    if you look closely, by any means
    except passing through one of these fords:
either God by his courtesy alone
    might have forgiven, or man by himself
    must have given satisfaction for his folly.
Look now into the abyss
    of the eternal counsel as far as you can,
    closely attentive to my speech.   96
Man with his limitations, afterward obedient,
    could never give satisfaction,
    through his inability to go down in humility
as far as he had risen in his presumption;
    and this is why man was prevented
    from compensating by himself.
Therefore it was necessary for God by His ways

to restore man to perfect life,
    I mean by one way [justice] or by both [justice and
        mercy].
But since a deed is more prized
    the more it displays of the goodness
    in the heart of the doer,   108
the Divine Goodness which puts Its stamp on the world
    was pleased to proceed by all His ways
    to lift you up, and, between the last night
and the first day, there has never been
    or will be so exalted and magnificent an act,
    either by one way or the other;
for, God was more generous to give Himself
    to make man able to redeem himself
    than if he had pardoned,
and all other ways would have been short
    of justice unless the Son of God
    humiliated Himself to become incarnate.   120
Now to fulfill well all your desires,
    I go back to explain a certain point
    so that you may see as I do.
You say, 'I see the water, I see the fire,
    the air, and the earth, and all their mixtures
    become corrupt and last only a short time.
And yet these things too were created,'
    so that if what I said were true
    they should be safe from corruption.
The angels, brother, and the perfect region
    in which you are, can be considered created
    as they are in their entire being,   132
but the elements you have named and the things
    made of them have received their form
    from a created power [a second cause].
The matter in them was created [directly],
    the forming power likewise
    in those stars which circle around them.
The rays and motion of the holy lights
    draw from the potential elements [of matter]
    the soul of every brute and of the plants.

But the Supreme Goodness breathes forth
    your life directly, and enamors it of Itself,
    so that ever after the soul desires It.   **144**
Hence you can infer from this
    your resurrection, if you consider
    how human flesh was made
when the first parents were formed."]

CANTO VIII

The Heaven of Venus

Venus, the heaven of divided love, is the last of those within the shadow of the earth. It has a second revolution, its "epicycle," in addition to the circling around the earth. In the same way, symbolically, the love of the souls here had an earthly as well as a heavenly center.

Dante is aware of his arrival in this heaven by the increased brightness of Beatrice.

The variations in the appearance of the souls here give a suggestion of the rapid and unpredictable movements of earthly love itself.

The world used to believe to its peril
    that the beautiful Cyprian goddess [Venus],
    turning in the third epicycle, radiated mad love.

Therefore the ancient people
    in their error not only did her the honor
    of sacrifices and of votive cries,

but revered Dione and Cupid,
    the former as her mother, the latter as her son
    who, they said, sat in Dido's lap;

and from her with whom I begin

they took the name of the star which woos the sun
    now from in front and now behind [as morning and
       evening star].   12

I did not notice my rising to it,
    but my lady who became more beautiful
    made me certain of being there.

And as a spark is seen in a flame
    or as one voice is distinguished from another
    if one holds its note and the other rises and falls,

so, in the light itself I saw other lamps
    move in a circle, more and less fast,
    in proportion, I believe, to their eternal vision [joy].

From a cold cloud a blast never descended so fast,
    whether visible as lightning or not,
    that would not appear slow or impeded   24

to one who had seen those divine lights
    come to us, leaving the dance previously begun
    among the lofty Seraphim.

And from within those who appeared in front
    "Hosanna" sounded so sweetly that never since
    have I been without desire to hear it again.

*The first soul to speak is that of a recent Charles Martel, whom Dante
knew personally. He points out how this heaven is moved by the
angels called "Principalities" whom Dante had addressed in the first
canzone of his* Convivio.

Then one came closer and began,
    "We are ready, all of us, for your pleasure,
    so that you may delight in us.

We turn equally in one circle and alike in our thirst,
    with the celestial Principalities
    to whom you in the world once said,   36

'You who, by intelligence, move the third heaven.'
    And we are so full of love that, to please you,
    a little pause will not be less sweet to us."

After my eyes had looked reverently

at my lady and she had contented them
and made them confident,

I turned to the light which had promised so much.
"Tell me who you were," were my words,
infused, as I spoke, with great affection.

And when I had said this how much larger
and brighter I saw it become
through the joy that was added to joy!   48

Thus changed it said to me, "The world below
held me only briefly; had that time been longer
much evil to occur would not happen.

My joy which radiates and envelops me
conceals me from you, so that I
am like a silkworm enclosed in its covering.

Much did you love me, and you had good reason,
for if I had been below longer I would have shown you
more than the leaves [i.e., the fruit] of my regard.

Charles tells of the power he had and would have had except for the "Sicilian Vespers," when the French were driven from Sicily. The mention of his brother brings up the problem of heredity. He states that in distributing talents Providence takes no account of family or rank. The variations in social or family needs demand differences in abilities: if inheritance were immediate and direct, all members of the same group would have the same characteristics, which Providence wisely prevents. Thus a generous father can produce an avaricious son. A recognition of this diversity should prevent trying to make a king of a born writer of sermons or directing into religion one born for a sword.

[That left bank bathed by the Rhone [Provence]
after it is joined by the Sorgue
awaited me in due time for its lord   60

and also that horn of Ausonia [Italy] which has
on its boundaries Bari, Gaeta, and Catona,
down from where the Tronto and the Verde empty
in the sea.

Already the crown of that land [Hungary]
which the Danube cuts after it has left
its German banks shone on my brow,

and beautiful Trinacria [Sicily]
>between Pachino and Peloro on the gulf
>which Eurus [the Sirocco] troubles most,
darkened not by Typhoeus, but by nascent sulphur,
>would still have awaited kings
>born of Charles and Rudolph through me,   72
if misrule, which always embitters
>subject peoples had not moved Palermo
>to cry out 'Let them die, die!'
and if my brother [Robert] had foreseen this
>he would already have avoided the greedy poverty
>of Catalonia, so that it would not hurt him.
For truly some provision must be made
>by him or others so that his bark,
>already laden, will not have an additional load.
His nature descending avaricious
>from a generous father would need such knighthood
>as would care little about hoarding money."   84
"Because I believe that the great joy
>your speech infuses in me, my lord,
>is seen by you in the Mind
where every good end has its beginning,
>it is more grateful to me, and I hold this dear also
>that you discern it by looking at God.
You have made me glad; but clear up for me
>(since by speaking you have made me doubt)
>how bitterness can come from sweet seed."
This I said to him, and he, "If I can show you the truth
>about what you ask, you will then face it,
>as now it is behind your back [not seen].   96
The good which revolves and satisfies
>all the kingdom you ascend, makes its providence
>a virtue of these great bodies,
and not only are natures foreseen
>in the Mind which by Itself is perfect,
>but their welfare as well.
Thus all the arrows shot by this bow [providence]
>are destined to fall at their allotted time
>like a thing directed to its mark.
If that were not so, the heavens in which you advance

would produce their effects in such a way
that they would not be works of [divine] art, but dis-
orders [accidents], 108
and that cannot be, if the intelligences
which move these stars are not defective
and the Prime Intelligence at fault for their imperfection.
Do you wish this truth to be cleared up further?"
"No, indeed," I answered, "because I see it is impossible
that nature should fall short in what is necessary."
Then he, "Now tell me, would it be worse for man
if he were not a social being on earth?"
"Yes," I answered, "and here I do not ask for a reason."
"And can that be, unless he lives below
diversely, for diverse duties?"
"No, if your master [Aristotle] writes well of this." 120
Having come to this point in his deduction,
the spirit concluded, "It is necessary then
that different aptitudes should exist in you,
so that one is born a Solon, another a Xerxes,
another a Melchisedech [a priest] and another
like him [Daedalus] who, flying through the air, lost
his son.
The celestial revolution which stamps
the wax of mortals carries on well its art,
but does not distinguish one family from another.
Thus it happens that Esau differs
from Jacob, and that Quirinus [Romulus] came
from so mean a father as to be attributed really to Mars. 132
A begotten nature would always
take the same course as its begetters
if Divine Providence did not prevent.
Now what was behind you is before you,
but to show my pleasure in seeing you,
I wish to provide you with a corollary.
Nature always succeeds badly
unless its fortune is suited to it,
like every seed out of its range,
and if the world below thought
of the foundation nature makes,
by following it, people would be better off; 144

but you direct into religion
    one born to bind on a sword,
    and make a king of a born writer of sermons;
thus it happens that your tracks leave the right road."]

CANTO IX

Cunizza, Folquet, and Rahab

Beautiful Clemence, after your [father] Charles
    had enlightened me, he told of the deception
    his race would experience,

but he said, "Be silent, and let the years pass."
    Therefore I can say only that just laments
    will follow the wrongs you have suffered.

And already the spirit of that holy light
    had turned to the Sun which requites it
    as to an all-sufficing good.

Oh, how deceived and impious creatures are
    who turn their hearts from such delight
    to look toward all that is vain!

Now behold! another of those splendors
    came toward me showing a desire
    to please me by its brightness.

Beatrice's eyes, fixed upon me
    as before, with sweet consent,
    reassured me in my wish.

"Oh happy spirit! satisfy my longing
    without delay, and give proof
    that my thought can be reflected in you!"

Thereupon the light which was unknown to me,
    from the depths in which it had been singing,
    spoke, like one happy to do good.

The new spirit, Cunizza da Romano, a sister of the cruel tyrant Azzolino, identifies herself. She does not complain of the influence of Venus which determined her fate since, like the others, she is happy to be where she is and oblivious to some phases of her past life, known, however, to others. After pointing out Folquet of Marseilles, Cunizza outlines certain events of local Italian history.

Folquet, a former bishop of Toulouse, who had instigated some of the worst cruelties of the Albigensian Crusade (although his conscience now is clear) becomes brighter and, interpreting Dante's unspoken question, identifies himself.

["In that part of the depraved Italian land
    which lies between Rialto and the springs
    of the Brenta and of the Piave,
a hill rises not very high
    from which once descended a torch [Azzolino]
    which devastated the country.
He and I came from the same root;
    my name was Cunizza, and I shine here
    because the light of this star dominated me.
Yet in my heart I accept with joy
    the cause of my fate, and am not distressed,
    which would seem strange to the crowd [who knew me].   36
The dear and shining gem of this heaven
    that is closest to me had great fame,
    and before his honor dies
this centennial year [1300] will be repeated five times.
    See how a man must excel on earth
    to live a second life after his death.
The crowd which the Adige and the Tagliamento
    enclose today do not think of that
    nor for being beaten does it repent.
But soon Padua, because her people are so stubborn
    against duty, will stain in the swamp [with their blood]
    the water which bathes Vicenza.   48
And, where the Sile and Cagnano unite,
    one [Riccardo da Camino] rules and holds his head high
    for catching whom [to murder him] the net is already
        made.
And Feltro will weep also for the crime [betrayal of guests]

of its impious pastor, which will be so shameful
   that for a similar one nobody ever entered Malta [a
      prison].
Very large would be the vat
   to hold all the blood of Ferrara,
   and weary he who would weigh it ounce by ounce,
which this priest so courteous, will sacrifice
   to please his party. But such a present
   probably suits the manners of the country.   60
Above are mirrors [angels] you call Thrones
   which reflect God's justice for us,
   so that these remarks seem merited."
Now she was silent and appeared then
   to be thinking of something else
   as she returned to the round where she was before.
The other joy [Folquet], already noted
   as a precious thing, appeared to me
   like a fine ruby on which the sun is shining.
Up there brightness comes from pleasure
   as laughter does here, but in Hell
   the shades darken outwardly as their minds are sad.   72
"God sees all and your vision is in Him,
   blessed spirit," I said, "so that no desire
   can hide itself from you.
Therefore, why does your voice which delights heaven—
   together with the song of the angels [the Seraphim]
   that make a cowl for themselves
of six wings—not satisfy my desire?
   I should not wait for your question
   if I could see in you as you see in me."
"The greatest basin into which the water pours
   from that sea which garlands the earth,"
   his words began, "extends   84
between its varied shores to the west
   so far [90 degrees] that it makes a meridian
   where first it is a horizon.
I was a dweller on the shore of that valley
   between the Ebro and the Macra which,
   after a short course, divides the Genoese from the
      Tuscans.

With almost the same sunset and sunrise [the same longitude]
    sit Buggea and the city [Marseilles] from which I came
    and which once [captured by Caesar] made its harbor
        warm with blood.
Those who knew my name called me Folquet,
    and this heaven is stamped by me
    as I was by it; for the daughter of Belus [Dido],   96
wronging both Sichaeus [her dead husband] and Creusa
        [Aeneas' wife],
    did not burn more than I
    as long as love befitted my locks,
nor that Rhodopeian [Phyllis] forsaken
    by Demophoön, nor Alcides [Hercules]
    when he took Iole to his heart.
Yet here we do not repent but smile,
    not at our sin, which we do not remember,
    but at the Power which ordained and foresaw.
Here we contemplate the art which adorns
    so great a work, and we discern the good
    whereby the world below turns to that above.]   108

*Folquet presents Rahab, the ex-harlot, now his companion and the first
and most typical representative of this heaven. Her story, related by
Joshua, tells how she saved certain Hebrew spies and for this service
was exempted from the curse on her city. Folquet reproaches the pope
and the clergy for abandoning the Holy Land to the infidels. Ecclesi-
astics are more interested, he says, in the canon law (the Decretals)
from which personal gain can be derived.*

But in order that your wishes
    conceived in this sphere may be borne away
    all fulfilled, I must proceed still further.

You wish to know who is in the splendor
    that is shining near me
    like a ray of sunlight on clear water.

Know that within it Rahab finds peace,
    and our order which she joined
    is characterized by her in the highest degree.

By this heaven, on which the shadow cast by your world

comes to a point, she was taken up
before any other soul of Christ's triumph.

It was fitting to leave her in some heaven
as a palm [trophy] of the great victory
won by lifting both palms [on the cross],

since she favored the first glory
of Joshua in the Holy Land
which concerns the pope's memory little.

Your city, planted by him [Lucifer]
who first turned his back on his Maker,
and whose envy is so lamented,

produces and spreads the accursed florin [coin]
which leads both sheep and lambs astray,
because it has made a wolf of the shepherd.   132

For this reason the Gospels and great doctors
are left aside, and only the Decretals are studied,
as is shown by their well-worn margins.

To this the pope and cardinals attend;
their thoughts do not extend to Nazareth
where Gabriel spread his wings.

But the Vatican and other chosen parts
of Rome which have been the cemetery
of the soldiery that followed Peter

will soon be free of this adultery [unholy union]."

CANTO X

The Heaven of the Sun

*The beginning lines of this canto are a prelude to the second division
of Paradise. The heavens now are beyond the peak of the earth's
shadow and symbolize a higher degree of spirituality and of bliss.*

By considering the great circles of the heavens, the equator and the

ecliptic, we can realize the marvel of Divine Providence which pro-
vides for an equal annual diffusion of light over the earth and for the
seasons. Through contemplation of the magnificence of the universe
we can gain some conception of its Maker.

Gazing at His Son with the Love
    which both eternally breathe forth,
    the first and ineffable Power

made everything that revolves through mind
    or through space and with such order
    that whoever thinks of it cannot fail to love Him.

Therefore, Reader, lift up your eyes
    with me to the lofty revolutions
    where one motion crosses another,

and there begin to contemplate the art
    of that Master who loves His creation so much
    that never are His eyes removed from it.   12

See how from there [the celestial equator] branches forth
    the oblique circle which bears the planets
    to satisfy the world that invokes them.

And if their course were not slanting
    many powers in heaven would be in vain,
    and almost all potency dead here below.

If the variation from a straight course were greater
    or less, much of the order of the world
    both above [the equator] and below would be imperfect.

Now, Reader, stay upon your bench
    thinking of what is touched upon
    if you would be happy before growing tired.   24

I have put food before you; now feed yourself,
    for the subject of which I have made myself a scribe
    turns all of my care to itself.

Dante now enters the heaven of the sun in which the light of the
great theologians or teachers is visible. This planet is in the constella-
tion of Aries, on the course which in spring makes it appear earlier
each day.

The greatest minister of Nature [the sun]

which imprints on the world the virtues of the heavens
   and with his light measures time for us,

conjoined with the region mentioned above,
   circled in the spiral in which
   he presents himself earlier from day to day.

And I was with him, but I was not aware
   of the ascent, any more than a man
   is conscious of a thought before it comes.   36

Beatrice [Revelation] is the one who leads us
   from good to better so suddenly
   that her action requires no time.

How bright must those souls have been,
   apparent, not by color but by brightness,
   in the planet into which I entered!

Though I call upon genius, art, or custom,
   I could not explain so that this could be imagined;
   but it can be believed, and may men long to see it!

And if our imaginations are inadequate
   for such great wonders, it is not surprising,
   for no eye ever saw light greater than the sun's.   48

Such, however, was the fourth household
   of the exalted Father who delights it
   by showing how He breathes and how He creates.

And Beatrice began, "Give thanks, give thanks
   to the Sun of the angels who, through grace,
   has lifted you to this visible sun."

No heart was ever so disposed to devotion
   and with more complete assent
   so ready to give itself up to God

as I became at these words,
   and all my love was so set on Him
   that it eclipsed Beatrice in oblivion.   60

This did not displease her; she smiled,
   so that the splendor of her laughing eyes divided
   among several things my mind before intent on one.

I saw many living and surpassing lights,

sweeter in voice than bright in aspect,
make a center of us and a crown of themselves.

Thus sometimes we see the daughter of Latona [the moon]
encircled, when the air is so damp
that it retains the thread [vapor] of which her belt is
made.

In the court of Heaven from which I return
are found many jewels so precious and beautiful
that they cannot [by description] be drawn from their
realm,   72

and among these was the song of those lights.
Whoever does not grow wings to fly there
may as well expect to have news from the dumb.

When, singing in this way, those blazing suns
had three times circled around us,
like stars near their fixed poles,

they seemed to be ladies not ending a dance
but silently waiting and listening
until they have heard the new measure.

And within one I noted this beginning:
"Since the ray of grace by which true love
is kindled and which then grows,   84

multiplied by loving, shines so clearly on you
that it leads you up these stairs
which no one descends without climbing again,

anyone who refused you the wine of his flask
to quench your thirst would be hindered,
like water when it fails to flow down to the sea.

You wish to know what plants provide
the flowers of this garland which all around gazes
at the fair lady who strengthens you for Heaven.

*The soul who addresses Dante, naming himself modestly after his
teacher, is that of St. Thomas Aquinas, the principal Catholic authority
on dogmatic theology.*

I was one of the lambs of the holy flock

that Dominic leads on the road
where they fatten well if they do not stray.

This one who is closest to me
on the right was my brother and master,
Albertus Magnus, and I am Thomas Aquinas.

If you wish to learn of all the rest
follow with your eyes behind my words
as I go over the blessed wreath.

The next flame comes from the smile of Gratian
who aided both courts [the religious and civil]
so that Paradise was pleased.

The next of those ornamenting our choir
was Peter [Lombard] who, like the poor widow,
offered his treasure [the *Sententiae*] to Holy Church.   108

The fifth and most beautiful light of all of us
comes from such love that the world below
is greedy to have news of it.

Within is the great mind [of Solomon] in which
was such profound wisdom that,
as truth is truth, an equal has never arisen.

Beside it see the light of the candle [Dionysius the Areopagite]
which in the flesh below saw deepest
into the ministry and nature of the angels.

In the next little light shines
that advocate of Christian times [Paulus Orosius],
of whose Latin Augustine made use.   120

Now if you are moving your eyes
from light to light, following my praises,
already you are eager for the eighth.

Within it rejoices, for seeing all good,
the holy soul [of Boethius] who, to those
who listened well, unmasked the deceitful world.

The body from which it was driven
lies below in Cieldauro [in Pavia],
and from martyrdom and exile it came to this peace.

See flaming, farther on, the ardent breath

of Isidore, of Bede, and of Richard [of St. Victor]
who, in contemplation, was more than a man.   132

The one from whom your eyes return to me
is the splendor of a spirit to whom,
in his grave thoughts, death seemed to come too slowly.

It is the eternal light of Siger who,
lecturing in the Vicus Straminum [in Paris],
demonstrated enviable truths."

Then as a horologe [clock] which calls us
at the hour when the Bride of God [the Church] rises
to sing matins to her Spouse that He may love her,

which pulls one part and thrusts another,
sounding "tin, tin" with such sweet notes
that the well-disposed spirit swells with love,   144

so I saw the glorious wheel move,
and voice answer voice in a harmony
and sweetness that cannot be known

except there, where joy becomes eternal.

CANTO XI

Eulogy of St. Francis

O senseless care of mortals! How false
are the arguments which make you
beat your wings toward the ground!

Some were following the law, some the priesthood,
others the aphorisms [of Hippocrates];
some tried to reign by force or fraud;

some took to plunder and some to civil business;
others, wrapped in the pleasures of the flesh,
were struggling, and some lived in idleness,

while I, freed from all of this,

in Heaven with Beatrice,
was thus gloriously received!

After each light had returned to the point
in the circle where it had been before,
it stopped, like a candle set in a candlestick;

and I heard that splendor
which first had addressed me speak,
smiling and becoming clearer.

"Just as I shine with the radiance
of the Eternal Life, so, looking into It
I learn the occasion of your thoughts.

You wonder, and wish to have explained
in such clear and explicit language
as will be plain to your understanding   24

my remarks above when I said
'Where they fatten well,' and 'An equal has not been
      born.'
Now here we must distinguish carefully.

The Providence that governs the world
with the wisdom by which every created [mortal] vision
is blinded before it reaches the bottom—

in order that [the Church], the bride of Him
who espoused her with loud cries and with His blood,
might go toward her beloved

secure in herself and more faithful to Him—
ordained two princes for her
who on this side and that would be her guides.   36

One [St. Francis] was all seraphic in his love,
the other [St. Dominic], through wisdom,
was a splendor of cherubic light.

I shall speak of one, although in praising him
the labors of both are included,
since they were directed to one end.

St. Thomas, a Dominican, now eulogizes St. Francis. In a long para-
phrase he describes the place where this leader was born, his marriage
with Poverty, his appearance at the papal court, the first and second
authorizations of his order, the attempt to convert the infidels, the

"stigmata" (traces of wounds like those borne by Christ), and then his
death and rise to Heaven from the arms of Poverty.

Between the Tupino and the stream which falls
    from the hill chosen by blessed Ubaldo [for a hermitage],
    a fertile slope descends from the high mountain

from which Perugia at Porta Sole feels cold and heat,
    and behind which Nocera and Gualdo weep
    because of their heavy yoke [the tyranny of Perugia].   48

On this slope where it breaks its steepness most,
    a sun [St. Francis] rose upon the world,
    as this one does from the Ganges.

Therefore let whoever speaks of this place
    not say 'Ascesi' [I have risen], which falls short,
    but 'Orient' [the dayspring], to name it rightly.

He was not yet far from his rising
    when the earth began to feel
    some comfort from his great virtue,

for, while still a youth, he opposed his father
    for the sake of a lady to whom as to Death
    no one unlocks the door,   60

and before his spiritual court,
    et coram patre,[1] he was united to her,
    and thereafter, from day to day, he loved her more.

She, deprived of her first husband [Christ],
    for eleven hundred years and more, until he came,
    remained obscure and despised and without a proposal.

Nor did it avail to hear that an emperor
    who frightened the entire world, found Amyclas with her
    undisturbed at the sound of his voice.

Nor did it profit her to be constant and unsubdued,
    so that when Mary remained below,
    she mounted with Christ upon the cross.   72

But that I may not proceed too obscurely,
    consider that in my diffuse speech
    Francis and Poverty were these lovers.

---

[1] "And before his father."

Love and marveling and sweet glances
    made their harmony and happy looks
    a source of holy thoughts,

so that the venerable Bernard
    first bared his feet, and ran after such peace,
    and while running seemed to himself too slow.

O unknown riches! O fruitful good!
    Egidius bared his feet, Sylvester his,
    following the groom, so pleasing was the bride!   84

Then that father and master went on
    with his lady, and with that little family
    girded already by the humble cord.

Nor did baseness of heart weigh down his brow
    for being the son of Pietro Bernardone [a tradesman],
    nor for appearing so marvelously despised.

But royally he declared to Innocent
    his stern resolve and from him
    received the first seal of his order.

After the poor folk [Franciscans] had multiplied behind him
    (whose marvelous life would be sung
    more fittingly in the glory of the heavens)   96

the holy will of this shepherd was adorned
    by the Holy Spirit, through Honorius,
    with a second crown [approval].

Then through thirst for martyrdom,
    in the presence of the proud Sultan,
    with others who followed him, he preached Christ;

but finding the people too unripe
    for conversion, not to stay in vain,
    he returned to the fruit of the Italian garden.

On the harsh rock between the Tiber and the Arno
    he received from Christ the last seal [the stigmata]
    which his limbs carried for two years.   108

When it pleased God who had chosen him
    for such good to draw him up to the reward
    which he merited by making himself lowly,

to his brothers, as to rightful heirs,

he recommended his most dear lady,
    and ordered them to love her faithfully.

And from her bosom [on the bare ground] his excellent soul
    wished to depart to return to its realm,
    and for his body wished for no other bier.

St. Dominic can be judged by this portrait of St. Francis. But the Dominicans, according to St. Thomas, have become greedy and violate the rule of the order; and this is the "going astray" to which he had referred.

Consider now how worthy his colleague was,
    who with him kept St. Peter's bark
    on a straight course on the deep sea;   120

and this was our patriarch;
    so that you can see that whoever follows him
    as he commands loads good wares.

But his flock has become greedy
    for new food, so that it cannot help
    straying into wild pastures.

And the farther the sheep go from him
    and are more remote and vagabond,
    the emptier they return to the fold.

There are indeed some who fear the harm
    and keep close to the shepherd, but they are so few
    that little cloth would make their cowls.   132

But, if my words are not obscure,
    if you have listened with attention,
    and if you recall what I have said,

your wish will be partly satisfied,
    because you will see the plant from which they come
    and you will know what my rebuke means,

'Where they fatten well, if they do not stray.'"

CANTO XII

St. Dominic

As soon as the holy flame [of St. Thomas]
    finished uttering the last word,
    the sacred millstone [circle of lights] began to turn

and did not complete its revolution
    before another [ring] encircled it and matched
    motion with motion, song with song—

a song which in these sweet throats
    surpasses those of our Muses, of our Sirens,
    as a direct ray surpasses its reflection.

As through a light cloud two rainbows appear,
    symmetrical and like in color
    when Juno commands her handmaid [Iris],   12

the one outside coming from the one within—
    like the speech of that wandering one [Echo]
    who was consumed by love, as vapor is by the sun—

making people here prophets [of the weather],
    assured by the pact God made with Noah
    that the earth never would be flooded again,

thus the two garlands of those eternal roses
    circled around us, and thus
    the outer corresponded to the inner.

*St. Bonaventura, in the outer circle of the Franciscans, returns the
compliment of St. Thomas by praising St. Dominic, the founder of the
Dominican order.*

When the dancing and great festival
    of the singing and the flashing
    of light with light, joyous and benign,   24

stopped at the same time and of one accord—
    as eyes are closed and lifted together
    by the impulse which moves them—

from the heart of one of the new lights
    a voice came which made me turn to it
    as the needle [of a compass] to the North Star,

and began, "The love which makes me beautiful
    leads me to speak of the other leader [St. Dominic]
    for whose sake so much good has been said of mine.

When one is mentioned, the other
    should be named: as they fought together,
    so should their glory shine.   36

The army of Christ which cost so much
    to rearm, moved slowly
    behind the banner [cross], timid, and few in number,

when the Emperor [God] who always reigns
    provided for this army, then in danger,
    through grace alone, not because of its worth,

and, as has been said, helped His spouse [the Church]
    with two champions, at whose acts and words
    the disbanding soldiers rallied.

In that place [Spain] where sweet Zephyr
    rises to open the new leaves
    with which Europe is reclothed,   48

not far from the breaking of the waves [of the ocean]
    behind which, because of their broad expanse,
    the sun, at intervals, hides himself from all,

lies the favored Calahorra under the protection
    of the great shield [of Castille], on which
    one lion is above and one below.

Within it was born the ardent lover
    of the Christian faith, the holy champion,
    benign to his followers, cruel to his foes,

and at his creation his mind was so replete
    with active virtue that in his mother's womb
    he made her a prophetess [through a dream].   60

After the marriage between him and the Faith
    had been completed at the sacred fount,
    when they dowered each other with mutual strength,

the lady [his godmother] who gave assent for him
    saw in a dream the marvelous fruit
    which was to come from him and from his heirs,

and that he might be construed as he was,
    a spirit from here [Heaven] made his name have
    the possessive form of the One to whom he belonged.

He was called Dominico [the Lord's],
    and I speak of him as of the husbandman
    whom Christ chose to aid Him in His garden.   72

Clearly did he appear a messenger and confident of Christ,
    for the primal love manifested in him
    was for the first counsel [poverty] that Christ gave.

Many times silent or awake he was found
    by his nurse on the floor, as if saying,
    'For this [hard and active life] I came.'

O father of him, truly Felix [happy]!
    O mother, truly Joan [the grace of the Lord]!
    if the names mean what people say.

Not for your world for which now men toil,
    following the Ostian or Taddeo [authorities on
        canon law],
    but for love of the true manna [knowledge],   84

he became in a short time a great doctor
    and went about the vineyard
    which soon withers if the keeper is at fault,

and he asked the Holy See, once kinder to the honest poor,
    (not in itself, but because of him [Boniface VIII]
    who sits there and now goes astray),

not for permission to spend two or three for six [to make
        a profit],
    not for the income of the first vacancy,
    not for *decimas quae sunt pauperum Dei*,[1]

but for freedom to fight against the erring [heretical] world
    for the seed [Faith] out of which grew
    the twenty-four plants [lights] that encircle you.   96

---

[1] "The tithes that belong to the poor."

Then with both learning and will
    and with apostolic leave he moved
    like a torrent forced out of a high spring,

and against the heretical thickets [growths]
    his attack fell, most vigorous
    where the resistance was greatest.

From him came diverse streams
    by which the Catholic garden is watered,
    so that its saplings stand more vigorous.

St. Bonaventura reproaches his own order for being divided into two groups, the Spirituales, who kept St. Francis' rule of poverty or made it more severe, and the Conventuales, who interpreted this rule freely.

If such was one wheel of the chariot
    on which Holy Church defended herself
    and conquered in the field of civil strife,   108

the excellence of the other [St. Francis]
    to whom Thomas, before my coming,
    was so courteous, should be clear to you.

But the track made by the circumference [of the wheel]
    is so abandoned that there is now mold [as on bad wine]
    where there was once a crust [as on good].

His followers who went straight
    with their feet in his tracks have turned about,
    so that the ones in front do not lead those behind,

and soon will be seen the harvest
    due to bad cultivation, when the tares [censured ones]
    will complain that the bin is taken from them.   120

I say, indeed, that by searching through our volume
    page by page, a leaf still might be found
    on which one might read 'I am as I was before,'

but not at Casale or Acquasparta [homes of the two factions]
    where followers so read the writing [rule]
    that one evades it and the other restricts it.

I am the life of Bonaventura
    of Bagnoregio, who in great offices
    always sacrificed the lesser [temporal] interests.

Illuminato and Augustino are here
    who were among the first of the barefooted [Franciscans],
    and who made themselves friends of God with their cord. 132

Hugo of St. Victor is here with them,
    and Peter the bookworm, and Peter of Spain,
    who down on earth gives light in his twelve little books.

Also Nathan, the prophet, the metropolitan [patriarch]
    Chrysostom, and Anselm, and that Donatus
    who to the first art [grammar] set his hand.

Rabanus is here, and at my side
    shines the Calabrian Joachim
    who was endowed with a prophetic spirit.

To emulate such a paladin,
    the ardent courtesy and respectful style
    of St. Thomas moved me, 144

and with me he moved all this company."

CANTO XIII

Solomon

*To visualize the situation of Dante and Beatrice surrounded by the
double ring of twenty-four doctors, the reader is asked to choose an
equal number of bright stars and to arrange them in the form of a
double crown.*

[Let whoever wishes to understand
    what I now saw imagine—and let him retain
    the image as firm as a rock while I speak—
fifteen stars which in diverse quarters
    enliven the heavens with so much brightness
    that it penetrates the density of the air;
and imagine the Wain [Great Dipper] for whose movement
    the depths of our heaven suffice both day and night

so that it does not disappear with the turning of its
  pole;
let him imagine the mouth of that horn [the Little Dipper]
  which begins at the axle [North Star]
  around which moves the wheel [daily rotation]   12
to have made of themselves two constellations
  like the one formed by the crown of the daughter
  of Minos [Ariadne] when she felt the chill of death,
and one constellation to have its rays
  within the other and both to circle
  so that one goes first and the other next,
and he will have, as it were, a shadowy image
  of the real constellation and of the double dance
  which revolved around the point where I was,
since it is as much beyond our experience
  as the heaven which exceeds [in speed] all the rest
  surpasses the current of the [stream] Chiana.   24
There they sang not a paean, not of Bacchus,
  but of the three persons in the divine nature,
  and It and the human in One Person.
The singing and the turning had fulfilled their measure,
  and these holy lights became attentive to us,
  rejoicing in one concern after another.
Then the light [St. Thomas] by which the marvelous life
  of the poor man of God [St. Francis] was narrated to me
  broke the silence of the harmonious spirits
and said, "Since one sheaf is threshed
  and its seed is stored away,
  sweet love invites me to beat out the other.]   36

*St. Thomas now takes up Dante's second question which was due to
the remark that Solomon's wisdom had never been equaled. St. Thomas
states that Adam and Christ must be excluded from the comparison,
since they were created directly by God and were therefore flawless.
Solomon, moreover, had asked only for kingly prudence, not for all
wisdom, and thus as a king only had no equal.*

*The world we see is a mere shadow of the divine idea which is trans-
mitted to the heavens (or to the angels governing them) and then to
the earth. The idea is perfect, but since matter is variable, imperfec-
tions and variations occur here on earth.*

[You believe that in the breast from which a rib
      was drawn to form the beautiful cheeks
      of her [Eve] whose palate cost the world so much,
and in that [of Christ] which, pierced by the lance,
      gave satisfaction for the past and future
      such that it outweighed every sin,
whatever light human nature was allowed
      to have was wholly infused
      by that Power which made both.
Therefore you wonder at what I said above
      when I related that the goodness inclosed
      in the fifth light [Solomon] did not have an equal.   48
Now open your eyes to what I answer, and you will see
      your belief and my remarks become for truth
      like the center of circles [one and coinciding].
What does not die and what can die
      is nothing but the splendor of that idea
      which our Lord in his love creates;
for that living Light [the Son, wisdom] which so streams
      from Its lamp [the Father] that It is never divided
      from Him nor from the Love [Holy Ghost], their third
            part,
in Its goodness focuses Its rays which are
      as if mirrored in nine subsistences [orders of angels]
      eternally remaining One.   60
Thence It descends to the ultimate elements,
      coming down step by step, until It produces
      only brief contingencies [perishable things],
and by these contingencies I mean
      generated things which the moving heaven
      produces with and without seed.
The wax [matter] of these and what molds it [nature of the
            heavens]
      are not always the same; therefore it [the divine idea]
            penetrates
      with more and less conformity to the ideal pattern;
whence it happens that trees of the same species
      bear better and worse fruit,
      and you are born with varying minds.   72
If the wax were exactly molded

and the heavens supreme [most propitious] in their
      power,
    the light of the seal would be all-apparent.
But Nature always gives it [the light] diminished,
    like an artist who is skilled in his art
    but has a trembling hand.
Yet if the warm love disposes and stamps
    the clear vision of the Primal Virtue
    all perfection is acquired there.
Thus once the dust was made worthy
    of all animal perfection;
    thus the Virgin was made pregnant.   84
Therefore I commend your opinion
    that human nature never was and never will be
    as in those two persons [Adam and Christ].
Now, if I did not continue farther,
    the words 'How was Solomon without an equal?'
    would form your question.
To make clear what is not apparent,
    think of who he was and the cause which moved him
    when he was told to ask.
I have not explained so [obscurely] that you cannot see
    that he was a king and asked
    for wisdom to· be a worthy one,   96
not to know the number of the motors [angels]
    here on high or whether *necesse* [an absolute premise],
    with a condition, ever produces a *necesse* [absolute con-
        clusion],
not *si est dare primum motum esse*,[1]
    or whether in half a circle a triangle
    can be made without one right angle.
Wherefore, if you note this and what I said,
    you will learn that the unequaled insight on which
    the arrow of my intention strikes is royal prudence.
And if you direct your clear eyes to the 'has risen'
    you will see that it relates only to kings,
    who are many, and the good ones few.   108
With this distinction accept my saying;

---

[1] "If a prime [uncaused] motion is to be admitted."

and then it can stand with what you believe
    about our first father and our Beloved One.]

We are admonished to be slow in our judgments and thus avoid the
errors of certain Greek philosophers criticized by Aristotle and certain
heretical theologians.

And let this be lead on your feet
    to make you move slowly, like a wearied man,
    both to the 'yes' and 'no' you do not see clearly;

for he is low among fools who,
    either in one case or the other,
    affirms or denies without distinctions;

because it happens many times
    that a hasty opinion inclines to error,
    . and later, feeling [pride] binds the mind.   120

Whoever fishes for the truth without knowing how
    leaves the shore more than vainly,
    since he does not return as he set forth;

and of that are clear proof
    Parmenides, Mellissus, and Bryson
    and many who went not knowing where.

So likewise did Sabellius and Arius and those fools
    who were like [polished] swords to the Scriptures,
    reflecting straight faces with distortion.

Let us not be too sure in judging,
    like those who estimate the ears
    in the field before they are ripe;   132

for I have seen all winter long
    the briar show itself stiff and rough
    and then bear a rose at its top;

and I have seen a ship run straight
    and swift on its way over the sea
    and perish finally on entering the harbor.

Let not dame Bertha or squire Martin,
    through seeing one rob and another make an offering,
    think they know them [their fate] in the divine counsel;

for one may yet go up and the other fall."

CANTO XIV

The Garment of Light—The Cross of Mars

The sound waves coming from St. Thomas in the ring and from Beatrice in the center remind Dante of the ripples in a round vessel.

In answer to Dante's question as interpreted by Beatrice, Solomon explains that after Judgment Day the brightness of the souls will remain but will not dazzle their bodily eyes, which will have increased powers. The souls look forward to the time when, with their bodies, they will be more complete and therefore still happier.

From the center to the rim, and from the rim to the center,
    the water in a round vessel moves,
      according as it is struck from without or within.

What I say suddenly occurred
    to my mind when the glorious life
      of Thomas became silent,

because of the analogy with the speech
    of him and of Beatrice who, after him,
      was pleased to begin as follows:

"This man has a need which he does not express
    either in thought or with his voice
      to go to the root of another truth.   12

Tell him if the light which makes your substance
    flowerlike will remain eternally
      with you as it is now,

and if it remains tell how,
    when you are again made corporeal,
      your vision will not be harmed."

As, impelled and drawn by greater joy,
    those who dance in a round at times
      lift their voices and rejoice in their movements,

so, at the ready and devout prayer,

the holy circles showed a new joy
by their turning and wondrous melody.   24

Whoever laments because here we die
to live up there, does not take account
of the refreshment of the eternal rain [of light].

That One and Two and Three which always lives
and always reigns in Three and Two and One,
uncircumscribed and circumscribing all,

was sung of three times by each of those spirits
with such melody that to hear it would be
a just reward for every merit.

And I heard in the divinest light [that of Solomon]
of the lesser circle, a modest voice,
like that of the angel to Mary,   36

answer, "As long as the festival of Paradise
exists, so long will our love
radiate around us such a robe [of light].

Its brightness corresponds to our ardor,
the ardor to our vision, and its intensity
depends, apart from our merit, on a gift of grace.

When our glorious and holy flesh
is reassumed, our persons
through being entire will be more acceptable;

therefore whatever gratuitous light
the Supreme Good gives us will be increased—
a light which fits us to see Him;   48

so that our vision must increase,
as well as the ardor lighted by it,
and the resultant radiance.

Like a coal that produces flames
but whose white incandescence shines through them
so that it maintains its visibility,

this effulgence which already encircles us
will be outshone by our flesh
which all this time the earth has covered.

Nor can so much light fatigue us,

for the organs of the body will be strong enough
    for all that can delight us."   60

So ready were both choirs to say "amen"
    that they truly showed their desire
    for their dead bodies,

perhaps not only for themselves but for their mothers,
    fathers, and others who were dear
    before they became eternal flames.

*Now a third ring shines around the other two, composed of souls
related to the Holy Ghost, wise in the things of the spirit, to complete
perhaps the symbolism of the Trinity. Then Beatrice and Dante rise
to the heaven of Mars. Here the soldiers of holy crusades appear,
ruddy with their love, on the white cross of their Faith.*

And behold! a light of equal brightness
    shone around what was there
    like a horizon growing bright,

and, as in early evening, stars
    appear faintly in the sky,
    so that their sight seems real and not real,   72

so I seemed to see new substances
    making a circle outside
    of the other two circumferences.

O true sparkling of the Holy Spirit,
    how suddenly glowing it became
    to my eyes which, overcome, endured it not!

But Beatrice showed herself so beautiful
    and smiling that her appearance must be left
    among the sights which overcame my mind.

Then my eyes gained strength to look up again,
    and I saw myself transported
    alone with my lady to more exalted salvation.   84

I was well aware that I had risen higher
    because of the enkindled smile of the star
    which seemed to 'me ruddier than usual.

With all my heart, and in that speech [silent prayer]
    which is one in all, I made to God
    such an offering as befitted the new grace.

And the ardor of the sacrifice
    was not exhausted in my breast
    before I knew the offering had been accepted;

for, with such light and such ruddiness
    splendors appeared to me within two rays
    that I exclaimed, "O Helios! [Sun] who dost so adorn
       them!"   96

As, distinct with lesser and greater lights,
    the Milky Way shows white between the poles,
    making the wise wonder about it,

thus constellated, those rays formed
    in the depths of Mars the venerable emblem [the cross]
    which the joining of quadrants in a circle makes.

Here memory overcomes my mind,
    for that cross flashed forth Christ,
    so that I cannot find a comparison;

but whoever takes up his cross and follows Christ
    will excuse me for what I omit
    when he beholds Christ flashing in that glow.   108

From tip to tip and between the top and bottom
    lights moved shining brightly
    as they met and passed by.

Thus, on earth, particles long and short,
    straight and aslant, fast and slow,
    changing aspect, are seen moving

through a ray of sunlight which streaks
    the shade [in houses] which men provide,
    with intelligence and art, for their protection.

And as a viol and harp, tuned in harmony
    with many strings, make only a sweet tinkling sound
    to one unfamiliar with the music,   120

so from the lights I saw in the cross
    a melody sounded which carried me away
    without my understanding the hymn.

Well was I aware it was a song of lofty praise,
    since "Arise and conquer" came, as to one
    who hears but does not fully understand.

So enamored was I with the hymn
  that until then nothing had ever bound me
  with such sweet ties.

Perhaps these words seem too bold,
  slighting the delight of the beautiful eyes
  which give rest to all my longing,   132

but whoever knows that the living stamps of all beauty
  [the eyes of Beatrice] have more effect the higher they
    are,
  and that I had not yet turned to them,

can excuse me for what leads to my self-accusation
  and see that I speak the truth and that
  the holy delight, which becomes purer

as it rises, is not disparaged here.

CANTO XV

Cacciaguida

A gracious will in which the love
  which breathes righteously is always manifest,
  as cupidity is in an evil desire,

imposed silence on that sweet lyre
  and quieted the holy strings
  tightened and relaxed by the hand of Heaven.

How could those substances be deaf to just prayers
  who, to encourage me to ask,
  joined together in their silence?

It is right that he should suffer without end
  who through desire for things that do not last
  deprives himself eternally of that love.   12

As in pure and clear skies

a sudden light darts from time to time,
  making eyes move that before were still,

a light which is like a moving star
  except that it lasts briefly
  and no star is missing from where it starts,

so, from the arm that extends to the right,
  a star of the constellation appearing there
  ran to the foot of the cross,

nor did this gem leave its ribbon,
  but through the radiant strip it moved
  like a torch behind an alabaster screen.   24

With like affection the shade of Anchises [Aeneas' father]
  advanced (if our greatest poet merits belief)
  when he saw his son in Elysium.

*The spirit so eager to see and to speak to Dante is Cacciaguida, the
poet's great-great-grandfather. He greets his descendant in the im-
pressive language of the Church.*

"O *sanguis meus,*[1] *o superinfusa*
  Gratïa Dei! sicut tibi, cui
  bis unquam coeli ianüa reclusa?"

So spoke that light, and I, attentive,
  turned my face to my lady,
  and on one side and the other I was amazed,

for a smile shone within her eyes
  such that I thought with mine to reach the depths
  of my grace and of my Paradise.   36

Then joyous to hear and see,
  the spirit added to his beginning
  words I could not understand, so profoundly did he speak.

Nor did he hide his meaning from choice
  but from necessity, for his thought
  rose above the range of mortals.

And when the bow of the ardent affection

---

[1] "O blood of mine, O grace of God lavishly poured forth! To whom
was Heaven's gate ever twice opened as to you?"

had so relaxed that his speech
 aimed at the mark of our intellect,

the first words I understood
 were "Blessed be Thou, Three and One!
 Thou that hast been so courteous to my seed."   48

And he continued, "The welcome and long-felt hunger
 derived from reading in the great book [of Fate]
 in which the white and black never change,

you have relieved, my son, within this light
 in which I speak to you, thanks to her [Beatrice]
 who endowed you with feathers for your flight.

You believe your thought flows [and is known] to me
 from the One [God] who is first, as from one [unity],
 when known, five and six [i.e., other numbers] derive.

Therefore you do not ask who I am
 and why I appear to you
 more joyful than any other.   60

What you think is true; for the great and small
 in this life gaze in the mirror
 in which thought is revealed before the thinking.

But in order that the sacred love in which I watch
 with perpetual vision and which makes me thirst
 with sweet desire may be better fulfilled,

let your voice, secure, bold, and joyous
 proclaim your wish, proclaim your desire,
 for which my reply is already decreed."

I turned to Beatrice and she heard
 before I spoke and smiled as a sign
 for me to enlarge the wings of my desire.   72

Then I began, "When the primal Equality appeared to you,
 love and understanding [ability to express it] became
 of the same measure for each of you,

since the Sun which illumined and warmed you
 with its heat and light is so balanced
 that all comparisons fall short.

But in mortals will and means [of expression],

for a cause manifest to you,
    have wings diversely feathered,

so that I, a mortal, feel this inequality
    in me, and therefore I give thanks
    only in my heart for the paternal welcome.   84

But I beg you, living topaz,
    adorning with your gem this precious jewel,
    that you satisfy me with your name."

*Cacciaguida tells first about his family, then about Florence in the
good old days. That city, as in Dante's time, heard the hours sounded
by the bells of the abbey near the city walls; no luxurious Sardanapalus
appeared then; the Roman hill of Montemalo had not been surpassed
by the splendor of the Florentine Uccellatoio; wives could count
securely on being buried at home, not in exile, and were not abandoned
by husbands on business trips to France; and such notoriously im-
modest or dishonest persons as Cianghella or Lapo Salterello were
almost unknown.*

"O leaf of mine in whom I delighted
    even while waiting for you, I was your root!"
    This was the beginning of his answer.

Then he added, "He from whom your family got its name
    and who for a hundred years and more
    has been circling the first ledge of the mountain

was my son and your great-grandfather.
    It is right that with your prayers
    you should shorten the long effort he has made.   96

Florence within its ancient walls
    (from which she still hears tierce and nones)
    lived in peace, sober, and chaste.

There were no bracelets then or coronets,
    no women with gaudy skirts
    or girdles to be seen more than their persons.

Not yet did a daughter's birth dismay a father,
    for the marriage age and dowry
    were not immoderate on one side or the other.

There were no houses empty of families;

not yet had a Sardanapalus come
　　to show what, in a chamber, can be done.　　　　108

Your Uccellatoio had not yet outdone [Rome's] Montemalo
　　which, surpassed as it has been in rising,
　　will be so too in its decline.

Bellincion Berti I have seen go forth
　　girded with leather and bone, and his lady
　　come from her mirror without a painted face.

I have seen a Nerli and a Vecchio
　　contented with bare leather,
　　and their womenfolk with spindle and with flax!

O fortunate ones! Each was certain
　　of her burial place, and none as yet,
　　because of France, was deserted in her bed.　　　　120

One kept watch beside the cradle
　　and, consoling, used the speech [of babies]
　　which makes new fathers and mothers glad.

Another, while drawing thread from the distaff,
　　told stories to her family
　　about the Trojans, Fiesole, and Rome.

A Cianghella or a Lapo Salterello [profligates]
　　would then have been a marvel,
　　like a Cincinnatus or a Cornelia now.

To so restful, to so fair a civil life,
　　to so trusted a citizenry,
　　to so pleasant a dwelling place,

Mary, invoked [at my birth] with loud cries, gave me,
　　and in your ancient Baptistry,
　　I became a Christian and Cacciaguida.

Moronto and Eliseo were my brothers;
　　my wife came from the valley of the Po,
　　and your surname was received from her.

Then I followed Conrad, the Emperor,
　　who girded me with his knighthood,
　　so much favor, by good deeds, did I gain.

With him I fought against the iniquitous faith

whose believers, through the shepherd's fault,
    now usurp your rights [to the Holy Land].   144

There, by that base people [the infidels]
    I was freed from your deceptive world
    the love of which corrupts so many souls,

and from martyrdom I came into this peace."

CANTO XVI

Cacciaguida's Florence

*Although recognizing the vanity of pride in birth, Dante cannot help
glorying in the merit of his ancestor; whereupon Beatrice, indulgent,
but aware of the failing, smiles. Dante asks Cacciaguida about the
date of his birth and about Florence in the old days.*

O insignificant nobility of birth!
    if it makes people boast down below,
    where our affections languish,

that will never be a marvel to me,
    for, where desires are not perverted,
    I mean in Heaven, I myself gloried in it.

It is indeed a mantle which quickly shrinks,
    so that unless we add [merit] from day to day,
    Time goes around it [diminishes it] with his shears.

With that *voi* [the polite form for "you"] which Rome
    first permitted and which the Romans
    now use least, my words began again.   12

Then Beatrice, who stood apart, smiling,
    seemed like her [the Lady of Malehaut] who coughed
    at the first recorded fault of Guinevere.

I began, "You are my father;
    you give me boldness to speak;
    you elevate me so that I transcend myself.

By so many streams my mind is filled
　　with joy that my ability to endure it
　　without bursting is another delight.

Tell me then, my dear forefather,
　　who were your ancestors and what years
　　marked your childhood.　　　　　　　　　　　24

Speak to me about the sheepfold
　　of San Giovanni, how large it was,
　　and who in it were worthy of the highest seats."

As a coal breaking into flame
　　at the blowing of the wind, so I saw
　　that light shine at my blandishments,

and as it became more beautiful to my eyes
　　so, with a sweeter and more lovely voice,
　　although not with our modern accent,

it said to me, "From the day when '*Ave*' was spoken [the
　　　　Annunciation]
　　to the time when my mother, now holy,
　　relieved herself of the burden I had been,　　　　36

this planet [Mars] had come to its Lion [Leo]
　　to be rekindled under its paws
　　five hundred and eighty times [in 1091].

My ancestors and I were born in the place
　　where the last ward is first reached
　　by the runners in your annual sports.

Let this suffice concerning my elders:
　　as to who they were and whence they came,
　　silence is more becoming than speech.

*Cacciaguida now gives an account of the city and of its former in-
habitants.*

[All those who could bear arms
　　between Mars [on the Arno] and the Baptist [Baptistry]
　　were a fifth of those living now.　　　　　　48
But the citizenry, now mixed
　　with Campis, Certaldos, and Figghines,
　　was once pure even to the lowest artisan.

O how much better it would be
    to have those people I mention as neighbors [not citizens]
    and to have your boundaries at Galluzzo and at Trespiano
than to have them within and to endure the stench
    of the villain from Aguglione and from Signa
    who already has his eye sharpened for barratry.
If the people who are most degenerate [the clergy]
    were not like a stepmother to Caesar [the temporal power],
    but benign, like a mother to her son, such a one   60
has become a Florentine and trades and changes money
    who would have been turned back to Simifonti
    where his grandfather used to go begging.
Montemurlo would still belong to its counts,
    the Cerchi would be in the parish of Acone,
    and perhaps in Valdigrieve the Buondelmonti.
Always the mingling of foreigners
    has been a source of evil to cities,
    as superfluous food to our bodies.
A blind bull falls more headlong
    than a blind lamb, and many times
    one sword cuts better than five.   72
If you look at [the towns of] Luni and Urbisaglia
    and see how they have gone, and how
    Chiusi and Sinigaglia go after them,
it will not seem hard to understand
    how families are destroyed,
    since even cities have an end.
All creations of yours have death
    like you yourselves; but this is not apparent
    in things that last long, since lives are short.
And, as the revolution of the moon, without rest,
    covers and reveals shores [with its tides],
    so Fortune does with Florence.   84
Therefore what I will say of the great Florentines
    whose fame is hidden by time
    should not seem marvelous to you.
I have seen among the Ughi, the Catellini,
    the Filippi, the Greci, the Ormanni, and the Alberichi,
    illustrious citizens, even in their decline.
And I have seen both great and of ancient origin,

the Sannella, the Arca, the Soldanieri
and the Ardinghi and the Bostichi.
Near the gate [of S. Piero] which now is burdened
with a new felony of such weight
that there will soon be a wreck of the boat,   96
dwelt the Ravignani, from whom
Count Guido descended, and all who since
have taken their name from great Bellincione.
Della Pressa knew once how to rule,
and Galigaio had in his house
the gilded hilt and pummel.
Notable once was the strip of vair [of the Pigli family],
the Sacchetti, Giuochi, Fifanti, Barucci,
and Galli; and those who blush for the [fraudulent]
bushel [measure].
The stock from which the Calfucci were born
was once great, and once the Sizii and Arrigucci
were drawn to the highest offices.   108
How great I have seen those, defeated by their pride,
and the golden balls [of the Lamberti family]
adorning Florence in all her great deeds.
Such were the fathers of those who now,
whenever the church [see of Florence] is vacant,
become fat by remaining in consistory.
The arrogant race [the Adimari family] which is fierce as a
dragon
after one who flees, and to one who shows his teeth
or purse is as gentle as a lamb,
already was coming up, but from people of mean stock,
so that Ubertin Donato was not pleased
that his father-in-law made him their kinsman.   120
Already Caponsacco had descended from Fiesole
to the market place, and already
Giuda and Infangato were good citizens.
I will tell something incredible but true:
into the inner circle [of the city] one entered
through a gate named for those of Pera.
Each one who bears the fair ensign
[of Hugh of Brandenburg] whose name and worth
the festival of St. Thomas keeps alive,

from him had knighthood and privileges,
   although there is one [Giano della Bella], siding with
      the people,
   who binds it [the ensign] with a border [fringe].   132
Already there were Gualterotti and Importuni,
   and the Borgo would be quieter
   if they had fasted for new neighbors.
The house [of the Amidei] which caused your weeping
   because of the just anger [feud] which has ruined you
   and made an end of your happy life,
was honored, both in itself and its allies.
   O Buondelmonte, how badly you avoided
   marriage with it at the instigation of another!
Many now sad would be happy
   if God had consigned you to the Ema [a river]
   the first time you came to the city.   144
But it was fitting that to the broken stone [a statue of
      Mars]
   which guards its bridge, Florence, in the last days
   of its peace, should offer a victim.
With those people and with others
   I saw Florence in such repose
   that she had no occasion to weep.
With them I saw its inhabitants
   so glorious and just that the lilies
   were never reversed on the staff,
nor made red by a party [the Guelfs]."]

CANTO XVII

The Prophecy

Like him [Phaëthon] who came to Clymene to be sure
   about what he had heard against himself [his father's
      identity]
   and who makes fathers wary with their sons,

so was I, and so I was felt to be
  by Beatrice and by the holy light
  which had first changed position for me.

Therefore my lady said, "Send forth the flame
  of your desire so that it may issue
  marked well by an inner stamp,

not because our knowledge grows through your speech,
  but to accustom yourself to express your thirst,
  so that someone may quench it."   12

"O dear root of mine, you who soar
  so that you perceive contingent [accidental] things
  before they exist—while gazing at the Point [God]

to which all time is present—
  as clearly as on earth we see that a triangle
  cannot contain two obtuse angles,

while I was with Virgil
  on the mountain that cures
  and while descending into the dead world,

I heard grave words about my future life.
  Although I have braced myself
  against the blows of fortune,   24

still I would be glad to hear
  what fate is bringing close to me,
  for an arrow foreseen comes more slowly."

Thus I addressed that light
  which had spoken first
  and expressed my wish as Beatrice desired.

Not in the ambiguous terms [of oracles] by which
  foolish people were entangled before the Lamb
  of God, who took away our sins, was killed,

but in clear words and precise terms
  that paternal love [Cacciaguida], made manifest
  and enclosed in its own light, replied.   36

"The contingencies, which do not extend [occur]
  outside of the volume of your material world,
  are shown wholly in the Eternal Vision,

but do not derive inevitably therefrom
    any more than a boat descending with the current
    gains necessity from the eye that mirrors it.

From it [the Eternal Vision], as an organ's sweet harmony
    comes to one's ear, there comes to my sight
    the future that is prepared for you.

*Cacciaguida predicts Dante's exile, his quarrels with his party, his
refuge with Bartolomeo della Scala, and the promise of the young Can
Grande della Scala, often indentified as the redeemer of Inferno I.*

Just as Hippolytus left Athens
    because of his pitiless and perfidious stepmother,
    so you will have to leave Florence. 48

This is wished for, this is sought
    and soon will be accomplished by him who plans it
    [in Rome] where Christ every day is bought and sold.

The blame will follow the offended party
    in popular clamor, as it is wont; but vengeance
    will give witness of the truth.

You will leave everything loved most dearly;
    and this is the arrow
    that the bow of exile shoots first.

You will learn how salty the bread tastes
    in others' houses, and how hard
    is the going up and down of others' stairs. 60

And what will weigh heaviest upon you
    will be the evil and senseless company
    into which you will fall in this valley,

a company which, ungrateful, mad, and impious,
    will turn against you; but soon they,
    not you, will blush for it.

Their ways will give proof of their brutishness
    so that it will be well for you
    to have made a party by yourself.

Your first refuge and first hostelry will show the courtesy
    of the great Lombard who [whose coat of arms]
    on a ladder bears the sacred bird [the eagle], 72

and who will have such regard for you
    that in deeds and requests, with you two,
    what is last among others will come first.

With him you will see that one [Can Grande]
    who at birth was so stamped by this strong star [Mars]
    that his deeds will be most notable.

People are not yet aware of him
    because of his age, since only nine years
    have these heavens turned around him,

but before the Gascon [Clement V] deceives the lofty Henry,
    sparks of his virtue will appear
    in his not caring for money or for idleness.   84

His liberality will be known,
    so that even his enemies
    will not keep silent about him.

Count on him and on his benefits;
    through him the fate of many will be transformed,
    rich and poor changing places.

And take written in your mind about him,
    but not to reveal . . ." and he said things
    incredible even to those who will witness them.

Then he added, "My son, this is the commentary
    on what was said to you; here are the pitfalls
    hidden within a few circlings of the heavens.   96

But I do not want you to hate your neighbors,
    since your life has a future
    far beyond punishment of their perfidies."

When by his silence the holy soul
    showed he had finished putting the woof
    on the web I had held out warped,

I began like a person who in doubt
    longs for counsel from someone who sees
    and who wills righteously and who loves.

"I perceive clearly, Father, how Time
    rushes toward me to give the blow
    that falls heaviest on him who is most heedless.   108

Therefore I must arm myself with foresight,
    so that if the dearest place [Florence] is taken from me
    I may not lose others through my verses.

Down in the world eternally bitter
    and on the mountain from whose fair summit
    I was lifted by my lady's eyes,

and afterward in Heaven from star to star,
    I have learned things which, if I relate them,
    will have for many a bitter taste.

And if I am a timid friend of Truth,
    I fear to lose life among those
    who will call this time 'ancient.' "   120

The light in which the treasure smiled
    that I had found there flashed
    like a golden mirror in the sunlight,

then answered, "A conscience darkened
    by its own or another's shame
    will indeed consider your speech harsh.

Nevertheless, all falsehood laid aside,
    make your entire vision manifest,
    and let there be scratching where the itching is;

for, if at first your words
    are bitter, when digested,
    they will leave a vital nourishment.   132

Your cries will be like the wind
    which strikes hardest the highest peaks;
    and that is no little mark of honor.

Therefore in these heavens, on the mountain,
    and in the woeful valley, only those souls
    known to fame have been shown;

for the mind of a listener is not quieted
    or confirmed in faith by examples
    which have hidden and unknown roots,

nor by arguments based on what is not apparent."

CANTO XVIII

The Heaven of Jupiter

Now that blessed mirror was rejoicing
    in its thoughts alone, and I was tasting mine,
    tempering the bitter with the sweet,

when the lady who was leading me to God said,
    "Change your thoughts, consider that I am near Him
    who lightens the burden of every wrong."

I turned at the dear voice of my comfort,
    and what love I saw then in her holy eyes
    I do not try to express,

not only because I do not trust my speech,
    but because my memory, without guidance,
    cannot extend beyond its capacity.   12

This much of the moment I can relate that,
    looking at her again, my affection
    was free from every other desire

while the Eternal Joy, which shone directly
    on her, contented me with Its aspect,
    reflected in her beautiful face.

Overwhelming me with the light of a smile,
    she said to me, "Turn and listen,
    for not only in my eyes is Paradise."

As here [on earth] we sometimes see feeling
    in faces, if it is so great
    that all the soul is absorbed by it,   24

so, in the flaming of the holy light [of Cacciaguida]
    to which I turned, I recognized its wish
    to talk a little further with me.

It began, "On this fifth branch of the tree
    which has its life from the top,
    and always bears fruit and never loses its leaves,

are blessed spirits who, below,
>before coming to Heaven were of great renown,
>so that every Muse would be enriched by them.

Cacciaguida names various champions of the Faith, Joshua, the suc-
cessor of Moses and conqueror of the Holy Land; Judas Maccabaeus,
who delivered the Hebrews from the tyranny of the Syrians; Charle-
magne, who restored the Empire and defended the Church; Roland,
William of Orange, and Rainouart (a legendary converted pagan),
characters in Old French epics; Godfrey of Bouillon, a leader of the
First Crusade; and Robert Guiscard, the Norman conqueror of southern
Italy.

Therefore look at the arms of the cross;
>the one I will name will move
>like swift lightning in a cloud."

36

I saw a light drawn along the cross
>at the naming of Joshua, immediately,
>nor was the word before the act.

And at the name of the lofty Maccabaeus
>I saw another move whirling;
>and joy was the lash of the top.

Then for Charlemagne and for Roland
>my attentive glance followed two of them
>as the eye follows a falcon in its flight.

Afterward William [of Orange], Rainouart,
>Duke Godfrey [of Bouillon], and Robert Guiscard
>drew my sight along that cross.

48

Then moving and mingling among the other lights,
>the soul that had spoken to me showed
>what an artist he was among the singers of Heaven.

Through the increased brightness of Beatrice, Dante is aware that he
has risen from the ruddy light of Mars into the temperate whiteness
of Jupiter, the heaven of Justice. The lights here first spell out the
words, Diligite iustitiam qui iudicatis terram ("Love righteousness, ye
that be judges of the earth"), and, after remaining for a while in the
form of the M (for Monarchy), change again into the imperial eagle.
Monarchy is the earthly representative of Justice whose ultimate form
is Empire.

I turned to my right side
    to learn my duty from Beatrice
    either by word or by sign,

and I saw her eyes so clear,
    so joyous, that her semblance
    surpassed her other and latest beauty.

And, as by feeling more delight
    in doing good, one notices
    from day to day the progress of one's virtue,   60

so I, seeing that miracle more lovely,
    became aware that with the heavens
    my circling had increased its arc.

And as a change comes soon
    in a pale lady when her face
    gets rid of the burden of shame,

so I saw a similar transformation when the whiteness
    of the temperate sixth star
    received me into itself.

I saw in that torch of Jove
    the sparkling of the love there,
    spelling for my eyes our speech.   72

And as birds, risen from a shore
    as if rejoicing over their pasture,
    make a flock, now round, now of another shape,

so, within the lights, holy creatures,
    while circling, sang, and in their figures
    formed now D, now I, now L.

First they moved while singing to their melody,
    then becoming one of these letters
    they stopped a little and were silent.

O divine Pegasea [Muse], you
    who make minds glorious and long-lived,
    and they, through you, cities and kingdoms,   84

illumine me so much that I may set forth
    their figures as I have conceived them;
    let your power appear in these brief verses!

They [the lights] showed themselves then in five times seven
    vowels and consonants; and I noted the letters
    as if they had been pronounced for me.

Diligite iustitiam were the first verb
    and noun of all the picture,
    qui iudicatis terram were the last.

Then in the M of the fifth word
    they remained arrayed so that Jupiter
    seemed silver there, patterned with gold.   96

And I saw other lights, descending on the top
    of the M, grow quiet there, singing, I believe,
    of the Good which moves them to Itself.

Then, as on striking burning logs,
    innumerable sparks rise,
    from which the foolish used to draw omens,

more than a thousand lights rose again,
    some much and some little, as the Sun
    by which they were kindled decreed,

and each having become quiet in its place,
    I saw the head and neck of an eagle
    represented by that patterned fire.   108

He who paints there has no one to guide him,
    but directs himself: from Him we recognize
    that [instinctive] power which designs a nest.

The other blessed souls who at first
    seemed content to form lilies on the M,
    with a slight motion, completed the imprint [of the
      eagle].

O sweet star, what quality and what number
    of gems showed me that our justice
    is an effect of that heaven you enrich!

Therefore, I pray the Mind, in which your motion
    and power are begun, to examine the place
    whence issues the smoke that obscures your rays,   120

so that, another time, It may be angry
    at the buying and selling in the temple
    which was walled by miracles and martyrdom.

O soldiery of Heaven whom I contemplate,
    pray for those who are on earth
    and are led astray by a bad example!

Once they were wont to make war with swords,
    but now it is done by taking away [through excommu-
        nication]
    the bread which the pitying Father locks up for no one.

But you who write only to cancel [excommunicate],
    consider that Peter and Paul, who died
    for the vineyard you lay waste, still live.   **132**

You can say, indeed, "My heart is so set [on money],
    on that one who lived solitary [the St. John on Floren-
        tine coins]
    and who for a dance was drawn to martyrdom,

that I know neither Paul nor the Fisherman!"

CANTO XIX

Divine Justice

The beautiful image [of the eagle] which the patterned souls
    had made in their sweet fruition
    appeared before me with outspread wings.

Each spirit looked like a small ruby
    in which a ray of sunlight burned
    and in my eyes was reflected.

What I must now describe was never reported
    by a voice or written in ink,
    or ever comprehended in any fancy,

for I saw and heard the beak speak
    and utter "I" and "mine"
    when the concept was "we" and "our."   **12**

And it began, "For being just and reverent,

I am exalted to that glory
   which cannot be surpassed by our desire.

On earth I left such a memory
   that the wicked people commend it,
   without, however, continuing its example."

As a single heat makes itself felt
   from many coals, so, from many loves
   a single sound issued from that image;

whereupon I, at once, "O perpetual flowers
   of the eternal joy, making the fragrance
   of all seem one to me,   24

relieve me of the great fasting
   which has long kept me hungry
   without my finding on earth food for it.

I know well that if Divine Justice makes its mirror
   in another heaven [that of the Thrones], yours, never-
         theless
   does not apprehend it through a veil.

Know how attentively I make ready
   to listen; know what that question is
   which has caused so long a fast."

As a falcon released from its hood
   moves its head and claps its wings,
   showing its desire, and making itself handsome,   36

so I saw that emblem which was woven
   of the praises of divine grace become such with song
   as only those who rejoice up there can know.

*The eagle now answers the question in Dante's mind. What troubles
the poet particularly is the justice of condemning virtuous pagans who
have no chance to know the Christian truth. The eagle points out
first that God's wisdom exceeds the capacity of the created to under-
stand it. It was because of his impatience to comprehend by his own
efforts, without grace, that Lucifer fell. Lesser minds cannot hope to
grasp all. Trying to understand divine justice is like looking into the
sea; only a little can be perceived.*

*We should be modest in our opinions. Whatever God wishes is just,
as if by definition. We should realize also that many who shout*

"Christ" will not be saved and that many virtuous pagans will be closer to God (possibly in the Garden of Eden) than they.

At the end of the canto the eagle delivers a severe judgment on the sovereigns ruling in 1300.

Then it began, "That one [God] who turned the compass
    around the limits of the world and in it
    made so variously things hidden and manifest

could not so impress his power
    on the universe that his Word [conception]
    should not remain infinitely greater.

And the proof is that the first proud one [Lucifer],
    who was the peak of all creation,
    through not waiting for light, fell unenlightened.   48

Thus it appears that every minor nature
    is a receptacle too scant for that Good
    which has no end and measures Itself by Itself.

Therefore our sight, which must be
    one of the rays of the Mind
    with which everything is replete,

cannot be by its nature so strong
    that its Source does not discern much
    beyond what is apparent to it.

Consequently the sight your world receives
    penetrates into eternal justice
    as the eye penetrates within the sea;   60

for, although at the shore the bottom is seen,
    on the main it is not, and nevertheless
    the bottom is there, its depth hiding it.

No light unless it comes from the Serene One
    [through revelation] is always untroubled; but dark is
        that
    shadowed by the flesh and its poison.

Now what conceals the living justice
    which has caused you wonder
    has been sufficiently revealed,

for you said, 'A man is born on the shore

of the Indus, and no one there
    speaks of Christ or reads or writes of Him,

and all this man's desires and acts are good,
    as far as human reason can see,
    and without sin in word or deed

he dies unbaptized and without faith.
    Where is the justice that condemns him?
    How is it his fault if he does not believe?'

Now, who are you who wish to sit
    in judgment a thousand miles away,
    with sight that reaches only a span?

Certainly for him who reasons with me
    there would be a wonderful chance for questioning
    if the Scriptures were not above you.   84

O creatures of the earth, O gross minds!
    The First Will which is good in Itself
    never moved from Itself, the Supreme Good.

Whatever is consonant with It is just;
    no created good can draw It to itself,
    but It, radiating, causes that good."

As the stork circles above her nest
    after she has fed her young
    and as the one fed looks at her,

so the gracious image moved its wings,
    impelled by so many counsels,
    and so I raised my eyes.   96

Wheeling it sang, "As my notes
    are to you who do not understand them,
    so is eternal justice to mortals."

Then those glowing flames
    of the Holy Spirit, in the banner
    that made the Romans revered, were silent.

It began again, "To this kingdom no one ever rose
    who did not believe in Christ
    either before or after He was nailed to the cross.

But observe: many cry 'Christ,' 'Christ,'

who at judgment will be farther from Him
    than some who do not know Christ,   108

and the Ethiopian will condemn [scorn] such Christians
    when the two companies are separated,
    the one forever rich, the other poor.

What will the Persians [non-Christians] say to your kings
    when they see that book [of Judgment] open
    in which is recorded all their infamies?

There will be seen among the deeds of Albert
    that one which soon will move the pen [of the recording
        angel]
    by which the Kingdom of Prague will be made desolate.

There will be seen the grief that he [Philip the Fair] brings
    to the Seine who, after falsifying the coins,
    will die from brushing against a wild boar.   120

There will be seen the pride that makes men thirsty
    and which makes the Scot and the foolish Englishman
    unable to remain within their bounds.

The luxury and evil life will be seen
    of him of Spain [Ferdinand IV] and him of Bohemia
        [Wenceslaus IV]
    who never knew or wished for valor.

The cripple of Jerusalem [Charles II of Anjou] will be seen,
    his good deeds marked by a I [one],
    while an M [a thousand] will mark the contrary.

The avarice and baseness of him [Frederick]
    who guards the Isle of Fire [Sicily]
    where Anchises ended his long life will be seen,   132

and, to indicate how insignificant he is,
    the writing for him will be in abbreviations
    which note much [sin] in little space.

And the foul deeds of his uncle [James of Majorca]
    and his brother [James II of Aragon], which have dis-
        honored
    such a great lineage and two crowns, will appear to
        everyone.

And he of Portugal and he of Norway

will be known there, and he of Rascia [a counterfeiter]
    who, to his harm, has seen the coins of Venice.

Hungary would be blessed if she did not allow herself
    to be mistreated longer, and Navarre blessed also
    if she armed herself [against France] with her
        mountains.   **144**

And all should believe that as a pledge of this [French mis-
        deeds]
    Nicosia and Famagosta [in Cyprus] are now lamenting
    because of their little beast [king]

which trots [on the path of crime] beside the others.

CANTO XX

Divine Grace

*The eagle names the souls in the lights that form its eye. Among them
are two pagans, Trajan and Ripheus. Dante wonders how these two
could have been saved and learns that both had faith in Christ.
Through the intercession of Gregory the Great, Trajan was allowed
to return to earth from Limbus to be converted to Christianity and to
die a second time. Ripheus, an inconspicuous character of the Aeneid,
permitted somehow to believe in Christ to come, shows how Divine
Grace is as unfathomable to our understanding as Divine Justice.*

When the sun which lights the whole world
    disappears from our hemisphere
    so that the day on every side is spent,

the sky, before enkindled by it alone,
    suddenly makes itself apparent
    with many lights [stars] on which one splendor [the sun]
        shines,

and this change came to my mind
    when the ensign of the world and of its leaders
    became silent in its blessed beak,

since all those living lights,
    shining much more brightly, began songs
    which have fallen and disappeared from my memory.   12

O sweet Love, clothed in a smile,
    how ardent didst Thou appear in those pipes
    which had the breath alone of holy thoughts!

After the precious and shining gems
    with which I saw the sixth heaven jeweled
    imposed silence on their angelic chimes,

I seemed to hear the murmuring of a river
    descending clear from stone to stone,
    showing the abundance of its high source;

and, as at the neck of a lute
    the sound takes its form, and as the breath
    within a pipe at the holes,   24

so, without delay or waiting
    that murmuring of the eagle
    rose through its apparently hollow neck.

There it became voice and issued
    through its beak in the form of words,
    for which my heart that inscribed them waited.

"The part of me which sees," it began,
    "and which in mortal eagles endures the sun,
    now must be inspected closely,

for, of the lights with which I am formed,
    those that make my eye sparkle
    were supreme in all their ranks.   36

The one that shines in the middle as the pupil
    was [David] the singer of the Holy Spirit
    who bore the Ark [of the Covenant] from house to house.

Now he knows the merit of his song,
    insofar as a result of his own counsel,
    by the reward which is equally great.

Of the five which make a circle for an eyebrow,
    the one closest to my beak [Trajan]
    consoled the poor widow for her son.

Now he knows how dear it costs

not to follow Christ by his experience
with the sweet life and with its opposite.

And the one [King Hezekiah] who follows in the circum-
         ference
    of which I speak, upon the upper arch,
    delayed his death by his true penitence.

Now he knows that eternal decrees [plans]
    are not violated when a worthy prayer
    turns todays into tomorrows down on earth [delays them].

The other [Constantine] with the laws and me [the eagle]
    became a Greek, and by giving [the Western Empire]
    to the shepherd [pope], with good intent, produced evil.

Now he knows how the wrong resulting
    from his good deed is not harmful to him
    although the world is destroyed by it.   60

And the one you see on the downward arc
    was William [II of Sicily], regretted by the land
    which weeps because of the living Charles and Fred-
         erick.

Now he knows how Heaven is enamored
    of righteous kings, and by his flashing
    he still is making that apparent.

Who down in the erring world
    would believe the Trojan, Ripheus, was the fifth
    of the holy lights in this circle?

Now he knows much about divine grace
    that the world cannot see, although even his sight
    does not penetrate to the bottom."   72

As a lark soaring in the air
    first sings and then is silent, content
    with the last sweetness which satisfies it,

so the image appeared to me
    under the imprint of the Eternal Pleasure
    by whose will everything becomes what it is,

and, although there in my doubt I was like glass
    [transparent] to the color that shows through it,
    this doubt did not endure to wait in silence,

but, from my tongue, "What things are these?"
    it urged with the force of its own weight;
    whereupon I saw a great revelry of flashing.   **84**

Then, soon, with a brighter eye,
    the blessed ensign answered me,
    not to keep me suspended in my wonder.

"I see that you believe these things
    because I say them, but do not see how,
    so that, although believed, they remain mysterious.

You do like those who apprehend a thing
    by name but cannot see its essence
    unless another discloses it.

Regnum coelorum[1] suffers violence [is moved]
    only from warm love and living hope
    which vanquish the divine will,   **96**

not as men overcome each other,
    but because it wishes to be overcome
    and, vanquished, it conquers with its own kindness.

The first and fifth life [souls] of the eyebrow [Trajan and
        Ripheus]
    make you marvel because you see
    the region of the angels embellished with them.

From their bodies they did not come, as you believe,
    as Gentiles, but as Christians, with firm faith
    in the feet [of Christ] to be pierced or already pierced;

for one returned to his flesh from Hell
    whence there is no direct return to good will,
    and that was a reward for the living hope [of Gregory]—   **108**

for the living hope which put power
    into prayers made to God to resuscitate him,
    so that His will might be changed.

The glorious soul of whom I am speaking,
    having returned to the flesh for a while,
    believed in Him who could aid him,

and, believing, was so enkindled with flames

---

[1] "The kingdom of the heavens."

of true love that, on his second death,
he was worthy of coming to this festival.

The other [Ripheus], through grace
which is distilled from so deep a spring
that no creature ever saw to the bottom, 120

put all his love below on uprightness;
wherefore, from grace to grace,
God opened his eyes to our future redemption,

and he believed in it and did not endure
from then on the stench of paganism
and reproached the perverse people for it.

Those three ladies [the Christian virtues] whom you saw
at the right wheel [of the chariot] replaced baptism
more than a thousand years before baptism.

O predestination! how remote your source is
from the vision that does not see
the First Cause entire! 132

And you, mortals, be careful
about making judgments, for we who see God
do not yet know all the elect;

and such a defect is sweet to us,
for our good is so refined in this good
that whatever God wishes we also want."

Thus, by that divine image,
to clear up my short vision,
a sweet medicine was given to me;

and, as a good lute player accompanies a singer
with the vibration of the strings,
and the song acquires a greater charm, 144

so, while it spoke, I recall
that I saw the two blessed lights [Trajan and Ripheus]
with the unison of blinking eyes

move their flames to the measure of the words.

CANTO XXI

The Rise to Saturn

The cold heaven of Saturn symbolizes the monastic life, the life of contemplation. The only warmth, a mere trace, comes from the constellation Leo. No song is heard here, no smile even of Beatrice brightens the severe atmosphere. But a ladder of golden light (Jacob's ladder) appears as a symbol of contemplation.

Already my eyes were fixed on the face
    of my lady, and my mind with them;
    withdrawn from every other concern.

She did not smile but, "If I smiled," she began,
    "you would become like Semele [on beholding Jupiter]
    when she was changed to ashes;

for my beauty which, as you have seen,
    on the steps of the eternal palace,
    is kindled more the higher the ascent,

if not tempered shines so much
    that your mortal sight in its flashing
    would be like a bough struck by a thunderbolt.   12

We have risen to the seventh splendor
    which, under the breast of the ardent Lion [Leo],
    radiates below its fused influence.

Let your mind follow your eyes
    and make of them mirrors for the figure
    which in this mirror [heaven] will appear."

Anyone who knew how my eyes
    loved to feed on the blessed countenance,
    by my paying attention to something else

would realize how pleasing it was to me also
    to obey my celestial escort,
    balancing one with the other.   24

Within the crystal which bears the name
   of the famed ruler [Saturn] under whom
   [in the Golden Age] all malice lay dead,

of a golden color on which sunlight shone
   I saw a ladder rising so high
   that my sight could not follow.

I saw also coming down the steps
   so many splendors that I thought every light
   in Heaven had been poured down it.

And, as by natural custom, the daws move together
   at the beginning of the day
   to warm their cold feathers,   36

then some go away without returning,
   others fly back to where they started,
   and still others delay, circling about;

thus a similar movement appeared to me
   to occur in that sparkling
   as soon as it reached a certain step.

And one light which stopped nearest to us
   became so bright that I said, thinking,
   "I see, indeed, the love that you point out to me."

But she from whom I await the how and when
   of speech and of silence, was still; wherefore I,
   contrary to my desire, did well not to ask.   48

She who understood my silence
   in the vision of Him who sees all
   said to me, "Set free your warm desire."

And I began, "My merit does not make me worthy
   of your reply, but for her sake
   who permits me to ask,

O blessed life, hidden within your joy,
   make known to me why you
   have placed yourself so near me,

and tell why the sweet symphony of Paradise
   which below sounds so devoutly
   is silent in this heaven."   60

"Your hearing is mortal, like your vision,"
he answered me, "therefore there is no song here,
for the same reason Beatrice has no smile.

Down over the steps of the holy stairs
I descended so far only to welcome you
with speech and the light that envelops me.

Greater love [than that of the other souls] did not make me
quicker,
for the same amount or more glows up above,
as the flaming makes manifest to you.

But the supreme charity which makes us ready servants
of the counsel which governs the world
allots [functions] here as you observe."   72

"I see well," I said, "O sacred light,
how love in this court is enough
for following the eternal Providence;

but this is what seemed hard for me:
why you alone among those with you
were predestined to this office."

*Dante's question about predestination incurs a check: even the angels
cannot give the answer.*

I had not reached the last word
before the light made an axis of its center
and whirled, like a swift millstone.

Then the love that was in it answered,
"A divine light is directed on me,
penetrating this glow in which I am contained,   84

whose virtue, combined with my vision,
lifts me so far above myself that I see
the Supreme Essence from which it is derived.

Thence comes the joy with which I shine,
because I match the clarity of my flame
to the clearness of my vision.

But that soul which is brightest in Heaven,
the Seraph which has its eye most fixed on God,
could not satisfy your request,

because what you ask goes so deep
    into the abyss of the eternal law
    that it is cut off from every created vision.   96

And when you return, report this to the mortal world,
    so that it will not presume any more
    to advance toward [understanding] such a goal.

The mind which shines here, on earth is dull;
    so consider if it can do down there
    what it cannot accomplish in Heaven."

His words imposed such limits
    that I gave up the question and restrained myself
    to asking humbly who he was.

"Between the two shores of Italy,
    not far from your native land, crags rise so high
    that thunder sounds much lower down.   108

They form a ridge, called Catria,
    beneath which a hermitage is consecrated
    which used to be devoted to worship only."

Thus he began his third speech,
    and continuing said to me,
    "There I became so firm in the service of God

that with food [for fast days] seasoned only with olive juice,
    I easily endured heat and cold,
    content with contemplative thoughts.

That cloister used to produce abundantly
    for these heavens, but now has become empty,
    as soon must be revealed.   120

In that place was I, Peter Damian,
    (and I called myself Peter the Sinner, in the House
    of Our Lady, on the Adriatic shore).

Little of mortal life was left for me
    when I was called to that [cardinal's] hat
    which is now passed on from bad to worse.

Once St. Peter and the Great Vessel
    of the Holy Spirit [Paul] came thin and barefooted,
    taking their food from any hostelry.

Now the modern shepherds want someone

to prop them on this side and that, so portly are they,
and one to lead and one behind to hold their trains. **132**

They cover their palfreys with their mantles,
so that two beasts go under one cloak.
O Patience, that endures so much!"

At these words I saw many little flames
descending and circling from step to step,
and every turn made them more beautiful.

Around this one they came and stopped
and uttered a shout [of reprobation] of such deep sound
that it would not be paralleled on earth,

nor did I understand it, the thunder so overcame me.

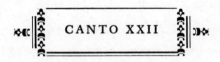

CANTO XXII

St. Benedict—The Heaven of the Fixed Stars

Dante is startled by the deafening cry of reprobation at the end of the last canto.

Oppressed by stupor, I turned to my guide
as a child does who runs
to where he feels most secure,

and she, like a mother who consoles quickly
her pale and breathless son
with her voice which is wont to reassure him,

said to me, "Do you not know you are in Heaven,
and do you not realize that Heaven is all holy,
and that what is done here comes from good will?

How the song would have changed you, or how I would,
if I had smiled, you can now imagine,
since this cry has so deeply moved you. **12**

If you had understood the prayers made in it [the cry],

the vengeance which you will see
before you die would be known already to you.

The sword up there does not cut hastily
nor slowly, except in the opinion of those
who, desiring or fearing, wait for it.

But turn now to the other lights,
for you will see many illustrious spirits
if, as I suggest, you look back."

As pleased her, I turned and saw
a hundred little globes of light
which embellished each other with mutual rays.   24

I stood like one who represses
the prick of desire and does not venture
to ask, fearing to go too far.

Then the largest and most lustrous
of those pearls came forward
to satisfy my wish,

and within it I heard, "If you saw
as I do the charity that burns among us,
your thoughts would have been spoken;

but that you may not retard
your high goal by waiting, I will reply
to the question you keep silent.   36

The summit of the mountain on whose slope
Cassino lies was once frequented
by deceived and ill-disposed people [pagans],

and I [St. Benedict] am the one who first took there
the name of Him who brought to earth
the truth that so exalts us.

And so much grace shone upon me
that I redeemed the surrounding villages
from the impious cult which seduced the world.

These other flames were all contemplative spirits,
kindled by that warmth
which gives birth to holy flowers and fruit.

Here is [Saint] Macarius, here is [Saint] Romualdus,

here are my brothers who within the cloisters
   stayed their feet and kept their hearts sound."

And I to him, "The affection that you show
   in speaking to me, and the kind looks
   that I see and note in all your ardors

have enlarged my trust as much
   as the sun does the rose
   that opens as fully as it can.

Therefore I beg you, and may you, Father,
   assure me if I can have such grace
   as to see you unveiled."   60

Then he, "Brother, your great wish
   will be fulfilled in the last sphere
   where mine and all others are realized.

There every desire is perfect,
   mature, and entire; there alone
   is every part where it always was,

because it is not a space and has no pole [revolution];
   and our ladder rises to it,
   extending up beyond your sight.

Up there the patriarch Jacob
   saw its top when it appeared
   so burdened with angels.   72

But no one now lifts his feet from the earth
   to climb it, and my rule
   has remained like waste paper.

The walls which used to be an abbey
   have become dens, and the cowls
   are sacks full of bad flour.

But heavy usury does not rebel more
   against the pleasure of God than that income
   which makes the hearts of monks so foolish;

for whatever the Church has in its keeping
   belongs to the [poor] folk who ask for it in God's name,
   not to relatives or to others still uglier.   84

The flesh of mortals is so soft

that on earth a good beginning is not enough
from the oak's sprouting to the forming of acorns.

Peter began without gold and silver,
and I with prayers and fasting;
and Francis started his convent humbly.

And if you look at the beginnings of each,
then see where each has strayed,
you will see white changed to brown.

But, through God's wish, help [to correct this]
would be less marvelous
than the Jordan turned back or the sea opened."   96

Thus he spoke, then drew back
to his company which assembled
and like a whirlwind rose.

Dante now ascends to the heaven of the Fixed Stars, entering the
constellation of Gemini, under which he was born.

The sweet lady moved me up that ladder
behind them, merely at a signal,
so did her virtue dominate me.

Never where we mount and descend naturally
has there been a motion rapid enough
to be compared to my flight.

As I hope to return, Reader, to that devout triumph
for the sake of which I often grieve
for my sins and strike my breast,   108

you could not have put your finger in the fire
and withdrawn it so quickly as I saw and was
in the constellation that follows Taurus.

O glorious stars, O light pregnant
with great virtue, to which I owe
all my genius, however it may be!

Under you I was born, and in you
was the sun, the father of all mortal life,
when first I breathed the Tuscan air.

Then when the grace was given me

to enter the lofty sphere that turns you,
    your region was allotted to me.   120

To you my soul now devoutly sighs
    to gain strength for the hard task
    which draws me to itself.

"You are so close to the ultimate salvation,"
    Beatrice began, "that your eyes
    must be keen and clear.

Therefore, before entering it, look down
    and see how great a world
    I have already put beneath your feet,

so that your heart, while rejoicing,
    may present itself to the triumphant throng
    which moves happily through this ethereal sphere."   132

I turned my eyes down through all the seven spheres,
    and I saw this globe of ours such
    that I smiled at its mean appearance;

and I approve that opinion as best which esteems it
    of least account; so that those who think
    of something else can truly be called righteous.

I saw the daughter of Latona [the moon]
    without the spots which once
    made me believe it was rare and dense.

The face of your child [the sun], Hyperion,
    I sustained there, and I saw how Maia [Mercury]
    and Dione [Venus] move about and near him.   144

Next appeared to me the tempering of Jupiter
    between his father [Saturn] and his son [Mars],
    and I saw clearly the varying of their positions;

and all seven showed me how great they are
    and how rapidly they move
    and in what remote regions they are placed.

While I was turning with the eternal Twins [the Gemini]
    there appeared to me the threshing floor [the earth]
    which makes us so fierce, from its hills to its river mouths.

Then, to the beautiful eyes [of Beatrice] I directed mine.

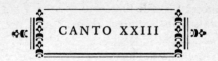

CANTO XXIII

The Triumph of Christ and Mary

*In this heaven, the starry sphere, a traditional symbol of the Church,
all the elect are assembled with the apostles and the evangelists. Dante
has a vision of the triumph among them of Christ and Mary.*

As the bird among the beloved leaves,
     having rested on the nest of her sweet brood
     during the night which hides things from us,

who, to see their longed-for faces
     and to find the food with which to feed them
     (which heavy task is a joy for her)

anticipates the dawn on the open branch,
     and with ardent affection waits for the sun,
     looking intently for the day to break;

so my lady stood erect and attentive,
     turned toward the point [the meridian]
     where the sun shows least haste,   12

and I, seeing her rapt and eager,
     became like one who, while waiting,
     wishes for something and satisfies himself with hope.

But there was little time between one "when" and the other,
     I mean the "when" of waiting and that
     of my seeing the heaven more and more resplendent.

Beatrice said, "Behold the army
     of the triumph of Christ, and all the fruit
     gathered from the circling of these spheres."

It seemed to me that her face was all aflame,
     and her eyes were so full of joy
     that I must forgo description.   24

As when, clear and full, Trivia [the moon]
     smiles among the eternal nymphs [stars]
     that paint the sky in all its depths,

I saw, above thousands of lights,
    a Sun [Christ] which kindled them all,
    as ours does the stars.

And through the living light
    the gleaming Substance shone so brightly
    upon my face that I endured it not.

O Beatrice, sweet and dear guide!—
    She said to me, "What overcomes you
    is a power against which there is no defense.   36

It is the Wisdom and the Power
    which opened the road from earth to Heaven
    for which there had been such long desire."

As fire [lightning] flashes from a cloud
    (through expanding so that it has no room)
    and, contrary to its nature, falls to the ground,

so my mind, in this feast of the spirit,
    becoming greater, transcended itself,
    and what it became I cannot recall.

"Open your eyes and see how I am [Beatrice said];
    you have witnessed things which have made you
    able to sustain my smile."   48

I was like one who is reminded
    of a forgotten dream and who endeavors
    in vain to bring it back to mind

when I heard this invitation, worthy of such gratitude
    as never to be extinguished
    from the book that records the past.

If now all those tongues sounded to help me
    which Polyhymnia with her sisters [the Muses]
    made richest with their sweet milk,

they would not come to a thousandth part
    of the truth, singing of the smile
    and how bright it made the holy face.   60

Thus, in presenting Paradise
    the sacred poem must leap,
    like one who finds his way cut off.

But whoever considers the heavy theme

and the mortal shoulders loaded with it,
will not find fault if they stagger under it.

It is not a voyage for a little bark
which the bold prow goes cleaving,
nor for a boatman sparing of himself.

In a scene similar to the one in the Garden of Eden, Christ and Mary reascend to the Empyrean, and St. Peter remains with his flock in the place of Christ.

"Why does my face so enamor you
that you do not turn to the beautiful garden
which blossoms under the rays of Christ?   72

There is the Rose [Mary] in which the Divine Word
became flesh; there are the lilies [apostles]
whose odor marked the good path."

Thus Beatrice; and I, wholly ready
for her counsel, again gave myself up
to the battle of my feeble vision.

As my eyes, covered by a shadow,
have seen a meadow full of flowers, under sunlight
that streamed bright through a rifted cloud,

so now I saw many throngs of splendors,
brightened from above by ardent rays,
without perceiving the source of the gleams.   84

O benign Virtue [Christ] that so stamps them,
Thou didst rise on high to make it possible
for my eyes, no longer sufficient, to see.

The name of the beautiful flower [Mary], which I invoke
morning and evening, constrained my mind
to gaze at its now greatest flame;

and when both my eyes had portrayed for me
the quality and the grandeur of the living star
which conquers up there as it did here below,

from within the heavens a torch [Gabriel]
descended circling, and girt her
with a crown [halo] and revolved around her.   96

Whatever melody sounds sweetest here below

and draws the soul most to it
would seem a cloud, rent, and thundering,

compared with the sound of that lyre
with which is crowned the beautiful sapphire [Mary]
by which this clearest heaven is so brightly jeweled.

"I am angelic love, circling the lofty joy
which emanates from the womb
that was the hostelry of Our Desire,

and I shall circle, Lady of Heaven, until thou
followest thy Son and makest the highest heaven
more divine by entering it."   108

Thus the circling melody scaled itself [ended],
and all the other lights
sounded the name of Mary.

The royal mantle of all the revolutions
of the world [the Empyrean], which is most fervid
and quickened most by the breath of God and by His
      ways,

had its inner shore so high above us
that from where I was
it still did not appear to me.

Therefore my eyes did not have the strength
to follow the crowned flame
which mounted after her Son.   120

And as an infant who, after he has nursed,
stretches his arms toward his mother
through gratitude which shows outwardly,

each of those bright souls stretched upward
with its flames, so that the great affection
they had for Mary was evident to me.

Then they remained in my sight
singing *Regina coeli*[1] so sweetly
that never has the delight left me.

Oh, the abundance stored

---

[1] "Queen of Heaven."

in the rich coffers of those
who were good husbandmen in sowing down below!

There [in heaven] they live and rejoice in that treasure
acquired in the Babylonian exile,
where gold was left aside.

There under the exalted Son of God
and Mary, and with the old
and the new council, triumphs in his victory

he [St. Peter] who holds the keys to such glory.

CANTO XXIV

The Examination in Faith

"O company chosen for the great supper
of the Blessed Lamb who feeds you
so that your desire is always satisfied,

if, through the grace of God, this one [Dante]
has a foretaste of what falls from your table
before death cuts time short for him,

consider his immense longing and refresh him
somewhat. You drink ever at the fount [of Truth]
upon which his thought is bent."

Thus Beatrice; and those happy souls
made spheres of themselves
on fixed poles, flaming like comets,

and, as wheels in clocks turn,
so that to someone looking
one appears still, while another flies,

so those lights, dancing
at varying speeds, slow and fast,
made me judge of their riches [joy].

From the one that seemed most beautiful

12

I saw a flame issue so joyously
that none was left there brighter,

and it moved around Beatrice three times
with a song so divine
that my fancy does not recall it; 24

therefore my pen leaps ahead in its writing,
for our imagination—not to say our speech—
is of too light a color for such deep folds.

"O my holy sister, you who so devoutly pray to us
through your ardent affection,
you release [bring] me from our round."

The holy fire, having stopped,
directed to my lady its breath,
which spoke as I have said.

And she, "O eternal light of the great man [Peter]
to whom our Lord left the keys
to the marvelous joy He brought below, 36

test this man, as you please,
on the grave and minor points of that faith
through which you walked on the water.

Whether he loves well and hopes well and believes
is not hidden from you, because your vision extends
to where everything is depicted,

but since this heaven makes citizens
through true faith, it is well he be called upon
to speak of it and to glorify it."

As the scholar arms himself, but does not speak
until the master proposes the question—
to reason about it, not to decide it— 48

so I armed myself with every argument
while she was speaking, to be ready
for such a question and such an examiner.

*St. Peter now conducts in the scholastic manner the examination in
Faith.*

*Comprehension of the Christian virtues must precede the direct vision
of God. Since these are essentially human, it is fitting that a man*

*should expound them. The blessed retain Love, but in a purified
form; Hope, however, has changed for them to fulfillment and Faith
to knowledge.*

["Speak, good Christian, make yourself clear,
        what is Faith?" I raised my face
        toward that light from which this came,
then turned to Beatrice and she quickly
        made signs that I should pour forth
        from my inner fount.
"May the grace which grants that I confess
        before the great Commander," I began,
        "cause my thoughts to be well expressed!"   60
And I continued, "As the true pen
        of your dear brother [Paul] who, with you, Father,
        put Rome on the good path, wrote for us,
Faith is the substance of things hoped for
        and evidence of things unseen,
        and this seems to be its essence."
Then I heard, "You think rightly
        if you understand why he [Paul] placed it
        among the substances and then in the evidence."
And I, "The profound things
        which favor me with their appearance here
        are so hidden from eyes below   72
that their existence is merely a belief
        on which their great hope is founded,
        and therefore is in the class
of substances, and from this belief
        we must argue without seeing more;
        therefore it contains the idea of evidence."
Then I heard, "If all that is acquired below
        through teaching were understood thus,
        the Sophists' minds would have no place there."
Thus breathed forth that kindled love;
        then it added, "The composition and weight
        of this money is covered well,   84
but tell me if you have it in your purse."
        Whereupon I, "Yes, so clear and sound
        that in its stamp nothing is dubious."

Then from the profound light
    which shone there, "This dear jewel
    on which every virtue is based,
whence did it come to you?" And I, "The abundant rain
    of the Holy Spirit which is diffused
    over the old and new parchments [Testaments]
is the argument that has proved it for me
    so sharply that compared with it
    every demonstration seems obtuse."   96
I heard then, "The ancient and new premises
    which make you conclude this,
    why do you hold them as divine?"
And I, "The proof that the truth is disclosed
    lies in the works [miracles] that followed for which
    Nature never heated iron nor struck an anvil."
He replied, "Who assures you
    that those deeds really occurred? Only the thing
    you want to prove confirms it."
"If the world turned to Christianity," I said,
    "without miracles, this fact is such
    that the others are not a hundredth part [as miraculous],   108
for you entered poor and hungry
    into the field to sow the good plant
    which was once a vine and now has become a thorn."
I having ended, the holy court
    resounded through the spheres a "God we praise,"
    with the melody that up there is heard,
and that lord who had drawn me
    from branch to branch in his test
    so that we were drawing close to the last leaves,
began again, "The grace which enlightens your mind
    has opened your mouth
    until now as it should,   120
so that I approve what has come forth,
    but now you must express what you believe,
    and whence your belief came to you."
"O holy father, you who see now
    what you once believed, so that you
    outstripped younger feet in [entering] the tomb [of
        Christ],"

I began, "you wish that I manifest
    here the essence of my ready belief,
    and you ask also about the cause of it,
and I answer, I believe in one God
    alone and eternal who, not moved,
    moves all the heavens with love and with desire,   132
and for such belief I have not only proofs
    physical and metaphysical, but that truth
    also gives it to me which rains down from here
through Moses, the prophets, the psalms,
    through the Gospels, and through you [apostles] who
        wrote
    after the ardent spirit made you holy.
And I believe in three eternal Persons,
    and these I believe one Essence, so unified
    and threefold that they agree with both *are* and *is.*
On the profound, divine state of being
    of which I speak now, the evangelical doctrine
    many times puts the seal.   144
This is the source, this is the spark
    which afterward grows into a living flame,
    and shines within me, like a star in heaven."
As the master who hears news that pleases him
    and embraces his servant, congratulating him for it
    as soon as the latter is silent,
so, blessing me while singing, the apostolic light,
    at whose command I had spoken,
    three times encircled me when I was silent,
so much did I please him with my remarks!]

CANTO XXV

The Examination in Hope

Before his examination in Hope, Dante expresses his greatest earthly longing, that is, to receive the poet's laurel crown in the city from which he had been exiled.

If it ever happens that the sacred poem
    to which Heaven and earth have set hand,
    and which has kept me lean for many years,

overcomes the cruelty which has barred me
    from the fair sheepfold where, a lamb, I slept,
    a foe to the wolves that war on it,

then with another voice and another fleece [a beard]
    I will return a poet, and on the font
    of my baptism I will receive the laurel crown;

because there I joined the faith
    which makes souls recognized by God
    and for which Peter circled my brow.   **12**

St. James, whose tomb in Galicia was a favorite shrine for pilgrims, greets St. Peter elaborately, perhaps to indicate the harmony between the Hope and Faith for which they stand. Then St. James examines Dante in Hope.

[Then a light moved toward us
    from the sphere whence had come [St. Peter] the first
    of the vicars that Christ left,

and my lady, full of joy, said to me,
    "Look! Behold the baron [St. James] for whose sake
    people down below visit Galicia!"

As when a dove alights near its mate
    and one lavishes affection on the other,
    circling and murmuring,

so I saw one great, glorious prince
    greet another, praising the food
    that up there feeds them.   **24**

After the greeting was over,
    each *coram me*[1] stopped silent,
    so fiery that my eyes were blinded.

Beatrice then said, smiling,
    "Illustrious soul, you by whom
    the generosity of our court was revealed,

make hope sound forth in this height.
    You know that you personified it as many times
    as Jesus bestowed most favor on three of you."

---

[1] "Before me."

"Lift up your head and be reassured,
 for what comes here from the mortal world
 must be ripened in our rays."   36
This comfort came to me from the second flame,
 so that I lifted my eyes toward the greatness
 which at first kept them lowered with excessive light.
"Since our Emperor, through his grace,
 wishes that before death you confront
 all his nobles in his most secret chamber,
so that having seen the truth of this court
 you may comfort in yourself and others
 the hope that causes righteous love on earth,
tell what it is, and how your mind
 blossoms with it, and whence it came to you."
 Thus the second light continued;   48
and that tender one who guided the feathers
 of my wings in so high a flight
 anticipated my reply.
"The Church Militant has no son
 with greater hope, as is written
 in the Sun that shines on all our host;
therefore he [Dante] was allowed to come
 from Egypt [the world] to see Jerusalem [Heaven]
 before his life's warfare was over.
The other two points which are not asked
 to learn but so that he may tell
 how greatly this virtue pleases you   60
I leave to him, for they will not be hard
 nor involve vainglory; so may he answer,
 and may the grace of God help him."
As a student, ready and willing,
 who, to reveal his learning,
 replies concerning what he knows,
"Hope," I said, "is a sure expectation
 of future glory which Divine Grace
 and precedent merit produce.
From many stars this light comes to me
 but the singer [David] of the Supreme Leader
 instilled it first in my heart.   72
'Let them hope in Thee,' he says

in his sacred song, 'those who know Thy name'
and who does not know it if he shares my faith?
You, afterward, in your epistle
also instilled it in me, so that I
am full [of hope] and shower it on others."
While I was speaking, within that flame
a flash broke forth,
sudden and repeated, like lightning;
then it breathed, "The love with which I still burn
for the virtue [hope] which followed me
even to the palm [of martyrdom] and the end of the
battle [of life]   84
wishes that I speak once more to you
who delight in it; it is my pleasure
that you tell what hope promises you."
And I, "The New and Old Testaments
set down the goal of the souls
God made friendly to Himself, and point it out to us.
Isaiah says that each will be clothed
in his home with a double garment [body and light]
and that home is this sweet life.
And your brother [John] far more explicitly
when he deals with the white robes
makes this revelation manifest to us."   96
Then near the end of these words
"*Sperent in te*"² was heard above us
to which all the choirs answered.]

*St. John, who is to examine Dante in Love, now appears as bright as
the sun. Dante, trying to confirm the legend that this saint went to
Heaven in the flesh, looks so intently that he becomes blind, like Love
itself.*

Then among these [carols] a light brightened
so that if [the constellation] Cancer had such brilliancy
the winter would have a month of a single day;

and as a happy maiden rises
and enters the dance (merely to honor
the bride, and not for any vanity),

---

² "Let them hope in thee."

so I saw the brightened splendor [St. John]
   come to the two who were turning
   as befitted their ardent love.   108

It entered then into the song and measure,
   and my lady kept her gaze on them,
   like a bride, silent and motionless.

"This is the one who lay upon the breast
   of the Pelican [Christ], and who was chosen
   from the cross for the great office [care of Mary]."

Thus my lady spoke, but no more after
   than before her words
   did she move her eyes from her fixed intent.

As one who looks and strives
   to see the sun partly eclipsed,
   who, to see, becomes unseeing,   120

so was I before that last flame
   while the words came, "Why do you blind yourself
   trying to see something not here?

My body is on earth and will be there
   with the others until our number
   is equal to the eternal purpose.

With both robes [body and light] in the blessed cloister
   are only those two [Jesus and Mary] who ascended;
   and this you shall report in your world."

At these words the flaming circle became quiet,
   together with the sweet concert made by the sound
   of the threefold breath [Peter, James, John],   132

just as, to avoid weariness or peril,
   the oars, at first driven through the water,
   rest at the sound of a whistle.

Oh, how greatly I was moved
   at not being able to see Beatrice
   when I turned to look at her

although near to her and in the happy world!

CANTO XXVI

The Examination in Love—Adam

St. John's examination in Love, carried on during Dante's blindness,
is brief, since the poet's whole life had been inspired by this feeling in
one form or another. Dante affirms that he loves God and the rest of
the universe insofar as it is like its Creator, since true love must be
kindled by the greatest goodness.

[While I was apprehensive because of my destroyed sight,
    a breath issued from the glowing flame
    that had quenched it, gaining my attention
and saying, "Until you have regained
    the sight you consumed on me,
    it is well to make up for it by speaking.
Begin then and say on what aim your mind is fixed;
    be certain that although your sight
    has lapsed, it is not destroyed,
because the lady, who through this divine region
    leads you, has in her glance
    the power of the hand of Ananias [to restore sight]."   12
I said, "May the cure come soon or late at her pleasure
    to the eyes that were gates through which
    she entered with the fire [love] that always burns in me.
The Good that contents this court
    is the alpha and omega of every scripture
    that love proclaims loudly or faintly."
The voice which had removed my fear
    at the sudden blindness
    gave me the care of speaking further
and said, "Certainly through a finer sieve
    you must sift; you must declare
    who directed your bow [love] to such a goal."   24
And I, "Through philosophical arguments
    and through the authority which descends from here
    such love had to be impressed in me;

for the Good, as Good, as when understood,
 kindles love, and all the greater
 in proportion to its degree of goodness.
Thus to the Essence in which such supremacy exists
 that all good found outside of it
 is only a ray of its own light,
the mind of everyone who discerns the truth
 on which this argument is founded
 must move more than elsewhere in its love.   36
Such truth is unfolded to my intellect
 by that one [Aristotle] who shows me the first love
 of all the eternal substances [souls].
The voice of the true Author unfolds it
 who said to Moses, speaking of Himself,
 'I will make you see all worth.'
You, too, unfolded it to me at the beginning
 of the lofty proclamation [gospel] that announces
  clearly
 to the world below the mystery of this place on high."
And I heard, "Through human reason
 and through authority agreeing with it
 your supreme love looks to God,   48
but tell further if you feel that other ties
 draw you toward Him, so that you may declare
 with how many teeth this love bites you."
The holy intention of the Eagle of Christ [John]
 was not hidden and I perceived
 where he wished to lead my profession.
Therefore I began again, "All these things whose bites
 can make the heart turn to God
 have concurred in creating my love;
for the existence of the world and my own,
 the death He bore so that I might live,
 and what all the faithful hope for, as I do, 60
together with the vivid assurance mentioned,
 have drawn me from the sea of perverted love
 and have placed me on the shore of the true.
The leaves which cover with foliage
 the garden of the Eternal Gardener, I love
 in proportion to the good brought to them by Him."]

After the examination Adam appears and answers Dante's questions about the nature of his sin, the date of his creation, the language he invented and spoke, and how long he remained in the Garden of Eden.

[As I was silent a sweet song
    resounded through Heaven, and my lady
    with the others said, "Holy, holy, holy."
And, as sleep is broken by a bright light
    when the visual spirit meets its splendor
    passing from membrane to membrane,   72
and the one awakened shrinks from what he sees,
    so undiscerning is his sudden sight
    until judgment helps him,
thus Beatrice banished every mote from my eyes
    by the radiance of her own,
    which shone for more than a thousand miles,
so that I then saw better than before;
    and as if amazed I asked
    about a fourth light I saw with us.
And my lady, "Within those rays
    the first soul ever created by the First Power
    gazes with joy on its Maker."   84
As a bough which bends its top
    at the passing of the wind, then rises
    through its own force which uplifts it,
so I did while she was speaking,
    and the desire to ask
    with which I was burning gave me assurance
to say, "O fruit, alone produced mature,
    ancient Father, of whom every bride
    is a daughter and daughter-in-law,
as devoutly as I can I beg you to speak.
    You perceive my wish
    and to hear you sooner I do not express it."   96
Sometimes an animal when covered up stirs
    so that its impulses are apparent
    because the covering moves with them;
and in a like way the first soul
    showed through his covering
    how happy he was to do me pleasure.
Then he breathed forth these words,

"I discern better your wish without its being uttered
    than you do what seems most certain,
because I see it in the truthful Mirror
    which reflects all things
    while nothing can reflect all of It.   108
You wish to hear how long it is
    since God placed me in the lofty garden
    where she [Beatrice] prepared you for the high stairs,
and how long it was a delight to my eyes,
    and the real cause of the great wrath,
    and the language that I created and used.
Now, my son, the tasting of the tree
    was not in itself the cause of so great an exile,
    but only the trespassing beyond the mark [disobedience].
In that place [Limbus] from which Virgil
    was sent by your lady I longed for this assembly
    during four thousand, three hundred revolutions of the
        sun,   120
and while I was on earth I saw it return
    to all the lights [stars] on its path
    nine hundred and thirty times.
The tongue I spoke was all extinct
    before the people of Nimrod
    began their impossible task,
for no product of the mind lasts long
    because of human fancy
    which changes as the heavens move.
For man to speak is natural,
    but whether this way or that,
    Nature leaves to him to do as he pleases.   132
Before I went to the infernal anguish,
    the Supreme Good from which comes the joy
    that enfolds me, was called 'I' on earth.
Later it was named 'El,' and that is fitting,
    for mortal speech is like a leaf on a branch
    which disappears when another comes.
On the mountain [Eden] which rises highest from the sea
    I stayed with life pure and disgraced [before and after
        the Fall]
    from the first hour to that which follows the sixth,
when the sun changes its quadrant."]

CANTO XXVII

The Wrath of Heaven

Adam's speech in the last canto is answered by a doxology in which all Paradise joins. The four "torches"—Peter, James, John, and Adam— stand before Dante, and when St. Peter refers to Boniface VIII and points out the corruption into which the papacy has fallen, the smile of Paradise changes to a blush of shame.

"Glory to the Father, to the Son,
 and to the Holy Spirit," all Paradise began,
 so that the sweet song inebriated me.

What I saw seemed a smile of the universe,
 and my intoxication came
 both through hearing and through sight.

O joy! O ineffable gladness!
 O life compact of love and peace!
 O riches, secure, without longing!

Before my eyes the four torches stood enkindled,
 and the one [St. Peter] who came first
 began to make itself more vivid.   12

It became [red] as Jupiter would
 if it and Mars, like birds of different color,
 exchanged their plumage.

Providence which here allots turns and offices
 had imposed silence everywhere
 on the blessed chorus,

when I heard, "If I change color
 marvel not, for while I am speaking,
 you will see all change.

That one [Boniface VIII] who on earth
 usurps my place, my place which is vacant
 in the sight of the Son of God,   24

has made of my cemetery a sewer

of blood and filth, so that the perverse one [Lucifer]
who fell from here is pleased."

With that color displayed by a cloud in the morning
or evening when the sun is opposite it
I saw all the heavens covered;

and, as a modest lady, sure of herself,
through another's fault becomes embarrassed
merely by hearing of it,

so Beatrice changed countenance;
and such an eclipse occurred in Heaven,
I believe, when the Supreme Power suffered.   36

Then his [St. Peter's] words proceeded in a voice
so transformed that his face
did not change more in color.

"The Bride of Christ was not nurtured with my blood,
nor with that of Linus and Cletus [early bishops of Rome]
to be used for acquiring gold;

but to gain this happy life
Sixtus, Pius, Calixtus, and Urban
shed their blood and many tears.

It was not our intention that part of the Christian people
[the Guelfs] should sit on the right hand of our successors,
and part [the Ghibellines] on the left,   48

nor that the keys entrusted to me
should become an emblem on a flag [of papal troops]
to lead a fight against the baptized,

nor that I should be a figure on a seal
for false and venal privileges,
because of which I often redden and complain.

Rapacious wolves in shepherd's clothes
are seen from here in all pastures.
O divine protection, why do you lie still?

The Gascon [Clement V] and Cahorsine [John XXII] are
          making ready
to drink our blood. O good beginning,
to what a base ending you must sink!   60

But high Providence which with Scipio
    defended for Rome the glory of the world,
    will soon bring aid, as I conceive.

And you, my son, who because of your mortal weight
    will go down again, open your mouth
    and do not hide what I do not conceal."

As our air sends down flakes
    of snow [in winter] when the horn
    of Capricorn is touched by the sun,

so I saw the ether above adorned
    with the rising triumphant vapors
    that had sojourned there with us.   72

My sight followed their forms
    until the intervening space in its vastness
    took away power to see further,

whereupon my lady, seeing me relieved
    of looking up, said to me, "Lower your eyes
    and notice how you have revolved."

*When Dante looks down again he observes that he has moved ninety
degrees so that he can see in the latitude of Jerusalem, the "first clime,"
from the eastern shore of the Mediterranean, almost, to beyond Spain.
He could have seen more except that the sun had advanced ahead of
him and did not illuminate the whole field of vision.*

From the time when I had looked first
    I saw that I had moved through the whole arc
    which the first clime makes from the middle to its end,

so that I saw, beyond Cadiz, Ulysses' mad course,
    and on the other side almost to the shore [Phoenicia]
    where Europa became a sweet burden,   84

and still more of this little threshing floor [the earth]
    would have been revealed to me except that the sun
    beneath my feet was a constellation or more ahead of me.

*The travelers now rise to the Primum Mobile. The movement of this
heaven, transmitted to the sun, furnishes the measure of time. Here
in the highest moving heaven there is another complaint against the
greed that corrupts the world and a reference to the lack of a respon-
sible temporal or suggestive force to guide the masses of men.*

My enamored mind, always paying court
    to its lady, was more eager than ever
    to look at her again,

and if nature or art has made a lure
    of human flesh or paintings of it
    to catch eyes and possess the mind,

all together they would appear as nothing
    compared to the divine pleasure that shone on me
    when I turned to the smiling face.   96

And the virtue bestowed by that look
    took me from the fair nest of Leda [Gemini]
    and lifted me into the swiftest of the heavens.

Its highest and lowest parts
    are so uniform that I cannot say
    which one Beatrice chose for my place;

but she who saw my desire
    smiled so happily that God seemed to rejoice
    in her countenance, and she began,

"The order of the universe, which holds its center [the earth]
    motionless and moves all the rest around,
    begins here as from its starting point,   108

and this heaven has no other location
    than in the Divine Mind where are kindled the love
    that turns it and the power it transmits.

Light and love enclose it in a sphere
    as it does the others; and of that region [the Empyrean]
    He that girds it is the only Intelligence [angelic force].

Its [the Primum Mobile's] motion is not controlled by an-
        other,
    but the others are regulated by it,
    just as ten by its half and fifth [its factors, two and five],

and how Time has its [unseen] roots in such a vessel
    and in the others its [visible] leaves,
    now can be manifest to you.   120

O cupidity, which so submerges mortals
    that no one has the strength
    to lift his eyes from its flood!

Well does the will blossom in men,
    but the continual rain [of suggestion]
    converts the good plums into bad fruit.

Faith and innocence are found
    only in children, but flee
    before the childish cheeks are covered [with beards].

One, still lisping, keeps the fasts
    who [older], with loosened tongue,
    devours any food under any moon,   132

and another, lisping, loves and listens
    to his mother who, with perfected speech,
    will want to see her buried!

Thus the white skin [of mortals] turns black
    at the first sight of the fair daughter [Circe, the Siren]
    of him [Apollo] who brings morning and leaves evening.

Consider, in order not to marvel,
    that no one governs on earth,
    so that the human family goes astray.

But before January is unwintered [falls in Spring]
    because of that extra day [in a hundred years] neglected
    [in calendars] down there, these high spheres will roar   144

so that the storm so long expected
    will turn sterns to where prows are,
    and the fleet will go straight;

and true fruit will come after the blossoms."

CANTO XXVIII

The Hierarchies of Angels

*In the Primum Mobile, Dante sees a symbolic picture of God in rela-
tion to the nine orders of angels. The image, the initial perception of
the truth, is first reflected in Beatrice's eyes. God appears as a point*

of exceeding brightness, the smallness signifying Unity. Around this
point rings of fire represent the various orders of the angels.

When, reproaching the present life
    of miserable mortals, she who elevates my mind
    to Paradise revealed the truth,

as a taper's flame when lighted
    behind someone may be seen in a mirror
    before coming into direct view or thought,

so that one turns to see if the glass
    tells the truth and perceives that it concurs
    as a song does with its measure,

thus my memory tells me that I looked
    into the beautiful eyes where Love
    made the snare to catch me;   12

and when I turned back, my eyes were struck
    by what appears in that sphere
    whenever one contemplates its revolution.

I saw a Point which radiated light
    so sharp that the eyes it dazzles
    must close because of its brightness.

The star that appears smallest from here [on earth]
    would seem a moon beside it
    if the two were placed together like the stars.

Perhaps as close as its halo seems
    to the light which paints it
    when the vapor around is thickest,   24

at such a distance around the point a circle of fire
    whirled so fast that it would have surpassed
    the swiftest motion that girds the world;

and this was circumscribed by another,
    and that by a third, and the third by a fourth;
    by the fifth the fourth, and by the sixth the fifth.

Above followed the seventh so widespread, indeed,
    that the messenger of Juno [Iris, the rainbow],
    if her circle were complete, would not contain it;

and so the eighth and ninth; and each

moved slower according as it was
more distant from the One; 36

and the circle least distant from the pure Spark
had the clearest flame, because, I believe,
it sinks deepest into Its truth.

My lady, who saw me in deep suspense,
said, "On that Point, the heavens
and all of Nature depend.

Look at the circle closest to it
and know that its movement is so fast
because of the fiery Love by which it is pierced."

*Dante wonders why the revolutions of the angels here do not cor-
respond to those of the heavens as seen from the earth, where the
least exalted are closest to the center. He learns that the smallest circle
(that of the Seraphim) corresponds to the largest and most exalted seen
from the earth (the Primum Mobile). Beatrice then names the various
orders of the angels. She points out also a fundamental concept: that
understanding must precede love and that this comprehension varies
according to one's merit or grace.*

[And I to her, "If the world were arranged
in the order I see in these circles,
what has been shown would have contented me, 48

but in our world of sense one can see
that the revolutions are more divine
as they are farther from the center;

so that if my desire is to have an end
in this wonderful and angelic temple
which has only Love and Light for boundaries,

I must still know why the copy
and the pattern do not correspond,
for, by myself, I contemplate that in vain."

"If your fingers do not suffice
for such a knot, it is no marvel,
so hard has it become by not being tried." 60

Thus my lady; then she said,
"Take what I tell you, and sharpen your wit
on it, if you want to be satisfied.

The material spheres are wide or narrow

according to the more or less of virtue
diffused through all their parts.
Greater goodness wishes to accomplish more good,
and a larger body contains more goodness
if its parts are equally perfect.
Hence this one [the Primum Mobile], which carries all the
    universe
with it, corresponds to the circle [of angels]
which loves most and knows most.   72
So, if you draw your measure
around the virtue, not around the appearance
of beings which seem circles to you,
you will see in each heaven a marvelous agreement
with its Intelligences [angels],
of greater to more and of smaller to less."
As the hemisphere of the air
remains splendid and serene when Boreas blows
from his gentlest cheek [from the northeast],
whereby the mists are purged and dissipated
which before obscured it, so that the heavens smile
with the beauty of all their regions,   84
so it was with me after my lady provided me
with her clear response and when the truth
appeared like a star in the sky.
And after her words had ceased,
not otherwise does molten iron sparkle
than the circles did.
Every spark followed in its path, and they were so many
that their number was greater than that reached
by doubling [in succession the squares of] the chessboard.
From choir to choir I heard "Hosanna" sung
to that fixed Point which holds them,
and always will, where they have always been;   96
and she who saw the questioning thoughts
in my mind said, "The first circles
have shown you the Seraphim and the Cherubim;
thus swiftly they follow in their paths [bound by love]
to resemble the Point as much as they can,
and they can, according as their vision is sublime.
These other loving spirits which go around them

are called 'Thrones' of the divine aspect
and they end the first triad [hierarchy].
You must know that all have delight
insofar as their sight penetrates
into the truth which quiets doubt.   108
Hence one can see how happiness
is founded on the act of beholding,
not on that of loving, which follows later,
and the merit which grace and good will beget
is the measure of the vision:
these are the steps from grade to grade.
The second triad sprouting thus
in the eternal Spring,
which no nightly Aries [no fall or winter] despoils
perpetually sing 'Hosanna' with three melodies
which sound in the three degrees
of joy that form the triad.   120
In that hierarchy are three divinities:
first the Dominations, then the Virtues;
the third order is that of the Powers.
Then, in the two penultimate dances [orders],
the Principalities and Archangels circle;
the last is for the pleasure of Angels.
These orders all gaze upward
and prevail downward so that toward God
all draw and are drawn.
Dionysius applied himself with such desire
to contemplating these orders
that he named them and divided them as I do,   132
but Gregory afterward differed from him,
so that when he [Gregory] opened his eyes
in this heaven, he smiled at himself.
And if such hidden truth was uttered
by a mortal on earth, do not marvel,
for he [Paul] who saw it here revealed it
with much more truth concerning these circles."]

CANTO XXIX

The Creation of the Angels

[When the children of Latona [the sun and moon]
  covered by the Ram [Aries] and by the Scales
  make the horizon their belt [rising and setting],
from the moment that the zenith holds them
  in balance to the time when both,
  changing hemispheres, are unbalanced,
for an equal time [a moment], with a smile on her face,
  Beatrice was silent, looking fixedly
  at the Point that had overcome me.
Then she began, "I tell, and I do not ask
  what you wish to hear, because I have seen it
  where every *where* and every *when* are centered. **12**
Not to acquire any benefit [for Itself] (which cannot be)
  but in order that Its splendor
  might declare as It shines '*Subsisto*,'[1]
the Eternal Love, in its eternity, outside of Time
  and every other limitation, as It pleased,
  disclosed Itself in new loves [angels].
Nor did It lie slumbering before,
  for neither 'before' nor 'after' existed previous
  to the moving of God over these waters [the Creation].
Form [mind] and matter [elements] united [in heavenly
        bodies]
  and separate issued into being with no flaw,
  like three arrows from a three-stringed bow, **24**
and, as in glass, in amber, or in crystal,
  a ray shines so that there is no interval
  between its coming and its complete existence,
so the triple effect shone forth
  from its Lord into being all at once
  without the distinction of a beginning.

---

[1] "I am."

Concreated was order and established
    for the substances, and these [the angels]
    in which pure act was produced were the highest.
Pure power [matter] held the lowest place;
    in between a bond tied up potentiality with act
    [spirit with matter] which never will be unbound.   36
Jerome wrote of the long ages
    after the angels were created
    before anything else was made;
but the truth [the contrary] is written on many pages
    by the writers of the Holy Spirit,
    as you will see if you look well.
And reason also perceives it somewhat,
    not admitting that the movers [of the heavens]
    should exist long without their perfection [activity].
Now you know when and where these loves
    were created and how; so that three flames
    of your desire are now quenched.   48
You could not count to twenty sooner than a part
    of the angels disturbed the substratum
    of the elements [the earth in their Fall].
The others remained and began the art
    which you discern, with such delight
    that they never stop their circling.
The source of the Fall was the accursed pride
    of him [Lucifer] you saw oppressed
    by all the weight of the world.
These you see here were modest, in recognizing
    that they owed their being to that Goodness
    which had made them ready for such great understanding; 60
wherefore their vision was exalted
    with illuminating grace and with merit,
    so that their will is complete and firm.
And I wish you would not doubt but be certain
    that receiving grace is a merit,
    because it is proportioned to the affection open to it.
Now, concerning this consistory
    you can observe much without further aid
    if my words have been comprehended.
But because on earth in your schools

you read that angelic nature
is apt to understand and remember and will,
I will speak further, so that you may see
the pure truth confused down there
by the equivocation of such writings.
These substances, since made joyous
by the face of God where nothing is concealed,
have never removed their gaze from it;
therefore their sight is never cut off
by a new object, and they have no need to remember
because of intercepted perception.]

*Beatrice denounces those preachers who entertain their congregations
with idle guesses instead of keeping to the Scriptures.*

Down below, people, although wide-awake, dream,
    believing and not believing to tell the truth
    (and the latter implies the greater fault and shame).   84

You do not go on one path in philosophizing,
    so greatly do the thought
    and love of show carry you astray.

And this is endured up here with less indignation
    than when Divine Scripture
    is left behind or twisted.

They [preachers] forget the cost in blood
    to spread it in the world
    and how pleasing is he who approaches it humbly.

To show off, each endeavors to invent,
    and his fancies are discussed,
    and the Gospel left in silence.   96

One affirms that the moon drew back
    at the passion of Christ, and intervened,
    so that the sun's light did not shine below,

and others that the light hid itself
    and therefore for the Spaniards and the Indians [Hindus]
    as for the Jews such an eclipse occurred.

Florence has not as many Lapos and Bindos [familiar names]

as such fables each year
shouted to this side and that from pulpits,

so that the sheep that do not know
return from pasture fed on wind;
and not seeing the harm does not excuse them.   108

Christ did not say to his first congregation,
'Go and preach nonsense to the world'
but he gave it a good foundation,

and that alone sounded on tongues,
and, in fighting to kindle faith,
they made the Gospels both lance and shield.

Now they go with jests and buffoonery
to preach and, provided people laugh loudly,
the cowl puffs up [pleased] and no more is required.

But such a bird [the Devil] is nesting in the tail
of the [preacher's] hood that, if the crowd saw it,
they would know in what kind of indulgences they
          trust.   120

In this way folly has increased on earth,
so that without proof of testimony
people flock to any promise.

On this [credulity] St. Anthony fattens his pig
and others, too, more swinish,
paying with unminted coin.

*Beatrice now returns to her explanation based on the Scriptures, and
tells of the number of angels and of their individuality.*

[But because we have digressed enough,
turn your eyes back to the straight road
so that our journey [discourse] may be shortened to the
          time [allowed].

The angelic natures mount to so high a number
that never did mortal speech
or concept go so far.   132

And if you consider what is revealed by Daniel
you will see that his 'thousands'
indicate no fixed number.

The First Light which shines on all

is received by them in as many ways
as there are splendors with which It unites;
therefore, since affection follows
the act of conceiving [the vision of God], the joy
of loving glows variously, greater or less, in them.
Consider the height and breadth
of the Eternal Worth, since It has made
so many mirrors in which It is divided [reflected],   144
remaining in Itself One, as before."]

CANTO XXX

The Light of Glory

*We now enter the final and only true Heaven. "As the stars fade and
vanish before the sun, so before the Eternal Light the nine circles of
angelic fire pale and disappear . . . ."*—CARROLL.

Perhaps six thousand miles away [on the Ganges] the sixth hour
[noon] is glowing, and this world [at dawn]
bends its shadows almost to a level bed,

so that here and there a star
in the middle of the sky, deep above us,
begins to lose its visibility on our low floor,

and, as the bright handmaiden of the sun [Aurora]
comes farther on, the heavens close off
light after light even to the most beautiful.

Not otherwise the Triumph which plays
around the Point [God] which blinded me,
seeming enclosed by what it encloses,   12

little by little disappeared from my sight,
so that my seeing nothing and my love
constrained me to turn my eyes toward Beatrice.

If what has been said of her up to now

were all included in one praise
it would be little for the present need.

The beauty that I saw transcends not only
all measure of ours, but I believe
that only its Maker enjoys it wholly.

At this point I grant that I am vanquished
more than ever a comic or tragic poet
by an incident of his theme;   24

for, as the sun to eyes which tremble most [are weakest],
so the recollection of the sweet smile
deprives my very mind of itself.

From the first day when I saw her face
in this life, up to this sight,
my song has not been prevented from continuing,

but now my pursuit which has followed
her beauty in my poetry must stop
as every artist at his utmost.

Thus I leave her to greater heralding
than that of my trumpet, which is bringing
its arduous theme to its close.   36

With the gestures and voice of an alert leader,
she began again, "We have advanced
from the greatest body to the Heaven of pure light,

a light intellectual, full of love,
love of the good, replete with joy,
a joy that transcends all sweetness.

Here you will see both hosts of Paradise [the angels and the
        blessed]
and one [the blessed] in the form
it will have at the last judgment."

As a sudden flash blinds the eyes
so that it deprives them
of the sight of the clearest objects,   48

so a vivid light shone around me
and left me swathed in such a veil
of its effulgence that nothing appeared to me.

"The love which quiets this heaven

always welcomes with such a greeting, in order
> to make the candle fit for its flame."

*Dante's vision is strengthened for a new kind of perception. He sees
the light of divine grace in the form of a river. Then his eyes having
received this grace, he has a vision of the blessed with their bodies as
they will be after Judgment Day, arranged in their places in the
white rose.*

No sooner had these brief words reached me
> than I felt myself
> surmounting my own power,

and such new vision was kindled in me
> that no light was too bright
> for my eyes to withstand.   60

And I saw radiance in the form of a river
> glowing between two banks
> painted with marvelous spring flowers.

From this river issued live sparks [angels]
> which settled everywhere in the flowers,
> like rubies set in gold.

Then, as if inebriated by the fragrance,
> they plunged again into the wondrous torrent,
> and as one entered another emerged.

"The great desire which now enflames
> and urges you to know about what you see
> pleases me more the more it grows;   72

but of this water you must drink
> before your thirst is satisfied."
> Thus the sun of my eyes spoke to me,

then added, "The river and the jewels which come
> and go from it, and the smile of the flowers
> are the shadowy prefaces of the reality;

not that the things are incomplete in themselves,
> but there is a defect in you,
> for your vision is not yet so exalted."

No infant ever turns his face so quickly
> to the milk if he awakens
> much later than his wont, as I did   84

to make still better mirrors of my eyes,
    bending down to the wave
    which flows so that we may be bettered in it.

And even as the eaves [lashes] of my eyelids
    drank in it, so it seemed
    to change its length into something round.

Then, as people under masks are transformed
    if they take off the semblance
    in which they disappeared,

thus the flowers and the sparks changed
    into a greater festival, so that I saw,
    made manifest, both courts of Heaven [the angels and
      the blessed].   96

O splendor of God through which I saw
    the lofty triumph of the true kingdom,
    give me power to tell *how* I saw it!

There is a light up there which makes the Creator
    visible to that creature who,
    only in seeing Him, has its peace.

And it extends in the form of a circle,
    the circumference of which
    would be too large a belt for the sun.

It is composed wholly of rays
    reflected on the top of the Primum Mobile,
    which gets life and power from it;   108

and as a hillside mirrors itself in water
    at its foot, as if to see itself adorned
    when rich in flowers and in verdure,

so, overlooking the light all around,
    I saw, as in a mirror, on more than a thousand tiers,
    all who have returned on high;

and if the lowest row gathers to itself
    so much light, how great is the width
    of this rose in its outermost petals!

My sight was not lost in the height
    and vastness, but took in all the extent
    and the quality of that joy.   120

There, neither nearness nor distance added
   or took away, for, where God governs immediately,
   natural law has no relevance.

Into the yellow of the eternal rose
   which expands and rises and breathes fragrance
   as praise to the Sun that makes perpetual spring,

like one who wishes to speak
   and is silent, Beatrice drew me, then said,
   "See how great is the assembly of the white robes.

See our city, how far it extends,
   see our seats so full
   that few more people are wanted.   132

*One seat is reserved for Henry VII, in whom Dante had placed his
hope for the restoration of the Empire.*

*With her last words Beatrice reproaches the world for its avarice, a
constant theme.*

In that great seat at which you look
   because of the crown placed above it,
   before you eat at this wedding feast,

will sit the soul, imperial below,
   of the lofty Henry who will come
   to set Italy straight before it is ready.

The blind cupidity which bewitches you mortals
   has made you like a child
   who dies of hunger and drives away the nurse.

In the divine forum [at Rome] will be a prefect
   [Clement V] who openly or secretly
   will not travel the same road with him,   144

but God will endure him [Clement] only a little while
   in the holy office, and he will be thrust down [to Hell]
   to where Simon Magus has his reward,

making him of Alagna [Boniface VIII] sink deeper."

CANTO XXXI

St. Bernard

In the form then of a white rose
    the holy company [the Church] which Christ with
        His blood
    made His spouse showed itself to me,

but the others [angels] who, flying, see and sing
    of the glory of Him who enamors them
    and of the goodness that has made them so numerous,

like a swarm of bees, at times lighting
    on a flower and then returning
    to where their toil is turned to sweetness,

descended into the great flower
    adorned with so many leaves, and then rose
    to where their love always dwells.   12

They all had faces of living flames,
    and golden wings, and the rest so white
    that no snow equals the whiteness.

When they sank into the flower
    from rank to rank, they bestowed
    the peace and ardor acquired as they flew,

nor did such a flying multitude
    between the flower and what was above
    obscure the vision of the splendor,

for divine light penetrates through the universe
    in proportion to its merit,
    so that there nothing can obscure it.   24

This secure and rejoicing realm,
    abounding in ancient and in new people,
    had eyes and love directed to one mark.

O Threefold Light which in a single star

scintillating in their sight so satisfies them,
look down here upon our storms!

If the barbarians coming from the regions [of the North]
covered by Helice [the Great Dipper] circling
with her son [Arcas, the Little Dipper] of whom she is
fond,

were amazed on seeing Rome
and her lofty monuments, when the Lateran [the papal
palace]
surpassed all mortal things,   36

I who had come from the human to the divine,
from Time to Eternity, and from Florence
to a people just and sane,

what amazement must I have felt!
Certainly it and my joy made me content
not to hear and to stand mute.

And as a pilgrim who gains fresh life
in the temple of his vow as he looks
and already hopes to report [at home] how it is,

so, through the living light,
I cast my eyes over the ranks,
now up, now down, and now around.   48

I saw faces persuasive of love adorned by the light
of Another and by their own smiles,
and with gestures graced by every dignity.

My sight had already taken in
the general form of Paradise,
but on no point had my eyes been fixed,

and I turned with rekindled desire
to ask my lady about things
that kept my mind in suspense.

*Beatrice's role as Revelation is now ended, since Dante is in the actual
presence of God, and she resumes her historical character as Beatrice
Portinari, whom the poet addresses from now on with the familiar
tu (for "you"). Her place is taken by St. Bernard, who was especially
devoted to the Virgin Mary and who represents Contemplation or per-
haps Intuition.*

I expected one thing, and another responded;
 I thought I would see Beatrice, and instead
 I perceived an old man, clad like those in glory. 60

Benign joy was diffused
 over his eyes and face, his mien kindly,
 as is fitting in a tender father;

and, "Where is she?" I said suddenly;
 whereupon he, "To fulfill your desire
 Beatrice sent me from my place.

If you look at the third row
 of the highest tier you will see her again
 on the throne her merit allots to her."

Without speaking I lifted up my eyes
 and saw her, making herself a crown [a halo of light]
 and reflecting from herself the eternal rays. 72

From the region of the highest thunder
 no mortal eye is so distant
 although plunged deep into the sea

as my sight there from Beatrice,
 but that had no effect on me,
 for her image came down unblurred.

"O lady in whom my hope is strong,
 you who for my salvation endured
 to leave your footprints in Hell,

in all the things that I have seen
 I recognize the grace and the virtue
 of your power and goodness. 84

You have lifted me from slavery to freedom
 by all those ways, by all the means
 through which you had the power to do so.

Continue your generosity toward me,
 so that my soul that you redeemed
 may be freed from my body pleasing to you."

Thus I prayed, and she, so distant
 as it seemed, smiled, and looked at me;
 then turned to the Eternal Spring.

And the holy old man said, "In order

that you may complete perfectly your journey
for which purpose prayer and holy love sent me,

cast your eyes over this garden,
for seeing it will prepare them
for rising higher in the divine radiance.

And the Queen of Heaven for whom I burn
wholly with love will grant us every grace,
since I am her faithful Bernard."

As a pilgrim, perhaps from Croatia, who comes
to see our Veronica [an image of Christ], and who,
because of his long-felt hunger, is never satiated,

but says in his thoughts as long
as it is shown, "My Lord, Jesus Christ, true God,
now was Thy countenance really like this?"   108

so I was while gazing at the living love
of him [Bernard] who in our world,
through contemplation, enjoyed that peace.

"Son of Grace, if you keep your eyes
only down here at this bottom," he began,
"this joyous life will not be seen by you.

Look at the rows as far as the most remote
until you see the Queen [Mary] sitting
to whom this realm is loyal and devoted."

I lifted my eyes and, as in the morning
the eastern part of the horizon
outshines that where the sun goes down,   120

so, as if rising from a valley to a mountain,
I saw with my eyes a part of the edge
dominating with its light all the rim;

and, as on earth at sunrise, the pole of the chariot [of the sun]
(which Phaëthon guided badly) is most enflamed
and on either side the light decreases,

so that pacific oriflamme [of Mary's] shone brighter
in the middle, and on either side,
gradually and equally decreased its light.

At that middle point, with wings spread,

I saw more than a thousand rejoicing angels,
    each distinct in effulgence and in function.   **132**

I saw there smiling at their games
    and at their songs, a beauty which became a joy
    in the eyes of all the other saints.

And if I had such wealth in speech
    as in imagining, I would not dare
    to attempt the least of the delight she gave.

Bernard, when he saw my eyes
    fixed and intent on his warm love,
    turned his toward her with such affection

that he made mine more eager in their gazing.

CANTO XXXII

The Mystic Rose

St. Bernard points out some of the souls that form the white rose. In the lower part are the children, the little folk who "hastened to the true life."

Intent on his delight, that contemplator [St. Bernard]
    freely assumed the office of teacher
    and began with these holy words:

"The wound that Mary healed and anointed
    the beautiful one [Eve] who is
    at her feet opened and enlarged.

In order, in the third row,
    Rachel sits beneath her
    with Beatrice, as you see.

Sarah, Rebecca, Judith, and the great-grandmother [Ruth]
    of the singer [David] who, in sorrow
    for his sins, said '*Miserere mei.*'[1]   **12**

---

[1] "Have mercy upon me."

You can see them from rank to rank
    as with the name of each I go downward
    through the rose from petal to petal.

And from the seventh row on,
    as down to it, Hebrew women
    divide all the petals of the rose.

According to the way their faith
    conceived of Christ they form the line
    by which the sacred stairway is divided.

On this side, where the flower is mature
    with all its leaves, are seated those
    who believed in Christ to come.   24

On the other, where the semicircles
    are broken by empty seats, are those
    who turned their faces to Christ already come.

And, just as on this side, the glorious seat
    of the Lady of Heaven and those below it
    make so great a division,

so, opposite her, does that of the great John
    who, always holy, endured martyrdom
    and the desert and then Hell for two years.

And beneath him, Franciș, Benedict, Augustine
    and others make a dividing line
    down to here from row to row.   36

Now marvel at the divine foresight, for both aspects
    of the Faith [the old Church and the new]
    will fill this garden equally;

and know that downward from the row
    which midway cleaves the two divisions,
    souls have a place through no merit of their own

but through that of others, under certain conditions;
    for all these are spirits released from the flesh
    [as children] before they could have a true choice.

Well can you see this by their faces
    and also by their childish voices
    if you look closely and listen to them.   48

The children enjoy varying felicity according to the grace they have received.

Pre-Christian infants were saved through their parents' faith in Christ to come; the others, in Christian times, through baptism.

[Now you wonder, and wondering, are silent;
 but I will undo the tight band
 by which your subtle thoughts are held.
Within the amplitude of this realm
 nothing can occur by chance
 any more than sadness, thirst, or hunger;
for whatever you see is established
 by eternal law, so that the ring
 fits the finger exactly.
Therefore, that those [little] people
 who hastened to the true life
 are more and less excellent is not *sine causa*.[2] 60
The King through whom this realm has rest
 in such love and in such delight
 that no desire ventures to have more,
creating all minds in His happy image
 endows with grace diversely, at His pleasure;
 and here let the fact suffice.
This is clearly and expressly noted for you
 in Holy Scripture in those twins [Jacob and Esau]
 who, within their mother, were stirred to wrath.
Therefore, according to the color
 of their hair, the light
 of grace must worthily crown them. 72
Thus, without merit for their conduct
 they are placed in various ranks,
 differing only in primal keenness [of spiritual sight].
In the early centuries
 the parents' faith alone sufficed,
 with innocence, to receive salvation.
Then, after the first ages were completed,
 males were obliged through circumcision
 to gain power for their innocent wings;

---

2 "Without cause."

but when the time of grace had come,
>without perfect baptism in Christ
>such innocence was held back there below.]   84

Dante shifts his gaze to the upper part of the rose.

Look now on the face [of Mary]
>which bears most resemblance to Christ,
>for its brightness alone can prepare you for seeing Christ."

I saw such joy rain upon her
>borne in the holy minds [of the angels]
>created to fly over that height,

that nothing I had seen before
>had kept me suspended in such wonder
>or revealed to me such likeness to God.

And that love [Gabriel] which first descended
>on her singing *Ave Maria, gratia plena*,[3]
>spread his wings in front of her.   96

The blessed court on all sides
>sang responses to the divine song
>so that every face became brighter.

"O holy father, you who endure for my sake
>to be down here, leaving the sweet place
>where you sit by eternal lot,

who is that angel which, with such rapture,
>looks into the eyes of our Queen,
>so enamored that he seems aflame?"

Thus again I had recourse to the learning
>of him [St. Bernard] who grew beautiful through Mary
>as the morning star does through the sun.   108

And he said to me, "As much confidence and grace
>as there can be in an angel or in a soul
>are in him; and we want it so,

because he is the one who brought the palm [of victory over
>others]
>down to Mary when the Son of God
>was willing to take on the burden of our flesh.

---

[3] "Hail, thou that art highly favoured."

But follow now with your eyes as I speak
    and note the great patricians
    of this most just and devout empire.

Those two [Eve and Rachel] who up there are happiest
    from being nearest to the Empress [Mary]
    are, as it were, two roots of this rose.   120

The one nearest her on the left
    is [Adam] the father whose bold tasting
    made the human race taste such bitterness.

On the right see the ancient father
    of Holy Church [St. Peter] to whom Christ
    entrusted the keys to this lovely flower;

and the one [John] who saw, before his death,
    the deplorable times of the fair Bride [the Church],
    won [by Christ] with the lance and with the nails,

sits beside him; and by the other
    that leader [Moses] rests under whom the fickle,
    ungrateful, and perverse people lived on manna.   132

Opposite Peter see Anna [the mother of Mary] so happy
    to gaze upon her daughter that she
    does not move her eyes while singing hosanna,

and opposite the greatest father of a family [Adam]
    Lucia sits, who sent your lady, when your eyes
    were bent down for your destruction.

But because the time which keeps you in slumber
    is flying, here we will stop, like a tailor
    who makes the gown according to the cloth he has,

and we will direct our eyes to the First Love,
    so that looking toward Him you may penetrate
    as far as possible through His light.   144

But, lest in moving your wings
    you should go back while believing to advance,
    grace must be obtained by prayer—

grace from that one [Mary] who can help you;
    and may you follow me with your affection,
    so that your heart will not be discordant

from my words." And he began this holy prayer.

CANTO XXXIII

The Beatific Vision

A prayer to the Blessed Virgin, later copied in great part by Chaucer, opens the final canto.

The stages of the Beatific Vision are, in ascending order, a comprehension of the world, a vision of the Trinity, and, as a final revelation, a view of the Incarnation.

"Virgin mother, daughter of thy son,
    humble and exalted more than any creature,
    goal established by Eternal Counsel,

thou art the one by whom human nature
    was so ennobled that its Maker
    did not disdain to become its creature.

Within thy womb was rekindled the love
    through whose warmth this flower
    has blossomed in eternal peace.

Here thou art for us a noonday torch
    of charity, and down below, among mortals,
    a living fount of hope.   12

My lady, thou art so great and so triumphant
    that whoever wants and does not turn to thee
    would have his desire fly without wings.

Thy benignity succors not only those
    who ask, but many times
    freely anticipates the request.

In thee is mercy, in thee pity,
    in thee magnificence, in thee whatever goodness
    can be found in creatures is resumed.

Now, this man who from the deep well
    of the universe up to here
    has seen the spiritual lives, one after another,   24

begs thee of thy grace for strength,
    so that he may lift his eyes
    still higher toward the ultimate salvation.

And I who never for my own sight longed more
    than I do for his, offer thee all my prayers,
    and may they not be insufficient,

in order that thou, through thine, mayst dispel
    every cloud of his mortality, so that
    the Supreme Pleasure may reveal Itself to him.

I pray thee further, O Queen! thou who canst do
    what thou wilt, that thou keepest
    his affection sound after so great a vision.   **36**

May thy protection overcome his human impulses.
    Behold Beatrice with so many of the blessed
    clasping their hands to aid my prayer."

The eyes [of Mary] venerated and beloved
    by God, fixed on him who prayed, showed
    how gratefully devout prayers are heard.

Then they turned to the Eternal Light into which
    we must not think any mortal vision,
    however clear, can ever penetrate so deeply.

And I who drew near to the goal
    of all desires, ended, as I ought,
    within myself, the ardor of my longing.   **48**

Bernard signaled to me and smiled
    so that I might look up, but I
    already had made myself as he wished.

For my sight, growing pure, penetrated
    ever deeper into the rays
    of the Light which is true in Itself.

From then on my vision was greater
    than our speech which fails at such a sight,
    just as memory is overcome by the excess.

As one who in a dream sees clearly,
    and the feeling impressed remains afterward,
    although nothing else comes back to mind,   **60**

so am I; for my vision disappears
    almost wholly, and yet the sweetness
    caused by it is still distilled within my heart.

Thus, in sunlight, the snow melts away;
    thus the sayings of the Sibyl, written
    on light leaves, were lost in the wind.

O Supreme Light that risest so high
    above mortal concepts, give back to my mind
    a little of what Thou didst appear,

and make my tongue strong,
    so that it may leave to future peoples
    at least a spark of Thy glory!   72

For, by returning to my memory
    and by sounding a little in these verses
    more of Thy victory will be conceived.

By the keenness of the living ray I endured
    I believe I would have been dazed
    if my eyes had turned away from it;

and I remember that I was bolder
    because of that to sustain the view
    until my sight *attained* the Infinite Worth.

O abundant grace through which I presumed
    to fix my eyes on the Eternal Light
    so long that I consumed my vision on it!   84

In its depths I saw contained, bound with love
    in one volume, what is scattered
    on leaves throughout the world—

substances [things] and accidents [qualities] and their
        modes
    as if fused together in such a way
    that what I speak of is a single light.

The universal form [principle] of this unity
    I believe I saw, because more abundantly
    in saying this I feel that I rejoice.

One moment obscures more for me than twenty-five centuries
    have clouded since the adventure which made Neptune
    wonder at the shadow of the Argo [the first ship].   96

Thus my mind with rapt attention
    gazed fixedly, motionless and attentive,
    continually enflamed by its very gazing.

In that light we become such
    that we can never consent
    to turn from it for another sight,

inasmuch as the good which is the object
    of the will is all in it, and outside of it
    whatever is perfect there is defective.

Now my speech, even for what I remember,
    will be shorter than that of an infant
    who still bathes his tongue at the breast.   108

Not that more than a single semblance
    was in the living light I gazed upon
    (for it is always as it was before),

but in my vision which gained strength
    as I looked the single appearance,
    through a change in me, was transformed.

Within the deep and clear subsistence
    of the great light three circles of three colors
    and of one dimension [the Trinity] appeared to
        me,

and one [the Son] seemed reflected from the other [the
        Father]
    as Iris by Iris, and the third [the Holy Spirit]
    seemed fire emanating equally from both.   120

O how poor our speech is and how feeble
    for my conception! Compared to what I saw
    to say its power is "little" is to say too much.

O Eternal Light [Father], abiding in Thyself alone,
    Thou [Son] alone understanding Thyself, and Thou
        [Holy Spirit]
    understood only by Thee, Thou dost love and smile!

The circle which appeared in Thee
    as a reflected light [the Son]
    when contemplated a while

seemed depicted with our image within itself

and of its own [the Circle's] color,
so that my eyes were wholly fixed on it.

Like the geometer who strives
to square the circle and cannot find
by thinking the principle he needs

I was at that new sight. I wanted to see
how the [human] image was conformed
to the [divine] circle and has a place in it,

but my own wings were not enough for that—
except that my mind was illumined by a flash
[of Grace] through which its wish was realized.

For the great imagination here power failed;
but already my desire and will [in harmony]
were turning like a wheel moved evenly   144

by the Love which turns the sun and the other stars.

GLOSSARY

ABSALOM.   Son of David; revolted against his father.

ACCORSO, FRANCESCO D'.   Italian jurist, thirteenth century; taught at Oxford.

ACHERON.   The first of the rivers of Dante's Hell.

ACHILLES.   A Greek hero of the Trojan War; according to a medieval legend he was killed because of his love for the Trojan Polyxena.

ACRE.   The last of the Christian strongholds in the East.

AEGINA.   An island, scene of a pestilence sent by Juno.

AENEAS.   Trojan hero of Virgil's *Aeneid*; founder of the Roman Empire.

AHITHOPHEL.   Absalom's counselor who incited him to revolt.

ALDOBRANDI, TEGGHIAIO.   Illustrious citizen of Florence, thirteenth century.

ALESSANDRIA.   Scene of the capture of the Marquis of Montferrat and Cavanese, who was kept in an iron cage until his death. His son attacked the town but was defeated.

ALEXANDER.   Among the tyrants. Alexander the Great of Macedon who invaded India, or perhaps Alexander of Pherae, a Greek tyrant of Sicily.

AMIDEI.   *See* Buondelmonte.

AMPHIARAUS.   An augur, one of the seven kings who besieged Thebes.

AMYCLAS.   A poor fisherman who was undismayed (since he had nothing to lose) when Caesar knocked on his door.

ANAXAGORAS.   A Greek philosopher.

ANCHISES.   The father of Aeneas.

ANTAEUS.   A giant defeated by Hercules.

ANTHONY, SAINT.   Founder of monasticism. Often represented with a hog at his feet. The monks of his order kept herds of swine.

APOLLO.   A Greek god; the sun.

AQUARIUS.   A constellation.

ARACHNE.   A Greek girl turned into a spider by Athena for presuming to compete with her in weaving.

ARGENTI, FILIPPO.   A rich and arrogant Florentine.

ARGO.   The first ship.

ARGONAUTS.   Sailors who accompanied Jason to Colchis after the Golden Fleece.

ARGUS. The guardian of Io; had a hundred eyes.

ARIADNE. Daughter of Minos; carried to heaven by Bacchus; her crown turned into a constellation.

ARLES. A city in southern France.

ARNO. A river that runs through Florence.

ARTHUR. Hero of the Arthurian romances.

ATHAMAS. A legendary Greek king.

ATTILA. A leader of the Huns; called the "scourge of God."

AUGUSTUS CAESAR. A Roman emperor.

AURORA. The dawn.

AVERROËS. A Spanish Moor, a scholar, and a philosopher.

AVICENNA. A Moslem doctor.

AZZOLINO DA ROMANO. A cruel tyrant of the thirteenth century; called "son of Satan."

BACHIGLIONE. A river at Vicenza.

BARBAROSSA. An emperor; destroyed Milan in 1162.

BEATRICE. Beatrice Portinari; (as an allegorical figure) Revelation, Theology, the Church. Her development in Dante's mind as a symbol is the subject of the *Vita Nuova*.

BEDE, THE VENERABLE. An English monk; author of a Latin history of the English.

BLACKS. A political party in Florence composed mainly of the old aristocracy.

BOETHIUS. A statesman and author, known also as St. Severinus. Wrote "On the Consolation of Philosophy."

BOLGIA. A name for the ditches of the eighth circle of Hell; plural, *bolge*.

BONIFACE VIII. A pope in Dante's time.

BONTURO. A notorious grafter referred to ironically by a devil in the ditch of the barrators.

BORSIERE, GUGLIELMO. A character known only through one of Boccaccio's stories.

BUONDELMONTE. Name of a Florentine family. One member forsook his betrothed of the Amidei family to marry a Donati. When he was murdered to avenge the insult, the deed caused a bloody feud in Florence.

CACCIAGUIDA. Dante's great-great-grandfather who, in the Heaven of Mars, prophesies the course of Dante's life.

CACUS. A fire-breathing monster killed by Hercules for stealing cattle.

CAHORS. A city in France, once a nest of usurers.

CAÏNA. A part of the ninth circle of Hell where traitors to kindred are punished.

CALLIOPE. A Muse whose song defeated that of the daughters of

King Pieros; the latter were changed to magpies for their presumption in challenging the Muses.

CAMILLA. A legendary warrior maiden.

CAPANEUS. One of the "seven against Thebes," a blasphemer.

CAPRICORN. The Goat, a constellation.

CAPRONA. A castle on the Arno River surrendered in 1289 to the troops of Florence and Lucca.

CASALODI. Lord of Mantua, persuaded by Pinamonte Bonacorsi to banish the nobles; later driven from the city.

CATILINE. A Roman conspirator.

CATO OF UTICA. A Roman philosopher and patriot.

CENTAUR. A creature with a man's head and chest and a horse's body.

CEPERANO. Supposed scene of a battle between Charles of Anjou and Manfred. The Apulian allies of Manfred deserted.

CERBERUS. A three-headed dog chained by Hercules for opposing his attempt to rescue Proserpine. Guardian of the circle of the gluttons.

CHARLEMAGNE. King of the Franks, a defender of the Church. The defeat of his rear guard under Roland is the subject of the medieval French epic, the *Chanson de Roland*. In the story Roland blew his horn so hard that his temples burst.

CHARLES OF ANJOU. Brother of St. Louis; king of Sicily.

CHARON. The boatman on the Acheron.

CHARYBDIS. A whirlpool off the Sicilian coast in the Strait of Messina.

CHIRON. A learned centaur, the preceptor of Achilles.

CHOSEN VESSEL, THE. St. Paul.

CICERO. A Roman philosopher and author.

CINCINNATUS. The Roman plowman dictator.

CIRCE. An enchantress who changed men into beasts.

CLEOPATRA. Queen of Egypt, mistress of Julius Caesar and of Antony.

CLOTHO. The Fate that spins the thread of life.

CLUNY. A town in France, the site of a famous abbey.

COCYTUS. A frozen pool at the bottom of Dante's Hell.

CONSTANTINE. A Roman emperor who removed the imperial government to Byzantium, fourth century.

CORNELIA. The mother of the Gracchi.

CYCLOPS. One-eyed assistants of Vulcan.

DAEDALUS. A legendary mechanic who fashioned wings for himself and for his son Icarus.

DEJANIRA. *See* Nessus.

DEMOCRITUS. A Greek philosopher.

DIDO. The mistress of Aeneas.

DIOGENES. A Greek philosopher.

DIONE. The mother of Venus.

DIONYSIUS THE AREOPAGITE. The supposed author of a work on the "Hierarchy of the Angels." Another Dionysius was a tyrant of Syracuse (407–367 B.C.).

DIOSCORIDES. The author of a treatise on plants and their properties.

DIS. One of the names for Satan.

DOMITIAN. A Roman emperor.

DRACHMA. A Greek coin and measure of weight.

ECHO. A nymph in love with Narcissus; consumed to a mere voice.

ELECTRA. The mother of the founder of Troy.

EMPEDOCLES. A Greek philosopher.

EMPYREAN. The highest of the heavens.

EPICUREANS. A name applied to freethinkers in Dante's time.

ERINYES. The Furies.

ETNA. A volcanic peak in Sicily.

EURYALUS. A legendary hero of the Trojan-Latin War.

EUROPA. A princess whom Jupiter, in the form of a bull, carried off.

FABRICIUS. A Roman consul famous for incorruptibility.

FARINATA DEGLI UBERTI. Ghibelline leader in the battle of Montaperti, 1260.

FELTRO AND FELTRO. Variously interpreted; possibly the towns of Feltro and Montefeltro between which Verona, the city of Can Grande della Scala, lies.

FIESOLE. A town on a hill near Florence where Catiline took refuge with his followers. According to tradition its inhabitants joined a Roman colony to found Florence.

FRANCESCA DA RIMINI. The aunt of Dante's patron, Guido Novello da Polenta.

FREDERICK II. Emperor of Sicily (1212–1250), long engaged in strife with the popes. He is supposed to have had leaden mantles melted on offenders against the throne.

FURIES. In Dante's work, symbols of madness or of remorseful terror.

GALEN. A Greek physician.

GALICIA. A province in Spain in which is located the tomb of St. James.

GALLEHAUT. The intermediary who brought Lancelot and Guinevere together.

GARISENDA. The name of one of the leaning towers in Bologna.

GASCONY. A province of southern France.

GENESIS. The first book of the Bible.

GERYON. A monster, the guardian of the circle of the fraudulent.

GIOVANNI, SAN. St. John; the name of Dante's church in Florence.

GLAUCUS. A fisherman who became a sea god.

GORGON, THE. Medusa, guardian of the City of Dis, symbol of Despair.

GRATIAN. The author of the *Decretum,* the leading textbook on canon law.

GUALDRADA. A Florentine renowned for her beauty and modesty.

GUERRA, GUIDO. A distinguished Florentine soldier, thirteenth century.

GUINEVERE. The wife of King Arthur, in love with Lancelot. The Lady of Malehaut interrupted an impassioned speech of hers with a cough.

HAMAN. An enemy of the Jews hanged on the gallows he had prepared for Mordecai.

HARPIES. Creatures with bird bodies and human heads.

HARROWING OF HELL. The descent of Christ into Limbo to release the Hebrews who had believed in His coming.

HECTOR. A Trojan hero killed by Achilles.

HELEN. The mistress of Paris; the cause of the Trojan War.

HERACLITUS. A Greek philosopher.

HERCULES. A mythological hero who defeated the giant Antaeus by holding him off the ground on which the latter's strength depended. *See also* Nessus.

HERMITAGE, THE. A monastery in the Tuscan Apennines.

HIPPOCRATES. A Greek physician.

HOLOFERNES. An Assyrian king whose head was cut off by Judith.

HOLY FACE. An image of Christ held in veneration at Lucca.

HOMER. A Greek poet, the author of the *Iliad* and the *Odyssey.*

HOMO. Latin word for "man."

HOUND. Dante's reference to a redeemer for Italy often identified as Can Grande della Scala.

HYPERION. Father of the sun.

HYPSIPYLE. A character in the *Thebaid* who pointed out the fountain of Langia to the thirsty Greeks.

ICARUS. The son of Daedalus. In spite of his father's warning, he flew too close to the sun; the wax with which his wings were attached melted, and he fell into the sea.

ILION. The citadel of Troy.

IPHIGENIA. Daughter of Agamemnon sacrificed by her father as the result of a vow.

IRIS. The rainbow.

ISIDORE, SAINT. Author of an encyclopedia called *Origines* or *Etymologiae.*

JACOB. A Hebrew patriarch; served twice seven years to obtain Rachel.

JASON. The leader of the Argonauts, who were amazed to see him compel two monstrous bulls to pull a plow.

JEPHTHAH. A Hebrew who vowed to make a burnt offering of whatever came from his house to meet him, and was obliged to sacrifice his daughter.

JOCASTA. A character in Statius' *Thebaid.*

JOSHUA. The successor of Moses and conqueror of the Holy Land.

JOVE. Jupiter, god of the Ancients. He was "mysteriously just" in striking down Phaëthon, who had lost control of the chariot of the sun.

JUDAS ISCARIOT. The traitor to Christ.

JULIA. The daughter of Caesar, wife of Pompey.

JUNO. A goddess.

JUPITER. *See* Jove.

LANCELOT. The lover of Guinevere.

LAWRENCE, SAINT. A Christian martyr of the third century.

LEANDER. The lover of Hero who used to swim across the Hellespont to see her.

LEDA. The mother of Castor and Pollux, the Gemini (twins).

LETHE. The river of forgetfulness.

LIMBO. The first circle of Hell.

LINUS. A legendary Greek poet.

LOMBARD, PETER. The author of the *Sententiae,* used as a manual of theology.

LOMBARDY. A province in northern Italy.

LUCAN. A Latin poet, author of the *Pharsalia.*

LUCIA, SAINT. St. Lucy of Syracuse, a third-century martyr.

LUCRETIA. Wife of Collatinus.

LYCURGUS. A king of Nemea. Blinded by grief at the death of his son, he was about to have Hypsipyle, to whom the child had been entrusted, put to death when her two sons rushed in to save her.

MACCABAEUS, JUDAS. A leader who delivered the Hebrews from the tyranny of the Syrians.

MAGPIES. *See* Calliope.

MAIA. The mother of Mercury.

MALEBOLGE. Evil pouches, the ditches of the eighth circle of Hell.

MALEBRANCHE. The collective name for the devils at the ditch of the barrators.

MANTUA. A city near which Virgil was born.

MARCIA. The wife of Cato.

MAREMMA. A woody and swampy region on the west coast of Italy.

MARS. The Roman god of war.

MEDUSA. One of the Gorgon sisters, the guardian of the City of Dis.

MICHAEL. An archangel.

Minos. Judge of the dead in classical mythology; also of Dante's Hell.

Minotaur. The offspring of Pasiphaë and a bull, conceived in a wooden cow.

Monferrato. *See* Alessandria.

Montaperti. The scene of a bloody battle between the Florentine Guelfs and the Sienese aided by the Ghibelline exiles.

Mordred. The treacherous nephew of King Arthur. When he was pierced by a spear, the sunlight shone through the wound.

Mosca dei Lamberti. A sower of discord.

Mucius Scaevola. A Roman who burned off his right hand for failing to kill Porsena, an enemy of Rome.

Muses. The goddesses of song and poetry.

Narcissus. A Greek youth who fell in love with himself after seeing his image in a pool.

Neptune. The god of the sea.

Nessus. A centaur. While trying to abduct Dejanira he was mortally wounded by an arrow from Hercules, her husband. To avenge himself he gave his shirt, poisoned by his blood, to Dejanira, who in turn gave it to Hercules, thus causing the latter's death.

Nicholas, Saint. According to a legend St. Nicholas threw money into the house of a poor neighbor to provide dowries for his three daughters.

Nimrod. The builder of the Tower of Babel in the land of Shinar.

Nisus. A legendary hero of the Trojan-Latin Wars.

Nones. The period from noon to 3:00 p.m.

Obizzo da Este. A thirteenth-century ruler of Ferrara.

Orosius, Paulus. The author of a compendium of universal history.

Orpheus. A legendary character considered by Dante as a philosopher.

Pallas. A Greek goddess. Also the name of a companion of Aeneas who helped this hero to gain possession of Latium.

Paolo. The lover of Francesca da Rimini, brother of her husband.

Paris. A Trojan prince.

Parnassus. A mountain sacred to Apollo and the Muses.

Pasiphaë. The mother of the Minotaur.

Penelope. The wife of Ulysses.

Penthesilea A queen of the Amazons.

Persephone. *See* Proserpine.

Peter, Saint. St. Peter's pine cone, a cone of gilt bronze originally about ten feet high.

Pettignano, Pier. A poor comb seller, regarded as a saint.

Phaëthon. Son of Apollo. When he tried to drive the chariot of the sun he lost control of the horses. The sky was scorched, as is apparent in the Milky Way. He was struck down by a thunderbolt from Jove.

PHILIP THE FAIR. A king of France who helped to transfer the papacy to Avignon, a crime in the eyes of Dante and other Italians. He died from a fall caused by a wild boar that brushed against his horse.

PHILOMELA. The sister of Procne who was wronged by the latter's husband. She was changed into a swallow.

PHLEGETHON. The river of blood, seventh circle of the Inferno.

PHLEGRA. The scene of the battle of the giants against Jove.

PHLEGYAS. A king of the Lapithae who, in a rage, set fire to the temple of Apollo. Guardian of the circle of the wrathful and the sullen.

PHOTINUS. A deacon of Thessalonica; supposed to have induced Anastasius II to deny the divinity of Christ.

PISTOIA. A town near Florence.

PLUTUS. The ancient god of wealth.

POLA. A city in northeastern Italy.

POLYCLETUS. A Greek sculptor.

PRISCIAN. A Latin grammarian of the sixth century.

PROSERPINE. The wife of Pluto, Queen of Hell. While picking flowers in the springtime in the valley of Henna she was carried off to the lower world.

PTOLEMY. A geographer and astronomer of Alexandria. Also the name of the king of Egypt in Caesar's time.

PYRAMUS. The mulberry turned red on being spattered with the blood of Pyramus, who stabbed himself when he thought Thisbe had been slain by a lion.

PYRRHUS. An enemy of Rome.

QUARNERO. A bay in northeastern Italy.

RACHEL. The wife of Jacob, who served fourteen years to obtain her; symbol of contemplation.

RASCIA. A state composed of some of the provinces that form the present Yugoslavia.

REHOBOAM. A king obliged to flee to Jerusalem after his tribute gatherer had been killed by the people of Israel.

RHEA. The wife of Saturn, mother of Jupiter. To protect the infant from Saturn, who devoured his children, she hid him, and had noises made to drown out the sound of his crying.

RICHARD OF ST. VICTOR. The author of a treatise on contemplation.

RINIER DA CORNETO. A powerful lord and highwayman, thirteenth century.

RINIER PAZZO. A highwayman, thirteenth century.

Roland. The hero of the "Song of Roland." To call for help he blew his horn so hard that his temples burst.

Romagna. A province in Northeastern Italy.

Rusticucci, Jacopo. Mentioned among the sodomites; his wife presumably drove him to his bad habit.

Saladin. The sultan of Egypt and Syria in the twelfth century.

Santafiora. The counts of that place in the Maremma lost much of their territory to Siena.

Saul. The first king of Israel; committed suicide by throwing himself on his sword.

Scipio. The Roman conqueror of Carthage.

Scylla. A rock on the Italian side of the Strait of Messina.

Semele. The daughter of the King of Thebes, loved by Jupiter. She insisted on seeing her lover in all his glory and was consumed to ashes.

Semiramis. A legendary queen of Assyria.

Seneca. A Latin moralist.

Sennacherib. A king of the Assyrians, killed by his sons.

Serchio. A river at Lucca.

Sextus. A son of Pompey, an enemy of Rome.

Sichaeus. The husband of Dido.

Siger of Brabant. A professor at the University of Paris. His unorthodox views were refuted by St. Thomas Aquinas.

Simon Magus. A Samaritan who offered money to the apostles. From him the name "simony" derives.

Strophades. Islands in the Ionian Sea.

Styx. One of the rivers of the ancient Hell; in the Inferno, a swamp.

Tagliacozza. The scene of a battle between Charles of Anjou and Manfred's forces. The battle was won by the strategy of Erard de Valéry, the French general.

Tarquin. The legendary last king of Rome.

Thales. A Greek philosopher, one of the seven wise men of Greece.

Theseus. A Greek hero; killed the Minotaur; attempted to rescue Proserpine from the lower world.

Thisbe. *See* Pyramus.

Tiber. The river that flows through Rome.

Tierce. The period from 6:00 a.m. to 9:00 a.m.

Tithonus. The husband of Aurora, the dawn. Dante refers to the moonrise as the "concubine" of Tithonus.

Titus. A Roman emperor who captured Jerusalem in a.d. 70. The defeat of Jerusalem was regarded as a vengeance for the Crucifixion.

Tristan. The lover of Yseult in the medieval romance.

TROY. The city involved in the Trojan War, the subject of Homer's *Iliad*.

TURNUS. A legendary hero of the Trojan-Latin War.

TUSCANY. A province of Italy of which the chief city is Florence.

TYPHOEUS. A giant supposed to have been buried under the volcano Etna.

UBALDINO. A cardinal accused of sympathy with the Imperial cause, placed by Dante among the heretics.

ULYSSES. The hero of Homer's *Odyssey*.

VENUS. The goddess of love. Wounded accidentally by Cupid, her son, she fell in love with Adonis.

VIRGIL. A Latin poet, author of the *Aeneid* and other works.

VULCAN. Jove's smith who forged the thunderbolts.

WHITES. A political party in Florence to which Dante at first belonged.

XERXES. A king of Persia who crossed the Hellespont with a vast army.

ZENO. A stoic philosopher.

Rinehart Editions